Group Dynamics and Team Interventions

Group Dynamics and Team Interventions

Understanding and Improving Team Performance

Timothy M. Franz

WILEY-BLACKWELL

A John Wiley & Sons, Ltd., Publication

This edition first published 2012
© 2012 Timothy M. Franz

Blackwell Publishing was acquired by John Wiley & Sons in February 2007. Blackwell's publishing program
has been merged with Wiley's global Scientific, Technical, and Medical business to form Wiley-Blackwell.

Registered Office
John Wiley & Sons, Ltd, The Atrium, Southern Gate, Chichester, West Sussex, PO19 8SQ, UK

Editorial Offices
350 Main Street, Malden, MA 02148-5020, USA
9600 Garsington Road, Oxford, OX4 2DQ, UK
The Atrium, Southern Gate, Chichester, West Sussex, PO19 8SQ, UK

For details of our global editorial offices, for customer services, and for information about
how to apply for permission to reuse the copyright material in this book please see our website at
www.wiley.com/wiley-blackwell.

The right of Timothy M. Franz to be identified as the author of this work has been asserted in accordance
with the UK Copyright, Designs and Patents Act 1988.

Library of Congress Cataloging-in-Publication Data

Franz, Timothy M.
   Group dynamics and team interventions : understanding and improving team performance /
   Timothy M. Franz.
      p.   cm.
   Includes bibliographical references and index.
   ISBN 978-1-4051-8677-3 (hardback : alk. paper) – ISBN 978-1-4051-8670-4 (pbk. : alk. paper)
1. Social groups–Psychological aspects.   2. Teams in the workplace.   3. Diversity in the
workplace.   4. Leadership–Psychological aspects.   I. Title.
   HM716.F73 2012
   302.3–dc23
                                        2011048256

A catalogue record for this book is available from the British Library.

Set in 10.5/13pt Minion by SPi Publisher Services, Pondicherry, India
Printed in Singapore by C.O.S. Printers Pte Ltd

3   2016

To Liz, Noah, Maddie, and Ethan

Brief Contents

Contents

Preface

I have been considering writing this book for some time. The primary reason for this is because, as an applied psychologist, I am often dismayed by the lack of communication between academics and practitioners. I work primarily in academia but also do some consulting. I also work with many practitioners. I find that academics often develop and use theory to understand groups and then design excellent interventions that are well communicated to other academics within the research journals. Unfortunately, practitioners seldom read research journals and care little for theory; what they instead want is a tool that works, regardless of why. In addition, practitioners seldom read academic literature. On the other hand, these same practitioners often have excellent ideas that are atheoretical; the reason(s) why they work often remain unexplained. This book is intended to bridge the gap between academic research about groups and real-life practice with teams. Academics who are preparing practitioners and practitioners who are interested in grounding their work in theory should find it useful.

A secondary and related reason for writing this book results from my many years of teaching undergraduate- and Masters-level Group Dynamic courses. Many of the undergraduate and graduate students with whom I've had the pleasure of working are interested in theory. They want to understand systems and have explanations, so they prefer to see the theory that explains how and why groups and teams work in the ways that they do. However, they do not want to stop at only understanding theory. Instead, they want effective theory- and research-based interventions that they can immediately apply to their work. Few texts have this dual emphasis. Instead, some books focus primarily on theory with only a little application (e.g., Forsyth's *Group Dynamics*, 2006 and Stangor's *Social Groups in Action and Interaction*, 2004) while other books focus primarily on application and practices with little mention of or linking to theory (e.g., Kayser's *Mining Group Gold*, 2011 and Wheelan's *Creating Effective Teams: A Guide for Members and Leaders*, 2005). These are all excellent books, and I've used each one in different classes as well as to generate and improve my ideas for team development exercises. However, they are almost at opposite ends of the continuum from science to practice. Again, this book is intended to bridge the gap.

As a result, I have grounded this book in two different perspectives that best illustrate how I think about applying the small groups and teams academic literature to improving team performance. First, I modeled it after the scientist-practitioner paradigm that is regularly discussed in applied psychology (e.g., Mellott & Mehr, 2007). Although this paradigm is often used to refer to graduate training programs (including graduate programs for industrial and organizational psychologists), it also applies to how individuals subsequently view the world in which they work. This paradigm emphasizes both science (i.e., research) and practice (i.e., application). Specifically, people who believe in this paradigm find that there is benefit to understanding and developing theory resulting from time spent working in the field, and similarly there is benefit to improving work in the field from time spent understanding and/or developing theory. It is this scientist-practitioner paradigm which I hope this book reflects.

The second key theoretical paradigm in which this book is grounded is the emphasis on both action and research, an idea he termed action research. Kurt Lewin (1946/1948), who was first and foremost an academic, was one of the first to discuss the concept of action research (Dickens & Watkins, 1999). His main premise when discussing action research was that for any applied field, such as group dynamics, there must be both basic scientific research that is working to understand general laws and principles as well as applied scientific research that is designed to solve a specific problem. He stated that "for any field of action both types of scientific research are needed" (p. 204). Furthermore, he believed that the research should guide action and action should follow research. Lewin was quite successful at combining his research with action. As a person who works in the tradition of Lewin, I have written this book with understanding research and taking action in mind; this book integrates theory and research with practice and action. Thus, conducting and understanding research about teams is a key feature to the book, and there are interventions in each chapter that can guide action.

As a result, I have organized the book around the concepts that are typically found in undergraduate and graduate group or team dynamics books. Unlike the theoretical books in group dynamics, however, I have also focused each chapter on specific ways to improve groups, which I term interventions, rather than only providing a summary of theories. And, unlike other applied books in improving team functioning, I have relied heavily on theory and empirical research to help select and explain successful interventions. This combination should help readers to better understand teams so as to guide successful application and intervention.

Thus, each chapter first summarizes some of the relevant theory and then provides steps to follow in several different interventions. As a result, practitioners can better understand the "why" of how groups work when intervening in their teams and also have readily available a list of several interventions that they can use to try to help them improve the effectiveness of the teams in their workplace.

Organization of This Book

Though groups are common today, we often see surface symptoms that show us that a group or team is not performing as well as it might be. These symptoms may include behaviors such as infighting or a rush to agreement, and show that teams need assistance and intervention to improve their performance. However, we often need to learn more about what specifically we need to do before we can intervene. Thus, the first step in intervening is assessment, which is discussed in Chapter 2 along with how to conduct a follow-up evaluation to determine the success of the intervention. Next, Chapter 3 focuses on some basic concepts necessary to understand group processes, such as the importance of the team task in understanding how to help a team. Finally, the remaining chapters of this book are organized around the input-process-output model of group functioning (Hackman & Morris, 1975). This theoretical model suggests that there are certain inputs, such as team member knowledge, personality, expertise, and confidence, that each individual brings to the team (Chapter 4). Then, once the team forms there are things that happen together – this is when group process occurs – and it is necessary to understand concepts such as cohesion, decision making, and problem solving. Finally, there are group outputs, which include concepts such as performance, productivity, and member satisfaction. These are discussed in the final chapter, Chapter 14.

For each chapter in this section, I summarize the main theoretical ideas necessary to understand group functioning. Then, in each chapter I suggest possible interventions that a practitioner might try if the assessment shows that a specific group or team has problems and needs intervention in that area. Although these interventions are included in one specific chapter, some could easily have been included in other chapters as well. Many interventions, to some extent, are integrative and thus have an impact that goes well beyond the specific material in any chapter. Finally, I end each chapter with a case study from a professional in the field discussing how one of the interventions was successful. Thus, by using this book practitioners should:

1. Understand the basic processes involved in assessing and evaluating teams;
2. Have a resource guide that can help them find measurement tools to use to assess and evaluate teams; and
3. Have a toolbox of interventions that they might use to help groups and teams perform better.

How to Use This Book

The book is focused on understanding how groups work and intervening to improve team functioning. It is intended for academics and practitioners who want to understand and then improve the teams with which they work. It differs from most academic texts in that it emphasizes assessment and intervention rather than just aiding understanding. It differs from most practitioner books because it is based on theory. As a result, this book can be used by a wide range of experts. Practitioners can use it as a guide to assessing teams in their organization. In addition, they may also use the book to plan a team training exercise that helps provide members with the skills necessary to improve team performance. Academics can use the text to teach team concepts in an upper-level or Masters-level group dynamics or team performance course. Regardless of who uses it, the reader is left with a set of assessment tools and interventions to improve team functioning.

To help academics and practitioners improve team functioning, many chapters summarize specific tools and interventions (i.e., Chapters 3 through 14), and each chapter ends with a case study, titled *Focus on Application*. The interventions provide simplified steps for how to improve groups and teams as well as the reference citation for the original source so that people can find more information as necessary. The case studies provide specific examples of how practitioners have used one of the interventions to solve real-life problems in groups and teams within organizations. They can be a guide for how practitioners should use that and other interventions, or a point of discussion for those who teach courses using this book.

In addition, each chapter ends with a resource list titled *Additional Resources* that might help readers. The list provides some of the resources that inform the theories and interventions included in that chapter. These lists are included because none of the chapters are a comprehensive review of the entire domain of research within that area; instead the chapters provide summaries of some of the key concepts that may be the most important for teams to consider when determining how to assess and intervene. Thus, the additional resources are designed to help users find more information than is provided in the chapter, including other potential interventions. For example, some of the additional resources will list specific assessment tools that can be used to assess the quality of team functioning. Other resources include online sites that provide additional information that might help to stimulate discussion or learn more about teams.

Finally, there are sample team development exercises at the end of each chapter that can be used as aids to improve depth of understanding about the concepts. The team development exercises include videos and video clips that illustrate concepts with an associated set of discussion questions, role play scenarios and instructions, assessment tools, and/or other team building exercises. These can be used in a college course or as part of a training program. As can be seen, the book remains focused on the intersection of theory with practice.

Acknowledgements

Although the words in this book are mine, I am indebted to many others for helping me fully develop all of the ideas within it. First, my philosophy about groups and teams has been strongly influenced by Jim Larson. The members of the Organizational Learning and Human Resource Development program at St. John Fisher have certainly reminded me to not only understand but, more importantly, apply the concepts about groups and teams to making the workplace better. These include the many current and former graduate students who have helped me to hone and develop my thinking. This also includes the faculty – especially my many conversations and debates with my friend Seth Silver – whose theoretical and applied contributions are too numerous to count. The reviewers provided invaluable feedback about how to make the book even better. And, thanks to the entire editorial team at Blackwell-Wiley. All of you were patient with me when I missed virtually every deadline. Finally, thanks to my family and friends for supporting me during the entire time that it took to complete this book. Without them, this book would not have been possible.

Part I

Introduction

Chapter 1

Introduction to Teams

During the 1980s, the space shuttle program was NASA's major thrust. Shuttles launched, carried astronauts to space, and then returned like airplanes, landing on a runway. The liftoff of the space shuttle Challenger on January 28, 1986 seemed typical of the many other successful shuttle flights. There were seven astronauts aboard the shuttle, including for the first time a person who was not trained as an astronaut, a teacher, Christa McAuliffe. Several seconds before liftoff, the shuttle engines ignited properly as they should have. At liftoff time, all three main engines were firing as the members of the team at NASA expected them to. Soon, the shuttle left its pad and cleared the tower. Its initial ascent was as predicted, showing nothing that caused anyone to have unusual concerns. This looked like any typical shuttle launch and another success for NASA.

Unfortunately, it did not turn out to be a typical liftoff. At 73 seconds into the launch the Challenger rapidly disintegrated, virtually exploding, and all seven astronauts aboard were killed as a result, including the person who NASA had billed as the first teacher-in-space. Why did the Challenger break apart? The simplest answer is also technical one. In short, it resulted from an engineering failure of the solid rocket boosters. Morton Thiokol was the supplier of these solid-rocket boosters. On the morning of the launch, the air temperature was unusually cold – 31 degrees Fahrenheit – which is far lower than is typical for Florida for that time of year. As a result of this low temperature, the O-rings in the boosters failed to seal properly, and caused a leak which quickly developed from a small plume into a full break up within a time period of just over a minute. This would appear to blame the explosion on a complex engineering issue that NASA could not have foreseen.

Group Dynamics and Team Interventions: Understanding and Improving Team Performance, First Edition. Timothy M. Franz.

Although the surface cause certainly did result from an engineering failure, the root cause requires one to delve into the group dynamics of NASA. As subsequent investigations revealed, Morton Thiokol and NASA had definitive evidence of this potential failure long before the fateful morning of the explosion. One engineer even wrote a memo suggesting that a failure like the one in the Challenger could lead to a loss of life. NASA even had ample opportunity to cancel the launch during several discussions with Morton Thiokol, the supplier of the rocker boosters. However, the key decision makers ignored these concerns and went forward anyway with the launch. Janis (1982) attributes this failure to a faulty group decision-making process, which he termed Groupthink (this is covered in more detail later in this book). Janis provides detailed evidence of how Groupthink is likely to have caused the Challenger disaster. Furthermore, Janis provides detailed methods designed to intervene in small groups such as NASA's launch team so as to help prevent these poor decisions. As a result of the Challenger disaster, NASA instituted several changes to help the launch team avoid a similar future disaster, some of which were even similar to those suggested by Janis. Did they work? In 2003, the astronauts in the space shuttle Columbia unfortunately faced a similar fate, though this time during reentry rather than at liftoff. Some scholars blame the Columbia disaster on the same symptoms of Groupthink that once again occurred at NASA (Ferraris & Carveth, 2003).

So, can teams be successful? The evidence is mixed. Some believe that teamwork can help organizations to perform beyond their expectations. Others are not so confident about the benefits of teamwork. Regardless of your bias, this book should help to provide you with a basic understanding of the way groups work and some tools to help you to make them work better.

Learning Goals for Chapter 1

- Differentiate a group from a team.
- Understand the importance of groups and teams in organizations today.
- Understand the nature of groups and teams in organizations today.
- Understand the goal of synergy and the reality of most teams.
- Know the input-process-output model of group functioning.

What Is a Group, What Is a Team?

One of the first questions with regard to understanding teams is to determine what a team is and how it differs from a group of people. A group can be defined as "two or more individuals who are connected to one another by social relationships" (Forsyth, 2006, pp. 2–3). This definition can be divided into its parts. The first part focuses on *two or more individuals*, meaning that groups can range from very small to very large. The second part of the definition is that there are members *who are connected to each other*, meaning that the members are somehow intertwined or networked. The third part, *by social relationships,* emphasizes the social nature of groups, regardless of their emphasis. In summary, members are seen and see themselves as part of the group because of their connected relationships.

On the other hand, a team can be defined as "an organized, task-focused group" (Forsyth, 2006, p. 159). This definition focuses more on the structure of the group and the task that the group is performing because teams, especially those in the workplace, have specific task requirements which the organization expects members to complete and are structured in a way that should help them meet those goals. A second concept that helps to distinguish the difference between some groups and teams is *entiativity* (Campbell, 1958), or the level of "groupness" among members; teams have high levels of interaction, interdependence, and belongingness that is typical of groups with high entiativity. It is this combination of structure, task focus, and high entiativity that typically distinguishes a team from any other group.

Katzenbach and Smith (1993; 2005) break down the differences between groups and teams even further. According to their classification system, a group includes the following:

- a strong, clearly focused leader;
- a system of individual accountability;
- a purpose that is the same as that of the broader organizational mission;
- outputs that are based on individual rather than collective work products;
- an emphasis on running efficient meetings;
- a system where members measure the group's effectiveness indirectly by its influence on others (such as financial performance of the business); and
- discussions where the group makes decisions and then delegates responsibility to members or others.

On the other hand, a team includes the following:

- a process of sharing leadership roles;
- a system with both individual as well as mutual accountability;
- a specific purpose that the team itself determines;
- outputs that are based on collective rather than individual work products;
- an emphasis on open-ended discussion and active problem-solving during meetings;
- a system where members measure the team's performance directly by assessing collective work products; and
- discussions where the group makes decisions and then does the real work together.

As can be seen in all of these definitions, there is overlap between what is a group versus what is a team. Although there is disagreement about the specific definitions (see Forsyth, 2006 for an excellent summary of this debate), I conclude that a team is a specific type of group, though a group is not always a team. There are many different social groups, such as Alcoholics Anonymous support groups, that may be high in interdependence but cannot be classified as a team because they do not have the task focus that is expected of teams. On the other hand, there are no teams that cannot also be classified as groups. One of the reasons to consider the nuances of these definitions is that there is considerable research about small groups, only some of which applies directly to teams. The rest of the research may or may not be generalized to teams – it is the reader who must carefully make that determination.

Team assessment: Are we a successful team?

The following questions are based on recommendations from Hackman (Coutu & Beschloss, 2009). Answering these questions can help you to quickly determine whether your team may or may not be as successful as it should be (Table 1.1).

This quick assessment can help you to assess how well your team is doing. Scores can range from 8 to 32. If your team scores closer to eight, your team is likely to be facing considerable issues with members and how they work together; its performance is definitely suffering and it is likely a detriment to the organization. If your team scores closer to a 32, it is likely to be helping the organization succeed. Scores in the middle represent teams that can improve performance but may not be holding the organization back.

Table 1.1   Criteria for Successful Teams.

Eight Criteria for Successful Teams	Strongly Disagree	Somewhat Disagree	Somewhat Agree	Strongly Agree
1. My team has problems coordinating tasks.	1	2	3	4
2. All team members are motivated to perform as a team.	1	2	3	4
3. My team is made up of the right members.	1	2	3	4
4. My team has clear goals and a compelling direction.	1	2	3	4
5. My team has clear boundaries.	1	2	3	4
6. My team has fewer than 10 members.	1	2	3	4
7. My team has a very stable set of members.	1	2	3	4
8. Organizations reward us as a team rather than us as individuals.	1	2	3	4

Teams in Organizations Today

As the previous space shuttle example illustrates, teams work together to send shuttles into space. They also operate on people, determine how to fight wars, decide who to hire for a position, and set the strategy for multinational corporations. In fact, organizations today require groups and teams to make far more decisions and perform many more tasks in organizations than ever before (Devine, Clayton, Philips, Dunford, & Melner, 1999; Guzzo & Shea, 1992). Furthermore, groups and teams at work are unlikely to go away any time soon (Kozlowski & Ilgen, 2006) because teams separated by time and distance can continue to function well with the rapid increase of technology that enables computer-mediated team meetings; individuals are expected to work in teams, and organizations expect greater outcomes from increasing their use of teams.

There are many reasons why people in organizations would want to work in teams (for a comprehensive list, see Zander, 1985). Five of the more common of these reasons include:

- *Preferences for Social Interaction.* Most people are social by nature and thus are attracted to working with others. A team provides them with this opportunity (Parks & Sanna, 1999).
- *Dividing Work.* Many tasks need to be completed quickly so as to provide organizations with a competitive advantage. However, these tasks can be very complicated and difficult for one person to complete in a timely fashion. It is much easier for team members to divide work among multiple people so that they can accomplish a greater volume of work at a faster rate (Stewart, Manz, & Sims, 1999).
- *Working Collectively to Effect Change.* Individuals often come together to plan and implement change when they think that any "one person acting alone cannot create that change" Additional members will continue to join if the group has a clear purpose with which they agree (Zander, 1985, p. 1).
- *Information Sharing.* Many complex problems require input from multiple individuals, and team members often know that they do not have the information that they need to solve these problems. Multiple members provide team members with the opportunity to increase the level of information and expertise on which to draw when compared with working alone (Franz & Larson, 2002).
- *Organizational Buy-In.* One important step to succeeding during an implementation phase is to get buy-in within all levels of an organization. Team members expect that decisions made with their participation get better buy-in among organizational members and improved commitment than will any individual decisions made by management (Scanlan & Atherton, 1981).

Although these factors affect what team members expect to get out of working in teams, they do not fully explain why most organizations have fully embraced teamwork. Social interaction, for example, is helpful to the individual members in a team. However, organizational leaders will typically look towards what that social interaction can actually provide the organization.

West (2004) provides a comprehensive list of reasons for what organizations might expect when using teams. This list can be summarized into four categories of expected organizational outcomes, including a) increased task performance, b) greater creativity, c) improved organizational learning, and d) higher employee engagement. First, organizations expect direct results in terms of task performance. Specifically, they expect teams to provide a greater quantity of work that is produced more quickly at a higher quality and is focused on the organization's goals and mission than what might be expected from those same individuals when they are working alone. Second, organizations expect greater creativity. In this case, teams are seen as resources for cross training and cross fertilization, which should result in more innovative ideas. Third, organizations expect improved organizational learning. This is because when members are working together they are more likely to learn the roles that other members perform in that team and can then pass that knowledge along when there is a change in team membership. Finally, organizations expect improved employee engagement. When people work together, they are expected to be more committed to the organization, involved in their work, and satisfied with their jobs.

As can be seen, organizations expect teams to improve organizational results, whether it results from task performance, innovation, learning, or engagement; that is the reason why organizations use teams to conduct work in so many different areas. Further, when companies today are rightfully concerned with losing their top talent, Hewlett (2009) recommends that well-functioning teams can help companies to retain some who otherwise might have "one foot out the door" (p. 24) by creating a stimulating environment with a sense of camaraderie. The type of teams these companies use include cross-functional work teams, project teams, management teams, leadership teams, task performance teams, and many other specific types.

Types of Groups at Work

There are several different ways in which organizations use teams. According to Larson and LaFasto (1989), there are three different types of teams. The first type of team is a problem-resolution team. These are teams that are set up to solve a specific type of problem. An example of a problem-solving team is a team that is tasked with the goal to determine what the annual employee survey scores mean and then decide on a set of actions to take based on their interpretations. The second type of team is a creative team. These are teams that are designed to come up with creative and innovative solutions to a problem. An example of a creative team is one that is designed to come up with a marketing plan for a new product. The final type of team is a tactical team. A tactical team implements solutions. An example of a tactical team is one that will create a new route for a more timely and effective delivery of products. Larson and La Fasto further state that any of these teams can either be standing teams – where members work together for considerable periods – or ad hoc teams – where members work together for a short period of time and where there is a definitive end goal.

As you might imagine, these three types of teams might often work together within an organization to solve and implement an organizational problem. For example, a creative team might brainstorm to come up with a large number of potential solutions. The creative team may then turn this large number of solutions over to a problem-solving team that then determines which one to implement. After coming up with the determination, the problem-solving team turns to the tactical team, which comes up with an implementation plan. It may not end there, though, and the tactical team may return to the other teams for advice – a new creative team and/or an existing problem-solving team if there is a lack of clarity with one portion of the implementation where the tactical team needs more information or guidance. Thus, each type of team serves its own purpose. Further, how the team is designed, who serves on the team, and the goal that it has should differ based the type of team that an organization should be using for the task.

The Input-Process-Output Model of Group Functioning

The input-process-output (IPO) model of groups (Hackman, 1987; McGrath, 1984; Steiner, 1972) has driven considerable work about group functioning. Although it is an imperfect model (Ilgen, Hollenbeck, Johnson, & Jundt, 2005), it provides at least a basic framework for understanding about how groups and teams work. According to the IPO model, teams have inputs that exist prior to formation, processes that occur when working together, and outputs that are produced. This model is summarized in Figure 1.1.

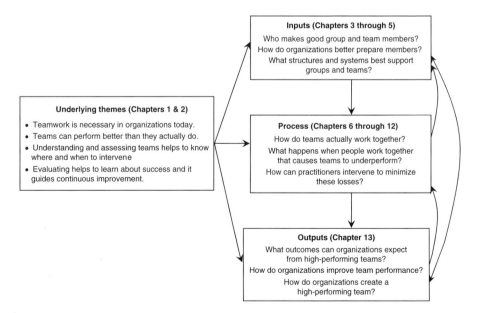

Figure 1.1   The Input-Process-Output Model as a Guide to Understanding This Book.

To provide a structure for evaluating teams and intervening to improve performance, this book is organized around the IPO model. Inputs include what team members bring, such as each person's competencies, motivation, and personalities, as well as factors resulting from the structure of the group team and/or organization, such as cohesiveness, the goals in the team, and how teams are supported and rewarded. These concepts are discussed in Chapters 3 through 5. Processes include many general concepts discussed in group dynamics, such as creative processes, decision making, problem solving, conflict, and leadership. These concepts are discussed in Chapters 6 through 12. Finally, outputs are the outcomes that can be expected from working in a team, such as productivity and member satisfaction. These concepts are discussed in Chapter 13. The IPO model can provide a framework that can help a practitioner to assess where to help group members improve their group outputs. For example, an assessment may show that increasing training of individual members may help inputs and thus improve process and outputs. On the other hand, it may be that members have the inputs to succeed, but a team needs structures to help them to improve processes. This also necessarily leads to some overlap across the book in terms of what appears in each section – it is impossible to discuss inputs and outputs without mentioning processes and vice versa.

Although the book chapters are organized around the IPO model, intervention to improve team performance is an underlying theme of the book. As stated earlier in this chapter, teams are used to improve organizational performance. However, they seldom reach the performance that can be expected of them. All is not lost, however. Specific interventions targeted towards specific team deficiencies in inputs and process can help to improve team outputs, and thus performance.

The IPO model is an excellent general organizing structure but is not without criticism. In fact, there have been recent updates to the IPO model that help to clarify some of these criticisms. For example, Guzzo and Shea (1990) suggest that inputs may not only have indirect effects on outputs through process but also direct effects, regardless of what happens within groups and teams. Littlepage and colleagues (1995) do provide evidence that some inputs seem to affect outputs directly rather than working through group process. Finally, Ilgen, Hollenbeck, Johnson, and Jundt (2005) recommend that process be defined much more broadly (they suggest the statistical term *mediator* instead) as well as considering the cyclical impact of group and team outputs on further inputs back into the team. The model above has been modified to include arrows on the far right, not included in the original IPO model, that show that processes and outputs can affect inputs, and inputs can directly affect outputs as well.

In Search of Synergy?

Organizations expect groups and teams to perform. Thus, one of the expectations of teamwork is for teams to outperform what might be expected of those same individuals when working alone. This expectation is called synergy, or the premise that the team is something greater than the sum of its parts. When a group or team achieves synergy, something magical occurs during the process of working together to create greater outputs that cannot be explained solely by the member inputs alone.

Unfortunately, teams may fail to perform as well as can be expected of them (Hill, 1982). This is typically because there is something lost when people work together and thus the team is not as successful as the individuals working alone might be. Steiner (1972) terms this problem *process losses*, which is any loss due to faulty processes of teams. These faulty processes might result from any number of team problems, such as unprepared team members, an inappropriate team structure for the task, poor coordination, miscommunication, faulty decision making, or high interpersonal conflict. And, this is only a small number of the reasons why teams struggle to reach their full potential.

In fact, J. Richard Hackman, a groups and teams researcher at Harvard, questions whether teams can be successful (see Coutu & Beschloss, 2009). According to Hackman, "Research consistently shows that teams underperform, despite all the extra resources they have. That's because problems with coordination and motivation typically chip away at the benefits of collaboration" (p. 100). In brief, Hackman says that some of the reasons for this include:

- *Coordination.* Teams have problems coordinating tasks. Working together requires a coordination of effort that is not found when working alone. Coordination problems may take away too much time and energy from the actual task work.
- *Motivation.* Team members often lack motivation to perform as a team. Teamwork requires extra steps that working alone does not require.
- *Membership.* Teams are often made up of the wrong members. Across the group, members need the knowledge, skills, and abilities to succeed when working together. Groups that do not have this required background diversity may fail.
- *Boundaries.* Teams seldom have clear boundaries. To succeed, teams need to know what they may do as well as what they may not.
- *Goals.* Teams often do not have a compelling direction. A team with a clear goal is more successful than one that does not know where it is heading.
- *Number of Members.* Teams often have too many members. There are times when people are placed on a team for the wrong reasons, and group process may slow down as a result.
- *Unstable Membership.* Team members change too often. Each time there is a change in a team member, the other members must acculturate the new member.
- *Reward Structures.* Organizations incorrectly reward individuals rather than teams. If an organization says it would like teamwork, it needs to reward teamwork.

Hackman's own conclusion is: "I have no question that when you have a team, the possibility exists that it will generate magic, producing something extraordinary, a collective creation of previously unimagined quality or beauty. But don't count on it" (p. 100).

The information in this book is designed to help practitioners to understand how teams work so that they can assess where there might be faulty processes. Then the interventions provided in many of the chapters can help teams with structured techniques that might help them avoid these losses in the future. It may be that teams that use this book get closer to, and maybe even attain, that goal of synergy that Hackman and others think is possible.

Improving Groups and Teams Requires Intervention

As the Dilbert cartoon in Figure 1.2 below shows, groups and teams often fail to reach their potential. This creates opportunities to intervene to develop the groups and teams so that their performance can improve. Organizational development is a field that emphasizes the use of social science principles to help teams and organizations improve their functioning (Spector, 2008). Organizational development practitioners often work through the use of tools and techniques that are designed to help them intervene and improve the functioning of the people within the organization. The intervention is generally a multi-stage process and is often described in terms of

DILBERT by Scott Adams

DOGBERT'S GROUP I.Q. FORMULA

THE INTELLIGENCE QUOTIENT OF ANY MEETING CAN BE DETERMINED BY STARTING WITH 100 AND SUBTRACTING 5 POINTS FOR EACH PARTICIPANT.

Figure 1.2   Dogbert Reflects on the Value of Using Groups at Work. DILBERT © (1991) Scott Adams. Used By permission of UNIVERSAL UCLICK.

the "medical model." A change agent, or the person guiding and implementing the change who is sort of like a physician, assesses, or "diagnoses," the problems that are occurring, intervenes, or "treats" those problems to help to improve functioning, and then evaluates, or "follows up" on the treatment to see what works.

This process of assessing, intervening, and evaluating, is part of a consultative approach to working with people. In organizational development, consultants may be internal and from within an organization or external and instead come from outside an organization. They provide expert assistance to support the groups and teams with which they are working. According to Reed and Francis (2003), the consultative approach should follow the following eight steps:

1. Gain awareness of the situation that is causing a requirement for intervention.
2. Find and analyze the facts about the situation.
3. Define the problem by trying to identify the root cause.
4. Generate alternative possible solutions for interventions that may improve the problem.
5. Select one intervention solution to implement.
6. Develop the action steps for implementing the intervention.
7. Gain acceptance for the intervention from stakeholders, or those who are affected by any implementation.
8. Intervene and evaluate the success of the intervention.

While Reed and Francis (2003) emphasize any consultative relationship, there are other resources that are designed specifically for people acting as consultants to groups and teams. Shonk (1982) and Reddy (1994), for example, focus solely on group-level interventions. According to Reddy, "group process consultation is the reasoned and intentional intervention by consultants into the ongoing events and dynamics of a group with the purpose of helping that group effectively attaining its agreed-upon objectives" (p. 8). In other words, it is organizational development at the level of the group rather than at the level of the organization. People in organizations often call this process team development.

This book integrates these organizational and group/team development principles with the core concepts from group dynamics. Chapters are organized around the IPO model, but the content of the chapters assumes:

a) Most groups and teams can improve at what they are doing.
b) It is necessary to understand the underlying concepts and theories about how groups and teams work to help to determine what is necessary to work towards improvement.
c) Assessing groups and teams can help to provide an understanding of the root causes for any issues that arise.
d) Intervention can allow many groups and teams to develop.
e) Evaluation helps to determine what has worked and pinpoint what has not so that the groups and teams can continually learn and develop.

Chapter Summary

Groups and teams are similar but somewhat different entities. Groups are two or more people who come together for a common purpose, while teams are groups that have a greater level of interaction and interdependency. Although social influence and group processes have been systematically studied for well over a century, teams are being used in organizations more today than ever before. This is because people tend to get many social benefits from working in groups and teams are expected to improve organizational performance over what might be expected if individuals are working alone. Unfortunately, teams often fail to provide the expected benefits because of the process losses that they all too often experience. This book is intended to provide practitioners with a) tools to assess teams, b) information to aid them with a basic understanding of how groups work, and then c) a list of many possible ways to intervene so that their teams might get closer to their potential.

Additional Resources

Baron, R. S., & Kerr, N. L. (2003). *Group process, group decision, group action. Mapping social psychology*. Buckingham, England: Open University Press.

Reddy, W. B. (1994). *Intervention skills: Process consultation for small groups and teams*. San Diego, CA: Pfeiffer & Company.

Shonk, J. H. (1982). *Working in teams: A practical manual for improving work groups*. NY: AMACOM: A division of the American Management Associations.

Worchel, S. Wood, W., & Simpson J. A. (1992), *Group process and productivity*. Newbury Park, CA: Sage.

Team Exercises

Exercise 1.1   Icebreaker – The Franz Group IQ Test

Step 1: Answer the questions on the following quiz individually.

THE FRANZ "GROUP IQ" TEST

This test consists of 15 questions that are designed to identify your group's intelligence. Make sure to respond to each question.

1. How many stripes are there on the flag of the United States?
2. What was little Miss Muffett eating?
3. What planet is closest to the sun?
4. How long is the Nile River in km?
5. Where, exactly, is Timbuktu (this answers requires more than just a continent)?
6. How did James Joyce die?

7. Who painted the Mona Lisa?
8. What is the distance from the earth to the sun (to the nearest million miles)?
9. What musical artist had his first US Top 40 hit in 1970, and has sung duets with k.d. lang, P.M. Dawn, Little Richard, Don Henley, Chris Rea, Tammy Wynette, Gladys Knight, RuPaul, Paul Young, and Eminem?
10. What was the longest running Broadway musical?
11. What was Muhammed Ali's name when he was born?
12. What are the two most expensive properties in the game of Monopoly?
13. What is the common name for the chemical sodium chloride?
14. In what town is Harvard University located?
15. How many defensive players must be on the line of scrimmage when the ball is snapped?

Step 2: Working as a team, discuss the quiz items and come to consensus about the answers.

Step 3: Score the quiz. Compare the individual scores to the team score. Compute your group IQ by subtracting the best member's score from the group score. If the group IQ score is negative, your group incurred some process losses and is performing at the level of the typical group. If the group IQ score is zero, you did great! At least your group did not have process losses. On the other hand, you did not have any process gains, either. If the group IQ score is positive, you did better than the typical group. However, did your group really have process gains and reach synergy? Synergy may only have occurred if your group answered a question that no individual member got correct (see Michaelsen, Watson, & Black, 1989; Michaelsen, Watson, Schwartzkopf, & Black, 1992; Tindale & Larson, 1992a, 1992b for a review of the debate around this).

Step 4: Discuss who did better? Why? Did the team answer any item that no individual could answer?

Exercise 1.2   What is a group? what is a team? are we a group? are we a team?

Step 1: Using the following list, work individually to determine whether the example fits the definition of a group and/or the definition of a team.

People waiting in line at a bus stop.
A professional basketball team.
A SWAT team
Seven employees working closely together for three months together on a project.
Four students working on writing a paper.
People sitting in a movie theater.
An online research team
A small sales company that includes two sales people, a president, an administrative assistant, a vice president of marketing, and a vice president of human resources and operations.

Step 2: Working as a team, discuss the list and come to consensus about what is a group versus what is a team

Step 3 (for existing teams only): Using the chart below, examine your team. How does it fit the ideal definition of a team? Where does it fall short? Where does your team need development so that you can move your team closer to the ideal?

A team:	How does our team match the ideal?	Where do we fall short?	What do we need to do to develop our team?
Is organized			
Is small			
Shares common goals and objectives			
Has a high level of interaction and interdependence			

Exercise 1.3   Worst group/best group

Step 1: Individual work (three to five minutes).

a) Have individuals think back to their worst group experience and write down what it was.
b) Then, have people list three to five characteristics that made it so bad.
c) Next, have individuals think back to their best group experience and write down what it was.
d) Have them list three to five characteristics that made it so successful.

Step 2: Group work (5–10 minutes)

a) Arrange people into groups of four to five.
b) Have groups come up with a common list of three to five characteristics that are common of the worst groups.
c) Have groups do the same for the best groups.

Step 3: Large Group Feedback (10–15 minutes)

a) Call the large group back together.
b) As a large group, come up with a list of the characteristics that make a group have problems that might lead to its failure.

c) As a large group, come up with a list of the characteristics that make a group succeed.

d) Contrast the list of items for the worst groups to the list for the best groups.

What was your worst group experience (briefly describe)?	What was your best group experience (briefly describe)?
What were the characteristics of that group that made it so bad? List 3–5.	What were the characteristics of that group that made it so bad? List 3–5.
1)	1)
2)	2)
3)	3)
4)	4)
5)	5)

Chapter 2

Methods of Assessing and Evaluating Team Functioning

Imagine that you are not feeling well, so you visit your physician. You are finally called into the waiting room, and the physician eventually hurries into the room to see you. The physician takes your blood pressure again, looks in your ears, looks down your throat, and then recommends you take Clindamycin, an antibiotic, to cure the problem. Unfortunately, you have not told your physician anything about your ailment. The physician did not take a history, conduct a physical examination, nor perform any tests. In other words, the physician did not perform a thorough assessment to determine the problem that needs treatment. My guess is that you would stop visiting that physician.

Just like physicians should complete assessments before prescribing any treatment, groups and teams should complete assessments as well to help them to determine the problems with which they are faced. This chapter reviews the basics of four different methods of conducting applied organizational research, including observation, focus groups, interviews, and surveys. There are many other books that provide far more detail than I intend to provide in this book (learning the details of assessment methods requires an expertise that is well beyond the scope of this book), a few of which are listed as *Additional Resources* at the end of each subsection. A practitioner who is less familiar with the methods summarized here may want to enlist the help of someone who is more of an expert in applied research and assessment. Instead, in this chapter I attempt to provide an overview of these methods in enough detail to outline the necessary steps in applied research to a) help a beginning practitioner try a small project, b) remind an experienced practitioner of what is necessary, or c) provide a structure for helping a novice discuss applied research and assessment issues with an expert.

Group Dynamics and Team Interventions: Understanding and Improving Team Performance,
First Edition. Timothy M. Franz.
© 2012 Timothy M. Franz. Published 2012 by Blackwell Publishing Ltd.

Learning Goals for Chapter 2

- Understand the importance of assessment and evaluation when intervening.
- Understand the steps involved in conducting applied assessment and evaluation research.
- Understand the basics of how to collect data with teams through:
    1. Observation
    2. Interviews
    3. Focus Groups
    4. Surveys

All interventions require some type of applied organizational research. One specific type of applied research is called assessment. This type of research is the key to understanding when and how to plan an intervention. The initial assessment should occur prior to planning any intervention and will help to determine what is happening and how to intervene. Unfortunately, practitioners all too often jump straight to the intervention without considering assessment. This can result in problems such as creating an intervention that fails to respond to the underlying problem. Without clear problem assessment, interventions will often fail.

A second specific type of applied organizational research is called evaluation research. This type of research is the key to determining whether an intervention was in fact successful. It is this follow-up evaluation that helps practitioners to determine (a) what worked, and (b) what didn't. As is the case in most interventions, nothing will be a complete success or a complete failure. Instead, most evaluations will demonstrate that an intervention will show some success. Concurrently, that same evaluation will demonstrate where the intervention failed. Follow-up evaluation then guides the practitioner as the organization continues to learn, assess, and intervene in the future. An excellent summary of different views of action research can be found in Rothwell and Sullivan (2005).

As a result, this becomes a circular process of assessment, intervention, and evaluation, a process summarized in Figure 2.1. The process begins with entry into the

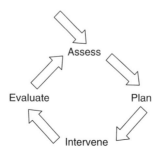

Figure 2.1   A Guide to the Research and Intervention Process.

organization and an initial assessment. After assessing, the practitioner plans how to intervene and then conducts that intervention. The final step is to evaluate successes and failures of the intervention. After evaluation, the process begins again, because the evaluation should also be a guide as to what to assess and how to intervene next.

Conducting the Initial Assessment

Assessing what is happening in a group is one of the most important steps in determining what subsequent steps to take to intervene. Once a practitioner becomes engaged on a project (whether serving as an internal or external consultant), it is necessary for him or her to gather information; Rothwell and Sullivan (2005) explain this as a process of collecting information about a problem to help identify a root cause. During the assessment stage, a practitioner uses appropriate applied research methods to collect detailed information about teams and then typically provides feedback about the results of this assessment. The assessment should focus on identifying the underlying problem and determining what needs to change (Tobey, 2005).

One common method of conducting an assessment is called a gap analysis (Franklin, 2006). In a gap analysis, the practitioner evaluates where a team wants to be and compares that to where the team currently is. This gap between this existing state and the desired state can help to determine what needs to change. Though a gap analysis is common, there are also many other techniques that can be used to conduct the initial assessment. Many assessment approaches, such as focus groups, may help organizations to reveal areas for improvement as well as specific ideas for improving. In addition, appreciative inquiry approaches focus on leveraging strengths. The choice of how to assess should depend on the specific needs of the team and organization.

Conducting the Follow-up Evaluation

Evaluation research should be conducted at the end of an intervention, which Rothwell and Sullivan (1995) term summative evaluation. It is designed to understand the overall results of an intervention. In an evaluation, the researcher uses social science methods to better understand the success (and failure) of a program. This program can be a training program, a social program, or a team intervention. Evaluation plans generally consider the stakeholders, or those who have interest in the success of an intervention. In small group interventions, the stakeholders might include (though are not limited to) the team members themselves, management, the leadership team in the organization, human resources representatives, the trainer, and/or a consultant involved in the project. The key in evaluation is to systematically review the effectiveness of the intervention as determined by these stakeholders.

The most common theory of understanding what type of evaluation to conduct is by Kirkpatrick (1994). Although designed specifically to evaluate training programs, it is certainly relevant to evaluating the success of many other programs interventions as well, and many of the interventions within this book have training requirements as part of their steps. The key to Kirkpatrick's view of evaluation is that it is for collecting information to "increase knowledge, improve skills, and change attitudes" (p. xvi). According to his model, there are four levels of analysis that a practitioner should emphasize when conducting this evaluation, including:

- *Reaction.* This is the first and most basic step of Kirkpatrick's model. This level is essentially a measure of customer satisfaction, or trying to determine what those who participated in the program liked and disliked about it. Reactions can help practitioners to improve the facilities, change delivery tactics, or make other similar changes. Unfortunately, satisfaction with an intervention does not predict its subsequent usefulness.
- *Learning.* Learning is the second level of Kirkpatrick's model. Usually evaluated using testing, this level determines whether those in the intervention actually changed their attitudes or increased their knowledge as a result of participating in the intervention. This level can show what people remember. Unfortunately, it fails to demonstrate whether people will actually use one of the interventions in their work.
- *Behavior.* This level, which is also called transfer, is the third level of Kirkpatrick's model. It is at this point that we see whether the intervention affects subsequent behavior in the workplace. Unfortunately, even if people behave in ways that are consistent with any intervention, it does not mean that these behaviors have an impact on the organization.
- *Results.* The final level of Kirkpatrick's model is results, and it emphasizes evaluating whether the intervention has any specific organizational impact, such as reducing turnover or increasing productivity. This final level is intended to demonstrate why the organization would want to continue to invest in an intervention that trains or develops groups and teams.

Follow-up evaluation research, whether using Kirkpatrick's model or conducted with another specific goal in mind, is important because it helps the practitioner to change and modify an intervention to make it more useful or discontinue using an intervention if the evaluation shows that it was unsuccessful.

The Steps in Applied Research

A summary of the steps in conducting applied assessment or evaluation research is provided in Table 2.1. These steps expand the "Assessment" and "Evaluation" components in the figure of the Rothwell and Sullivan (2005) model to provide a set of guidelines for how to assess and evaluate. These general guidelines can be used as a step-by-step method for conducting most applied research projects.

Table 2.1   A General Guide to the Steps in Conducting Applied Research.

1.	Set Objectives/Clarifying the Research Question.
2.	Determine Research Method.
3.	Select or Create Measurement Instruments.
4.	Consider Reliability and Validity.
5.	Choose a Sample.
6.	Consider Schedule, Location, and Facilities.
7.	Collect Data.
8.	Organize and Screen the Data.
9.	Analyze the Data.
10.	Report the Results.
11.	Act on the Information.

The first step of an applied research project is that it must have clear objectives that guide its methods. Clarifying the objective is necessary to conducting good applied research, and drives all the choices after it. One consideration here is determining who are the stakeholders and what do they need. It is always a good rule to begin the project with the end in sight – what is it that all stakeholders need to know at the end of the project and how will the project get at this information.

The objective helps the applied researcher to determine the method, including whether to choose surveys, interviews, focus groups, or even multiple methods of data collection. Summary descriptions of each of these methods follow.

After identifying the project objective and appropriate method, the practitioner should next identify or create measurement instruments necessary to get the data. It is always better to identify existing measures as long as they are reliable and valid. However, there are times when existing measures will not provide project-specific information. In these cases, it is best to carefully construct measurement tools. Creating measurement tools is beyond the scope of this book, but this chapter includes a brief summary of how to identify and select existing measurement tools.

It is at this point that a practitioner should consider the reliability (i.e., repeatability) of the measurement tools as well as their validity (i.e., accuracy). These two terms are often confused, but are distinct. Reliability means a measure will give similar responses over repeated measurements. On the other hand, validity means that a measure will give the response that is intended. The following example may help to clarify this difference: Imagine that a 250-pound person stood on a scale three times. The scale showed 180 pounds the first time, 179 the second, and then 181 the third. This scale is extremely reliable – its reliability is greater than 99%. Although the person may be quite pleased about the results, the scale is clearly not accurate, or in other words, it is not a valid measure of weight in pounds because it does not truly reflect the actual weight of a 250-pound person. Another example might be taking the SAT to get into college. A high school student may take the SAT three times and get very similar, albeit low, scores. The student may also have severe test anxiety, and the standardized testing environment makes the student very nervous. Thus, the reliable score (i.e., consistent over time) may not be a valid predictor (i.e., accurate) of college performance for that student. Determining reliability comes first – if a measure is reliable, the second step is to determine its validity. If the measure is not reliable, we are already confident it is not valid because it cannot be accurate if the measure provides dramatically different results.

Concurrently, a practitioner should also consider the people from whom data will be collected, or participants. The broad pool of people of interest is called the population. However, it is often difficult to collect information from all members of the population. Thus, research is often conducted on a sample, or a subset of the population. There are many different ways to sample, but the two key questions to consider when sampling include whether the sample is representative of the members of the organization and whether there is a relevant group to which one might compare the sampled participants. Carefully screen participants so that they do in fact represent the population that is being studied.

These are the *when and where* details that must be determined prior to collecting data. Some considerations include collecting data during or outside of work hours (e.g., lunch), where and how do people return instruments, is face-to-face versus online data collection best, and so on. Once again, the project objectives should help guide the answers to these questions.

Once steps 1–6 have been completed, a practitioner can move forward with actually getting the information he or she needs.

After collecting the information, the next step is to move it forward. This step also requires some planning on how it might be analyzed and reported (the next two steps). In addition, the data need to be screened for accuracy; anything that is clearly unreasonable needs to be considered carefully prior to using that data. Screening can help to identify two problems:

Typographical errors and outliers. A typographical error is when the person who entered the data into a computer format mistyped a value, for example a "3" for gender, when "1" represents a female participant while a "2" represents a male participant. Neglecting to screen for typographical errors may lead to an interesting discussion where you are required to explain how your assessment yielded a third gender in the team! Screening should also search for outliers, which are unusually high or low values for a response. How to determine an outlier is well beyond the scope of this text.

Like the previous step, this step requires some planning about how the data are going to be reported. Qualitative data might be analyzed according to key themes that participants discuss. Quantitative data should be analyzed using appropriate descriptive statistics and possible inferential statistics. At this point, those who are inexperienced with statistical analyses might solicit the help of a behavioral scientist or statistician who is trained in analysis. Finally, reporting tabulations of numbers is insufficient; it is the researcher's job to also interpret what the data mean. The purpose of applied research is to learn about generalities rather than identify specifics about a person. Although each person's individual opinion about the assessment and evaluation is certainly important in some circumstances, it is not the individual but the tendency of the typical individual in which the researcher is interested.

Imagine, for example, that 99 participants report performing subsequent behaviors that suggest an intervention is successful while only one reports behaviors that suggest that it failed. This intervention was likely a success, because the tendency of the group was to act in accordance with the intervention. The researcher might want to consider what happened to the lone individual, but it is clear that the intervention caused most people to change their behavior. Thus, it is less important to understand one person's response than it is to get a sense of how a larger group responded.

The second to last step is disseminating the results to project stakeholders. The two most common ways to deliver results are through presentations or written reports. Regardless of which method is appropriate for the stakeholders, it is necessary to consider the knowledge level and preparation of the audience so as to make sure not to provide too much detail or discuss the information at a level which is beyond their understanding. This may even make it necessary to prepare several different reports or presentations to different groups of stakeholders.

The final step is for the stakeholders to plan an action and then act on the information. Action may include making changes in the organization, ending some process in the organization, or changing an intervention to make it more successful.

Voluntary Participation, Confidentiality, and Anonymity

There are some guidelines that researchers use to help participants feel at ease with data collection. These include voluntary participation, providing confidentiality, and/or ensuring anonymity. Voluntary participation means that all participants should be given the opportunity to refuse to participate. The guarantee of voluntary participation is common within basic and academic research. In fact, most Institutional Review Boards – the committees that determine whether academic research is ethical – will not allow a study to go forward unless the researcher explicitly (usually in writing) commits to the guarantee of voluntary participation of those who will participate.

This is not always the case with applied research. Applied research projects within organizations often do not fall under the purview of Institutional Review Boards. In addition, participants within organizations are often being paid to participate as well as being expected to participate as part of their job responsibilities. Because of this, some might feel that they should have the right to force participants within their organization to respond. However, this type of coercion will likely only lead to poor data; if potential participants have grave concerns about participating, they will not provide accurate information. If the information from participants is inaccurate, the corresponding project results will also be inaccurate, as will any subsequent organizational decisions based on that information.

Along with voluntary participation comes a guarantee of confidentiality. This means that the researcher, or research team, knows who the participants are but pledges to withhold any identifying information in summaries and analyses of the data (and keeps this pledge even in difficult situations). Like voluntary participation, this can only increase the quality and meaningfulness of the data because people are more likely to provide honest and accurate information. Like voluntary participation, guaranteeing confidentiality is a necessity regardless of whether the project is applied or not.

Even better than guaranteeing confidentiality is finding ways to provide participants with complete anonymity, or collecting data using methods that ensure that even the researcher himself or herself has no idea who submitted information. Although creating procedures to create anonymity are not possible in every research situation, it is an admirable goal when possible and participants typically feel more comfortable to express themselves in ways that provide honest opinions and improve the quality of the data.

Methods of applied research   Although there are many different methods that can be used to assess the core problems in a group and evaluate the success of interventions, three of the most common and most useful applied methods are summarized in this chapter. They include conducting observation, individual interviews, focus group interviews, and surveys. The first three methods are often *qualitative*, or methods where analyzing the data is, at least in part, based on the researcher's interpretation of the information. A final method of assessing groups is through the use of surveys. These are often used to collect *quantitative* data, which means the method of data collection tends to emphasize numerical information and is less affected by individual interpretation, although they are used to collect qualitative data as well. Thankfully, there are also many reliable and valid assessment tools that have already been designed to provide evidence about a certain phenomenon that can be included in a survey. An example of a one of these tools is the Thomas-Kilmann Conflict Mode Instrument (Thomas & Kilmann, 1974). Although assessment tools are somewhat imperfect (i.e., they do not have perfect reliability and validity), practitioners can easily find many tools with acceptable levels of reliability and validity that already exist rather than creating their own. A final type of quantitative research is experimentation, although it is seldom used in applied settings, and as a result I do not discuss it further in this book.

One of the underlying premises of organizational research is that by conducting the research, organizations will learn something useful so that they may make positive change. These changes are often called interventions. Organizations use evidence-based reasoning to make informed changes rather than simply intervening without any knowledge of what, how, why, or when to intervene. In fact, many feel that research alone is a type of intervention (Harvey & Brown, 2001). There is merit to this; simply asking people for information may make them feel better about working for the organization because it seems that the organization cares. There is a corresponding problem resulting from this as well. If organizations continually ask for information but do not act on that information, research participants may quickly become jaded and frustrated (Mastrangelo, 2008).

Using Observation to Conduct Team Research

To the novice researcher, observation seems to be one of the simplest ways to conduct research; you just sit down and watch teams, no different than watching people walk through a park in the city or within the local mall. The reality of collecting information through observation, however, is much more difficult than that. Collecting data through observation requires making some very specific research choices, preparing ahead of time, and then making possibly subjective choices about what the observations mean.

How to observe and analyze information from those observations

Regardless of the difficulties of conducting observation, it is a tool that is worth knowing for the team researchers. In fact, the basic idea about one of the classic studies about group performance, Triplett's (1898) study of social facilitation, was gathered when Triplett was observing how bicycle racers go faster when working against one another than when working alone. His follow-up experimentation was conducted in a much more systematic manner, but observation was at the heart of how he was able to generate his ideas.

The process for gathering information through observation is described in detail in Table 2.2. As you can see in the table, the process starts with a review of what, specifically, needs to be known about this group or team. This helps the observers to know what it is they are looking for while observing. If the observers do not have this guidance, than the observations will likely lack clarity because of the broad range of possibilities and the outcomes of the observation will be far less meaningful than if the observers are given clear guidance. On the other hand, skilled observers should be given some flexibility to observe unexpected, *but related*, behavior with the team. This is because virtually no plan is perfect; as applied researchers, we are always modifying our plans to account for the unexpected.

Table 2.2   Steps in Conducing Observation Research.

1.	Determine What it is You Will be Observing.
2.	Determine Who to Observe, Where it is You Will Be Observing, and When to Observe.
3.	Determine How to Record Data.
4.	Determine Whether You Should Do Participant Observation, Unobtrusive Observation, or Something in Between.
5.	Have More Than One Person Observe.
6.	Test Run.
7.	Observe.
8.	Code the Data as Necessary.

After coming up with the goals for what will be observed, the plan needs to get into specifics, such as the who, where, when, and how much. As with all research, these choices should be made in ways that are consistent with the overall research question. The next step is to determine how involved you should be as part of the research. Some recommend that the observer be a participant, while others recommend that the observer be completely unobtrusive, or like a fly on the wall. Both choices have advantages and disadvantages. Finally, the observer should make a determination about whether, if possible, there is more than one person who can collect the observation data.

After the preliminary decisions above are made, the researcher should take a test run of the system. This will help him or her to learn about any problems with the choices or other areas that he or she has neglected to consider, such as a problem with the location or video taping equipment. Once these problems are solved, it is time to carve out the necessary time to make the observations and then analyze the observation data.

Observation can be a task that is completely overwhelming if an observer does not know ahead of time specifically. The applied research needs to first examine the research question carefully and then make sure that what he or she observes matches the needs of the question.

Second, it is important for the researcher to identify who should be observed, and this depends on the question. Does, for example, the question focus on roles? If this is the case, the researcher should be observing all team members (and not guests or ad hoc members. If, on the other hand, the question focuses on leadership, then the observers should be encouraged to focus on the team leaders. In addition to whom, the researcher also needs to find a location that is convenient for the team, not the researcher. Finally, the researcher must answer the question of when to observe. Typically, a sample of a team's behavior is often all that is needed. Thus, if a team is working together for a long period of time, it is unnecessary to watch every interaction among members. Instead, the researcher should pick, ahead of time, some times which are more or less random at which to observe. The team, however, should have advance notice so that the members are not surprised and upset by the appearance of an observer. After a short time during observation, most people will start to ignore the presence of the observer.

Third, the researcher needs to determine how to record the observation data. There are three main methods of recording information from observations: Audio, video, and notes. Unfortunately, the method (as always) depends on the situation. In teams where the researcher has an existing, strong relationship based on trust, audio or video recording can be excellent ways of collecting detailed information. There are many situations where the information is sensitive or the observer does not have a preexisting relationship based on trust. In these cases, it is usually best to take notes rather than impose a recording device on the team.

Fourth, the researcher needs to make a careful decision about how much those being observed know about the research that is being conducted. One of the controversies in conducting observation research falls from, on one side, those who believe in unobtrusive observation to, on the other side, those who recommend participant observation. Unobtrusive observation means that those being observed likely do not even know that they are being observed. Proponents of unobtrusive observation say that the primary benefit of this type of observation is creating a real-life situation where people act as if they would normally act because they are not aware of being observed. Participant observation is when the observers themselves are active parts of the group or team. Proponents of participant observation believe that observers are much more informed and can gain details that they otherwise may not know if they are part of the team. As always, I recommend allowing the research question and the specific situation to dictate whether you choose unobtrusive observation, participant observation, or something in between.

Although not always possible, it is helpful in providing reliable and valid results if more than one person conducts the observation. The observation notes and content from the two observers can be compared to verify that they are finding the same information, Further, if they don't agree they can then go back to their notes or the recording and make a determination through review and discussion. My one piece of additional advice here is to break up and clarify all the roles. If observation is the method being used to collect data about the success of a team intervention, then the person who is observing should be different from the one conducting the intervention. In addition to the competing time demands, it is also very difficult for anyone to separate the roles of research/evaluator from consultant and collect unbiased information about the success of one's own intervention.

If at all possible, make sure to work with your observation partner to test run your observation methods! A short test run may yield problems with your observation choices and more areas that might need to be observed. It is better to learn of these concerns during a small test run than when halfway through a study.

After the core choices are made, it is time to conduct the observations. Make sure to be wary of time. Observations, as well as the subsequent analysis of these observations, may take a considerable amount of time out of one's daily schedule.

Finally, as with any qualitative research, the research and/or observer must make sense of the observations. One way to make sense of this vast amount of information is to put codes to the data. These codes then help to provide a structure for analyzing the information. A second way is through theme analysis, which is discussed in more detail in the next section (see Atkinson & Coffey, 2002, for a comparison of observation and interviewing methods).

Additional Resources for Observation

Sanger, J. (1996). *Compleat observer: A field research guide to observation* (Qualitative Studies Series). NY: Routledge.

Using Interviews to Conduct Team Research

Like observation, conducting individual interviews is seemingly one of the easiest ways to collect information from people. Unfortunately, it is in fact quite difficult to create quality interview questions that probe for the necessary information and takes time and practice. Furthermore, analyzing the information resulting from interviews can be quite cumbersome, especially when interviewing a large number of participants; in these situations it might be best to use quantitative surveys instead of interviews because large quantitative data sets are often easier to analyze than large qualitative data sets.

How to conduct interviews and analyze interview information

There are three broad categories of interviews: Structured, semi-structured, and unstructured. These really can be organized on a continuum. On one end of the continuum are structured interviews. These provide all the questions that the interviewer must ask on the form and the interviewer is then not allowed to stray from any of those questions. These are excellent tools to help provide reliability when conducting a large number of interviews with many interviewers (e.g., the United States Census). Unfortunately, structured interviews do not allow experienced researchers to probe for more information or follow-up on an interesting line of thought from one or two participants. On the other end of the continuum are unstructured interviews, where the interviewer does not necessarily plan questions at all. These allow interviewers the flexibility to follow the flow of the interview and investigate any interesting thought patterns that might result. However, they provide virtually no means for establishing reliability, because the flow of questions often differs considerably from one interview to the next. Thus, both fully structured and unstructured interviews have drawbacks that I find difficult to accept when assessing to determine what intervention to conduct or evaluating the success of interventions. This is because a set of core questions is necessary to provide the needed reliability, while a skilled interviewer also needs the flexibility to follow-up on discussion points to learn about information that he or she may not have initially considered.

This leads to a third type of interview – called semi-structured – which is at the middle of the continuum between fully-structured interviews (with reliability yet little flexibility) and unstructured ones (with flexibility yet little reliability). The question then instead becomes how much flexibility is necessary, and the answer depends on the goals of the project as well as the skill and expertise of the interviewers. In semi-structured interviews the interviewer has a core set of key questions while allowing that same interviewer the flexibility to move off the form. I am personally a fan of using semi-structured interviews because the technique balances the need for reliability with the need for flexibility and as a result recommend it to practitioners. Thus, Table 2.3 provides a summary of some basic steps to consider when

Table 2.3   Steps in Conducting Semi-Structured Interviews.

1. Create Interview Questions.
2. Revise and Fine-Tune Questions to Create an Interview Form.
3. Schedule Interviews.
4. Conduct Interviews.
5. Analyze Qualitative Interview Data.

conducting a semi-structured interview. These add more detail to the steps in the "general" applied research model previously described and summarized in Table 2.3.

The first step in interviewing is to brainstorm a list of all possible questions and/ or identify existing measures that ask possible questions. If creating new interview questions, it is a better starting point to generate many questions when trying to brainstorm for the final list. Good questions are usually conversational, short, clear, easy to ask, and open-ended (i.e., answers such as yes or no are not possible). Questions should use terms and phrases that are relevant to the interview audience while avoiding jargon that the interview participants would not know. It sometimes helps to create questions that ask participants to list or rank things of importance.

After identifying a long list of questions, the second step is to narrow that list and create a final survey interview form. Try to identify and revise questions that appear several times. In addition, make sure to eliminate questions that do not fit the project objective and sequence the questions logically. Finally, it is always best to get feedback about the questions from other professionals and test the questions in the interview with one or two potential participants prior to using it for all interviews. It is at this point that the interview questions can be revised before it is too late.

Next, schedule the research interviews. Make sure you have a good estimate of how long the interview might take so you can schedule accordingly. In addition, it is important to find a location and time that is convenient for *the participant*, not for the interviewer while at the same time making sure that the interview is in a location where the participant will have few interruptions. It might even be best to ask the participant to turn off computer prompts and cell phones as necessary.

Fourth, conduct the interviews. In a semi-structured interview, the interviewer should follow the interview form, but should also feel the flexibility to move beyond or outside of it when necessary. This flexibility allows the interviewer to probe for information and also to lead the discussion in a direction that is relevant to the research question (it is always important to keep it on topic rather than just allow the discussion to simply move in any direction that it flows). However, the interviewer should eventually move back to the interview form to continue the discussion after following up. An additional consideration at this point is how to collect the interview data. The interviewer can either take notes or tape record the interview. There are benefits and drawbacks with each choice: Taping the interview provides the richest data, but also gives many participants concerns about confidentiality and anonymity. On the other hand, participants have fewer concerns with note-taking (especially when they have a chance to see the notes at the end to guarantee that their name is not on it), but the process of taking notes can a) create some pauses that slow the flow of discussion and b) block some cognitive processing so that the interviewer might forget to follow-up on an important point.

The final step is to make sense of the information. Although there are several ways to analyze qualitative interview information, one of the most common methods is called a theme analysis. In this type of analysis, the practitioner can code the interview data for key ideas or themes that have been discussed by multiple participants. These themes can be generated ahead of time from theory or preexisting knowledge about the problem. On the other hand, these themes can be generated while reading and reviewing the interviews (a process called grounded theory). Regardless of analysis method, qualitative analysis should be systematic and verifiable, but should also continually develop as analysis occurs.

Additional Resources for Interviewing

Dick, B. (2005). Grounded theory: a thumbnail sketch. Available at: http://www.scu.edu.au/schools/gcm/ar/arp/grounded.html.

Lee, T. W. (2003). *Using qualitative methods in organizations*. Thousand Oaks, CA: Sage.

McCracken, G. (1988). *The long interview: Qualitative research methods series vol. 13*. Thousand Oaks, CA: Sage.

Oishi, S.M. (2002). *The survey kit, vol. 5: How to conduct in-person interviews for surveys* (2nd edn). Thousand Oaks, CA: Sage.

Using Focus Groups to Conduct Team Research

A focus group is a process designed to gain depth of understanding from a group of people rather than interviewing one individual. In a focus group, a moderator asks interview questions and then works to elicit the feelings, attitudes, and perceptions of the participants. Two advantages of focus groups over interviews include: a) there are some synergies or disparities that may occur in a focus group interview as participants together discuss an issue and b) the researcher can collect information from a greater number of people in less time than if all the people were interviewed individually.

How to conduct focus group interviews and analyze focus group interview information

Designing focus group interviews is, in many ways, conceptually similar in design to individual interviews. The major difference is in the process of actually conducting the focus group. This is because the researcher is interviewing multiple people at once, and thus he or she must have skills in understanding and facilitating groups in addition to those required in designing the project, creating the interview form, and analyzing the

Table 2.4   Considerations when Conducting Focus Group Interviews.

1.   Selecting Focus Group Size.
2.   Setting the Environment.
3.   Producing Participation.
4.   Eliciting Elaboration.
5.   Keeping the Discussion Focused.

information. These facilitation skills take time and practice to develop; it can be quite difficult to ask questions, move the group along, keep the topic focused, balance participation, decide where to elicit more information, and record notes about what was said all at the same time. These additional considerations are listed in Table 2.4.

The first step is to determine the size of the focus groups that are necessary. Typically, it is best to have between six and ten people in the focus group. This group size allows members to work together and generate new ideas while allowing time and specific opportunities for each member to speak and contribute. A group of more than ten people can become difficult to manage, and the facilitator may not have the time or ability to draw information out of quiet members.

The second step in focus group interviews that is above and beyond a one-on-one interview is to set the environment. The focus group moderator must facilitate the session to create an informal and open conversational environment. This is important because people are more likely to reveal their opinions, feelings, and attitudes when they feel more comfortable.

Another role of the moderator is to find ways to elicit information from participants. These skills become increasingly important when one or more members are very vocal or exceedingly quiet.

In addition, the focus group moderator is to find ways to encourage focus group participants to elaborate on why they have said what they have said. This requires probing for more information. Questions such as "Can you tell me more?" or "Can you explain that to me?" can help the moderator to draw out important information from the participants.

Often, groups move quickly from a topic that is of interest to a discussion that is tangential. A final role of a moderator is to carefully steer the conversation back to the topic. Although the tangents may be interesting, they often reveal little information that is important to the project objectives.

Additional Resources for Focus Groups

Krueger, R. A. & Casey, M. A. (2000). *Focus groups: A practical guide for applied research* (3rd edn). Thousand Oaks, CA: Sage.

Morgan, D. L. & Krueger, R. A. (1997). *The focus group kit (vols 1–6)*. Thousand Oaks, CA: Sage.

Puchta, C. & Potter, J. (2004). *Focus group practice*. Thousand Oaks, CA: Sage.

Using Surveys to Conduct Team Research

A survey is a standardized method of collecting information from a set of people. Often, not all the people of interest are surveyed (otherwise it would be called a census, not a survey). First, the researcher must know about the parameters of the group that will be surveyed. All the people to whom the researcher would like to generalize is called the *population*. In organizational settings, the population might be the entire organization, or it might be as small as a work team. This depends on the question that the applied researcher is trying to answer. Second, the researcher must select a *sample*, or a subset of the members of the population. This sample must be selected in a way that answers the research question while at the same time representing an approximation of the characteristics of the population. One of the best tools for selecting sample participants is by doing so randomly, although there are other methods of selecting samples from the population as well.

How to conduct surveys

Once a practitioner has decided that a survey is the best tool to solve the assessment or evaluation problem, the next step is to create the survey. This section focuses on quantitative survey design – that is, creating and administering surveys that help researchers collect numbers that represent the necessary information. The steps that expand on the general model in Table 2.1 are summarized in Table 2.5. There are two ways to get the items that are necessary to create a survey: a) create and write items that are tailored to the research problem or b) identify and obtain existing items or instruments that past research has shown are reliable and valid.

As in creating items for an interview or focus group questionnaire, the best choice is always to find existing items rather than creating them. There are two main reasons for this. First, existing items have usually been revised and improved, leading to better reliability and validity than items that a researcher creates. The second is that creating and testing items takes far more time than finding existing ones. However, there are many assessment and evaluation projects that ask questions that are so specific that the practitioner will have to create at least some items for the project. The next two sections summarize how to identify and create survey items.

The first step in creating a survey is to determine the general theoretical constructs, or concepts, that are necessary for the survey. For example, a survey might ask about

Table 2.5 Considerations when Conducting Quantitative Surveys.

1. Determining What to Survey.
2. Identifying Existing Measures.
3. Create Other Necessary Items.
4. Survey.
5. Organize Information.
6. Analyze the Data.

organizational commitment, job satisfaction, and/or employee engagement. However, it is important to limit the concepts to only to those that are most important to the research question. When thinking about what to ask, one rule is to only ask about concepts and information that will guide subsequent action. One reason for this is that surveys with more concepts take more time to create than surveys with fewer. More importantly, however, is that surveys take time for participants to complete. Longer surveys, of course, may yield more information. However, longer surveys may also reduce the response rate to the point where they might make the survey results meaningless.

The second step is to, where possible, search to identify and obtain reliable and valid measurement items. If, after conducting an exhaustive search trying to identify existing items, concepts still remain, create the necessary items to survey these concepts. Next, distribute the survey using online, face-to-face, telephone, or mail methods. Then, the research must screen and organize the information in order to improve the quality of the data. The final step is to analyze the data using a mix of descriptive and inferential statistics as necessary for the target audience.

Identifying and evaluating existing instruments

There are many quantitative surveys, instruments, tests, and other tools that have already been created that are designed to conduct some of the specific assessments and evaluations that a practitioner might need to perform. Some of these existing instruments are excellent resources for an applied researcher. Unfortunately, others have not been well designed. The difficulty, then, becomes first identifying where to find relevant instruments and second identifying which ones have acceptable reliability and validity. Fortunately, Ponterotto (1996) provides an excellent summary of finding and reviewing these instruments. Unfortunately, this at times takes some detective work within a library.

According to Ponterotto (1996), the first step in the process is to locate which instruments may be relevant for the assessment. Many critiques and validation studies of instruments are included in several resources, such as Mental Measurements Yearbook or Test Critiques (more of these reference books are located in the *Additional Resources* section that follows at the end of this chapter). These publications, and others like them, provide reviews of the instruments, including information about reliability and validity. Although the reviews themselves will not give the items on the instruments, they will provide information about where to obtain them. In addition, there are other books that will provide the exact items on the instruments, such as the Directory of Unpublished Experimental Measures. Finally, there are articles published in journals, such as the Journal of Applied Psychology, Educational and Psychological Measurement, and the Academy of Management Journal where practitioners may also find instruments to use to assess individual as well as team functioning.

The second step in the process is to evaluate the reliability and validity of the instrument, often called its psychometric properties. As stated previously, there are many instruments that are available for use. However, some are well designed tools with empirical research to support their use while others have limited usefulness because they lack reliability and/or validity. It is the responsibility of the practitioner to carefully select tools that have acceptable psychometric properties for the specific research question which they are trying to solve.

The final step is to obtain the actual instrument. This step often requires contacting the author or copyright holder in order to gain permission to use it. Some instruments require the practitioner to pay for using them, while others may simply be used for free. As a result of this, there are many possible assessment tools that a practitioner might use. This book provides a small sampling of these assessment tools within the text of each chapter.

Creating items that are tailored to the specific research question

A complete explanation of how to create survey items is well beyond the scope of this book. In fact, entire books, such as volume 2 of *The survey kit* (Fink, 2002), have been devoted to the nuances of writing survey items. Furthermore, creating good assessment and evaluation tools (i.e., ones that are valid and reliable) requires developing the skill through practice – that is one reason why it is always best to find existing measures that will work for the project. However, this will not always be possible. At times, the practitioner will be forced to write his or her own items because of the specific nature of the questions involved in the assessment or evaluation project. A brief summary of this process follows.

The first step in developing items for the survey is to clearly define the concepts that have been identified as requirements for the survey. Once these concepts have been identified, the next step is to brainstorm and draft a laundry list of items that might measure these concepts. After creating the laundry list, the practitioner should then reexamine all items about a concept and eliminate the ones that are redundant, revise the remaining items so that they are in conversational English and only measure one concept (i.e., good survey item writers work hard to avoid double-barreled items, or ones that measure two concepts at the same time). Finally, the completed set of survey items should be piloted, or tested with a very small sample of the population (actually, a good rule for all applied research), before being used with the entire group.

Collecting survey data

Once the survey has been created, tested, and revised, it is time to administer the survey. There are four methods to administering surveys: Face-to-face, telephone, paper and pencil, or online. Each of these has advantages and disadvantages, and the practitioner must evaluate the tradeoffs and select the most appropriate method for the project. Briefly, the methods are listed in order based on their advantages and disadvantages. Face-to-face methods have many disadvantages. They are typically are the most expensive, take the most time from survey design to completed data set, and require the most training of those administering the survey. However, face-to-face methods have specific advantages, such as they often have the highest response and honesty rates whereas online methods may have the lowest of each (Fink, 2002). At the other end of continuum are online methods, which are usually the least expensive to administer (especially with inexpensive online survey programs such as *SurveyMonkey* and *Zoomerang*), take the shortest time, and require the least training to administer, but also have the lowest response and honesty rates.

How to analyze survey information

After completing the survey, the next step is to organize and then analyze the survey information. Organizing the information is necessary because the vast amount of information must be in an analyzable format before it may be analyzed. This step requires screening the data to make sure every survey is usable and the responses are reasonable and then organizing it into a format so it may be analyzed. Although it is possible to conduct analyses by hand, I don't recommend this because of the vast numbers of easy to use computer programs available to help with analysis, such as Excel and SPSS.

For many applied audiences, it will be sufficient to conduct *descriptive statistics*, or statistics that describe only the characteristics of the data that have been collected (Mertler & Vannatta, 2005). These statistics can help to understand what intervention to use or how well the intervention worked. Common descriptive statistics and when they should be used are listed in Table 2.6. However, any judgments resulting solely from using descriptive statistics should be made with caution – these judgments are best made by using inferential statistics. *Inferential statistics* are those that help a researcher to draw inferences from the sample to an entire population (Mertler & Vannatta, 2005).

Table 2.6 Types of Data and Relevant Descriptive Analyses.

Type of Data	Definition	Appropriate Descriptive Analyses
Categorical (Nominal)	Numbers that represent categories (e.g., coding men as "1" and women as "2")	Percentages, Frequency Table, Pie Chart, and Frequency Chart
Ordinal	Numbers that represent order or ranking (e.g., the top performer gets a "1", the second a "2" and so on)	Percentages, Frequency Table, Pie Chart, Frequency Chart. In Some Cases, an Average (Interpret these with caution)
Numerical (Interval & Ratio)	Numbers that have order and equal intervals between them (e.g., temperature and weight)	Average, Minimum, Maximum, Percentiles, Median (or 50th Percentile)

Additional Resources for Surveys

Buros Institute. *Mental measurements yearbook*. Highland Park, NJ: Mental Measurements Yearbook.

Fernandez-Ballesteros, R. *Encyclopedia of psychological assessment*. Thousand Oaks, CA: Sage.

Fields, D. L. (2002). *Taking the measure of work: a guide to validated scales for organizational research and diagnosis*. Thousand Oaks, CA: Sage.

Fink, A. (2002). *The survey kit* (2nd edn). Thousand Oaks, CA: Sage.

Goldman, B. A., Mitchell, D. F., & Egelson, P. E. (1996). *Directory of unpublished experimental mental measures*. Washington, DC: American Psychological Association.

Guion, R. M. (1998). *Assessment, measurement, and prediction for personnel decisions*. Mahwah, NJ. LEA.

Hersen, M. (2003). *Comprehensive handbook of psychological assessment*. Hoboken, NJ: John Wiley & Sons, Inc.

Keyser, D. & Sweetland, R. C. (1991). *Test critiques*. Austin, TX: Pro-ed.

Maddox. T. (2003). *Tests: A comprehenseive reference for assessments in psychology, education, and business*. Austin, TX: Pro-ed.

Mental measures. Washington, DC: American Psychological Association.

Reddy, W. B. (1996). *Group-level team assessment: A 10-step sequence to a committed team*. San Diego: Pfeiffer & Company.

FOCUS ON APPLICATION

Improving the team that got along too well: Jeffrey A. Jolton, PhD, Kenexa

The practitioner

Jeffrey A. Jolton, PhD, is a Director of Consulting at Kenexa, providing thought leadership and strategic direction for several of Kenexa's largest global projects. He has over 18 years of extensive consulting experience with organizational, leadership, and individual assessment, and is considered a leading expert in assessment-based change and research. He has provided innovative and insightful guidance to a number of organizations throughout his career including Accenture, CVS Caremark, Ernst & Young, Hewitt Packard, HSBC, General Electric, Johnson Controls, PricewaterhouseCoopers, and Xerox. A regular presenter at conferences,

Jeffrey has also published over 30 articles, book chapters, and publications on including topics on employee engagement, effective leadership, and global HR practices. He holds a Doctorate and a Master of Science degree in Industrial and Organizational Psychology from Ohio University.

The symptom

A mid-sized custom manufacturing firm, which specialized in the design and manufacturer of precision screw machined components and assemblies, was looking to grow and increase customer satisfaction. The president was concerned that although they had strong engineers working at the firm, they were not creating the high quality and innovative solutions he felt the engineering teams were capable of producing. Individually he saw some impressive work, but when teams were assembled, things just didn't seem to be "clicking." He called me in to assess the situation and provide solutions that would help promote his strategic business goals.

Assessing the problem

We started with some general interviews with engineers and their managers. The general impression was that people enjoyed working together, and that cooperation seemed very important to the engineers. The managers, however, confirmed that the engineers were smart, and did some great independent work, but were not producing as expected at a team level. One manager wondered aloud: "Is this the kind of place where one head is better than many?"

I established a battery of assessment tools to measure critical thinking, job knowledge, personality, and interpersonal skills. We then examined these results at the individual and team levels. What was striking was how similar the individual profiles were among the engineers. We also learned that indeed this was a group of very smart people, but they tended to be focused in their breadth of knowledge, and so perhaps innovation was limited because they were not considering things outside their area of expertise (and, more importantly, if everyone had the same background, they were all drawing from the same area). The other factor was that on the personality and work styles measures almost all the engineers came out as being very conflict adverse, and when interacting with others they would put cooperating and getting along ahead of expressing an opposing viewpoint or disagreement.

Intervening: What did you do?

We first determined that more diversity of thought and personality style would benefit the team and its innovation. The company had been using an assessment profile to find and hire talented engineers, and it seem that profile was working perhaps too well, bringing in people who all fit the "cookie cutter" nature of the profile. We adjusted the hiring profile to also focus on broader competencies that would serve the role (critical job factors) rather than just specific skills. We also suggested that they select engineers who were more open to conflict, liked debating, and less adverse to risk taking. The expectation was that over time, this greater mix of engineers would enhance the diversity of teams and increase innovation.

Once we adjusted the selection profile, we started working with the teams themselves to help alter some of the dynamics. Awareness of the problem is always helpful, so we first reviewed the assessment results alone with each engineer, pointing out the strengths and weaknesses their profile revealed and how it affected their team and their work. We then met each team of engineers and shared a team profile, underscoring the fact they valued cooperation over conflict, and how this was actually creating greater risks for the team (e.g., groupthink). We then formalized roles for each team meeting, so that within the team there was always someone playing one of the key roles:

- Devil's advocate, whose job was to argue against ideas.
- Master of ceremony, whose job was to make sure everyone spoke up and brought their own ideas to the table.
- Judge, whose job was to evaluate the team dynamics in the meeting and call out behaviors they were trying to break (e.g., if the devil's advocate wasn't really countering ideas, or if people were being too quiet).

At the end of each meeting, the judge provided a verdict on the team dynamics, what worked, what didn't, and served as a mechanism to provide on-going feedback to the teams. When appropriate, the meetings also had a "librarian" whose job was to find and share an article or research or innovation outside the knowledge base of the team to inspire new directions. Roles were rotated for each meeting.

The teams adopted the new roles quickly, and although at first they struggled with the devil's advocate role, within a few weeks they reported feeling like they were getting better ideas and directions from the sessions. In a six-month follow up, which was conducted after a few new engineers were hired, the teams reported greater energy and more positive dynamics. One engineer said, "All this time I thought I was helping the team by agreeing with everything. Now I see how much opportunity we missed!." The business has grown significantly, and is now considered an innovation leader in its field.

Final Comments: Triangulating to Find Answers

Furthermore, a practitioner may also find that they need to use multiple methods to triangulate, which is a process of learning about a phenomenon – in this case, a team – by using more than one method of collecting assessment and evaluation information. For example, an organizational survey may generate some concerns by showing significantly lower employee engagement scores among a certain set of work teams than the previous year's survey results. After the survey, the practitioner may follow-up with focus group interviews to learn more detail. On the other hand, a practitioner may conduct a focus group interview and learn about some safety concerns. To determine how widespread or isolated the problem is, that same practitioner may then conduct an organizational-wide assessment. As can be seen, this chapter provides the outline for conducting this research and ways to learn more about becoming an assessment and evaluation expert. These mutli-method approaches to assessment and evaluation are called triangulation.

Chapter Summary

In this chapter, I have briefly reviewed four different methods of assessing and evaluating groups and teams, including interviews, observation, focus groups, and surveys. Interviews are typically one-on-one sessions where the interviewer learns about what is happening through dialogue, which helps researchers to learn about perceptions among group and team members. In observational research, the applied researcher works to learn about the group or team by observing key concepts and themes that can help her or him to learn about processes and behaviors. Focus group interviews are more efficient than one-on-one because multiple people are being interviewed at once, and are also an excellent research tool for gaining multiple perspectives and perceptions during an interview. But, they also require skills in facilitating groups. Finally, surveys are quick ways to get a snapshot of the attitudes and opinions of many individuals in a relatively quick time frame. Regardless of which specific method of collecting data, the process of applied group research follows a fairly structured pattern that is consistent with reliable and valid research.

Each of these three has its place and may be used in applied group research. Thus, it is important for practitioners to become expert at all four methods so that they have more opportunities and choices for ways to assess and evaluate team functioning. However, regardless of which method, the main point of this chapter is that to determine what is the proper intervention requires a thorough assessment of the problem. In addition, to determine whether the intervention worked (and concurrently what did not!) and what might be next requires a thorough evaluation of the outcomes.

Additional Resources

Bader, G. E., Bloom, A. E., & Chang, R. Y. (1994). *Measuring team performance: A practical guide to tracking team success.* San Francisco: Pfeiffer.

Brannick, M. T., Salas, E., & Prince, C. (1997). *Team performance, assessment, and measurement: Theory, methods, and applications.* Mahwah, NJ. LEA.

Cooper, D. R., & Schindler, P. S. (2006). *Business research methods* (9th ed.). Boston: McGraw Hill.

Davidson, E. J. (2005). *Evaluation methodology basics: The nuts and bolts of sound evaluation.* Thousand Oaks, CA: Sage.

Kirkpatrick, D. L. (1994). *Evaluating training programs: The four levels* (2nd ed.). San Francisco: Berrett-Koehler Publishers, Inc.

Ponterotto, J. G. (1996). In F. T. L. Leong & J. T. Austin (eds.) *The psychology research handbook: A guide for graduate students and research assistants.* Thousand Oaks, CA: Sage.

Rothwell, W. J. (2005). *Practicing organization development: A guide for consultants.* San Francisco: Pfeiffer.

Sommer, R., & Sommer, B. (2002). *A practical guide to behavioral research: Tools and techniques.* New York: Oxford.

Tobey, D. D. (2005). *Needs assessment basics.* Alexandria, VA: ASTD Press.

Team Exercises

Exercise 2.1   Finding an assessment tool

Step 1:   Using a search engine on the internet, find assessment tools to learn about team conflict, team communication, and team member diversity awareness.

Step 2:   Assess the reliability and validity of the tools you find. Check for information about the tools within Mental Measurements Yearbook, if possible.

Step 3:   Using an academic literature search engine, find assessment tools to learn about conflict, team communication, and team member diversity awareness.

Step 4:   Assess the reliability and validity of the tools you find. Check for information about the tools within Mental Measurements Yearbook, if possible.

Step 5:   Contrast the reliability and validity information about the different tools.

Exercise 2.2   Deciding on a choice of research method

The president from a local non-profit organization calls you and requests your assistance regarding some problems she is having in her organization. The president explains that in the last six months the performance of her leadership team has significantly decreased, their employees are calling in sick to work, and turnover is at an all-time high. You know that these issues are potentially symptoms of a larger issue around group inputs or processes. She explains that she would like you to conduct a survey to determine what some of the issues might be that are causing these problems. As a groups and teams consultant, however, you know that there are many other data collection tools available to you that you might use to get at the root cause. How would you research this situation using the information in this chapter? You know that your research is going to help her determine what steps to take to develop her team. Consider:

- How you would assess the issues facing this team?
- How you would later evaluate whether any intervention was successful?

Part II

Inputs

Chapter 3

Team Theories and Concepts

Imagine that you lead a five-person engineering team where one of the team members is named John. Although John has incredible technical skills, he comes to meetings late. He commits to design work during meetings but then never completes it. He never lends a hand when others are behind when completing challenging tasks. Another person on your team is named Sue, who is almost John's polar opposite. Sue is always early for meetings and comes prepared. She not only completes the work to which she commits, but also goes above and beyond. Finally, she is always willing to help others so that the team can succeed. Next, imagine that your boss just informed you that one person on your team had to go. I am quite confident that you would keep Sue around and let John go. Sue is prepared for working in a group or team while John is not.

Individual preparation for group and team work is one of the many basic team concepts that team members must understand in order to work more effectively in groups and teams. These concepts include structural issues about how groups work, how groups differ than individuals, and how members are influenced in teams. This chapter reviews some of these basic team theories and concepts so that team members have the background knowledge necessary for them to become part of a highly effective team.

Learning Goals for Chapter 3

- Know basic team concepts that help to understand a team.
- Understand how teams develop and be able to identify the developmental stage of a team.

Group Dynamics and Team Interventions: Understanding and Improving Team Performance, First Edition. Timothy M. Franz.

- Understand team member socialization.
- Understand different team structures and their impact on team performance.
- Understand the importance of team member fit.
- Understand individual versus team tasks and know how to improve group work depending on the tasks.
- Understand group roles and role problems and how to improve group performance by modifying roles.

Assessing Team Member Effectiveness

As Chapter 2 stated, assessment and evaluation are both starting and ending points of a continual cycle of evolution to improving teams. Thus, all remaining chapters within this text begin with one possible assessment tool that you may use as the starting point to getting information about some of the key points within the chapter. It is important to note that I have only chosen one possible assessment from the vast literature available to students, researchers, and practitioners; there are many others. The tools within this text may be an excellent starting point for your team. However, your team may also need to identify other assessment tools that are not listed in this book. You can find these tools using the methods that you have already read in Chapter 2.

Knowledge of team member preparedness can help a team in at least four different ways (Cannon-Bowers & Salas, 1997). First, information about how prepared members are helps that team (or someone outside of that team) to diagnose its problem areas and then the team members can work together to solve those problems. Second, knowing these problem areas can help a team to list its strengths and weaknesses, so members within that team know when to use skills and abilities – often referred to as competencies – within their team versus when to reach outside of the team for help with competencies that are not found within the team. Third, this knowledge about problem area as well as strengths and weaknesses can help to guide decisions about individual member as well as overall team training. Finally, knowledge about team member effectiveness is an effective first step at providing relevant and meaningful feedback to the team about its own members.

Loughry, Ohland, and Moore (2007) designed an overall measure of team member effectiveness (Table 3.1). This measure has two versions: An 87-item survey as well as a short form that contains 33 items. For the purposes of this book, the short version is all that is necessary. The items in the assessment tool are designed to get at an overall picture of the team members' readiness for working in a team and individual teamwork abilities. Further, the scale can be further divided into five subscales including (a) eight items about contributing to the team's work (Items 1–8); (b) ten items about interacting with teammates (Items 9–18); (c) seven items about keeping the team on track (Items 19–25); (d) four items about expectations of quality (Items 26–29), and (e) four items about having relevant task-related knowledge,

Table 3.1   Loughry, Ohland, and Moore's Measure of Team Member Effectiveness – Short Form.

Item	Strongly Disagree	Disagree	Somewhat Disagree	Neutral	Somewhat Agree	Agree	Strongly Agree
1. Did a fair share of the team's work.	1	2	3	4	5	6	7
2. Fulfilled responsibilities to the team.	1	2	3	4	5	6	7
3. Came to team meetings prepared.	1	2	3	4	5	6	7
4. Completed work in a timely manner.	1	2	3	4	5	6	7
5. Did work that was complete and accurate.	1	2	3	4	5	6	7
6. Made important contributions to the team's final product.	1	2	3	4	5	6	7
7. Kept trying when faced with difficult situations.	1	2	3	4	5	6	7
8. Offered to help teammates when it was appropriate.	1	2	3	4	5	6	7
9. Communicated effectively.	1	2	3	4	5	6	7
10. Facilitated effective communication in the team.	1	2	3	4	5	6	7
11. Exchanged information with teammates in a timely manner.	1	2	3	4	5	6	7
12. Provided encouragement to other team members.	1	2	3	4	5	6	7
13. Expressed enthusiasm about working as a team.	1	2	3	4	5	6	7
14. Heard what teammates had to say about issues that affected the team.	1	2	3	4	5	6	7
15. Got team input on important matters before going ahead.	1	2	3	4	5	6	7
16. Accepted feedback about strengths and weaknesses from teammates.	1	2	3	4	5	6	7
17. Used teammates' feedback to improve performance.	1	2	3	4	5	6	7
18. Let other team members help when it was necessary.	1	2	3	4	5	6	7
19. Stayed aware of fellow team members' progress.	1	2	3	4	5	6	7
20. Assessed whether the team was making progress as expected.	1	2	3	4	5	6	7
21. Stayed aware of external factors that influenced team performance.	1	2	3	4	5	6	7

(continued)

Table 3.1   (cont'd).

Item	Strongly Disagree	Disagree	Somewhat Disagree	Neutral	Somewhat Agree	Agree	Strongly Agree
22. Provided constructive feedback to others on the team.	1	2	3	4	5	6	7
23. Motivated others on the team to do their best.	1	2	3	4	5	6	7
24. Made sure that everyone on the team understood important information.	1	2	3	4	5	6	7
25. Helped the team to plan and organize its work.	1	2	3	4	5	6	7
26. Expected the team to succeed.	1	2	3	4	5	6	7
27. Believed that the team could produce high-quality work.	1	2	3	4	5	6	7
28. Cared that the team produced high-quality work.	1	2	3	4	5	6	7
29. Believed that the team should achieve high standards.	1	2	3	4	5	6	7
30. Had the skills and expertise to do excellent work	1	2	3	4	5	6	7
31. Had the skills and abilities that were necessary to do a good job.	1	2	3	4	5	6	7
32. Had enough knowledge of teammates' jobs to be able to fill in if necessary.	1	2	3	4	5	6	7
33. Knew how to do the jobs of other team members.	1	2	3	4	5	6	7

skills, and abilities (Items 30–33). Team members can be given this assessment tool prior to starting team work, after team work has been completed, or anytime during the team's work. By using this instrument as an assessment tool among the members within a team, you can get a general picture of where each team member stands relative to the others within the team. With the results in hand, you can start to better prepare all members for group and team work (another more thorough measure of the climate around diversity can be found in Kossek, Zonia, & Young, 1996).

Each member of the team should complete the survey and rate his or her own team competencies. To score the team member effectiveness survey, calculate an average of the scores for all 33 items on the scale to get a general sense of team competency. Members who score higher on the scale have greater team competency than those who score lower. Further, the scale can be scored by dividing it into the five subscales described above to understand specific team competencies, including contributions to the team's work (Averaging items 1–8), interacting with teammates (Averaging items 9–18), keeping the team on track (Averaging items 19–25), expectations of quality (Averaging items 26–29), having relevant task-related knowledge, skills, and abilities (Averaging items 30–33). In all categories, scores closer to "7" indicate greater team member effectiveness while scores closer to "1" indicate members who are less prepared for teamwork.

Team Formation and Development

Teams progress through stages in their development. Understanding a team's place in its developmental progression can help team members as well as consultants to help that team to improve its functioning and move further along in its developmental progression. Although there is considerable research about team development, two different authors have developed stage theories that provide an easy to understand summary of team development processes.

Tuckman (1965) has designed what is by far the most well-known theory of group development. He suggested that groups proceed through four to five specific stages: Forming, storming, norming, performing, and adjourning. The first stage is forming. This is the initial meeting time where members may learn more about one another, define their task and goals, and identify the opportunities and challenges which they might face. Because this is a time of initial learning, members are primarily focused on their individual behavior rather than on integrated team behavior; often, they are not yet functioning as a team.

According to Tuckman, the second stage through which a team progresses is storming. The primary way to identify this stage is though the increase in the level of team conflict. It is often a contentious and unpleasant stage that is difficult for many members. This is because team members have started to confront one another, understand where they have similar and possibly overlapping roles and possibly identify issues around leadership and other similar group facilitation responsibilities.

The third of Tuckman's group development stages is norming. This is the period of time when a team starts to resolve many of the problems with which it struggled in the previous stage. Group members have now had the time to get to know each other better and learn each others' strengths and weaknesses. They have more clearly defined team roles and agreed on task processes as well as expected social behavior within and possibly outside of the team. They may even start to gain detailed knowledge of what one another can do for the group and start to create a meta-cognition knowledge structure that extends beyond each member (Larson & Christiansen, 1993).

In Tuckman's original work, the fourth and last phase of development was performing. At this point, teams moved into a stage where they could attain a level of performance that was at or possibly even above what was initially expected of it. This is because the team has solved most of its problems around communication, conflict, and other group process losses that diminished its ability to succeed to the level of its potential.

Tuckman (see Tuckman & Jensen, 1977) reviewed the research about group development and as a result added adjourning as the fifth and final stage. With this, they recognized that not all groups remain intact. There are a variety of reasons for this, such as the organizational hierarchy disbanding the group but also a group completing its project so that the members may move on to different work or the ad hoc nature of some project teams.

Wheelan (2005) recommends an integrated theory of group development. Like Tuckman, she has four stages to development, including dependency and inclusion, counterdependency and fight, trust and structure, and productivity and effectiveness. She also includes a phase like Tuckman's adjourning, which she calls final. Although this model seems linear, it is more inclusive because it does not imply that groups must progress through the stages in order. Further, she states that not all groups attain the final stage because they get stuck in the earlier stages (see Wheelan, 2009).

There are reasonable critiques of these stage theories. The primary critique is that stage theories presuppose that groups and teams progress though these stages in order (Gersick, 1988; Ancona & Caldwell, 1988), meaning that the second stage can only occur when it follows the first, the third follows the second, and further. However, groups and teams often cycle around through the stages without necessarily following the order, and there are certainly many theories that do account for this. In addition, groups and teams can easily slip into early phases when they face considerable changes within or outside of the group, such as the addition of new members, a new project, or a structural change within the organization. Because of this, I recommend interpreting the stage theories like Tuckman's more loosely than originally designed. If team members can recognize some of the symptoms that are occurring, they may be more aware of what they can accomplish and how they need to develop or change.

Other scholars have tried to solve this same problem by developing and clarifying Tuckman's original model. Morgan, Salas, and Glickman (1993), for example, created the TEAM model. It describes a series of nine rather than five developmental stages. In their model, teams can spend differing periods of time within each stage. The model also includes periods where teams might re-enter later stages that are similar to earlier ones. Finally, the model includes both task and interpersonal factors in team development. Additionally, Gersick (1988) recommends a model of development that is evolutionary, or punctuated equilibrium (see also Dennis, Garfield, & Reinicke, 2008), where teams go through quick and rapid changes and these are followed by times of relative stability. Finally, Karriker (2005) provides an example of a cyclical model that builds upon Tuckman's linear model. Karriker suggests that, in intact groups, performing can impact storming in a process she describes as recycling.

Team Member Socialization

Equally important to the development of the entire team together is the socialization of team members who are later integrated into the team. Most of the team development literature assumes that members all start together and the entire team develops together. Unfortunately, this is not the case. People get promoted, change jobs, move, or change teams in other ways. When this happens, new members often join a team. These members need to be socialized so that they fit the team.

Socialization is the process through which members adjust over time to the actions and values of the group. It is when new team members learn how to act appropriately within the team. When team members' expectations are met through the socialization process, organizations have many positive outcomes, including increased trust (Porter, 1997), improved performance and effectiveness (Rentsch & Hall 1994), and reduced absenteeism (Porter & Steers, 1973). It is clear that the "the nature and quality of the interactions between newcomers and insiders are major determinants of adjustment and other socialization outcomes" (Major, Kozlowski, Chao, & Gardner, 1995, p. 419). During this socialization process, a newcomer integrates organizational values and their underlying assumptions into his or her own value system (Major *et al.*, 1995).

The important question about socialization becomes how to socialize new members so that the group or team can continue to function. Major and colleagues (1995) provide a list of potential answers to this. According to their longitudinal research with graduating seniors from a large Midwestern university, two major factors predict socialization:

- Leader-member exchange (see also Graen, 1976) is the quality of the dyadic relationship between a leader and each of his or her subordinates. Members who have a positive relationship with their leader are more likely to be socialized so that they fit the team than members who have less positive exchange relationships.
- Team-member exchange (see Seers, 1989) is a parallel concept extrapolated to the team level, or the quality of the team member relationships within the team. The process is similar, but at the level of the team members rather than with the leader and subordinate.

In leadership exchange as well as team member exchange, higher quality exchange relationships are predictive of the quality of the socialization process. Positive exchange relationships are ones where the expectations of the two people involved in the relationship are consistent. For example, if a team leader has clarified her expectations of the role that a new team member should take on within a team, and that new team member understands and agrees to perform that role, the leader and the team member will have, at least on this level, a positive exchange relationship. Thus, organizations that develop high quality team-member and leader-team relationships around expectations and roles will better socialize newcomers into their teams.

Person-Organization Fit

Socialization is effective if people, to at least some extent, fit the culture and values of the team. This is often called person-organization (P-O) fit. Kristof (1996) defines P-O fit as "the compatibility between people and organizations that occurs when: (a) at least one entity provides what the other needs, or (b) they share similar fundamental characteristics, or (c) both" (p. 6; see also O'Reilly, Chatman, & Caldwell, 1991). The concept behind P-O fit is that people are more motivated, stay longer, perform better, and so on, if they fit the values of the organization. On the other hand, if someone does not fit, he or she is more likely to leave, be more frustrated, have lower performance, and/or feel of lower value to the organization. As a colleague recently put it, the key to person-organization fit is to "get the right people hired and have them in the right seats" (M. S. Bryson, personal communication, May 21, 2009). The person-organization fit literature says that the right person is the one that matches, or fits, the values of the organization.

Hollenbeck (2000) has generalized this concept of person-organization fit to fit when working in teams. According to Hollenbeck, many of the critical aspects of fit "are manifested at the team level" (p. 534). This means that not only must organizations find and select employees who fit the values of the organization, teams must also find members within or outside of the organization who specifically fit the values manifested within the team. Hollenbeck recommends determining whether the culture is divisional, functional, centralized, decentralized, misaligned, or adaptive (see Table 3.2). Next, Hollenbeck recommends matching different personality types, as measured by the Big Five taxonomy, to these structures in order to see greater

Table 3.2   Hollenbeck's Recommendations for Matching Structure to Personality Type.

Organizational/Team Structure	Matching Necessary Team Member Personality Trait
Divisional: Roles in the team tend to be broad and unspecified.	Cognitive ability: A broader term than intelligence, team members need to have the ability to learn and use a wide variety of skills to succeed.
Functional: Roles in the team tend to be narrow and well defined.	Agreeableness: Team members need to be eager to help and sympathetic towards others to succeed.
Centralized: One person in the team is generally responsible.	Extroversion: Team members need to be sociable, assertive, active, and talkative to succeed.
Decentralized: The team has no clear leader or coordinating structure.	Conscientiousness: Team members need to be disciplined, plan, and have self-determination to succeed.
Misaligned: Dynamics and values within the team do not match those within the organization.	Emotional stability: Team members need to be stable and able to deal with stress to succeed.
Adaptive: The team is open and ready for change.	Openness to experience: Team members need to be ready to engage in novel and innovative patterns of behavior to succeed.

Adapted from Hollenbeck (2000).

team success. Although personality is only one part of the person, many of the other components (e.g., values and culture) are detailed in Chapter 4. Table 3.2 explains these matches between structure and personality.

ASA model

One of the most common theories within the person-organization fit literature is Schneider's (1987) Attraction-Selection-Attrition (ASA) Model. Schneider outlined the process through which a person might come to fit the organization. According to Schneider, the *people make the place* within an organization. The process through which this works is as follows, and is diagrammed in Figure 3.1. The founding leader of an organization defines the organization's initial culture. This initial culture then attracts people with similar values while those who have dissimilar values are not attracted to it. Once potential employees interview, organization members next select those who fit the values and pass on applicants who do not fit. Finally, employees who fit the culture typically stay within that organization and subsequently attract new members, while those who find over time that they do not fit move on to other organizations.

Halfhill, Nielsen, and Sundstrom (2008) applied Schneider's ASA model to attraction, selection, and attrition within work teams. Similar to Hollenbeck's concepts of person-organization fit, Halfhill and colleagues used some of the personality measures from the Big Five personality taxonomy to understand differences among team members. They found that group members who fit the minimum team expectations for agreeableness and conscientiousness had higher ratings of performance than those who did not meet the minimum expectations.

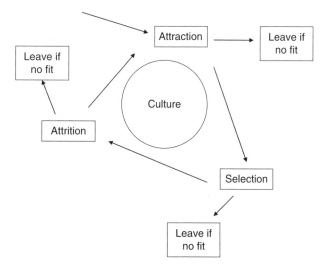

Figure 3.1   A Diagram of Schneider's ASA Model.

What this person-organization fit literature means for work teams is that the team members themselves come to set the culture of the team (which is, of course, embedded within the organizational culture). Members who fit the core values and expectations within team will stay and perform well. On the other hand, those who do not fit the core values and expectations will be far less likely to stay. Given the importance of person-organization fit, personnel selection processes become essential for identifying high-performing team members. These team selection processes, like any others, certainly need to account for the knowledge, skills, abilities, and other key characteristics that are required to complete the tasks for the job. But, the typical selection procedures used in organizations are unlikely to be enough when finding team members (Klimoski & Jones, 1995). Instead, team selection processes need also to consider team competencies, or the knowledge, skills, abilities, and other characteristics that make for a good team member.

Cannon-Bowers and Salas (1997) classify how organizations should identify new team members. According to Cannon-Bowers and Salas, selection criteria need to consider four different categories of competencies:

1. Transportable competencies, or those competencies that fit a variety of task and team situations.
2. Task competencies, or those that are related to specific tasks that may be required for the job regardless of which team a person is working with.
3. Team-contingent competencies, or those that are specific to a particular team but may not generalize to other teams.
4. Context-driven competencies, or those that depend on both the specific task and the specific team.

According to Cannon-Bowers and Salas, meeting these needs requires team members to be selected for their task and team competencies. In addition, they recommend that organizations conduct specific training programs, such as role plays and task simulations, which are designed for specific teams. Finally, they recommend that team management and development structures, such as rewards and recognition programs, be designed to reward team behavior.

Stevens and Campion (1994; 1999) provide a detailed list of some of these competences required for staffing work teams, which are detailed in Table 3.3. They used these competencies to determine the content for a teamwork selection test (Stevens & Campion, 1999). According to their study, the list of competencies helped them to develop a valid and reliable teamwork test. This list could help team members to identify the subset of competencies

The Team Task

Often, an intervention that works for one group at one time will not work for a different group or even that same group at another time. One reason for this situational

Table 3.3   Stevens and Campion's Competencies for Teamwork.

Area	Sub Category		KSA
Interpersonal Competencies	Conflict resolution	1.	Recognize and encourage desirable conflict while discouraging undesirable conflict.
		2.	Recognize the type and source of conflict and implement an appropriate resolution strategy.
		3.	Find win-win solutions rather than identify win-loss ones.
	Collaborative problem solving	4.	Identify situations requiring participative group problem solving and utilize the proper degree of participation in the group.
		5.	Recognize the obstacles to collaborative problem solving and implement appropriate corrective actions.
	Communication	6.	Understand communication networks and use decentralized networks to enhance communication where possible.
		7.	Communicate openly and supportively.
		8.	Listen nonevaluatively and use active listening techniques.
		9.	Maximize the consonance between nonverbal and verbal messages and recognize and interpret the nonverbal messages of others.
		10.	Engage in small talk and greetings and recognize the importance of these behaviors to the team.
Team Self-Management Competencies	Goal setting and performance management	11.	Establish specific, challenging, and accepted team goals.
		12.	Monitor, evaluate, and provide feedback on team as well as individual performance.
	Planning and task coordination	13.	Coordinate and synchronize activities, information, and tasks among team members.
		14.	Help establish task and role assignments for team members and balance the workload.

specificity is due to the task that a group is completing. Knowledge of the task type can help groups and teams to decide on the types of supports they may need. Further, real teams need to be assigned tasks that are only appropriate for teamwork (e.g., Saavedra, Earley, & Van Dyne, 1993) rather than creating something that is not a real team to work on an individual task (e.g., Stagl, Salas, & Burke, 2007).

McGrath (1984) provided one of the most detailed typologies of different group tasks. According to McGrath, tasks can be divided into four major categories: Generate, choose, negotiate, and execute. Each of these task types has specific characteristics that define how groups and teams might work when faced with such a task. The differences among these four task types are detailed in Table 3.4. The table also includes a brief summary of some of the task-specific considerations that are necessary for groups and teams when faced with these tasks.

Straus (1999) tested how groups differed in terms of their procedures when using different tasks. Although the test of the model was somewhat limited, she found that "patterns of agreement, disagreement, and process communication correspond to the needs for member interdependence in group tasks" (p. 180). As a result, high performing teams need to carefully consider a type of intervention that will help them to succeed on the specific task, rather than just accepting any intervention tool to move the team forward.

Table 3.4   McGrath's Task Typology and Considerations for Teams.

Task Type	Task Type Definition	Task-specific Considerations for Teams
Generate	Teams generate a set of unique ideas, such as brainstorming tasks. Outcomes can be creative ideas or actions for planning.	This is a collaborative task where all members have the opportunity to contribute to help the team succeed. Thus, generation tasks require little or no time or structures for groups to spend on coordination or consensus. Teams must manage individual differences to succeed.
Choose	Teams are required to make a decision among several choice alternatives. Choices can be intellective, where there is an identifiable and demonstrably correct answer, or judgmental, where there is no correct response.	Choice tasks have only one outcome so agreement is required through either consensus or compromise. To help increase the chances of success, choice tasks may require structured activities to regulate discussion, especially when the task is judgmental or when no one member is able to solve the problem.
Negotiate	Teams must determine among right and wrong answers. Choices may require the negotiation of conflicting viewpoints or the negotiation of resources and interests.	Conflict is an inherent part of the nature of this task. Thus, negotiation tasks may require conflict management and/or other interventions and strategies to improve the chances for success.
Execute	Teams must complete a set of tasks, whether those tasks have cognitive or psychomotor requirements. Teams may also be competing with other teams.	These tasks require post-decision execution after the initial decision has been made and require considerable coordination among team members. Procedures that help teams to coordinate will improve their success.

Setting Team Goals

Goal setting is one of the most researched areas of work behavior. One reason for this is that setting goals is a powerful driver of behavior; goal setting is a powerful way of motivating individuals. Guzzo, Jette, and Katzell (1985) found that goal setting interventions have a large effect on increasing organizational performance. A complete discussion of the goal setting literature is well beyond the scope of this book; Latham and Locke (2007) provide an excellent recent brief review of the goal setting literature with ideas about new developments in the literature as well as a guide for future directions for academics as well as broad advice for practitioners.

One of the most common simple applications of the goal setting literature in the popular press is setting and understanding SMART goals, or goals that are specific, measureable, attainable, relevant, and time bound. This acronym helps to remind individuals that a) specific goals provide more guidance than broad, overarching goals; b) measureable goals help individuals to know when they have attained those goals; c) attainable goals (though they should be challenging) are more motivating than goals that are easily attained or those that are completely unattainable; d) goals that are relevant to one's own plan are more motivating than irrelevant goals that are set by someone else; and e) finally, goals should have a time stamp in them to help to provide a deadline. As you can see, the SMART acronym provides a quick way to easily remember how to set goals, even though it is an imperfect tool (e.g., Clutterbuck, 2008). Using the SMART acronym helps individuals to design goals that meet their organizational goals while helping them to find meaning and understanding around their goals.

Though there has not been much research on team goals, the findings are similar – group goal setting increases performance (see Pritchard, Jones, Roth, Stuebing, & Ekeberg, 1988). However, team goal setting provides an added issue than individual goal setting. Team members must have common goals that do not conflict with their individual goals. This means that they must work together to set their goals or together understand the goals that were set for them. In fact, Campion, Papper, and Medsker (1996) found that teams where members had high goal interdependence had higher member satisfaction as well as higher employee and management judgments of performance than teams where members had goals that were independent of one another. Thus, goal congruence among members rather than goal conflict is a characteristic of successful work teams.

In addition to team task congruence, team members must be confident that they are truly completing a team task. It is too common for an organization to use a team to perform a task that is in fact an individual task. According to Arthur and colleagues (2005), teams must perform a detailed task analysis not only on the overall task but also on the sub tasks, to determine how to work together as a team. Figure 3.2 details the workflow patterns they identified. As you progress from Pattern 1 to Pattern 5, the level of entiativity required (remember from Chapter 1 that entiativity is the level of "groupness") increases. Pattern 1 is individual work – work is received and can be completed by an individual. No entiativity, or teamwork, is necessary at

Team Workflow Pattern	Description	Illustration	RESPONSE
1. NOT a Team Task/Activity.	Work and activities are **NOT** performed as a member of a team; they are performed alone outside the context of the team. Work and activities are performed by an individual working **ALONE**, **NOT** in a team.	Work Received by Individual 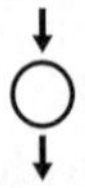 O Work Leaves Individual	①
2. Pooled/Additive Interdependence.	Work and activities are performed separately by all team members and work does not flow between members of the team.	Work Enters Team 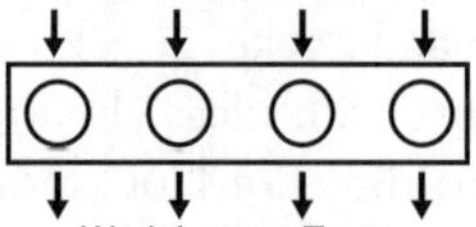 O O O O Work Leaves Team	②
3. Sequential Interdependence.	Work and activities flow from one member to another in the team, but mostly in one direction.	Work Enters Team 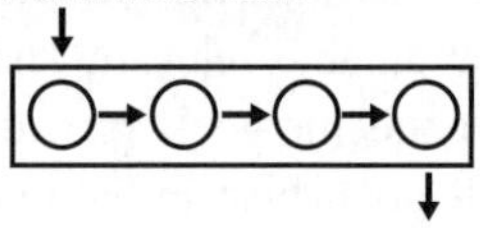 O→O→O→O Work Leaves Team	③
4. Reciprocal Interdependence.	Work and activities flow between team members in a back-and-forth manner over a period of time.	Work Enters Team 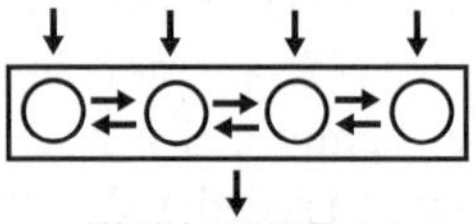 O⇄O⇄O⇄O Work Leaves Team	④
5. Intensive interdependence.	Work and activities come into the team and members must diagnose, problem solve, and/or collaborate as a team in order to accomplish the team's task.	Work Enters Team 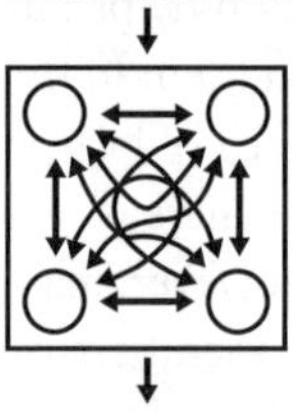 O O O O Work Leaves Team	⑤

Figure 3.2   Arthur *et al.*'s Five Individual/Team Workflow Patterns. (*taken from Arthur, Edwards, Bell, Villado, & Bennet, 2005*).

all. Pattern 2 is division of labor – all members perform activities and then through coordination these activities are added together at the end, which requires only a small amount of entiativity. Patten 3 is requires more coordination because work must flow from one member to the next, like in a factory line. Patterns 4 and 5 require far more interdependence, whether it is reciprocal (Pattern 4) or complete (Pattern 5). These two patterns are far more consistent with how I defined teamwork at the beginning of the book. If teams are used with workflow patterns like that in Pattern 1, then team goals and individual goals might conflict, creating problems within a team. On the other hand, if individuals are used to try work in patterns like that in 4 and 5, the individuals might quickly feel overwhelmed and overloaded. Teams will be much more successful with these tasks.

Member Identity and Roles in Teams

Different members take on different roles within groups and teams. Benne and Sheats (1948) provided one of the most thorough descriptions of the different types of roles within groups. They classify roles into three categories: Those that help the group or team complete its task, those that help the group or team to maintain positive interpersonal functioning, and those that focus on the needs of specific individuals. These are called *Task Roles, Group Maintenance Roles,* and *Individual Roles,* respectively. These roles are detailed in Table 3.5.

According to Benne and Sheats, groups need both task and maintenance functions to succeed. The task functions help groups with their task-specific performance. However, groups also need to learn and practice techniques to help knowing what these roles are, identifying who acts in each role, and possibly assigning roles to members can help groups to set goals, understand conflict, plan, develop, learn, and improve.

One of the common problems with working in groups and teams is when members take on the individual roles that so commonly lead to process losses and reduce group performance. There are many different recommendations for dealing with difficult member, including techniques such as coping with the problem, venting among other team members, reporting the problem to management, asking for third-party intervention, or confronting (de Leon, 2001). In fact, de Leon demonstrated that teams will work to avoid conflict and direct confrontation, reserving that for the last step. Ultimately, most methods of resolving problems with members who take on roles that cause difficulty fall into three broad categories:

- *Accept*: teams can ignore, cope with, or accept members who act in the difficult, individual roles. If the difficult member is performing in a way that does not ultimately hinder team performance more than dealing with the resulting problem would, acceptance might be the best initial solution.
- *Confront*: Members can confront the situation either indirectly through discussions with management, hiring a consultant, or engaging a mediator or directly through talking with the difficult member. This is the next choice for teams after acceptance and should be used when the problem role hinders group performance.
- *Exclude*: The final way that teams can deal with members who take on difficult, individual roles is to exclude the member who has taken on the difficult, individual role. This can be done informally through ostracizing the member or formally through removing the member from the team. This should be used as a last resort because it will at least for a short period of time hinder group performance.

Table 3.5   Benne and Sheat's (1948) Group Roles.

Task Roles: These help a group to complete its task	Group Maintenance or Social Roles: These help group members with the interpersonal functioning of the group	Individual Roles: These are selfish roles that emphasize the goals of an individual over those of the group
Initiator/Contributor: Starts discussion and provides direction. Provides new goals or new definition of the problem.	**Encourager:** Praises contributions, accepts ideas, and agrees with others.	**Aggressor:** Expresses disapproval or attacks others.
Information Seeker: Asks for clarification and works to seek necessary facts from others within the group.	**Harmonizer:** Resolves conflicts by mediating differences of opinion, relieves tension.	**Blocker:** Stubbornly resists changes and new ideas within the group.
Information Giver: Responds to queries for information. Offers facts based on authority.	**Compromiser:** Operates within a conflict to work to find win-win or other compromised solutions to group differences.	**Recognition-Seeker:** Constantly working to seek recognition for personal contributions rather than group success.
Opinion Seeker: Works with others to gather opinions and values within the group.	**Gatekeeper/Expediter:** Works to keep communication channels open by facilitating the participation of others.	**Self-Confessor:** Uses the group setting to contribute non-task related information about personal matters.
Opinion Giver: Provides opinions to the group that are pertinent to the discussion.	**Standard Setter:** Expresses high-quality standards for the group.	**Playboy:** Openly displays non-involvement.
Elaborator: Works with others to spell out suggestions and develop them further, such as identifying the risks of an alternative.	**Group Observer and Commentator:** Analyzes and comments on group process and progress.	**Dominator:** Constantly trying to take over the group by asserting perceived superiority.
Coordinator: Reduces conflict through issues-based activities and clarifies the relationships among ideas and suggestions.	**Follower:** Passively accepts the ideas and serves as a member of the audience.	**Help-Seeker:** Calls forth sympathy responses from others within the group in order to call attention to him or herself.
Orienter: Defines the position of the group with respect to its goals.		**Special Interest Pleader:** Pleads for ones own biases by cloaking them in requests for the underdog or common person.

Table 3.5   (cont'd).

Task Roles: These help a group to complete its task	Group Maintenance or Social Roles: These help group members with the interpersonal functioning of the group	Individual Roles: These are selfish roles that emphasize the goals of an individual over those of the group
Evaluator/Critic: Helps the group by providing constructive critique of group task work as compared to its standards.		
Energizer: Keeps the group action-oriented and focused on the importance of the task and tries to get higher-quality activity.		
Procedural Technician: Expedites goal activity by keeping the group on track with activities such as keeping time, comparing to agenda.		
Recorder: Records suggestions and ideas, takes minutes, and records the decisions within the group.		

Regardless of the types of functional, interpersonal, or individual roles that members take on within a group or team, all members may have to deal with additional role issues, including role ambiguity, role overload, and role conflict (see Örtqvist & Wincent, 2006, for a recent meta analysis of these concepts):

- *Role conflict*: Incompatibility among the multiple roles expected of team members, either from within or outside of the team. For example, teams may have multiple leaders; one leader may request one task while another leader requests the team stop what they are doing and complete a different task.
- *Role ambiguity*: Uncertainty about what to do within the team. For example, a new team member may not know the role expectations of other long-term members.
- *Role overload*: Too much work within a role. For example, members of a new cross-functional team may be asked to take on additional team-related responsibility while keeping all of their existing individual duties.

Role conflict, ambiguity, and overload cause team members to reduce the quality and/or quantity of their contributions because they are unclear about what to do. These problems all cause different types of role stress (Örtqvist & Wincent, 2006).

To improve group functioning, Benne and Sheats (1948) recommend role analysis and role training. The first step in understanding and improving roles is for the group or team to conduct an analysis, whether that analysis is formal or informal. This is necessary because task requirements are a function of how well the group is completing its task while interpersonal requirements are a function of how mature a group is. Thus, groups that are early in their development require more time with members acting in interpersonal roles than those that are more mature. Similarly, groups that are starting a task require more time with members acting in task roles than those which are nearing task completion. Informally those taking on the group observer role can be used to assess role actions among members within a group. Formally, an outsider can take a checklist, like that found in Exercise 3.1, to assess the roles of members within a group or team.

All of this presupposes that members understand the different roles described by Benne and Sheats. This is why Benne and Sheats recommend additional training about understanding the different group roles. In this training, members should a) learn the differences between roles versus personalities, b) gain basic skills training around the behavior expected when acting in different roles, c) participate in specific role-play sessions when members can take on and then gain initial comfort and practice within each role, and then d) take specific, structured times to act as the role of group observer so that all members can assess and help other group members to develop their skills at understanding roles within the group and know how to modify ones own behavior to improve.

Three Interventions to Improve Initial Team Functioning

Development processes that work to improve inputs can help groups and teams to determine where to focus efforts. "Although not a cure-all for an organization's ills, team development can improve the team's goal-setting skills, ability to establish clear responsibilities ... to ultimately improve the team's contribution to the overall organization performance" (Shonk, 1982, p. 2). This section provides summaries of three of these interventions that can focus group and team members about how to improve inputs so that members are more prepared to work together.

Conducting a role analysis

Because understanding roles is essential to teamwork, one way to improve groups and teams is to conduct a role analysis. French and Bell (1984; see also Buckham, 1987 and Table 3.6) recommend conducting a role analysis so team members can perform their work more efficiently and effectively. A role analysis can help a team to solve some of the problems when members of groups and teams first start working together because individual members will know ahead of time what roles they should and

Table 3.6 A Summary of the Steps Involved in Role Analysis.

Step	Procedure
1.	In a meeting, the team: a) appoints a recorder; b) determines the goals for the role analysis; b) reviews the following role analysis procedures; and c) sets ground rules for the role analysis process, including providing an opportunity for developing open and honest communication as well as developing a constructive and cooperative mindset.
2.	During that meeting or a subsequent meeting: a) Each team member discusses his or her roles within the team including a description of his or her working relationships with other members of the team. b) One team member records the information on a flipchart. c) The team discusses each member's roles as well as expectations for how those roles will support the goals of the team and the team leader.
3.	After the meeting, each team member creates a written summary of his or her roles as well as the expectations for how the roles will support the initial goals.

Adapted from Buckham (1987).

should not be taking on during the team process. This will immediately help group and team members to have role clarity and understand their obligations to the team.

Although a role analysis can be conducted by someone within a team, French and Bell recommend that the role analysis be conducted by a skilled facilitator. This is because the facilitator can provide positive as well as constructive feedback during the session with less fear of how he or she might be perceived by other team members in the future. These analyses can be conducted by someone within the organization but outside of the team or by a consultant who is expert in providing facilitation and feedback to groups and teams. The steps involved in conducting a role analysis follow.

Defining team goals

As described earlier, goal setting is one of the more effective methods of motivating people. Wegge and Haslam (2005) find in their research that setting group goals is "robust strategy for improving work motivation and brainstorming performance in groups (p. 401). Adams (2008) provides a four-step model of team building that will create high-performing teams. Adams suggests that one of the requirements of creating a high-performing team is to focus that team on its goals. According to Adams, the four steps will help team members to put in the extra, discretionary effort that is required for high performance because it provides a structure for enhancing communication and trust. The result is successful collaboration that will focus the team on its goals rather than on dysfunctional individual behavior. Further, these successful teams take time after any team-building activity for lessons learned – this allows the team to learn and improve. These steps are summarized in Table 3.7.

Table 3.7   A Summary of the Steps Involved in Setting Goals for Team Building Interventions.

Step	Procedure
1.	Organize a meeting of those who will be facilitating the team goal setting strategy as well as those who are on the team. In this meeting: a) The team can set objectives for the team-building event. b) The team and the facilitator together can define the challenge with which the team is faced. c) The facilitator can learn more about the challenge including how to break it into sub tasks.
2.	Within one month, conduct the team-building challenge.
3.	Within one month, debrief the team to help the team members to learn about themselves and their work within the team. Ask members: a) What did you learn about yourself? b) What factors promoted good teamwork? c) What factors prevented good teamwork? d) Which of the factors you listed were relevant to the working environment? e) How can you best apply what you have learned in this effort? f) What is your future plan based on this learning? g) What outcomes can you expect as act on this plan?
4.	Finally, within about two months revisit the learning from Step 3 as well as the success in acting on the plans from Step 3.

Adapted from Adams (2008).

Table 3.8   A Summary of the steps involved in a task analysis.

Step	Procedure
1.	Create a spreadsheet with four columns. Label the first column Team Task, the second Importance, the third Team Relatedness, and the fourth Team Workflow Pattern. This can be completed on paper, on a flipchart, or on a white board.
2.	Establish the overall task for the team as well as all of the subtasks. Write each of the subtasks in the first column in order.
3.	The next step is to rate the importance. Working together, rate the importance of each of the tasks on a 1 to 5 scale, where 1 is not at all important while 5 is of highest importance.
4.	Fourth, rate team relatedness, which is the extent to which successful team performance requires the team members to work together in order to optimally perform the task. Working together, rate the relatedness of each of the tasks on a 1 to 5 scale, where 1 is Not required to work with others at all for optimal performance while 5 is Very much required to work with others for optimal performance.
5.	Finally, rate the team workflow pattern using Figure 3.2. Subtasks that are of high importance and have high relatedness should use Pattern 5. On the other hand, subtasks that are of low importance and have low relatedness should be completed individually to prepare for subsequent teamwork. Use this chart as a resource for completing the overall task.

Adapted from Arthur, Edwards, Bell, Villado, and Bennet (2005).

Conducting a task analysis

As described earlier, Arthur and colleagues (2005) provide a list of the workflow patterns that are required for individual versus team tasks (Table 3.8). Their assumption is that all tasks performed by team have a variety of subtasks. At least some of these tasks should be completed by individuals while others should be completed as teams. To get the most value from teamwork, a team should conduct a detailed task analysis to break down which of the subtasks should be completed.

FOCUS ON APPLICATION

Re-learning to work together at the YMCA of Greater Rochester

The practitioner

Fernan R. Cepero, PHR, MA, MS is Vice President of Human Resources and Chief Diversity Officer for the YMCA of Greater Rochester. Fernan has also served an Employee Development Manager for The Perrier Group of America where his responsibilities included recruiting, employee development, and ensuring effective succession planning. Prior to assuming this position he served as Human Resource and Employee Development Manager for Xerox. He was responsible for the creation and implementation of a People Development Strategy, where in, he developed and maintained a pool of management talent to meet the company's long-term needs. Fernan is also certified to administer the Myers-Briggs Type Indicator (MBTI)®, the FIRO®, the Kirton Adaptation Innovation®, and The PROFILOR®.

The symptom

The YMCA of Greater Rochester was experiencing tremendous growth in 2002; the most aggressive in the last 40 years of their 150-year history at that point. In the midst of the expansion YMCA core communities of practice, work teams found themselves struggling with personal differences, finding strengths to leverage, and balancing commitments to the organization's growth and changing goals against the demands of their everyday assignments, roles, and tasks. I was called in to examine the work team's needs that were arising from pressures of unprecedented growth. I recognized that teams often underestimate the importance of group dynamics and team development. The work team members knew that the success of the organization's first 150 years resulted from teams where members worked well together they concentrated on problem solving and operational improvement. At the core of work teams at the YMCA of Greater Rochester are ten key operational principles rooted in organizational development:

1. Empowerment – We will empower knowledgeable people to take action and make decisions without fear.
2. Quality – We will commit to continuous improvement of our programs and services.
3. Fun – We will encourage humor and fellowship to create an environment where great things can take place.
4. Diversity – We will seek out, value and develop the capabilities of all people for the benefit of all concerned.
5. Accountability – We will expect that every unit and individual must have clear and measurable purposes: rewards and consequences will match performance.
6. Growth – We will establish an environment which fosters the development of individual and institutional growth to their fullest potential.
7. Innovation – We will remove all barriers to allow for the highest level of creativity, innovation, and flexibility.
8. Teamwork – We will work together, combining our ideas and skills to improve the quality of our work.
9. Integrity – We will always act in an ethical and honest manner in all dealings and relationships in and outside the organization treating everyone with courtesy, fairness, dignity, and respect.
10. Member Focus – We will recognize that members are the purpose of our work and will take personal responsibility to ensure that all members and potential members receive a timely, efficient, and courteous response to their needs.

Assessing the problem

Interviews and focus groups were conducted with members of the YMCA communities of practice (health and wellness, childcare, member services, aquatics, and facilities).The needs assessment analyzed if the members feel like insiders or outsiders; do they feel that they belong; do they want to belong; do they genuinely fit in. The key focus areas included:

*   Team membership and Inclusion Influence, Control, and Mutual Trust
*   Synergy and Mutual Loyalty
*   Team Relationships and Camaraderie
*   Identity with the Team and Organization

Intervening: What did you do?

1. Administered the MBTI® Team Report that included a summary of the team's personality types, team strengths and challenges, the individual's contributions to the team, and discussions on team and individual problem-solving, conflict-handling and communication styles, and the organization's influence on the team.
2. Administered the DiSC® Workplace Report
   a. Results designed to help build better relationships in the workplace.
   b. Helped to build upon the MBTI® results and to better understand work team member style better and appreciate the style of those they work with.
3. Administered the Least Preferred Coworker Scale (LPC)® – The LPC Scale assumes that people whose leadership style is relationship-oriented tend to describe their least preferred coworkers in a more positive manner, while those whose style is task-oriented rate them more negatively.
4. Facilitated a review of the fundamentals of teamwork from Glenn Parker's Team Players and Teamwork.
5. Led workshops about Dr. Jerry B. Harvey's The Abilene Paradox and Dr. Irving Janis' Groupthink to encourage and foster productive argumentation and conflict.
6. A considerable amount of time was spent observing the group process in order to better understand how the team was interacting. Observing how the team worked served several purposes:
   a. It helped identify patterns of interaction that could have become problems if they persisted.
   b. Observation helped to distinguish for the team members between the content of a discussion and the methods used during the discussion.
   c. Observation also gave tangible examples of skills which they were trying to develop, for example testing for understanding and consensus decision making.
7. Employee satisfaction surveys were and continue to be administered every two years to monitor the group dynamics, the synergy, and changes in the syntality of work teams.

The group work helped the teams to re-focus on the YMCA of Greater Rochester values of caring, honesty, respect, responsibility, fun, and friendship. The work teams' dynamics and roles were again congruent with these values that now influence operations and give YMCA employees a sense pride in their teams and in their organization proving that teams are most dynamic when their purpose is aligned with a clear vision unifying their efforts. Overall team satisfaction increased as well.

Chapter Summary

There are many basic team concepts that affect to team functioning. This chapter provided guidance with some of these basic team concepts, including:

- understanding formation and development processes and finding ways to improve upon it;
- socializing new team members;
- understanding the value of selecting fit;
- defining team member competencies;
- understanding different team tasks and how to take steps to improve the work conducted by individuals versus the work conducted by teams; and
- understanding team complications that are caused by differences in roles.

Team members who understand these basic team concepts can help to create higher functioning teams.

Additional Resources

Arrow, H., McGrath, J.E., & Berdahl, J. L. (2000). *Small groups as complex systems: Formation, coordination, development, and adaptation*. Thousand Oaks, CA: Sage Publications, Inc.

Biech, E. (2001). *The Pfeiffer book of successful team-building tools: Best of the annuals*. Pfeiffer.

Lencioni, P. (2005). *Overcoming the five dysfunctions of a team: A field guide for leaders, managers, and facilitators*. San Francisco, CA: Jossey-Bass.

Team Exercises

Exercise 3.1   Identifying team roles

Step 1. Divide the group into small groups of about four to five. Select one person from each small group to serve as observer.

Step 2. Give one pack of 100 3 × 5 index cards and one roll of masking tape to each team. Give the teams the following instructions:

> Your goal is to build a house that is the tallest and most appealing. You may only use the index cards and tape supplied; you may not use anything else to build your house. You have 20 minutes in which to plan and build your house. I will provide no other instructions other than those that are written here. When time is called, the observers will judge the houses and make a determination about which of them is tallest and most appealing. Do not start talking or working until I tell you to do so.

Step 3. Give the observers a check sheet with the roles from Benne and Sheats. The observers should record notes about:

- Who acts in which roles (each person that they observe may perform several different roles).
- What behavior they performed that made the observer categorize them in that role.

Step 4. Allow the groups to build their houses and the observers to record names and behaviors. Call time at 20 minutes.

Step 5. After the 20 minutes is done, have the observers make the determination about which house is the tallest and most appealing.

Step 6. The facilitator should then have the observers report about the roles and related behaviors they observed.

Step 7. Team members should be given time to reflect and respond about why they behaved in the way that they did.

Note: An alternative to this exercise is to randomly assign roles ahead of time.

Chapter 4

Understanding Culture and Diversity

I worked at another university prior to arriving over 12 years ago at my current institution, St. John Fisher College. At the previous university, it was completely acceptable – even encouraged – for members of other departments to use the microwave oven in our psychology laboratory. After two months at my new place, I told a colleague from another department that he could certainly use it to warm up his lunch. When someone in my department complained at one of our group meetings that other departments were in the laboratory using our microwave, I sheepishly admitted that I said he could. I clearly violated a strong cultural norm in my new team and not only created discomfort for myself, but also the interloper who used our microwave!

As the previous example suggests, one input to how groups and teams function is the larger organizational culture in which the team is embedded. Another is understanding the differences among members within (and also beyond) the team. Understanding and working in different cultures as well as working with members from diverse backgrounds is a core requirement for success as a project team.

Fortunately, Myers (1996) provides a tool to understand how team members are reacting to cultural differences (Table 4.1). Myers (1996) recommends the use of a formal team diversity assessment process. According to Myers, conducting a diversity awareness assessment is the first step in any intervention because the assessment tool alone will start the organization on the path to better cultural awareness because team members will be more aware of how they react to differences.

To conduct the assessment, use the self-scored instrument below. Hand the instrument to all the members of the team and have them complete the items. After they have completed the items, have them add up their score (the meaning of these

Group Dynamics and Team Interventions: Understanding and Improving Team Performance,
First Edition. Timothy M. Franz.
© 2012 Timothy M. Franz. Published 2012 by Blackwell Publishing Ltd.

Table 4.1 Diversity Awareness Assessment.

Instructions: Circle the appropriate number using the following scale: (1) = Strongly disagree, (2) = Disagree, (3) = Neither agree or disagree, (4) Agree, and (5) = Strongly agree.

1.	Our team has a stated vision.	1	2	3	4	5
2.	The vision is accepted by all.	1	2	3	4	5
3.	The vision is understood by all.	1	2	3	4	5
4.	It includes reference to diversity.	1	2	3	4	5
5.	It considers the values and needs of each of its members.	1	2	3	4	5
6.	Our team environment supports diversity.	1	2	3	4	5
7.	Our team encourages members to be open with one another.	1	2	3	4	5
8.	Team members help one another.	1	2	3	4	5
9.	Our team promotes the sharing of success.	1	2	3	4	5
10.	Our team encourages individual interaction across diversity lines.	1	2	3	4	5
11.	The team members are open to differences of opinion.	1	2	3	4	5
12.	There is appreciation of the talents and skills of each individual.	1	2	3	4	5
13.	Members can count on one another, irrespective of their diverse backgrounds.	1	2	3	4	5
14.	The team is able to deal with interpersonal problems and conflicts.	1	2	3	4	5
15.	Team members feel secure in bringing up problems and conflicts.	1	2	3	4	5
16.	The team members can determine whether their problems are diversity-related.	1	2	3	4	5
17.	There is a system in place for addressing problems and conflicts.	1	2	3	4	5

scores is on the next page). The next step is to have a facilitator start a discussion about what culture and diversity mean, including some reflection and sharing (if team members are comfortable) about their scores.

Learning Goals for Chapter 4

- Know how to conduct a diversity assessment.
- Define organizational culture.
- Understand and identify artifacts, espoused values, enacted values, and assumptions.

- Define and understand the nature and value of diversity.
- Understand social categorization and ingroup/outgroup differences. Know the biases caused by these differences.
- Conduct a cultural assessment.
- Know the importance of 360-degree feedback to understanding differences.
- Define and know the steps to the Conversity technique for improving the understanding of differences.

To score the diversity assessment, use the following scoring key:

---

81 to 85: Congratulations! Your team has successfully integrated diversity awareness into the team's values and operating norms, making it possible to capitalize on each other's differences. You should try to share the lessons learned from your team's experiences with other groups in your organization that may not be as far along.

75 to 80: Very Good. Your team is making progress and has all the ingredients for even greater success. Focus on the areas which received lower scores from team members. Address these areas with the entire team to find out what can be done to improve. Develop specific action plans and take the team assessment again in a month or two to track your improvement.

61 to 75: Room for Improvement. Your team has some core strengths but clearly there are areas for growth and improvement. Review the areas that received the lowest scores and put them on the agenda at the next team meeting. At the same time, look at one or two areas that received the highest scores and have the team focus on how these strengths have been achieved. There may be some cues for building the other areas. Set specific targets for areas to improve and agree on a plan to get there. Make sure the team recognizes the advantages of improving – that there will be a greater sense of teamwork and harmony, as well as better work performance overall. Set a specific date for the next team assessment and for a follow-up analysis of the results at that time.

60 or Less: Your team may already be running into problems. The team assessment provides you with a starting point on which to focus. Pick one or two specific areas that received low scores on the assessment and focus your team's efforts there. Don't try to accomplish everything overnight. Instead, plan for progress in small steps, retaking the assessment test as the team progresses. Even though a journey of small steps can seem like a marathon when you are standing at the starting line, the destination makes every step worthwhile. Think about bringing in an outside facilitator to help your team start moving toward being a high performing diverse work team.

Taken from Myers (1996).

A Brief Background On Culture

Culture is one of the most difficult concepts for members within and outside an organization to identify. This is because culture is a concept that a) is unique to any one group or organization, b) is something that is learned over time, and c) includes a shared understanding among group or team members that is often not explicitly explained or written down. Schein (2004) defines culture as "a pattern of shared basic assumptions that was learned by a group as it solved its problems of external adaptation and internal integration, that has worked well enough to be considered valid and, therefore, to be taught to new members as the correct way to perceive, think, and feel in relation to those problems" (p. 17).

As you can see, Schein's understanding of culture includes feelings, thoughts, and behaviors that are expected within an entire organization or even within an organizational unit or group or team. Breaking this definition down provides a basic understanding of what makes up the culture of a group or team, including:

- Knowing about the culture in a group or team includes having a shared understanding of what it is by members within the group or team.
- Those outside the group or team may not ever have a full understanding of the group or team's culture.
- The culture in a group or team developed over time; the group or team did not start with the understanding of its culture that it now has.
- The culture has resulted from the group or team working together in action, such as problem solving and decision making.
- It involves more than just thoughts (cognitions), but also includes feelings (affect) and expected appropriate behaviors.

Though the concept of culture is difficult for insiders to state and even more difficult for outsiders to know, there are four different ways to identify and understand culture. These include:

- Artifacts, which are the written displays of culture. According to Schein, these are the surface-level ways to identify culture. Artifacts include visible signs of culture, including environmental factors such as manners of dress, signs on the wall, how people display emotions, and the ways people address one another.
- Values, which are what the group or team believes is important. These are different from artifacts because they are not as easily identifiable; they are instead stated rather than displayed as artifacts. Identifying values requires more depth of understanding of the group or team than identifying artifacts. There are two different types of values – espoused values versus enacted values.
    - Espoused values (Schein, 2004) are the values stated by those within an organization, especially those within leadership roles. An example of an espoused value might be for sales representatives to be completely honest with customers about the uses of a pharmaceutical product.
    - Brunsson (1989; see also Argyris & Schön, 1978) discusses the differences between espoused values versus enacted values. Enacted values are the values that people actually follow within the organization. These are often better indicators of organizational culture because they show what organizations actually value in the actions of its people rather than what is stated. An

example of an enacted value that differs from an espoused value may be allowing pharmaceutical sales representatives to "stretch the truth" about the effectiveness of a product even though the organization publicly states that it strives for complete honesty. According to Brunsson, the discrepancy between espoused and enacted values can help to provide information about misunderstandings within an organization.

The impact of violations of values depend on whether there is correspondence between espoused versus enacted values. Violations of espoused values are typically only a problem to the organization if that stated value is in fact enacted as well or if it becomes publicly known that an organizational member violated an espoused value.

- Assumptions are the underlying values that have been transformed over time into a shared and implicit understanding of how people should act. Assumptions are different from values because they are part of a shared social validation system and are typically **not** explicitly stated. Instead, assumptions are underlying ways to think, feel, or behave that are taken for granted. Many who have joined a group or team after these assumptions have been established may never know about the events that occurred to drive them. Violations of assumptions are often the most challenging for organizations to deal with because there is often little or no written policy explaining them but people are still expected to act consistent with them anyway. An example of an assumption is organizational expectations for how to dress. An organization may not have an explicit dress code. However, there is likely an implicit assumption that people working in the organization will not come to work in their pajamas (in most organizations, that is!).

Schein (1990) provides a summary list of seven relevant dimensions of culture. These include: a) the group or team's relationship to its external environment, b) the nature and rate of activity within the group or team, c) the nature of how the group or team defines truth, d) orientations towards time, e) assumptions about human nature and whether people are basically good, neutral, or lazy, f) the nature of the correct ways for people to interact, and g) assumptions about whether homogeneity or diversity is preferred. Decisions about the dimensions are usually first defined by the original leaders and then modified through experience over time. Current concepts of culture are socialized into new group or team members through the procedures described in previous chapters.

Schein's work identifies within-organization or within-group culture. Hofstede (2001), on the other hand, focuses specifically on understanding differences among cultures, typically at the level of a society. According to Hofstede, there are five different dimensions of culture that can define a society, including power distance, individualism versus collectivism, masculinity versus femininity, uncertainty avoidance, and time orientation. Hofstede uses these dimensions to classify differences in culture among different societies. Table 4.2 provides summaries of the meaning of each of these dimensions. These dimensions have become some of the common ways to describe cultural differences.

Table 4.2   Hofstede's Five Dimensions of Culture.

Hofstede's Cultural Dimension	Definition
Power Distance (low versus high)	The extent to which the less powerful members of organizations and institutions (like the family) accept and expect that power is distributed unequally. People in high power distance societies prefer larger perceived differences between people at different levels of an organization than those in low power distance countries.
Individualism versus Collectivism	The degree to which individuals are integrated into groups. People in individualist cultures prefer to work individually and tend to identify with their own characteristics while people in collectivist cultures prefer to work in groups and teams and tend to identify with the group's characteristics.
Masculinity versus Femininity	The distribution of roles between the genders. People in masculine cultures tend to prefer assertive and competitive behavior while those in feminine cultures tend to prefer cooperative and caring (socio-emotional) behavior. This difference is more pronounced for men than it is for women.
Uncertainty Avoidance versus Uncertainty Acceptance	The society's tolerance for uncertainty and ambiguity. People in uncertainty-avoidant cultures tend to have strict procedures and laws to avoid uncertainty and provide some structure to an environment than those in uncertainty-accepting cultures. People in uncertainty-avoidant cultures also tend to be more emotional and more motivated by an inner nervous energy.
Long-term Orientation versus Short-term Orientation	The society's view on time and whether to look to the near or distant future when considering the importance of issues when making decisions. People in long-term orientation cultures tend to make decisions where the long-term implications have more importance while those in short-term orientation cultures are more concerned with short-term implications.

A Brief Background On Diversity

If culture is the shared set of assumptions that we hold, diversity is, in part, the differences in these assumptions. Most organizations today state that they want to recruit and retain a diverse workforce because of its potential to create value for an organization. In fact, in many organizations today you will see artifacts that explicitly state this value, such as signs that say "Celebrate Diversity!" This is because diverse workforces are expected to provide benefits to an organization, including (see Mannix & Neale, 2005 for a summary of the psychological research about team diversity):

- greater resources;
- more knowledge;
- different skills and expertise;
- the ability for teams to understand and work with others from different cultures.

These are all important and necessary ways through which diverse teams may positively contribute to an organization. The organizations that succeed in harnessing members with different skills, abilities, and backgrounds are likely to be far more successful within a diverse marketplace than those that do not. Thus, the promise of diversity is one with which most groups and teams in organizations can easily agree.

Unfortunately, the reality of performance in diverse groups and teams is not nearly so positive as the promise of results or the rhetoric within organizations; it often fails to meet the goals for which many hope. The research evidence shows that diversity is, in fact, at best a mixed blessing. Diverse groups and teams also have considerably more problems than those that are not diverse, including:

- miscommunication;
- conflict;
- subgrouping, coalitions, and cliques;
- attraction and commonalities among similar members.

These problems are a reality that many diverse groups and teams in the workplace must face. Diversity in the workforce has the potential to provide many benefits but also has the risk of creating as many problems.

Regardless of the promise of or struggle with diversity in teams, we live in a global economy that is rapidly changing. The "increase in globalization of markets and economies brings cultural diversity" (Jackson & Ruderman, 1995, p. 5) into a growing number of organizations. According to Gabel and Brunner, there are over 63,000 multinational corporations and 821,000 foreign subsidiaries that employ approximately 90 million people around the world (Gabel & Brunner, 2003). This globalization along with improvements in global communication is changing the way we perform work.

Further, the workforce in most communities is becoming far more diverse as well. There is an increasing number of women and people of color in the workforce (Jackson & Ruderman, 1995). According to the US Department of Labor (1999):

> Immigration trends, coupled with varied birth rates, will bring more diversity to the American workforce. In 1995, the United States was estimated to be 83% white, 13% black, 1% American Indian, Eskimo, and Aleut, and 4% Asian and Pacific Islander.

10% of Americans, mostly blacks and whites, were also of Hispanic origin. Nearly one in eleven Americans was foreign born. ... By 2050, minorities are projected to rise from one in every four Americans to almost one in every two. ... In fact, after 2020, the Hispanic population is projected to add more people to the United States every year than will all other groups combined (p. 3).

And, these are only the statistics for differences regarding race; there are many other changes to the American workforce as well. For example, the education rate is rising, there will be more immigrants in the workforce who are arriving to the United States ready to work, and the average age of the workforce is increasing. The bottom line is that regardless of whether diverse groups lead to higher or lower performance, all team members today must learn to work in culturally diverse groups and teams if our organizations are to succeed in today's competitive global community. Culturally diverse teams are a reality in today's business environment and this will not be changing.

The term diversity, unfortunately, means many different things to many different people. In fact, it all too often becomes a surrogate term for differences due to race and gender, issues which have been quite salient and easily identifiable as the work-place has rapidly changed during the last 30 or 40 years (Jackson & Ruderman, 1995). Diversity, however, means understanding differences regardless of what they are, and this understanding of the concept is much broader than just understanding cultural differences that are due to race and gender.

Loden (1996) provides a summary diagram that helps to understand the broad array of these cultural and personal differences that make up the members of a diverse workforce. According to Loden, there are sixteen different components of diversity (see Figure 4.1). Others categorize differences into three theoretical per-spectives about what it means to be a diverse workforce: the trait perspective, the expectations perspective, and the differential power perspective (McGrath, Berdahl, & Arrow, 1995). The trait perspective is the presumption that differences are related to the underlying attributes, or characteristics, of a person. The expectations perspec-tive presumes that differences are related to differential expectations of the way members of another group act. Finally, the differential power perspective presumes that differences are related to differential access to resources.

Understanding the Impact of Diversity on Groups and Teams

Differences among people have an impact on work because of social identity. Social identity is a psychological concept that describes how we make sense of whom we are as well as whom others are in our social world; it is one of the core theories in social psychology and helps to describe the origins and consequences about how we organize and classify people (Brewer, 1995).

According to Social Identity Theory (see Tajfel & Turner, 1986), we classify people to help us to organize the complex information in our world. In many ways, the

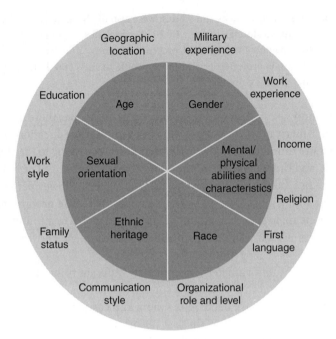

Figure 4.1   Loden's Components of Diversity (from Loden, 1996).

basic process of classifying social information is not much different than the way we classify information that is not social. Imagine the way we classify furniture – we organize in our heads information about chairs, for example. We have an example, or exemplar, of what a chair should be. If you imagine what a chair looks like, it is likely that it will have four legs and a seat and a back. However, not all chairs look like this. In fact, some desk chairs have only one central leg or post, some living room chairs have wing backs, and so on. But, by using the central information from the classification system, we can generalize to other members of the group. This type of classification and organization of information into representative groupings is actually a very useful cognitive processing and memory tool. If people had to remember every detail of, for example, every chair, our mind would be cluttered with so many facts that most would have trouble remembering anything at all.

Tajfel and Turner expanded this paradigm of classification to understand the processes of identification and classification of social information. The theory of social identity argues that people organize and classify information about social identity based on how well individuals fit the social group as well as how well they feel that the social group contains relevant information. Thus, people organize and classify people in similar ways to the ways that they organize and classify inanimate objects.

Further, Tajfel and Turner demonstrated that classification a) is something that people do automatically, and b) causes people to make value judgments as a result. They term this the minimal group paradigm. In minimal group paradigm demonstrations and research, people are divided up into groups randomly. These same people are often even told that they were organized randomly. However, once they have been arranged into groups, people tend to automatically prefer the members that they have been grouped with (termed the ingroup) while do not prefer the people with whom they have not been grouped (termed the outgroup). One possible reason that people perform this grouping is to maintain their self-esteem; they look to their ingroup to gain a positive view of themselves while at the same time find ways to denigrate the outgroup.

As you can see, these ingroup and outgroup differences are one of the potential causes of biases such as stereotyping and prejudice. This is because people classify themselves and others into ingroups and outgroups on all types of features – whatever feature may be most salient or identifiable at the time. Unfortunately, physical differences (such as race, gender, etc.) are easily classifiable and people all too often may use them to lump others into groups. Once this categorization occurs, other cognitive biases can contribute to an exacerbation of perceptions of differences. Some of these include confirmation biases, the fundamental attribution error, illusory correlations, the self-fulfilling prophecy, and similar-to-me errors. All of these are explained below.

- Confirmation biases are the tendency for people to search for and then interpret information that is consistent with their pre-existing viewpoints (Darley & Gross, 1983). If, for example, I assume that all college professors are geeks then I will look for evidence of that among my peers and even bias the way I see certain behavior to verify my view.
- Fundamental attribution errors (Jones & Harris, 1967) are "a tendency for perceivers to underestimate the impact of situational factors and to overestimate the role of dispositional factors in controlling behavior" (Manstead & Hewstone, 1996). Once we have classified people into the outgroup, it is easy for us to assume that their behavior is due to their traits and internal characteristics rather than the environment or situation. Thus, if a college professor mumbled and looked uncomfortable in front of her or his class, the fundamental attribution error would cause me to assume that this is because the professor is a geek (an internal attribution) rather than is having a bad day or has the flu (an external attribution).
- Illusory correlations (Hamilton & Gifford, 1976) are "when an individual perceives a correlation between two classes of events which in reality are not correlated or which are correlated to a lesser extent than perceived" (Manstead & Hewstone, 1996). In many ways, people are programmed to see associations among events. This is an excellent way to learn – without the predisposition to association people would be unlikely to learn anything. However, it becomes a problem when these associations, or correlations, are false. For example, if I see a college professor and then see that professor trip, I might assume there is a correlation between being a professor and clumsiness, which is more evidence for my assumption that college professors are geeks.

- The self-fulfilling prophecy (Rosenthal & Jacobson, 1966) is a process that occurs when people make an initial assumption about a person. Then, they act in a way that causes the others to behave in a way that is consistent with that expectation. For example, I might meet a college professor. Because I assume the professor is a geek, I only ask questions that then elicit and confirm my assumption. It is important to note that this professor may or may not meet the criteria, but I have set up the situation so that it fulfills my initial expectations.
- Similarity-attraction (Izard, 1960) is a core theory within social psychology. According to the theory, people are more attracted to those who are similar to them. A related concept is the similar-to-me error – the research shows that people give more positive evaluations of those who are similar to themselves (Baskettt, 1973). Thus, if I am a college professor, I am more likely to like (and recruit) other college professors.

As can be seen, breaking others into categories and then making assumptions about the members of these categories can adversely affect judgments and lead to biases.

So far, the chapter has focused on how people interpret and perceive individual differences of others. However, these issues manifest themselves within groups and teams in a way that is different than the interpretations and perceptions of individuals with whom we may or may or may not be working. Once people are together in a group or team, there is an entirely new process of understanding the impact of the diverse makeup of groups and teams. The process is described by the terms group heterogeneity and group homogeneity. Group homogeneity/heterogeneity is the overall representativeness of differences within a group. Homogonous groups are ones where there are few differences among members. On the other hand, heterogeneous groups are ones with considerable differences among members. These two concepts are at polar opposites of a continuum – groups can be completely homogenous, very heterogeneous, or anywhere in between.

Jackson and colleagues (1991) conducted a classic study examining the effects of levels of homogeneity and heterogeneity on organizational outcomes, such as promotions and attrition. What they found was that dissimilarity, especially dissimilarity due to education and industry experience, led to a significantly higher level of attrition. However, this was also influenced by status. Specifically, dissimilarity had a larger impact on those of lower status within the organization. This effect of dissimilarity is not limited to attrition. Tolbert, Andrews, and Simons (1995) point out that dissimilarity leads to negative attitudes about those who are in the minority (women in academia, in their study), especially as the minority group becomes more powerful and a larger (though not majority) percentage of the group (see also DiTomaso, Cordero, & Farris, 1996).

This leads back to the question from the beginning of this section: Are diverse (heterogeneous) groups more successful or are non-diverse (homogenous) groups more successful? As always, the answer is that it depends. Mannix and Neale (2005) sum up the impact of diverse teams well. Diverse teams are successful when a) they are working on tasks that require exploration, innovation, and creativity, b) when there is organizational support for working in diverse teams and strong superordinate goals – or goals that go beyond any one team member and bond members together around a "greater" goal that are beyond those that might divide a team, and c) when members who are in the minority group have the backing of strong organizational members or coalitions. Diverse groups and teams certainly have the potential to improve organizational functioning, but whether they can reach their potential depends on the process within and beyond the group and team. The salad bowl is a better metaphor for understanding and making sense of diverse groups than is the melting pot metaphor. According to Raghuram and Garud (1996):

> The salad, as a metaphor, is more appropriate than the melting pot because a salad preserves the diversity and integrity of its ingredients. At the same time, the appeal of a salad is enhanced or diminished by how it is mixed. It is precisely this processual aspect that lends diversity its allure. Whether or not a group benefits from diversity depends on the processes that unfold (p. 175).

Three Interventions to Understand Culture and Improve Performance in Diverse Groups and Teams

As the review of the theories and research about culture and diversity demonstrate, effective groups and teams must try to integrate members into the culture, must work to change the culture for the positive, and must value and integrate diverse teams into the tasks where they will be successful. This is not always a simple task. The next three interventions provide some structured opportunities to make groups and teams more successful at understanding and changing culture as well as getting members working in diverse work groups and teams that are highly successful.

Deciphering culture

Many leaders within organizations state that they want to change the culture. This is a very long process that is beyond the scope of this book. However, culture change requires understanding the culture of an organization so that team members know what it is that they need to change. A culture change assessment can be used to solve conflicts and resolve differences by identifying how the values and assumptions within the team help or hinder performance.

Schein's steps involved in a culture assessment are described in Table 4.3. Most of the work involved is in determining the underlying values and assumptions within the team or organization. Once these are identified, the team can use them to better understand what values and assumptions are causing friction that reduces the ability of team members to perform.

Table 4.3 A Summary of the Steps Involved in a Culture Assessment.

Step	Procedure
1.	Gain leadership commitment. According to Schein, this is necessary for any culture change assessment or process to be successful.
2.	Select groups to interview. This requires working with contacts within the unit or organization to determine who is representative of the organization and who will have the required level of openness and trust to provide useful information.
3.	Select a setting for the interviews. Make sure the setting is comfortable and there is space on the walls (flip charts, whiteboards, etc.) for notes. It also helps to have a set of break out rooms available as well.
4.	Explain the purpose of the meeting. A leader or authority should explain why people are at the meeting, and then the meeting should continue after the leader or authority has left the room.
5.	Describe the concept of culture. A facilitator should introduce the concept of culture, including artifacts, values, and assumptions so that team members have a shared understanding of the concept.
6.	Elicit descriptions of the artifacts. Start with a member who has joined the group most recently, and have her or him describe what they first noticed. A good question is "What is going on here?" Others can join into the discussion. Then, break these artifacts into logical categories (e.g., dress code).
7.	Identify espoused values. A question to start the discussion is "Why are you doing what you are doing?" Ask this question about some of the artifacts to get at values and beliefs. Check for consensus around values.
8.	Identify shared assumptions. Assumptions are one of the most difficult parts to get at. Start with listing the artifacts and values, and then try to find out what causes conflict that is not covered within the artifacts and values. The first assumptions may be triggers for a new range of insights not covered during the previous discussions.
9.	Identify cultural aids and hindrances. Break the group into two subgroups. The subgroups should spend time refining the current and identifying new assumptions as well as categorizing the assumptions about whether they will help or hinder the team.
10.	Report assumptions and analysis. The final step is to gain consensus. The subgroups come together and each report findings. Together, they examine the similarities and differences and come to consensus around assumptions and constraints.

Adapted from Schein (2004).

The literature on culture assessment and change is mixed. Advocates of culture change write volumes about the methods, procedures, and techniques designed in changing culture. On the other hand, critiques argue that culture is difficult and slow to change, and most efforts to do so fail. Like Harris and Ogbonna (1998),

I take a moderate view on culture change procedures. If the organization follows a structured set of procedures **and** the leadership is leading the change **and** the followership is willing to take part in the change, a culture assessment and change process can be successful. Good facilitators and consultants, whether internal or external, need to be well-versed in change methods to take advantage of leaders and followers who are ready for change.

Improving understanding of differences through a 360-degree feedback process

Diversity initiatives are often used in organizations to better understand the ways that different people react to differences. Curtis and Dreachslin (2008) studied the impact of diversity training initiatives on organizational performance. They did this by reviewing the literature about the effectiveness of diversity initiatives that was published from 2000 to 2006. Some of their key findings included:

- Racial and gender diversity had neither a positive or negative impact on performance per se. When racial diversity had a negative impact on team processes, it was mitigated by training and development initiatives.
- There were few direct effects at all of diversity interventions on performance because context is crucial to determining the nature of diversity's impact. A highly competitive team context exacerbated negative effects of racial diversity, whereas racial diversity enhanced team performance when organizations fostered an environment that promotes learning from diversity. In general, gender diversity was less problematic than racial diversity.
- Different aspects of organizational context and some group processes moderated diversity–performance relationships (Curtis & Dreachslin, 2008, pp. 129–130).

In summary, their findings show that, unfortunately, there is little evidence that the diversity interventions that they studied –those that focus on understanding differences – can help subsequent organizational performance (though they do not hinder performance, either).

On the other hand, Polzer (2008) finds that one way to improve the communication among members of different groups is to conduct 360-degree assessments. A 360-degree assessment, or what is also called multisource feedback, is a process where a team member receives anonymous feedback from bosses, peers, subordinates, and sometimes customers (Table 4.4). This information is summarized and then fed back to the member in a way that helps them to make changes to behavior as well as develop leadership and team member behavior (see Atwater, Brett, & Charles, 2007). According to Polzer, "sharing honest self-assessments and appraisals of one another through 360-degree feedback can help [group] members achieve interpersonal congruence (p. 21). What this means is that group or team members can understand where their understanding of themselves and others is congruent with others and where it is not.

Table 4.4   A Summary of the Steps Involved in 360-degree or Multisource Feedback.

Step	Procedure
1.	The first step in a 360-degree feedback process is to set up the context for performing 360-degree evaluations to help to build trust in the process. This includes defining the administrative process that the team will be following. • Clearly explain the purpose of the 360-degree feedback session to every member of the organization. This includes explaining the source of the 360-degree feedback instrument and how the findings will be used. • Communicate the confidentiality and anonymity of the process. Anonymity and confidentiality, however, can have limits (one of the raters may say something that identifies him or her), and these need to be explained as well. • Choose the raters. In most cases, these should be chosen by the person being rated. The person being rated should be coached to a) choose people he or she knows well, b) choose some that are supporters and some that are not, and c) choose multiple people in each category, where possible. • Make sure the questionnaire is designed to capture the unique views of customers. • Discuss up front how the person being rated will receive support for personal development and performance improvement. • Focusing on similarity rather than diversity.
2.	Design the questionnaire so that there is meaningful input to the 360-degree process. • Make sure the instructions for all components of the process are clear. Training to improve the process may be necessary. • The questionnaire items need to be designed carefully so that they are valid and reliable. • Carefully consider alternative possibilities for the response alternatives (choices). Many 360-degree instruments only consider frequency of behavior, but another good additional choice is quality of the behavior being conducted. Also make sure to have a "not applicable" choice alternative.
3.	Determine the process and design for providing feedback. There are many formats for providing feedback to the person being rated and some consideration should be given to how the feedback should be given. • The information should be analyzed across respondents and organized into central themes. • The themes and concepts presented on the report should be ones that can be developed within the person being rated.

Table 4.4   (*cont'd*).

Step	Procedure
	• All feedback reports should have self assessments as well as the information provided by others. There can be considerable information, and the person being rated will likely need help to sift through the meaning of these findings. Provide written (verbatim) comments, but make sure that a skilled facilitator is working with the person being rated to help him or her understand the meaning of the comments within the perspective of the entire report; people can easily focus too much on one negative comment rather than seeing the larger issues.
4.	Unfortunately, too many multisource feedback processes end after the feedback report. However, the process must also provide meaningful support for improvement, development planning, change, and improvement.
	• Know what areas of development to recommend and specifics about how to develop that area. • Follow up regularly during post-assessment to track the person's areas of success and other areas of development.

Adapted from Van Velsor (1998).

The process described above is only one of many processes to conduct 360-degree feedback assessments. It has become a popular tool within organizations and can be a successful way to provide members of groups and teams with feedback. A recent literature review by Morgeson, Mumford, and Campion (2005) answers many of the common questions about multisource feedback. Their conclusions suggest that if conducted well, 360-degree or multisource feedback is a promising innovation when developing people.

Conversity (ASTD)

A more recent initiative being used in organizations to help people of different backgrounds work together is termed Conversity (Wildermuth & Gray, 2005, Table 4.5). According to Wildermuth and Gray, successful diversity training programs:

- require long-term intervention and reinforcement;
- are customized to the specific group of participants;
- use active learning and experiential procedures such as role playing; and
- focus on gaining a comprehensive set of skills, including problem solving, conflict resolution, communication, and feedback.

They find that long-term diversity training that changes attitudes is far more successful than the typical one-seminar diversity training seminar that many organizations use.

The Conversity program takes into account these four suggestions and, essentially, turns diversity on its head. Instead of focusing on differences, Conversity emphasizes similarities.

Although there is not yet any independent research about the success of Conversity as a specific intervention, the concepts that it recommends are clearly consistent with the research. Randel and Earley (2009), for example, found that team members who tend to notice and think about the similarities between them and other members have higher performance than those who notice and think about differences. Similarly, Luijters, van der Zee, and Otten (2008) found that team members who perceive similarity are more likely to identify with their team than those who perceive differences. Finally, noticing similarities appears to have an even stronger

Table 4.5   A Summary of the Steps Involved in Conversity.

Step	Procedure
1.	Select the facilitators for the Conversity program. The facilitators need to be able to control the environment while concurrently developing and encouraging respectful communication. Look for seasoned facilitators who are aware of their own biases and tendencies, have leadership and facilitation skills, and are committed to learning as well as developing the learning in others.
2.	Prepare the environment, including the group, the training room and seating, the refreshments, and the materials (many of the Conversity exercises require specific materials).
3.	Verify the leadership commitment to valuing differences. Make sure that the leaders truly want to.
4.	Prepare for four modules of Conversity training, including:
	a) Create a safe environment while respecting legal rights. Get members to think out of the box, including providing an understanding of categorization and how it affects personal and professional relationships. Work to get participants to seek common ground with members of other groups.
	b) Work to understand culture and its impact on our assumptions. Have participants examine their own cultural values and assumptions.
	c) Work to understand stereotyping. Have participants understand their own stereotypes. Have participants discuss the origins of stereotypes and the impact of stereotypes on decision making. By the end, participants should begin to question and even discard stereotypes.
	d) Work to understand discrimination and prejudice and connect them with real-life experiences. Learn to recognize the subtle methods of discrimination, such as body language.
5.	Gain commitments from participants about how they will change their behavior in the future. Work with participants to develop a process to communicate these changes with their supervisors and coworkers.

Adapted from Wildermuth and Gray (2005).

impact at improving team performance when members are thinking about value differences (Homan, van Knippenberg, Van Kleef, & De Dreu, 2007). Thus, ASTD's Conversity approach is based on a solid research foundation.

FOCUS ON APPLICATION

Using conversity to improve team performance: Sequetta F. Sweet, Atteuq Potential Unlimited, Inc.

The practitioner

Sequetta F. Sweet founded *Atteuq Potential Unlimited, Inc.* in 2005. The company provides Performance and Talent Management consulting with emphasis on Human Resource Training, Development, Organizational Learning and Change. The ultimate objective is to assist in improving individual and organizational performance – *unleashing potential and driving performance*. Services are provided in the following areas: Leadership Development, Performance Management, Management, Project Management, Customer Service, Diversity & Diversity Management, Executive Coaching, Communication, Assertiveness, Dealing with Difficult Personalities, Systems Analysis & Design, Software Development, and Microsoft Office Products.

Prior to starting *Atteuq*, Sequetta enjoyed a nearly 25 year career in corporate America and the Information Technology (IT) industry working to hone her leadership, business, and IT skills. She served in IT roles such as: Requirements/System Analyst, Systems Engineer, Database Administrator (DBA), Project Manager, Process Engineer, and Applications Development Manager. She has worked at fortune 500 companies in both Rochester, NY and Boston, MA. She currently serves as an adjunct instructor at Monroe Community College in the Office and Computer Programs department.

Sequetta is currently a doctoral candidate in Executive Leadership at St. John Fisher College in Rochester, NY focusing her dissertation in Entrepreneurship and Entrepreneurial Learning (expected graduation August 2012). She serves as a graduate assistant to the program and is currently involved in a field experience in Entrepreneurship with the College's Bittner School of Business. Sequetta holds a Masters of Science in Organizational Learning and Human Resource Development from St. John Fisher College and a Bachelors of Science in Computer Science from Rensselaer Polytechnic Institute in Troy, NY.

Sequetta is happily married to Charles, a semi-retired home remodeling and repair professional.

The symptom

African American and Hispanic nurses, certified nursing assistants (CNAs), and food service workers in a nursing home were experiencing racial slurs from patients. Employees' complaints were falling on deaf ears. Lower-level employees had also lodged complaints that senior and mid-level managers were not approachable or engaging (they did not speak to them in the hallways and they had a way of not acknowledging them.) and were unfair in their disciplinary practices. The lower-level employees felt that they were not valued. The fact that an overwhelming number of employees at the senior and middle management level were white (99%) while an overwhelming percentage of employees at the lower levels of the organization were African American and Hispanic (between 80% and 90%) caused some to conclude that racism existed in the organization. For this reason I was engaged to deliver diversity training to about 50 senior and mid-level managers and 150 staff members.

Assessing the problem

Prior to engaging me the organization decided to face the issue head-on by holding a series of focus groups. All employees of the organization were required to attend. The question "Does racism exist here?" was asked. Some sessions were uneventful because the issue of race was barely addressed or the participants felt there were no issues with race there. Several other sessions, however, were exceptionally emotional, as discussions of racism often are. At these sessions black and Hispanic employees gave poignant stories of how they had been mistreated by employees in the organization. The management team came to a rousing conclusion that racism existed in the organization.

The results of the sessions were then shared with me. I was briefed by the executive director. I met several times with senior management team and others in the organization and asked questions about the organization. My conclusion was that, like in most, if not all organizations, the employees in this organization have difficulty accepting others with differences, not just

racial differences. I developed my training to address accepting all differences rather than having a focus on race.

Intervening: Using the conversity technique

Remembering the impact that the "sensitivity" sessions of the 1980s had
caused me to avoid the use of them. "Sensitivity" sessions focused mainly
on the issue of race. Diversity is so much broader than race. Additionally,
in "sensitivity" sessions the issue of race was confronted openly by blacks
telling their feelings, why they are the way they are, and trying to convince
whites of the injustices to which blacks have been subjected. I learned that
it is nearly impossible for someone to truly understand what it is like to
"be black" without actually being black. In my experience, the sessions left
both blacks and whites with an empty feeling knowing that nothing was
really accomplished. This is usually the end-result of a discussion on differences. But people can be positively affected by conversations about
similarities. This is the focus of the Conversity intervention. With
Conversity, participants are encouraged to focus on what they have in
common rather than on their differences.

During the session, I paired participants with someone they did not know
well. They had a normal conversation in which they sought for hidden similarities in each other. Asked to go beyond the obvious and search for common hopes, dreams, fears, and interests, the participants engaged each
other by asking and answering questions for 15–20 minutes. In all of the 18
sessions where the Conversity technique was used, the participants wanted
more time to engage in these conversations. The conversations seemed to
flow. The feeling in the room was extraordinary; one of connection, bond-
ing, camaraderie, and relationship. People could not stop talking. People
who had never even said "hello" to each other or who were normally quiet
were drawn into the exchange. Though conversations would start out with
the mention of birthdays, birthplaces, number of children, and more surface kinds of dialogue, if given enough time many participants would ven-
ture into the deeper, more meaningful talk of hopes, dreams and life aspirations. This is where the real learning began and where true connections
were made in the workplace. Participants began to learn that we are more
the same than different and their relationships can then be developed to
assist in improving team interaction and thus, team performance.

The Conversity technique is an excellent approach to use for teambuild-
ing. Team members can be given a chance to interact one-on-one with each
other regularly, but more purposefully using this technique.

Chapter Summary

This chapter examined the impact of organizational culture and group and team member diversity on performance. Culture is the shared basic assumptions learned by a group as it solved its problems. It is identified through the artifacts, values, and assumptions within a group or team. There are two different types of values: espoused and enacted. The discrepancy between the espoused values and enacted values can provide additional understanding about the strength of the culture within an organization. Culture is something that is initially created by an organization's founding member(s) and is learned over time and can be changed if necessary, though the change process is slow.

Diversity is the different values and cultures among members, and is more than simply an understanding of black versus white. It is necessary in today's multicultural and global society to understand how to work with those of varying backgrounds. The promises of a diverse workforce include a greater understanding of customers, more information from varied backgrounds, and improved social benefits for all. The reality of diverse groups and teams, however, differs from the promise. Diverse groups and teams can struggle because of differing values, the underlying social identities, stereotypes, and prejudices. However, diverse groups and teams appear to be able to succeed if they focus on superordinate goals, the task is one that requires creativity and identity, they are supported within the organization, and they are given enough time to develop their own norms and standards.

Additional Resources

Burke, W. W. (1994). *Organization development: A process of learning and changing*. Reading, MA: Addison Wesley Publishing Co.

Jackson, S. E., & Ruderman, M. N. (1995). *Diversity in work teams: Research paradigms for a changing workplace*. Washington, DC: American Psychological Association.

Mannix, E., & Neale, M. A. (2005). What differences make a difference? The promise and reality of diverse teams in organizations. *Psychological Science in the Public Interest, 6,* 31–55.

Schein, E. H. (2004). *Organizational culture and leadership* (3rd ed.). San Francisco: Jossey Bass.

Wildermuth, C., & Gray, S. (2005). *Diversity Training*. Alexandria, VA: ASTD Press.

Team Exercises

Exercise 4.1   Take the Implicit Associations Test

One way to help to understand the way we see people of different cultures is to take the Implicit Association Test (IAT). The IAT tests implicit (rather than explicit) biases. Implicit biases are ones that are deep within our thought processes, often ones we don't even know about. Because they are so deeply rooted in our thought processes, they are often beyond our cognitive control.

Step 1:   Go to: https://implicit.harvard.edu/implicit/.
Step 2:   There are many different versions of the IAT. Pick one of the IAT tests and then take it. Examine your results and reflect about what it tells you about your implicit biases.
Step 3:   Pick another IAT and examine your results.
Step 4:   Without necessarily sharing your results, share how the IAT made you feel about your understanding of other groups. How did your score make you feel? What did you learn about your implicit biases? How will it change your reactions to others who are different from you.
Step 5:   Read the project web page at: http://www.projectimplicit.net/generalinfo. php.

Exercise 4.2   What is diversity?

Break into small groups and discuss the following case: Your organization has grown over the past 12 years from a small privately-owned company and 80 employees in one location to a large publicly-traded corporation and 1,700 employees spread across 25 offices in three countries. Most of this acquisition has occurred through purchasing small companies. As it has grown, the organization has been working to get the support systems in line with the new organizational structure that is being developed. Customers, the public, and employees have recently started complaining about the lack of women and people of color with leadership positions. In addition, the senior leadership team has realized that it now needs a new position designed to help employees to integrate all the different organizational cultures from the multiple locations into one new cultural identity. To head this effort, they are hiring a new Director of Diversity. You are part of a team that has been appointed by the senior leaders to hire this new director-level position. You have a list of four people from whom to choose, including:

- An Asian man who was born and raised among the Main Line suburbs of Philadelphia, PA. He has a Master's degree in Industrial-Organizational Psychology and five years of experience in Human Resources after earning his Master's degree.
- An African-American woman who was born in the city of Rochester, NY, a mid-sized city in upstate NY. She withdrew from high school and five years later earned her GED. She has 35 years of experience and has worked herself up from an Administrative Assistant to the Director of Human Resources at a mid-sized (300 employee) company. She is currently enrolled in a bachelor's degree program part-time and should earn her degree within the next two years.

- A Caucasian man whose birthplace is unknown. He was raised by mixed-race foster parents in the Marcy Projects in Brooklyn, NY. He has a degree in Business from the City College of New York. He has 10 years of experience and is currently the Manager of Human Resources at a competitor.
- An Indian woman who just completed her doctoral degree this month in Human Resources Development. She was raised in a wealthy household and worked as a customer service representative for six years before moving to the United States to earn her degree. She is the first woman in her family to attend graduate school.

Given this information, rank order the four candidates.

Chapter 5

Preparing the Environment for Teamwork

Most people have had the experience of working on a group project in school. The way that it is supposed to work is that the group members come together. They carefully read over the assignment. They decide on the best method for responding to that problem. They divide up the work and then come back together to organize and arrange it. Then, each member gets a grade. However, it often does not work as well as this (the professor's) expectation. Instead, each individual member is getting her or his own grade for the project. What often happens is that the person in the group who is most concerned with earning an "A" does almost all of the work. This is because the group work is not in alignment with the individual needs.

Designing a proper reward system is one of the areas where it is necessary to prepare the environment for teamwork. Thus, the final set of inputs considered in this book is at the level of the organization. The three major categories include group and team rewards and recognition, creating an organizational structure that supports groups and teams, and garnering leadership support for teamwork.

As always, the first step in making change is assessment. Wageman and colleagues (Wageman, Hackman, & Lehman, 2005) created a detailed assessment tool that they titled the "Team Diagnostic Survey" (Table 5.1). The survey is a theory-based tool that helps teams to assess all areas of their team development. To establish the reliability and validity of the survey, they examined the tested the tool with 1,202 team members from 140 different work teams. They compared each item on the assessment tool to team effectiveness. They found that the Team Diagnostic Survey "can be used to diagnose the strengths and weaknesses of work teams" (p. 395). Only a select subset of five of the categories is listed here – those that apply to diagnosing the organizational environment. A full version of the Team Diagnostic Survey is

Group Dynamics and Team Interventions: Understanding and Improving Team Performance,
First Edition. Timothy M. Franz.
© 2012 Timothy M. Franz. Published 2012 by Blackwell Publishing Ltd.

Table 5.1 Assessing the Organizational Environment: The Team Diagnostic Survey.

TDS Item	Highly Inaccurate	Inaccurate	Neither Inaccurate Nor Accurate	Accurate	Highly Accurate
Rewards and Recognition					
1. Excellent team performance pays off in this organization.	1	2	3	4	5
2. Even teams that do an especially good job are not recognized or rewarded by the organization. (R)	1	2	3	4	5
3. This organization recognizes and reinforces teams that perform well.	1	2	3	4	5
Information					
4. It is easy for teams in this organization to get any data or forecasts that members need to do their work.	1	2	3	4	5
5. This organization keeps its teams in the dark about information that could affect their work plans. (R)	1	2	3	4	5
6. Teams in this organization can get whatever information they need to plan their work.	1	2	3	4	5
Education/Consultation					
7. Teams in this organization have to make do with whatever expertise members already have – technical training and support are not available even when needed. (R)	1	2	3	4	5
8. When something comes up that team members do not know how to handle, it is easy for them to obtain the training or technical advice they need.	1	2	3	4	5
9. In this organization, teams do not receive adequate training for the work they have to do. (R)	1	2	3	4	5
Material Resources					
10. Teams in this organization can readily obtain all the material resources that they need for their work.	1	2	3	4	5
11. Scarcity of resources is a real problem for teams in this organization. (R)	1	2	3	4	5
Focus of Leader's Attention					
12. Leaders coach individual team members.	1	2	3	4	5
13. Leaders help team members learn how to work well together.	1	2	3	4	5
14. Leaders get the team set up right – clarifying its purpose, picking members, structuring the task, setting expectations, and so on.	1	2	3	4	5
15. Leaders run external interference for the team – getting resources, securing outside assistance, removing roadblocks, and so on.	1	2	3	4	5

These five sections of the Team Diagnostic Survey are taken from Wageman, Hackman, and Lehman (2005).

available online at http://research.wjh.harvard.edu/TDS. Wageman and colleagues provide multiple sources of evidence that demonstrate that the Team Diagnostic Survey predicts team performance and the ability of teams to manage themselves. In addition, Liu, Pirola-Merlo, Yang, and Huang (2009) found that the Team Diagnostic Survey predicted team performance within Taiwanese teams as well.

When using the Team Diagnostic Survey, a team's score is computed by averaging member responses on each of the five subdimensions listed above with relevant reverse scoring (i.e., when there is an "R" behind the item, the item is worded in the opposite direction and the numbers need to be changed in the opposite direction so that a 1 becomes a 5, a 2 becomes a 4, etc.). After finding your team's results, you can determine whether you need to focus on team rewards, organizational structure, or leadership when determining how best to support the team.

Team Structure: Matching Tasks with Goals, Feedback, and Rewards

One of the problems with using groups and teams is that many support structures within organizations are designed around individuals. Too many organizations organize teams and then rely on individual goals and reward systems. However, "teams, just like individuals, respond to both external and internal rewards" (Harrington-Mackin, 1994, p. 132). Rewards, just like goals, need to be set differently for teams than for individuals.

Saavedra, Earley, and Van Dyne (1993) provide some of the most compelling evidence to demonstrate this relationship between tasks, goals, and rewards. They conducted a research study where they examined the relationships between tasks, goals, and feedback on group performance. Their main finding was that groups performed better when they had a group goal combined with a group task combined with group-level feedback. Further, they found that the second highest performance was on individual tasks with individual goals and individual-level feedback. Clearly, there is an interdependence among these concepts. If an organization wants individuals to perform best, it should use individual feedback and reward systems. On the other hand, if an organization wants teams to perform well, it should use team feedback and reward systems (see also Pritchard, Jones, Roth, Stuebing, & Ekeberg, 1988). Regardless of the system, however, it must be perceived by team members as a legitimate way to disperse compensation and incentives (Aime, Meyer, & Humphrey, 2009).

Katz (2001), like Saavedra and colleagues, stresses the importance of designing team reward systems. She classifies team compensation systems into five different team-based compensation categories, including:

- *Pay equality*: Each member of the team receives the same pay.
- *Pay equity*: Each member is compensated according to individual performance.
- *An individual/group hybrid with a group threshold*: After the team as a whole reached a certain target, members' pay rates rose relative to their individual performance.

- *An individual/group hybrid with an individual threshold*: Once every member of the team hit an established target, pay rates for each would rise according to their individual performance.
- *A relative ratio*: Team members are paid for individual performance, but once the highest paid earns a predetermined level more than the lowest paid, some of the high performers' subsequent earnings are transferred to the low performers to reduce the pay gap within the team.

In her research she found that the two individual/group hybrid systems led to higher performance than the other three systems. This is likely to occur because the two hybrid systems account for team performance while at the same time providing a method of rewarding individuals while holding them accountable to the team.

Though Katz as well as Saavadra and colleagues provide the recommendations about reward systems, Harrington-Mackin (1994) provides advice about how specifically to create team reward structures. The majority of these ideas examine the way that individual and team reward systems interact. First, the reward system must be congruent with the culture in the organization and with the overall management style. Second, if the evaluation system stresses one set of priorities [such as teamwork] and the reward system stresses another [such as individual work], the reward system will win out. Third, the reward system must focus on the accomplishments of the team, not individuals. Fourth, reward and recognition systems geared to individuals are in direct conflict with the idea of teams. Fifth, if the organization is going to give rewards, it is best to do so at the end of a team project, rather than on an annual basis. Finally, reward systems should make teams accountable to the organization as a whole, as well as to the team. As you can see, Harrington-Mackin is in favor of rewarding teams for teamwork while rewarding individuals for individual work. The chapter in her book provides even more details about recommendations than are summarized here as well as additional advice about rewarding teams.

Organizational Structure

Just as tasks, goals, feedback, and rewards must consistently support groups and teams, the organizational structure must also be organized in a way that supports groups and teams as well. Unfortunately, there is no one-size-fits-all organizational structure that will serve as a panacea to allowing groups and teams to succeed. Instead, an organization must consider whether its current structure can provide teams with the information and authority to succeed.

According to Mohrman and Quam (2000) "For some team advocates, self-management and the elimination of bureaucracy and hierarchy are part of the definition of a team. In fact, in team-based organizations teams perform a number of tasks previously handled by managers, including lateral integration with other teams and internal leadership tasks" (p. 21). This does not, however, mean that teams lack structure and leadership. In fact, Mohrman and Quam clarify this by stating that teams are an integral part of the formal organizational structure and hierarchy. They further state that "the entire enterprise must be rethought to design the workings of the organization to support the performance of an array of interacting teams" (p. 21). They suggest that team effectiveness depends on how well management can provide the teams within the organization with a consistent direction. They suggest that the role of the organization structure is to provide teams with:

- *Direction*: "Teams must have a clear understanding of strategy, their goals must be aligned with the other parts of the business unit, and there must be processes for adjusting strategy and goals in a dynamic environment" (p. 26).
- *Relevant communication*: "Teams need access to a broad range of information, not only about their own activities but also about the activities of the broader organization" (p. 26).
- *Authority in decision making*: "Clear team boundaries can be defined by charting key decisions, indicating where teams have authority to make decisions, what input they are expected to get, how they participate in decisions where they do not have final authority, and how decisions get escalated" (p. 26).

Many of the structural characteristics that support teams can be provided by making a change in the organizational structure that emphasizes methods of empowering work teams. Thomas Furman (1988), a former executive at United Technology Corporation, recommends this as one step in a process of changing an organization. According to Furman, making change requires creating a vision, developing a shared vision, taking initiative, empowering others, and gaining support within the organization. Kirkman and Rosen (1999) define an empowered team as one that feels potency, meaningfulness, autonomy, and impact. Potency is where team members must feel that they have the competencies to act. Meaningfulness is when team members must feel a sense of purpose and care about their tasks. Autonomy is where team members must feel that they are able to act when necessary on the tasks that are relevant to their job. Finally, impact is when team members must feel that what they do has some impact on the organization.

However, empowering a team requires a significant amount of time and work by senior management. To accomplish this, "develop work processes and capture team synergies. Typically, the rollout of organizational efforts to install empowered work teams begins with visionary statements by top management, the formation of work teams, team-building exercises, and a variety of efforts to establish team identity" (p. 55).

Leadership Support

Just as the organizational structure must support teamwork, the leadership within the organization must also support teamwork (Topchik, 2007). In fact, "empowered employee teams are frequently used in both education and business arenas to improve quality and facilitate organizational change. However, teams do not always achieve their goals due to a lack of leadership support" (Olson, Olson, & Murphy, 1998, p. 35). Olson and colleagues strongly urge management to "model teamwork at the Management Level and practice what they preach" (p. 37). This leadership support can take four different forms, including emotional support, informational support, instrumental support, and appraisal support. Emotional support is providing a sympathetic understanding and empathetic response to issues that the team may face. Informational support is making sure that teams have the necessary information to do their work. Instrumental support is providing support with the tasks that the team faces, including helping an overloaded team member. Finally, appraisal support is helping teams to find alternative ways to assess and then solve a problem while at the same time not providing a specific solution. These support behaviors help, as Winum and Seamons (2000) say, because the "senior management team must 'walk the talk' to gain credibility and avoid hypocrisy" (p. 89). Leadership support is especially crucial because leaders are the ones who choose how to allocate resources to groups and teams (Conger & Fulmer, 2003).

Gaining leadership support can be difficult when making changes to an organization. As part of his model of change, Kotter (e.g., Kotter & Cohen, 2002) recommends creating a sense of urgency to help to drive change within an organization. One way to accomplish this is by identifying and highlighting significant performance gaps within the organization (Cohen, 2005).

Initial Planning Processes

The final consideration for groups and teams before starting is to set the stage prior to working together. This includes setting norms and confirming expectations of one another. The expectations should be set around process (how groups and teams should work together) as well as interpersonal behavior (how people should act towards one another). In addition, groups and teams can help make their time together go more smoothly if they appoint a facilitator ahead of time.

Norms are "shared group experiences about appropriate behavior" (Muchinsky, 2009, p. 260). Groups and teams that have well-defined norms for successful performance are more effective than those that do not have them because norms regulate expected social behavior (e.g., see Baron, Kerr, & Miller, 1992; Levine & Moreland, 1990). One reason for this is because groups and teams with strong norms, especially norms for critical task behavior, help groups to improve information sharing, and this leads to success with group tasks (Postmes, Spears, & Cihangir, 2001). Further, group norms can help groups and teams to become more cohesive (Eys, Hardy, & Patterson, 2006).

Helping groups and teams to set norms when they start working together can improve their chances for success. Setting norms can help members to eliminate at least some of the time spent during the storming phase during group development, so that members can more quickly focus on task behavior and reach the performing stage sooner. Scott, Mitchell, and Birnbaum (1981) recommend a three-step process for how norms are identified and communicated within an organization. The steps include:

- Group members either explicitly define the norms or implicitly define them by describing behaviors that are consistent with the norms.
- Group members determine whether others follow the norms.
- Group members recognize and reward those who follow the norms while punishing or ostracizing those that do not.

Three Interventions to Prepare a Team for Teamwork

Planning the structure of a group session

As part of the preparation for facilitation, Kayser (2011) recommends considering four steps when planning for a group (Table 5.2). Using these four steps can help a group to short circuit some of the process losses and focus its work on the task outcomes rather than wasting time on problems.

After following these four steps, the group and the group's facilitator is ready to work with the group. Kayser also recommends setting meeting agendas, a topic which will be covered in detail in the Appendix in this book, which is about improving group meetings.

Creating norms for groups

Setting norms ahead of time, just like creating the structure ahead of time, can help groups and teams to eliminate many of the problems and conflicts that might arise later (Table 5.3). This is because the group or team has already made decisions about how members will act when working together. Further, it reduces conflict because the group has explicitly stated how members will act. Finally, it serves as a reminder about how people should act towards one another.

Chapter 3 reviewed some of the basic team processes, including team development. One of the stages in team development is storming. This stage of group development occurs because team members are learning how to work with one another and are defining roles, setting norms, and determining standards of behavior. When members fail to agree or have different expectations, there is often conflict. Taking time to set norms ahead of time can save groups considerable time later when they are moving towards the performing stage.

Table 5.2   A Summary of the Steps Involved in Planning the Structure of a Group Session.

Step	Procedure

Before starting a group session

1. *Determine the session's purpose and desired outcomes.* Kayser recommends defining a clear purpose to help reduce confusion, irritation, and arguments. Ask the following questions:
   - Why are we here?
   - What outcomes are we trying to accomplish?

2. *Determine whether a group session is even necessary.* This question follows the purpose because once the purpose is decided, the group can then decide whether a group session is even necessary. Kayser finds that 15% to 25% of meetings are completely unnecessary. In some cases, electronic communication can save time and eliminate these unnecessary meetings.

3. *Determine who should attend.* The main question for this section is to ask "Who are the appropriate people to invite?" Kayser's general principle is to "select the fewest number of people required to achieve the designed outcomes." (p. 59). Unnecessary attendees makes group facilitation more difficult and can cause disruptions in the group.

4. *Determine the "macrocomposition" of the group and its potential chemistry when members come together.* Kayser recommends stepping back and making sure all the interested parties are represented. More importantly, he says that the facilitator should try to understand some of the dynamics of the group ahead of time including:
   - Has the group worked together?
   - Which people in the group will be enthusiastic while which will not?
   - Have there been any problems with group process before?
   - Are there any disruptive members?
   - What is the tenor of the group? Is it more task oriented or fun loving and interpersonal?
   - What is the level of support about the task?
   - Which members are most influential
   - What are the factors that prevent those who have less power from contributing?

Adapted from Kayser (2011).

Appreciative inquiry and culture change

Appreciative Inquiry (AI) is an organization development philosophy that is rooted in the positive psychology movement, meaning that it focuses on strengths rather than deficits. The methods of appreciative inquiry can help groups, teams, and organizations to move forward with changing culture. This appreciative inquiry process was first described by Cooperrider and Srivastva (1987). The basic premise of appreciative inquiry is to emphasize strengths and areas for development rather than focus on

Table 5.3 A Summary of the Steps Involved in Setting Ground Rules.

Step	Procedure
1.	At the group's first meeting, set aside a period of time – usually 15–20 minutes – to establish ground rules.
2.	This session should be facilitated by someone who can remain unbiased about the ground rules.
3.	Open the floor to suggestions from the group for ground rules. Record the ground rules on a flipchart. Some areas to consider when setting ground rules are: <ul><li>Attendance and promptness</li><li>Disagreements and conflict</li><li>Participation</li><li>Interruptions and outside communication</li><li>Conversational courtesies</li><li>Confidentiality</li><li>Completing group assignments outside of the group time</li><li>Breaks</li><li>Rotation of responsibilities</li><li>Meeting places and times</li><li>How decisions will be reached</li></ul>
4.	Modify, add, and change the ground rules when people make suggestions for improvement.
5.	When all group members agree on the ground rules, post them on the wall for the current and any future meetings.
6.	On a regular basis (monthly, quarterly, etc., depending on how often the team meets), revisit and modify the ground rules as necessary.

Adapted from Scholtes, Joiner, and Streibel (2003).

deficits and gaps in performance. Cooperrider and Srivastva recommend that appreciative inquiry "research should begin with appreciation, should be applicable, should be provocative, and should be collaborative" (Bushe, 1998, p. 41). According to Cooperrider and Whitney (n.d.):

> AI involves, in a central way, the art and practice of asking questions that strengthen a system's capacity to apprehend, anticipate, and heighten positive potential. It centrally involves the mobilization of inquiry through the crafting of the "unconditional positive question".

Thus, appreciative inquiry works towards getting people directed towards the positive aspects of the organization rather than having them dwell on the negatives.

AI has grown considerably since 1987. Although there are now hundreds of appreciative inquiry interventions, one of the major concepts driving most of them results from Cooperrider's "4-D" model: Discover, Dream, Design, Destiny.

Table 5.4   A Summary of the Steps Involved in Small Group Appreciative Inquiry.

Step	Procedure
1.	*Discover*: A facilitator has team members recall their best experience when working on a team. The facilitator works in a round-robin fashion by having each member, in turn, describe their best experiences and any supporting evidence for those experiences.
2.	*Dream*: The facilitator then works with the team to create a list of the concepts from the experiences that describe the attributes – including exploring what it is about the team member, the situation, and the task – of an effective team.
3.	*Design*: The facilitator works with the team by using the "peak" experiences to design what this team thinks would be an ideal team experience.
4.	*Destiny*: Finally, the facilitator invites members to publicly commit to the team design that they have created.

Adapted from Bushe (1998).

According to Cooperrider (1998), organizations using an appreciative inquiry approach should consider four different steps to improvement. These include:

- *Discover*: Discovery is the research phase of the 4-D method by determining what the positive opportunities for change are.
- *Dream*: Once the basic positive opportunities have been discovered, the next step is to dream a purpose and vision that can drive the organization forward.
- *Design*: In the design phase, the organization defines propositions for how people will work together toward the future of the organization.
- *Destiny*: At this point, the organization puts into place structures and procedures that support the design and dream.

Bushe (1998) used the basic appreciative inquiry paradigm to create a specific 3-step process when working with small groups and teams. In his model, he uses appreciative inquiry principles to move teams forward in their success. The steps involved in the Bushe model are summarized in Table 5.4.

There is considerable research showing that using appreciative inquiry can improve the effectiveness of groups and teams. The Appreciative Inquiry Commons hosted by the Weatherhead School of Management at Case Western Reserve University is an excellent, up-do-date resource for the considerable research that has been conducted during the 1990s and 2000s. Most of this research shows the positive impacts that appreciative inquiry tools – especially when designed around the 4-D method – can have on organizations and teams. In a meta-analysis, Bushe and Kassam (2005) find the effectiveness of appreciative inquiry's transformative potential is due to "(a) a focus on changing how people think instead of what people do and (b) a focus on supporting self-organizing change processes that flow from new ideas" (p. 161).

FOCUS ON APPLICATION

Changing to a team culture: Suzanne Piotrowski, Leader, Strategic Practices McArdle Ramerman & Co

Suzanne M. Piotrowski, MS, HRD, RODP has close to 20 years of experience in organization development and effectiveness across a variety of sectors, including higher education, not-for-profit, healthcare, and Fortune 100 manufacturing. She has served as both an internal and external consultant. Suzanne brings strategic skills, human resources development skills, strong process focus, collaboration, creativity, and innovation to her clients and their projects.

Clients describe Suzanne's work as engaging and her style as energetic. Her extensive experience includes assessment, design, and facilitation of organization development and human resources processes. Particular areas of interest include: personality type and its impact on leadership and group dynamics, facilitation, strategic planning, and leadership development.

Background

A North American company having grown rapidly in recent years with expected continued growth had been experiencing remarkable economic success as well as growing pains. During this time, operations staffing increased 110% and administration increased by 45%.

The symptoms

Senior leadership was experienced with "caring about people, customers, its reputation, and its services," they were also experiencing issues surrounding team dynamics within their own ranks, which in turn was negatively impacting the organization. These team dynamics specifically included strained relationships and lack of teaming between key leaders; chronic conflict avoidance; and prolonged leadership decision-making. They were a reflection of growing pains and the current state of the leadership relationships.

The company's top leadership recognized that they could not continue to avoid their leadership team issues if they were to grow in line with their vision for the future. Initially, they partnered with our company with the purpose of creating a leadership development program.

Assessing the problem

During our conversations, we encouraged the team to embark on a needs assessment in the form of qualitative interviews and a survey to create greater clarity around the root causes and drivers of the issues they were experiencing. The goal was to help them create a path for leadership effectiveness. To ensure actions taken were not perceived or experienced as shallow and temporary, we partnered from the beginning with them to co-create the plan. This fostered consultant client relationship as well as set the foundation for buy in and support.

One feature of the multifaceted assessment approach was a qualitative interview process. We solicited feedback from interview participants on the culture, challenges to being effective, and vision for the future. We also asked for feedback on each of the key leaders. We asked participants to identify both clear areas of strength as well as areas for improvement for each leader.

A key to success was that leaders communicated their desire for candid feedback up front to all participants in person and via email. Interviewers also reiterated the purpose and intent of those questions during the interviews. Each interviewer ensured that interview participants were given the same information, confidentiality was a condition of the experience, and the questions were co-constructed by their leaders in their interest of getting a clear feedback picture as a place to begin their own leadership development. Participants were told that the information would be used to provide feedback to their leaders, inform the development of a meaningful leadership development program, and provide guidance on attending to other organization effectiveness issues. Participants were guaranteed that they would have the themes, patterns, results, and recommendations shared with them at an upcoming leadership retreat.

The resulting recommendations were the first phase of a multi-year organizational effectiveness process that will fundamentally change leadership. The cornerstone for organizational change is leadership change beginning with leadership development for the top fifty leaders.

The intervention

A comprehensive organizational leadership assessment was created using the qualitative methods of interviewing and a survey. Our consultants conducted 18 interviews over two weeks with a cross section of senior leadership, administration and operations representatives.

How did you use the technique and how did it work?

The needs assessment process we co-created with our client allowed us to get feedback from representatives from all the key stakeholder groups. Partnering to co-create our process was an important step at the outset. The partnership we were able to form with our client fostered buy-in from the start as well and ensured good organization communication and shared ownership for getting to results. Face to face interviews also fostered trust and transparency in our communications all along the way. This transparency continues as we progress in the three-year plan.

We find organizational assessment to be the critical step in ensuring breakthrough results are achieved from subsequent OD/OE and leadership development activities/interventions and work in the system.

We were informed by our experiences with systems theory, OD intervention and action research principles, family systems theory, and especially appreciative inquiry. We know that in addition to overall communication, consultant interview experience, and organization change expertise, developing strong and evocative questions leads to successful results. We ensured a balance between identifying current challenges and dreaming future possibilities.

Patterns and themes emerged quickly from each process and we were able to use them to create strategic and targeted recommendations for moving forward. In addition to leadership development, the assessment findings pointed the way to a systems approach to change, confirming what we suspected, but the client did not. While findings confirmed leadership development as a need and top priority, strategic planning, succession planning issues, and organization design also emerged and provided a solid framework for architecting the recommended changes. The architecture also provides a data-based and strategic lens for organizational development choices over three years.

At a follow up retreat held immediately after the assessment, all participants engaged in a debriefing and discussion of the overall key results. We worked closely with leadership to help them prepare for their leadership role at the retreat. The most impactful component of the retreat occurred when each of the key leaders authentically articulated their individual commitment to their personal change, their team change and the commitment to immediate and continued development for the organization. They started the retreat with a heartfelt thank you to all participants, description of the feedback they received as individuals, and what they planned to do with it for their own development. They were specific in sharing their individual commitments to honoring the feedback and used that time to model the way. They then explained how each member of the group would be supported in their leadership development. Participants in the interviews and survey reported positive feelings about their inclusion in this process and increased respect for their senior leadership for using this approach. Senior leaders reported that they highly valued the candid feedback they received. The leaders are receiving both individual and group leadership development coaching to support the change process. Leadership development for the top 50 is underway and strategy, succession, and organizational design will be developed during the next two years. Participants continue to report satisfaction in seeing how their positive feedback influenced recommendations, priorities, and their own leadership development.

Chapter Summary

The final inputs that must be considered for groups and teams to succeed are the structural inputs that can help the group to succeed or, if that support is not provided, prevent that same group from succeeding. This support comes in the form of an organizational structure that supports groups, leadership that believe in groups, and goals and rewards that are aligned so that group rather than individual success is the outcome.

Many groups and teams start without support in one or more of these areas. A thorough assessment, such as the one at the beginning of the chapter, can help a group or team to identify the structural areas of support where they might need to put the most emphasis. Once the area(s) of intervention are identified, the next step would be for the group or team to work with others to change the supporting structure using the interventions discussed in this book – planning group structures, creating team norms, or using appreciative inquiry to change organizational or team culture – to properly align the systems with the group or team needs so that groups and teams have a greater chance of success in an organization.

Additional Resources

Argyris, C., & Schön D. A. (1978). *Organizational learning*. Reading, MA: Addison-Wesley Pub. Co.

Bolman, L. G., & Deal, T. E. (2003). *Reframing organizations: Artistry, choice, and leadership*. Hoboken, NJ: Jossey-Bass.

Case Western Reserve University (n.d.). *The appreciative inquiry commons.* Retrieved from: http://appreciativeinquiry.case.edu/.

Duke Corporate Education. (2005). *Building effective teams.* Chicago: Dearborn Trade Publishing: A Kaplan Professional Company.

Schein, E. H. (2004). *Organizational culture and leadership* (3rd ed.), San Francisco, CA: Jossey-Bass.

Team Exercises

Exercise 5.1   Coming up with a team name

When creating several new teams, one way to jump-start the process of creating a team culture is to have each team determine a team name. Here are the steps.

1. Divide a larger group into its relevant subgroups (1 minute).
2. In teams where members do not know one another, have each team member introduce him/herself to the group (5 minutes).
3. Have each team member come up with a list of three possible names that they think represent the values and competencies of the team (under 5 minutes). For each name, the member should have a brief explanation about why she or he thinks this name represents the team.
4. Once all members have their list, members in each group should go round-robin to present the name and explanation with no analysis or critique by any members of the team, including the one presenting the information (5 minutes).
5. The team should then use the information from members to create one team name that represents the team along with an explanation of why it represents the team (5–10 minutes).
6. Each team should present its name back to the larger group, along with the explanation (5 minutes).
7. These names should be used to identify any team outputs in the future.

Part III

Processes

Chapter 6

Improving Small Group Communication and Trust

I was in the grocery store the other evening with my three kids, who have reached the age where they can help with shopping. We were in a bit of a rush, so we were working as a team to get the groceries checked off the list and into the cart. All three kids were working their way through the store to get specific items. At one point, I left my oldest at the delicatessen counter and instructed him to get sandwich pepperoni for the calzones I intended to make that night. He showed up with sliced turkey. Unfortunately, turkey calzones are not as tasty as pepperoni ones, so we had to go back, which slowed us down.

Communication errors like this can slow down group and team performance. In addition, communication and trust are two overlapping yet interrelated concepts. Communication is the process of reciprocal information sharing within groups and teams. Good communication processes – the right message through the correct medium with as little interference as possible to the proper receiver – can certainly help groups and teams to yield higher performance. There is even evidence that poor team communication, along with the subsequent conflict and distrust that it causes among members, impacts the performance of the overall organization (Creed & Miles, 1996) as well as organizational financial performance (Johnston, Reed, Lawrence, & Onken, 2007).

Like communication, improving trust within groups and teams can also help groups with improving their performance. Trust is based on the expectation of and confidence in a person following through on a course of action (Lewicki & Bunker, 1996). Communication and trust are interrelated because communication is a social factor that impacts the level of trust (Cook & Cooper, 2003) and the evidence shows that undistorted, truthful, and candid communication can increase trust (Mishra, 1996).

On the other hand, distorted communication can break down trust (Mishra, 1996). Thus, when trust breaks down in groups and teams, it is often a result of poor

Group Dynamics and Team Interventions: Understanding and Improving Team Performance,
First Edition. Timothy M. Franz.
© 2012 Timothy M. Franz. Published 2012 by Blackwell Publishing Ltd.

communication and improving communication processes is a way to improve trust. This chapter examines some of the major theories around understanding and improving communication and trust. It is important to note that there have been many volumes written about understanding and improving small group communication processes. This chapter only highlights a few of the major concepts.

Learning Goals for Chapter 6

- Understand the communication process
- Know verbal and nonverbal communication modes
- Determine how trust is formed and know the barriers to communicating in small groups and maintaining a high level of trust
- Have a set of tools to Improve group communication
- Be able to intervene to positively impact group communication processes

Team Communication Assessment

Before diving into a communication and/or trust intervention, it is of course necessary to evaluate the current level of communication within a group or team. Baker, Amodeo, Krokos, Slonim, and Herrera (2010) developed a tool to measure teamwork attitudes

Table 6.1   TeamSTEPPS Communication Assessment.

Item	Strongly Disagree	Disagree	Neutral	Agree	Strongly Agree	
1. Teams that do not communicate effectively increase their risk of committing errors.	1	2	3	4	5	Item 1 Score
2. Poor communication is the most common cause of reported errors.	1	2	3	4	5	Item 2 Score
3. Adverse events may be reduced by maintaining an information exchange with the team.	1	2	3	4	5	Item 3 Score
4. I prefer to work with team members who ask questions about information I provide.	1	2	3	4	5	Item 4 Score
5. It is important to have a standardized method for sharing information when handing off work.	1	2	3	4	5	Item 5 Score
6. It is nearly impossible to train individuals how to be better communicators.	1	2	3	4	5	6 - Item 6 Score
					Total	

This subscale is adapted from Amodeo, Baker, and Krokos (2009). See the Agency for Healthcare Research and Quality (n.d.) at http://teamstepps.ahrq.gov/ for the complete TeamSTEPPS measure.

which is a part of the larger TeamSTEPPS program (Team Strategies and Tools to Enhance Performance and Patient Safety) within the Department of Defense (Table 6.1). They designed the assessment tool to improve patient safety within healthcare teams, and focused on five key areas of team attitudes that are related to performance, including: team structure, leadership, situation monitoring, mutual support, and communication. Further, Amodeo, Baker, and Krokos have a website devoted to using the TeamSTEPPS measure to train team members after assessment. Because this chapter is focused on communication, it only includes the communication subscale – the rest of the measure and all supporting documents are available for use online.

The TeamSTEPPS measure was designed to create a valid and reliable instrument to measure teamwork attitudes. Inter-item reliability is acceptable. In addition, their research demonstrates that the TeamSTEPPS measure can be used as a valid measure to assess core constructs of teamwork within healthcare, and they suggest modifying the measure, as it has been in this book, for use outside of healthcare. To use the TeamSTEPPS measure of communication, first write the scores for Items 1–5 in the right column. Subtract the score for Item 6 from six (because it is a reverse-scored item). Next sum the values in the right column. The valid range of this measure is six to 30. Communication attitude scale scores closer to 30 mean more positive attitudes towards strong and effective team communication while scores closer to six mean less positive attitudes towards strong and effective team communication. Thus, the lower the scores on the TeamSTEPPS communication scale, the more important it is to intervene within the team.

A Brief Background on Small Group Communication

When many discuss communication, they often are referring to how we tell others information. However, sending information is only one the first part of the communication process. Shannon and Weaver (1949), who were engineers studying the phone system, provide a classic description of the communication process. According to Shannon and Weaver, there are at least four main components of the communication process, including:

- *Sender*. The sender is the person/organization sending information who initiates a communication process.
- *Message*: The message is the information contained within the communication process.
- *Receiver*: The person or organization that receives the information.
- *Noise*. Shannon and Weaver's original idea was about understanding the cause and impact of electronic noise within the phone system as a medium for communication. Now, the term noise within a communication model is more closely associated with all the factors, interpersonal ones or those that are caused by the medium, that cause a message to be miscommunicated.

Although the Shannon and Weaver (1949) model of transmission of information is a classic, it is not without fault. For example, Maras (2001; 2008), like many others,

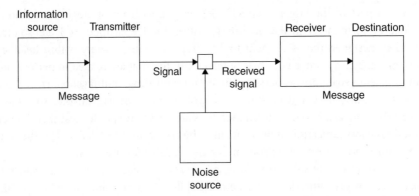

Figure 6.1   A Diagram of the General Communication Model (taken from Maras, 2008).

discusses deficiencies with the description of the basic communication model that is typical of work based only on Shannon and Weaver (Figure 6.1). Specifically, one of the major critiques is the model's focus on the unidirectional transmission of messages, rather than on reciprocal exchange of information. Maras, like others, argue that information exchange (a back and forth, or reciprocal, process) is much more descriptive of understanding the communication process than is the one-way process described by Shannon and Weaver.

A second major deficiency identified by Maras (2001; 2008), as well as others, is that the model fails to account for the situational specificity of the communication process, or how members understand language because of what is occurring within a group or team at that moment. For example, the acronym OT may mean "off-topic" during one conversation, such as an email conversation that has gone off topic, or it may mean "overtime" in another, such as a discussion about football. Thus, the Shannon and Weaver model can help group and team researchers and practitioners to recognize the nature of the communication process within teams as long as they also recognize that communication processes are both reciprocal and situational.

Verbal communication in small groups

Verbal communication means the information communicated by the words that someone uses. There are two messages within verbal communication – the denotative and the connotative (see Fiske, 1982). The denotative message is representative of the specific facts involved in any communication message. Denotative meaning is usually the most obvious meaning created by the words, or semantics, of the message. Deciphering the denotative message is typically quite easy for the receiver because it does not require any knowledge of the context or situation – everyone would have the exact same denotative meaning given the same facts.

On the other hand, the connotative meaning represents not only the words and semantics, but also the emotional. Thus, connotative message necessitates understanding the situational information to make sense of the message. Deciphering the connotative message requires higher-order, or second-level, processing because the receiver has to understand something about the context and/or situation in order to fully understand the underlying meaning of the message. Most importantly, the connotative meaning is interpreted, and this means that different people might have considerably different understandings of the meaning given the exact same denotative information.

There are times when the denotative meaning of a sentence is clear and everyone understands it in the same way. For example, I can say the seemingly simple phrase "That was a really great consultant who taught our class about how to improve our communication skills today." Without specific contextual information leading to an alternative interpretation, this would mean that the speaker appreciates the knowledge, skills, and/or abilities about the communication processes that the trainer helped her or his audience to improve. In this case, the speaker might say this with feeling and excitement, getting ready to use some of the skills immediately upon returning to regular work. In fact, anyone reading this sentence completely out of context (i.e., without the other cues from the situation) would certainly interpret this as a message with positive feedback.

However, there are times when the denotative message and connotative meaning lead to different interpretations of the same communication. Using the prior example, it may be that that communication skills training program was terrible, and everyone in the room knew it. The speaker may instead stress "a really great consultant" in the sentence, and say it with sarcasm rather than excitement. Unlike the previous example, the denotative message this time, or the simple reading of the words, is inconsistent with the connotative meaning, and most receivers will likely attend to what the sentence connotes (that the speaker was terrible) rather than what the simple words mean. However, some may misinterpret the cues (the speaker's tone) and completely misinterpret the message. Almost anyone who has failed to communicate sarcasm in an email message (or missed the sarcasm in one sent to them) can easily understand the difference between the denotative message (the dictionary definition of the words) and what was actually meant to be inferred within the email message.

Nonverbal communication in small groups

Nonverbal communication is clearly tied to the denotative and connotative meanings described in the previous section. This is because it is often by attending to the nonverbal content, such as the sarcastic tone in the previous example, that a receiver can help to interpret the true underlying meaning of a message. According to Goldhaber (1974), nonverbal communication is the flow of "messages which are not spoken" (p. 134), which includes vocal cues such as tone as well as nonvocal cues such as space and time.

Table 6.2   Modes of Nonverbal Communication.

Area	Explanation	Example
Facial Expression	Communicating information through the use of muscle movements of the face.	A smile typically means that a person is happy while a frown typically means a person is upset.
Oculesics	Using eye movement and eye behavior to communicate information.	Gazing into a person's eyes may represent love and attention while looking away may represent a lack of caring and inattention.
Vocalics	Often called paralanguage, these are using voice inflection, tone, pitch, tempo, and so on.	Speaking quickly can mean that a person is very excited about a subject while speaking slowly may mean that a person is thinking.
Kinesics	Using body movement (other than eye movement and facial expressions) to communicate information	Sitting upright usually means that a person is more attentive than slouching.
Proxemics	Using space and distance to communicate information.	Speaking very closely with someone usually indicates a sense of informality and intimacy while standing further away often indicates a more formal and less close relationship.
Chronemics	Communicating information through the use of time.	Constantly arriving to a meeting late can communicate the message that a) a person is very busy, or b) a person does not care about attending the meeting.
Haptics	Using touch to communicate information	Touch can communicate many messages, such as love or power. For example, people who have high power tend to touch those who have low power.
Clothing/ Appearance	Communicating information through clothes and appearance, whether purposeful or not.	Wearing traditional business attire communicates a more formal message at work than does wearing business casual attire.
Olfactics	Communicating information through a sense of smell. Much less explicit than many of the others.	Realtors might bake chocolate chip cookies when showing a house to increase prospective buyers feeling and sense of this house becoming a home.

Adapted from Myers and Anderson (2008).

Nonverbal communication definitely serves a function in aiding people when trying to understand the meaning of a message. In fact, different researchers have estimated the amount of information provided with nonverbal cues in contrast to the amount of information provided by verbal cues. According to Goldhaber (1974), these estimates range from as low as only 7% of the meaning and information in a message provided by nonverbal information (with, of course, the other 93% of the information from verbal communication) to as high as 93% of the meaning and information provided by nonverbal information. Regardless of whether the true estimate is high or low (and it is more likely in the middle and the amount depends on the type of information in the message), it is clear that nonverbal information is, at times, essential to understanding communication.

Nine different areas of nonverbal communication are summarized in Table 6.2. The difficult problem comes in interpreting the nonverbal cues within these nine areas. For example, some people suggest that crossed arms mean that a receiver is unwilling to listen to a message. On the other hand, it might also indicate that a person is cold. I might be in a meeting with my arms crossed. I know that my arms are crossed because I am cold, while my colleagues might interpret this as defensiveness. These two different understandings could potentially become a source of misunderstanding and conflict if the implicit interpretation of the nonverbal cue is not made explicit by probing questions. Unfortunately, there is no easy solution to understanding nonverbal information, other than to be aware of the types of information that is communicated, the functions of nonverbal communication, and knowing that meaning is created in the receiver and this meaning is not necessarily the same as the message that was sent.

Common Barriers to Small Group Communication

Misinterpreting communication messages, whether caused from misunderstanding verbal or nonverbal information, are often a cause of many problems within groups and teams. These problems might result in conflict, a lack of creativity, poor problem solving, frustration with leadership, or many other group process problems when group and team members try to work together. Although there are many different communication problems which a group or team might face, this text classifies them into four major categories: Poor interpersonal communication, team network structures, poor listening, and member communication apprehension.

Poor interpersonal communication

Quality interpersonal communication can increase the performance of small groups and teams. Quality communication includes understanding standard messages, being able to properly assess nonverbal communication, and being sensitive to the speech patterns of other people. On the other hand, poor interpersonal communication is caused by misinterpretations of messages, nonverbal information, and speech patterns (Bienvenu, 1971).

A study of dyadic communication patterns in married couples serves as a foundation for understanding similar communication problems in small groups. Bienvenu (1971) studied 316 people who either attended college or a vocational school. He measured their communication skills and compared the scores for speakers who were good communicators to those who were poor communicators. He found that six areas predicted good versus poor communication. These included:

- *Reflecting a sense self concept* – speakers who have the ability to present a positive sense of their self-concept are better at interpersonal communication than those who present information that demonstrates a poor self concept.
- *Clarity of expression* – speakers who are able to evoke an accurate picture or representation are better at interpersonal communication than those who cannot present an accurate picture.
- *Listening* – speakers who clearly reflect that they are listening are better at interpersonal communication than those who seem like they are faking attention.
- *Coping with angry feelings* – anger is, of course, a frequent cause of communication breakdowns (p. 386). Speakers who are better at managing their anger rather than expressing it are better at interpersonal communication than those who become visibly upset.
- *Self disclosure* – speakers who reveal some information about themselves and in turn get to know other people are seen as more truthful and better at interpersonal communication than those who do not self disclose.
- *Empathy* – speakers who generate a sense of empathy, or show that they can understand another person's feelings, are better at interpersonal communication than those who cannot show empathy.

Bienvenu (1971) used this information to develop an interpersonal communication inventory that has been widely adopted by researchers wishing to better understand interpersonal communication within groups and teams. For example, in the book *Team-Based Project Management*, Lewis (2004) uses the characteristics of good interpersonal communication to describe how teams may communicate better. Further, Penley and colleagues (Penley, Alexander, Jernigan, & Henwood, 1991) use Beinvenu's concepts as a basis for understanding communication and making recommendations for managers when communicating with their work groups.

Team structure and communication networks

Different team communication and organizational structures impact the rate and quality of their communication. These structures are often called communication networks. These networks control the flow of information through the group or team. First, whether a group or team has an open or closed communication network affects the quality and timing of communication. Second, the nature of how people are connected within a communication network affects communication. Finally, how centralized the network is, or whether one person seems to be central within the network, affects communication. The ability of groups and teams to use different communication networks have been formally studied since as early as 1950 and then were studied regularly in the 1960s and 1970s (e.g., Bavelas, 1950; Goldhaber, 1974; Leavitt, 1951; McKenzie, 1966).

Five different communication network patterns are diagrammed in Figure 6.2 (see Goldhaber, 1974). In each of these networks, the circles represent a person within the network while the lines and arrows represent to whom each person communicates. These networks can first be divided into two categories – constrained or unconstrained/open. Constrained communication networks are represented by the first four diagrams: The wheel, circle, chain, and Y. Constrained networks do not allow fully open communication. Instead, they have requirements about who is allowed to speak to whom. On the other hand, unconstrained communication networks, like those depicted in the final diagram, allow open communication among all members.

There are two subcategories to the constrained networks: Centralized and decentralized. The wheel and the Y are centralized networks. This is because one person is at the center of the node and all communication and information must flow through him or her. On the other hand, the circle is completely decentralized, meaning that no one person is in the center. Information must flow through many different members, depending on who starts the message and who needs or receives the information. The chain is in between, because information must pass through certain people more than others. Specifically, the center person tends to be the most central while the two ends are the not central. The two others – the 2nd and 4th person – are partially central.

Often, group and team members want to know how to structure their communication using the "best" type of network. Unfortunately, as is typically the case, each

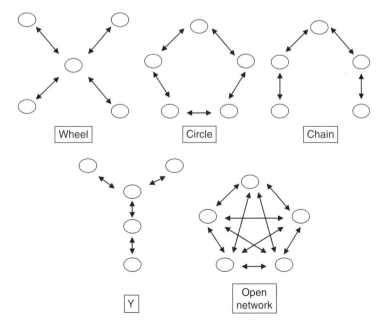

Figure 6.2   Five Communication Network Patterns.

Table 6.3   Borgatti's Summary of When to Use Different
Communication Networks.

Desired Outcome	Simple Task	Complex Task
Fewest messages	centralized	centralized
Least time	centralized	decentralized
Fewest errors	centralized	decentralized
Most satisfaction	decentralized	decentralized

network gives groups and teams certain advantages and disadvantages when trying
to communicate. Some of the key findings include:

- The open network allows for a completely free flow of information, but can be
  slowest and also can have the greatest number of biases (e.g., see group polarization and Groupthink in Chapter 9).
- Those at the center of the wheel and Y networks are most likely to be perceived
  as the leader of the group or team. This can be helpful if the person at the center
  has the competencies of a leader, but can be problematic if the person has not yet
  developed his or her leadership skills and abilities.
- Group morale is higher in decentralized and open networks.
- Centralized networks typically make faster decisions and the fewest number of
  decision errors.

As can be seen in the few findings listed here, the "best" depends on what the
group or team desires (or what organizational structures have been imposed on a
group or team). If a group is looking to gain buy-in, decentralized and open networks are probably best. If decisions need to be quick and accurate, then centralized
networks are probably best, as long as the person at the center has the competencies
to help the group succeed. A quick way to understand this is summarized by Borgatti
(1997) and organized in this book into Table 6.3 (see Bavelas, 1948; Bavelas, 1950;
Leavitt, 1951). As can be seen in the table, which to use first depends on what the
desired outcome is (e.g. a quick decision or greater satisfaction) and second on the
complexity of the task; more complex tasks have different communication demands
than simple ones. Thus, if a group or team is working on a complex task and wants
to avoid errors, a decentralized structure might be best. On the other hand, if a group
or team is working on a simple task that it wants to complete quickly, it might be best
to use a centralized structure.

Poor listening

A second common issue around miscommunication has to do with poor listening.
Ralph Nichols (Nichols & Stevens, 1957; Nichols, 1960), who is often called "The
Father of Listening" noticed that although many people studied how to understand

and improve sending messages, few studied the reception. In fact, he claims that most people are notoriously "bad listeners" (Nichols & Stevens, 1957, p. 3) even though approximately people spend 45% of their day listening. This amount has increased with more current research, especially if interpersonal listening (listening to others) and mass listening (listening to news broadcasts) are considered together.

Nichols summarized his research into the 10 bad habits of listening. For each of these ten habits, Nichols suggests ways for individuals to improve their listening. These 10 habits and ways to improve listening are summarized in Table 6.4.

Although Nichols began his research and writing over 50 years ago, his concepts are still relevant today. In fact, a recent book by Michael Nichols (2009) revisits many of the same concepts that Ralph Nichols discussed. The ability to listen well is certainly still relevant to groups and teams.

Communication apprehension/social anxiety

Communication apprehension is the fear and anxiety that is produced when a person is required to speak in front of other people (McCroskey, 1977). Though not called communication apprehension, the concept was discussed before McCroskey – in 1974, for example, it was referred to as communication or speech anxiety and an unwillingness to communicate (e.g., Burgoon & Burgoon, 1974). In his classic measure of communication apprehension, the PRCA-24, McCroskey divides communication apprehension into four categories that are distinct yet related representations of apprehension: Interpersonal, group, meeting, and public speaking. Interpersonal communication apprehension is discomfort when speaking with others, group communication apprehension is discomfort during group discussions, meeting communication apprehension is discomfort within a meeting, and public speaking communication apprehension is discomfort when presenting in front of a large group. All four together create an overall understanding of communication apprehension.

Regardless of the source – interpersonal, group, meeting, and/or public speaking communication apprehension – communication apprehension can cause problems within groups and teams because members who are apprehensive are unlikely to share the information that is required for the group to be completely successful. For example, Comadena (1984) finds that communication apprehension is a predictor of performance in groups performing a creativity task. Specifically, the more the communication apprehension among the members of the group, the lower is the group's performance. One reason for this is because people with communication apprehension have a lower sense of self efficacy, or doubt their ability to succeed on a task, than those with less communication apprehension (Hopf & Colby, 1992). This lower sense of efficacy likely affects the collective efficacy of a group.

Communication apprehension is related to lower group performance. However, group members can likely improve through training. Dwyer (2000) demonstrated that college students with high communication apprehension can be trained to self-manage their apprehension through many different methods, including clinical

Table 6.4 Nichol's 10 Bad Habits.

Ten Bad Listening Habits	Explanation	Improving Listening
Calling the Subject Dull	Some messages are important but not necessarily exciting. Poor listeners decide that a subject is dull before even hearing it. If this is the case, they are likely to ignore any important information (e.g., thinking that research is boring so look at email during a talk).	Good listeners sift through a message for any information that they might be able to use.
Criticizing the Speaker	Not every speaker's delivery skills are exemplary. Poor listeners spend energy criticizing a speaker's delivery rather than focusing on the content (e.g., being distracted by the number of "ums" and "ahs" rather than listening to the content).	Good listeners avoid focusing on the speaker's mannerisms or delivery and instead focus on content.
Getting Overstimulated	Everyone has certain topics which get them overly excited – either for better or worse. Poor listeners get overly focused on one part of the message with which they disagree and then they lose focus and miss the information that follows (e.g., the speaker mentions a political argument from the point of view of the Democrats while the speaker is a strong Republican, and the speaker does not hear the subsequent message that may or may not disagree).	Good listeners withhold all evaluation until they completely comprehend the message.
Listening Only For Facts	Most messages contain many facts that are used as evidence to support key themes. Poor listeners write down or focus on minor facts that they hear in a message (e.g., in a talk about the importance of the relative distance of planets within the solar system, the listener focuses only on the exact number of miles between the Earth and the Sun).	Good listeners organize the facts into the key themes and important concepts rather than just listing the facts.
Trying To Outline Everything	Outlining can be a good way to summarize information. Poor listeners always try to rigidly outline a message (e.g., outlining all message information even the question and answer information that is tangential or unrelated to the main point of a message).	Good listeners instead work flexibly with trying to organize information, because there are times when the information contained in a message is not presented in a linear fashion.

	Poor Listeners	Good Listeners
Faking Attention	Many listeners fade out of attention when listening to a message. During these periods, poor listeners fake attention rather than spending their cognitive energy to interpret and organize the information (e.g., staring at a speaker while instead reflecting about where the listener went out the previous night).	Good listeners instead use their cognitive energy to keep renewing their focus on the important information in the message.
Tolerating Distraction	Most situations that require listening include distractions from within and outside of the environment in which the message is being delivered. Poor listeners tolerate these distractions and allow them to prevent their focused listening (e.g., tolerating a speaker who speaks so quietly that the listener can't hear the message).	Good listeners work to eliminate all environmental distractions so that they may instead focus on the message content.
Choosing Only What's Easy	Most people have been in a situation where a speaker is trying to deliver a complex or nuanced message. Poor listeners avoid the difficult and complex content and instead only listen for what they find easy to understand (e.g., avoiding the statistical information in a presentation	Good listeners instead work to understand what they can in the difficult and complex rather than avoiding it and becoming inattentive.
Letting Emotion-Laden Words Get In The Way	Many messages have words that contain some words that evoke emotion within people. Poor listeners let the connotative meaning within some words affect their ability to interpret the message (e.g., hearing a derogatory word right before hearing a professional speech).	Good listeners put aside their emotions and instead focus listen for the themes to get to the important part of the message.
Wasting the Differential Between Speech and Thought Speed	Listening is far faster than speaking, so there is a differential between the listener's ability to think about a message and a speaker's ability to communicate it. Poor listeners waste this time thinking about irrelevant information (e.g., during a slow part of a message starting to make a mental list of the tasks for the next part of the day).	Good listeners use this extra cognitive ability to analyze the message and make connections with other information, a technique that will improve understanding and retention.

interventions such as systematic desensitization and rational-emotive therapy to other methods such as skills training, exercise to manage and reduce anxiety, and interpersonal support for the apprehension. Because most communication apprehension occurs at the individual level (even though this can reduce performance), these interventions are also at the individual level.

Methods of Improving Communication

Just like there are many methods of improving communication apprehension, there are many methods of improving the overall communication process. Most of these methods fall into two different categories. First, individual group and team members may need to improve their own interpersonal communication through techniques such as active listening or listening training. These were discussed in the previous sections. Second, there are also tools that organizations can use to improve overall information dissemination, such as newsletters, email updates, or town hall meetings.

A newsletter is a corporate communication tool that is designed to share information on a regular basis to many team members at the same time. Newsletters are excellent tools to share upcoming changes and best practices. The Engineering Design Center at Coca-Cola, for example, used biweekly newsletters to communicate information about methods regarding how to improve quality (Houston & White, 1997). As with most newsletter projects, these allowed the organization to implement a change project, in part, by keeping team members informed about the organization's goals and values.

One drawback of newsletters and is that they do not allow immediate feedback through questions and answers. Organizations have many other tools that can help with this, including large-scale organizational meetings (often called town hall meetings). These provide team members with a time for a specific face-to-face update while at the same time allowing them to ask questions and learn more about the organization. Parametric Technology Corp, for example, uses town hall meetings to help provide team members with an "understanding of the key business issues and can provide increase employee feedback up the hierarchical ladder" (Woodward, 2006, p. 58). In fact, companies that regularly use town hall meetings financially outperform those that do not.

These organizational communication tools do not have to be used individually to help groups and teams within the organization to succeed; organizations that use a multifaceted approach are likely to be even more successful, because they are communicating information through multiple channels. Maynard (1997), for example, discusses how the software company Synergex improved information sharing throughout the entire organization by using biweekly open forums, biweekly team meetings, lunch and learn sessions, and an employee newsletter. Synergex was able to survive an economic downturn as a result of their multifaceted approach to communication. These tools are one reason that the organization could keep team members informed and regain their trust after layoffs and then, in turn, motivate team members. Synergex had one of its most successful years after implementing a multi-faceted communication strategy. Technology is changing the way organizations communicate, and all of these tools can also be modified so that they are successfully used in virtual environments.

Gaining Trust

Mayer, Davis, and Schoorman (1995) define trust as being vulnerable to the actions of another team member as well as expecting that another team member will perform as expected. Trust is an essential component for team success (Mayer, Davis, & Schoorman, 1995), especially among teams that begin to manage themselves (Politis, 2003). This is because team members, and to a lesser extent group members, require a level of interdependency to succeed, and the members cannot attain the necessary level of interdependency unless those members can trust one another.

There are many different predictors of what causes trust in teams. First, knowledge exchange improves trust and performance (Politis, 2003). Commitment to the team and strong interpersonal relationships also improve trust (Nandhankumar & Baskerville, 2006). Lau and Liden (2008) found that trust in leadership predicted trust among coworkers. Wilson, Straus, and McEvily (2006) found that inflammatory remarks by members led to reduced trust. Avolio, Jung, Murry, and Sivasubramaniam (1996) find that shared leadership predicts trust. Finally, Costa (2003) finds that the perceived trustworthiness of other members, cooperative behavior among members, and the propensity to trust others predicts trust while increased monitoring behaviors reduces trust.

Trust among team members leads to many benefits for groups and teams. For example, members who work in a trusting environment are more satisfied with their team and are more likely to want to continue to work with that team (Costa, 2003; Golembiewski & McConkie, 1975). In addition, members who trust each other are more likely to share information and are more likely to learn from their past experiences as a team (Zucker, Darby, Brewer, & Peng, 1996). Finally, a trusting environment enhances member cooperation (Coleman, 1990) and increases organizational citizenship behaviors (McAllister, 1995). When taken together, what this all means is that a trusting team environment positively affects team and subsequently organizational success (Costa, 2003; Mayer, Davis, & Schoorman, 1995).

Unfortunately, trust can break down because of the actions of members. Bies and Tripp (1996) provide a list of actions within teams that violate trust. One subset of negative actions affects the group members' expectations about the civic order and procedures. These actions include: rule violations, changes in the rules, breaches of contract, shirking responsibilities, broken promises, lying, stealing ideas, disclosing confidential information, and an intolerable boss. Another subset of negative actions that reduce trust affects the group members' identify within the group. These include public criticism, being wrongly or unfairly accused of a negative action or event, and an insult to the person or the group. The severity of the impact of these negative actions depends on the situation and the cognitive appraisal of the other members (i.e., the attribution about what those members thought was the meaning behind the action).

When trust within a group or team has been violated, members react in ways that may be unhealthy to effective group functioning. Bies and Tripp organize these into seven different categories, ranging from behavior that can have little impact such as doing nothing or fantasizing about revenge, to other actions that can definitely cause process losses within a group, such as social withdrawal. The remaining three – private confrontation, identity restoration, and attempts at forgiveness – have mixed impacts, depending on the situation. Regardless of the reaction, trust needs to be rebuilt to restore the group or team to full functioning.

Whipple (2009) provides seven different strategies that team members can use to improve trust, including: be open, be honest, be ethical, honor commitments, communicate, be consistent, and have integrity. The theme connecting all of these strategies is that members must pull together and get along. Whipple suggests that these seven standards are the minimum requirements for gaining trust, and without them leaders and their teams will fail. In fact, Whipple says that applying these ideas will lead to lower burnout and reduced turnover.

Interventions to Improve Communication and Trust

As this chapter has demonstrated, many groups and teams face problems that result, at least in part, from poor communication, miscommunication, and mistrust. Because communication and trust issues are so common, there are many different interventions that are designed to improve communication and/or trust. I have picked three of the more common and/or more effective interventions, including active listening, creating collective communication competence, and using a Workplace Covenant to build trust in work groups.

Active listening

One of the more common training programs for groups and teams that is designed to improve communication is listening. Listening is one of the processes that help teams to communicate better and improve their shared mental models, or shared understandings of norms, expertise, and knowledge (Kline, 2005). One specific communication and listening processes is called active listening. "Active listening is a process in which the listener receives messages, processes them, and responds so as to encourage further communication" (Comer & Drollinger, 1999, p. 18). In fact, a Google search on the term "active listening" when this book was still a manuscript yielded 675,000 hits. This technique is so popular because it is effective and also is easy to train and use.

Knippen and Green (1994) recommend a five-step process to using active listening. These are detailed in Table 6.5.

Table 6.5 A Summary of the Steps Involved in Using Active Listening.

Step	Procedure
1.	*Determine when to use active listening.* There are times when a dialogue necessitates activities such as problem solving and decision making, and then there are other times when a dialogue requires listening. A good rule of thumb is that active listening is necessary when there are strong feelings that are being communicated.
2.	*Select an appropriate active listening technique.* Knippen and Green recommend becoming skilled at four different active listening techniques, including:
	a. Restating/paraphrasing by echoing back to the team member what she or he is saying.
	b. Summarizing by feeding back a message to clarify and/or demonstrate understanding.
	c. Explicitly responding to non-verbal cues from the other team member, especially when the non-verbal cues appear to directly contradict the verbal message.
	d. Acknowledging the feelings that have been expressed by another team member even if you do not agree with or understand the reasoning for those feelings
3.	*Use the technique selected.* Use whichever of the four techniques above in the conversation with the member.
4.	*Evaluate the communicator's response.* This begins a feedback loop – monitor how the member is reacting to your listening technique.
5.	*Take appropriate action.* This is the second part of a feedback loop – when you monitor how one is reacting, make sure to either continue with the technique you are using or modify it for the situation. This monitoring of feedback and re-alignment of active listening techniques will take time and practice to improve.

Kippen and Green recommend four different response possibilities in their five-step process. There are, however, other skills that can help improve active listening. Boyd (2007), for example, includes three additional skills for improving listening, including asking open-ended questions rather than yes/no ones, making sure to spend your time listening first and advising second (if at all), and being sure to commit fully to the conversation, including closing off all other distractions such as phones and email. Comer and Drollinger (1999) include three other active listening skills. First, they recommend monitoring one's own responses carefully to encourage the communication process to continue. Second, they recommend working to monitor your voice tone, inflection, and volume during the conversation; because of the intensity of the feelings being presented, voice becomes an important method of communicating a commitment to listening. Finally, they recommend maintaining appropriate personal body language, including eye contact, facial expressions, and head nodding. Using these skills as well as the step-wise recommendations by Knippen and Green can help members to better communicate with one another.

Table 6.6 A Summary of the Steps Involved in Building Collective Communication Competence.

Step	Procedure
1.	*Spending time together*. When team members spend more time together, they are more likely to communicate effectively with each other because they are building relationships.
2.	*Task talk*. Discussing the task is as important as building relationships because if teams only focus on relationship building, the actual work will suffer.
3.	*Practicing trust*. When team members openly talk about their desire for trust and the consequences of violating trust, team communication is more competent.
4.	*Openly discussing communication differences*. Communication competence is built when team members use non-threatening language to openly address the differences in ideas as well as the differences in the ways that different members express those ideas.
5.	*Communication processes*. Thompson identified four team communication processes that lead to communication competence, including:
	a. Demonstrating presence occurs when members actually focus their communication on the team when necessary while eliminating anything that gets in the way of open communication (or even creates a perception of getting in the way).
	b. Reflexive talk is when team members reflect on what they have been hearing and provide that feedback back to the group.
	c. Backstage communication, which happens behind the scenes, helps to increase collective communication competence because it provides an opportunity to share more detailed information, including discussion of any strong emotions that would be inappropriate to express in front of the entire team.
	d. Humor and shared laughter creates collective communication competence because it can "relieve stress, support group ideals, integrate ideas, and show support for common values and… can be used to bring out potential problems before they become big problems. Joking and laughing can help to build a sense of community and cohesiveness within a team" (p. 289).
6.	*Communication processes to avoid*. Not only did Thompson find the communication processes that helped to develop collective communication competence, she also found four processes that hindered the development of collective communication competence. These included:
	a. Jockeying for power: When multiple team members try to take over a team process and jockey for power, interpersonal relationships within the team suffer.
	b. Communicating boredom: When one or more team members show blatant disinterest it leads to the member being ostracized and isolated.
	c. Debating expertise: Debates of expertise are often focused on developing a sense of ego rather than debating true differences in knowledge, and these lead to tension and boundaries that hinder team communication.
	d. Sarcasm and negative humor: Sarcasm and humor that is at the cost of another team member destroys interpersonal relationships and diminishes trust.

Adapted from Thompson (2009).

Creating a team that communicates

According to Jablin and Sias (2001), communication competence is the total set of abilities and resources which a team has available to use during a communication process. These abilities and resources include background information, knowledge about how to communicate, as well traits and abilities about how to understand information while communicating. Communication competence is necessary because if the team can improve its skills and abilities at communicating, they can determine information needs, communicate more freely, generate more innovative ideas, motivate team members, understand additional labor needs, and avoid ingroup-outgroup biases (discussed in Chatper 4). In sum, teams that are competent at collaborative communication can be more successful.

Thompson (2009) examined communication competence within an interdisciplinary research team. To study this, she used an approach called grounded theory, where the researcher begins without a preconceived theory at the beginning of the study and then builds the theory through a close examination of the data. Specifically, Thompson used qualitative research methods and conducted an in-depth, four-year, longitudinal ethnographic investigation of an interdisciplinary research team. During that time, she interviewed 12 members of the team, and used considerable other data from a larger investigation of communication and collaboration processes within that team. The team was led by five principal investigators (PIs), 14 co-investigators, and nine graduate students, and the participants represented 12 disciplines.

Her study revealed the five processes that teams should consider when trying to build collective communication competence. In addition, her study revealed four communication processes that teams should avoid because they hinder the development of collective communication competence. These steps are detailed in Table 6.6.

Thompson's study revealed that when a team uses these skills, it creates collective communication competence and improves performance through shared learning, improved trust, and strong interpersonal relationships.

Workplace covenant

Finally, a recent intervention designed to improve communication and trust is the Workplace Covenant by Silver (2008). The covenant is successful because it includes three phases that are necessary for improving team functioning, including creating charters, facilitated dialogue, and feedback about performance (Table 6.7). The process provides a structured, facilitated method of two-way dialogue, which can occur within teams or between a team leader and the other members, that provides a safe

Table 6.7   A Summary of the Steps Involved in the Workplace Covenant.

Step	Procedure
1.	An independent facilitator introduces the process of the Workplace Covenant. After the introduction, the facilitator separates the team leader from the other team members. The team leader works alone while the team members work together.
2.	The team leader works on a draft of his or her obligations and expectations, including:
	a. Creating a list of obligations, thinking about what the leader owes the team.
	b. Creating a list of expectations, thinking about what the team should be doing for the leader.
	c. Rating both lists in terms of a checkmark (doing well), a question mark (not sure), or an up arrow (could improve).
3.	The team works together to draft a similar list of expectations and obligations, including:
	a. Creating a list of obligations, thinking about what the team owes the leader.
	b. Creating a list of expectations, thinking about what the leader should be doing for the team.
	c. Rating both lists as previously described
4.	Next, the facilitator has the team leader rejoin the team, and then the facilitator works with the lists to merge them into two lists: The team leader's covenant (obligations) to the team and the team's covenant (obligations) to the team leader.
5.	The team leader signs his or her covenant and the team signs their covenant.
6.	The facilitator conducts regular feedback sessions every 1-3 months by reviewing the covenants, rating performance as previously described, and modifying the covenant as the workplace demands and team members change.

place for feedback. According to Silver, the Workplace Covenant communication process creates a sense of empathy, mutual respect, goal alignment, and partnership, which all lead to a trusting relationship.

Unfortunately, there has been little research specific to the claims of the Workplace Covenant as of this point. However, team charters improve performance (e.g., Matheiu & Rapp, 2009), team dialogue and communication improves performance (e.g., Stanton, 1996), and feedback improves performance (e.g., DeShon, Kozlowski, Schmidt, Milner, & Wiechmann, 2004), and all these tools are incorporated into the covenant process. Thus, it is no surprise when clients of Silver's, such as Steve Sauer of Toshiba Business Solutions of New York recommend the process because its structures provide a method of "honest communication" (Silver, 2010).

FOCUS ON APPLICATION

The workplace covenant

The practitioner: Seth R. Silver, Ed.D.

Dr. Seth R. Silver is an independent management consultant, working as Silver Consulting, Inc. He has consulted to many for-profit and non-profit organizations, including the American Red Cross, Bosch Security Systems, Cape Cod Healthcare, Manulife Financial, SUNY Alfred State College, and Toshiba Business Solutions. His expertise is in transformational leadership, employee empowerment, "Workplace Covenants", and culture change. Seth is also an Assistant Professor in the Graduate Human Resource Development Program at St. John Fisher College, and has published articles in several popular and academic journals. Seth received his Doctorate in Human Resource Development from The George Washington University.

The symptom

There was strife and discord within the School of Education at a Canadian University. The HR director and her HR consultant colleague described the situation to me over the phone. Jim, the dean of the School, was a "very nice man", arguably too nice, but not really acting as a "leader", and not dealing effectively with "problem faculty". The School was growing fast, from no students to over 700 in just over four years. The School of Education now had 30 full time faculty, and 15 adjuncts. There were, apparently, three or four faculty noted for being particularly negative, disrespectful to colleagues, disruptive at meetings, and one person, even outright insubordinate to Jim as well as to the Associate Dean. The HR Director and HR consultant made it clear that Jim and the School needed immediate help, and that they were looking for some type of "intervention". Dismissal of the problem faculty was not an option – all had tenure and their behavior to this point had not yet crossed the line where termination could be defended to the union.

Assessing the problem

The first step in the diagnosis was to interview the dean, Jim, and learn his perspectives of the problem, its history, his role in the dynamic, and his goals. In brief, he acknowledged he had let the faculty problems go on too long; that one person in particular was the ring leader and instigating the others; that he needed to be a better leader; and that he needed to re-gain some lost confidence in his own ability to lead this group. Following, I interviewed one-on-one the three "problem" faculty, to learn their perspectives and their ideas for improvement. Not surprisingly, they pointed fingers of blame at Administration, notably Jim; they saw their disruptive behaviors as justified and not understood; and they expressed their strong desire to see Jim removed as dean. Finally, I held two focus groups with "neutral faculty." Their recommendations, in brief, were for the disruptive faculty to "get over it", "grow up", start being civil, and for Jim to get firm and deal with the problem staff. They also suggested Jim listen more to faculty in general, communicate better, and be more demonstrably appreciative of the hard work and accomplishments of the faculty, who were admittedly stretched pretty thin and putting in a lot of extra time.

The feedback from all sources was then analyzed for themes, and summarized in a *School of Education Climate Report*. The themes included *Good News, Bad News and Issues,* and *"Recommendations."*.

Intervening: What did you do?

Following are the topics/activities covered during the one-day off-site "Team Development" workshop:

1. A brief review of the *Climate Report*, with each of the 38 participants sharing a short comment on the Report, and one "hope for today's workshop"
2. A presentation on the "Top 10 List of Organizational Best Practices", inspired by the *Fortune 100 Best Places to Work* List.
3. An "Image Exchange", in which the different units exchanged perceptions.
4. *The Workplace Covenant,* which is a three hour process whereby two parties exchange mutual Obligations, Expectations, Feedback and Advice.

The process helped the faculty and staff see themselves as 'one' group, with a relatively common set of attitudinal and behavioral obligations to the Administration, and expectations of Administration. It was also a needed and healthy conversation for all of the faculty to discuss how well (or not) they had recently performed to these obligations. Appropriately, they noted areas where they had been weak or inconsistent and needed to improve. The faculty and staff also outlined the expectations they had of Administration, and again appropriately provide feedback to the three administrators on areas that head been going well and areas that could improve.

The three administrators had a similar conversation. They concurred on a set of reasonable obligations to the faculty and staff, provided self-feedback; and they outlined a set of expectations along with the accompanying positive and constructive feedback.

This Covenant exchange turned out to be a turning point for this group. It was 'healing' for each party to publicly admit their own mistakes and short-comings. It was helpful and insightful for both parties to lay out what they owed, and what they expected, as these lists tended to be close in content with the other party's corresponding lists. Finally, it was a symbolic way to hit "re-set" in the faculty-Administration relationship when both parties publicly stated their commitment to the newly created Covenant, signed it, and agreed to use them as a way to keep the relationship on track going forward.

Based on follow up calls made at six months and then one year later, the School of Education continues to function quite well. In fact, three of the four "problem faculty" have now become strong vocal advocates for Jim and his leadership (and it is worth noting that soon after the workshop, Jim went out of his way to help each with career-related goals they had, including letters of recommendation, support for time off, and public recognition of their academic work). The one person considered the 'ring leader' voluntarily decided to seek employment elsewhere, concluding she had no 'allies' left, and that Jim was not going to be removed no matter what she did/said. The HR director and her consultant colleague attribute the climate change in the School to the workshop process, and in particular to the Workplace Covenant.

Chapter Summary

Good communication processes and trust can lead to more effective teams and reduced process losses. The communication system includes a back-and forth communication process between communicators (senders) and those who are getting the content of the message (receivers), and includes some level of noise that obfuscates the meaning of the message. And, the main goal is a joint understanding of meaning in the receiver, because what the sender intends to communicate is only important if a) the receiver truly gets the underlying meaning and b) the sender knows that the receiver has accurately interpreted the message. The receiver can only understand the message if it is clear. It is important, however, to consider the verbal and nonverbal messages that are communicated within a communication system because when there is a perceived conflict between the verbal and nonverbal messages, the receiver may interpret the meaning in a way that is not intended.

Trust and communication are clearly related processes. When communication processes fail, trust is often lost. If a team loses trust, then a quick intervention is necessary or performance may quickly decline. To build trust requires, among other processes, rebuilding an open and honest communication process. Some interventions include, but are not limited to, active listening, improving communication competence, and the Workplace Covenant, a process that allows open communication and trust building in a facilitated environment. Teams will definitely benefit from improved communication, even if trust has not declined.

Additional Resources

Myers, S. A., & Anderson, C. M. (2008). The *fundamentals of small group communication*. Thousand Oaks, CA: Sage Publications.

Scholtes, P. R., Joiner, B. L., & Streibel, B. J. (2003). *The team handbook* (3rd ed.). Madison, WI: Oriel, Inc.

Team Exercises

Exercise 6.1   Active listening exercise

This exercise helps groups and teams to understand the importance of active listening. In it, one group member will tell a story while the others will listen to the story. It only takes approximately 20 minutes and includes a period of time in which to introduce the process of active listening. The steps are as follows:

Round 1: Tangents

1. Break a larger group into small groups of three to four members.
2. Have each group pick a speaker. The others are listeners.
3. The speaker should come up with a two-minute story.
4. The listeners' job is to try to listen, find some pertinent information, and take the story on a tangent.
5. Stop the groups when two minutes is up.

Round 2: Irrelevant communication

1. Have each group pick a new speaker. The others are again listeners.
2. The speaker should come up with a two-minute story.
3. The listeners' job this time is to mention completely irrelevant information during the story and take the conversation in an entirely new direction.
4. Stop the groups when two minutes is up.

Round 3: Active listening

1. Introduce the process of active listening.
2. Have each group pick a third speaker. The others this time are active listeners.
3. The speaker should come up with a two-minute story.
4. The listeners' job this time is to try to actively listen, using some of principles that have been introduced about active listening.
5. Stop the groups when two minutes is up.
6. After all three rounds have finished, have groups reflect about the differences between the three sessions, including:
    a. What it felt like to be a story teller in each group.
    b. What it felt like to be a listener in each group, including what the story was about.
    c. Examples of real-world discussions when they have been a part of a group that a) has gone on a tangent, b) has moved on to irrelevant
7. Share some key information from the small groups to the larger group.

Exercise 6.2   Communication networks exercise

This exercise can help groups to learn about and understand the importance of how different communication networks impact decision quality trying to get a message across members and then make a group decision. It takes about 20–30 minutes and requires some preparation. The steps are as follows:

1. Prepare a short (e.g., 5–10 item) multiple choice quiz about the content of this chapter.
2. Break a larger group into small groups of five members each.
3. Each group gets assigned a different communication network (open communication, the Wheel, the chain, the circle, and the Y) that members must use to communicate all information about the quiz from member to member. They must then organize their chairs far enough apart so that they can't hear the conversations of those next to them in their network (except for those using an open communication network, where all members can talk to each other). Members are only allowed to communicate information with members to which they are connected by arrows in the network (for example, members can't just loudly announce information so all can hear it).
4. Groups then take the quiz and come up with a group decision for each item. During the quiz, a facilitator should track the time it takes for each group to complete the quiz and the number of items each group gets correct.
5. After all groups have finished, have groups reflect about the network they used, including:

    a.   What worked well when using this type of network to take a quiz and what didn't work well when taking the quiz.

    b.   Examples of real-world groups that they have been in that are organized in a network like this and how well the network worked.

    c.   Examples of the types of tasks groups perform or environment in which groups work where this type of network would be successful.

6.   Share some key information from the small groups to the larger group.

Chapter 7

Improving Creativity and Innovation

Many groups and teams are required to be creative and innovative in order to be successful. Organizations, for example, use marketing and/or advertising teams to determine how to position a product. Teams that are creative and innovative can help organizations to better position that product and then enhance company sales. Further, as discussed in earlier chapters, groups and teams are often working within a dynamic and changing environment. For example, medical research teams are faced with many changes, from changing viruses to changing regulatory requirements. The teams that can innovatively and creatively work within these changing environments will be more likely to come up with meaningful and lasting solutions. Finally, idea generation and solution generation are stages of decision making, another requirement of many groups. It is clear that effective teamwork requires creativity and innovation.

Learning Goals for Chapter 7

- Understand the foundations of individual creativity.
- Understand the additional causes of group and team creativity.
- Improve individual as well as group and team creativity.

This chapter has three major sections. It begins with an assessment tool designed to assess the support for innovation within teams. The second section discusses the research and theories about innovation and creativity. The first half of that section focuses on individual creativity while the second half focuses on group creativity.

Group Dynamics and Team Interventions: Understanding and Improving Team Performance,
First Edition. Timothy M. Franz.
© 2012 Timothy M. Franz. Published 2012 by Blackwell Publishing Ltd.

This is because innovation and creativity is in part an individual input and in part a group process. The chapter ends with a section describing three different intervention tools that can help groups and teams to improve their innovation and creativity.

Assessment

Anderson and West (1998) created a 38-item measure of the climate for innovation within a work team. Their assessment tool, which extended some of their earlier work (1994), measures four different subconcepts that are all incorporated within their concept team innovation (Table 7.1). These four concepts include: Vision for innovation, safe participation, task orientation towards innovation, and support for innovation. They tested the measure on 155 managers from 27 different hospital teams. The following assessment tool lists only those eight items that were designed to measure support for innovation. To score this assessment, add the scores across the eight items. Scores closer to 40 indicate strong support for innovation while scores closer to 8 indicate little support for innovation. For information about the items that are designed to assess the other three subconcepts concepts, see Anderson and West (1998).

A Brief Background on Individual Creativity

Creativity is important because the outcomes of creative and innovative processes within groups and teams can help to improve performance and productivity as those organizations move forward. Creativity is alternatively defined as a process (how to

Table 7.1   Team Support for Innovation Assessment.

Item	Strongly Disagree	Disagree	Neutral	Agree	Strongly Agree
1. This team is always moving toward the development of new answers.	1	2	3	4	5
2. Assistance in developing new ideas is readily available.	1	2	3	4	5
3. This team is open and responsive to change.	1	2	3	4	5
4. People in this team are always searching for fresh, new ways of looking at problems.	1	2	3	4	5
5. In this team, we take the time needed to develop new ideas.	1	2	3	4	5
6. People in the team cooperate in order to help develop and apply new ideas.	1	2	3	4	5
7. Members of the team provide and share resources to help in the application of new ideas.	1	2	3	4	5
8. Team members provide practical support for new ideas and their application.	1	2	3	4	5

Taken from Anderson and West (1998).

be creative) and/or a product (a creative outcome). The definitions in the product group focus on ways to measure and assess creative outputs while those in the process group emphasize knowing and creating the systematic, structured procedures through which individuals and teams can be more creative (Treffinger, 1993). Feldhusen (1993) bridges the gap, by defining creative thinking as a process of adaptive thinking and reqonceptualization that results from "a cognitive activity that may result in a creative production that is perceived as new and useful" (p. 31). According to Isaksen and colleagues (1994), behaving creatively is neither mysterious, magical, nor linked to some sort of madness, as it is often thought to be. Instead, creativity is a "natural part of being human that is not reserved for people with a special gift" (p. 4). Creativity is a complex process that can be understood and improved with practice. In addition, it can be enjoyable as well as yielding important results.

On the other hand, innovation is "the result of creativity which emphasizes the product or outcome" (Isaksen *et al.*, 1994, p. 381). On the continuum of definitions of creativity between process and product, the definition of innovation clearly falls only at the product or outcome. Creativity is generating unique outcomes. Innovation, on the other hand, is when those outcomes produce useful and meaningful outcomes. According to Kaufamann (1993), creativity is a necessary but not sufficient condition for innovation. Innovation requires more, because it is the process of putting the creative product to use.

Creativity and innovation differ from problem assessment and problem solving, although the processes are linked (Treffinger, 1993). Creativity emphasizes breaking boundaries, finding creative problem solving approaches, and understanding and improving the nature of generating novel outcomes. Problem assessment is the act of structuring the nature of the problem. Finally, problem solving is trying to find a single "best" answer to a problem. The processes are different – understanding problems and solving them requires working within boundaries while creativity often requires working outside or beyond them. However, these three processes are not interdependent, but instead are interwoven. Generating creative solutions is part of the creative problem-solving process.

Group and team creativity first results from individual creativity. Individual creativity is the act of producing relatively novel ideas or products. It is also an individual process of creative cognition, where creativity depends on the successful workings of the mind (Smith, Gerkens, Shah, & Vargas-Hernandez, 2006). It results from characteristics of the people involved as well as the process they use to be creative. In addition, it depends on the intended outcomes as well as the context (e.g., culture) in which the creative actions are working. According to Sternberg (2006), this individual creativity includes the following five components:

1. Creativity involves thinking that is aimed at producing ideas or products that are relatively novel and that are, in some respect, compelling.
2. Creativity is neither wholly domain specific nor wholly domain general. The goal is to gain the knowledge one needs to make creative contributions.
3. Creativity can be measured, at least to some degree.

4. Creativity can be developed, in at least some degree.
5. Creativity is not as highly rewarded in practice as it is supposed to be.

A theme within this list is that individual creativity is something that scholars and practitioners can understand and then train and develop.

According to Simonton (2006) creativity requires improving the cognitive processes that underlie the creative process. The cognitive processes that underlie creativity appear to be very consistent with general critical thinking, or complex, higher-order thinking (Halpern, 1998). Both critical thinking and creativity require complex, novel, higher-order thought.

In addition to complex, novel, higher-order thought, individual creativity involves removing the internal blocks to creative thinking (Isaksen *et al.*, 1994). These barriers result from the person, the problem-solving process, and the environment. According to Isaksen, personal blocks result from resistance to using imagination, the inability to tolerate uncertainty, the unwillingness to consider other viewpoints, relying on strong customs or habits, imposing unnecessary constraints on oneself, and fear of failure (e.g., I am not a creative person, an explanation that assumes creativity results from on inborn traits that cannot be changed). Barriers in the problem-solving process result from using processes that inhibit creativity (e.g., I don't know how to be creative, an explanation that assumes creativity can be learned or improved through practice or the use structured processes). Finally, barriers in the environment result from fixed ways of thinking in a team or organization (e.g., this is the way we always do it here).

Improving the individual creative process comes from removing these barriers (Isaksen *et al.*, 1994). Thus, improving creativity requires a focus on the person, the process, and the environment. The first step is to create an environment for creativity, or an environment that is challenging, allows for freedom, trust, and openness, provides time for creative endeavors, encourages playfulness and humor, encourages positive conflict, supports idea generation, encourages debate, and allows for risk taking. The second step is to break the personal barriers and work with people to show that they can be creative. Finally, the third step is to teach people a 'toolbox' of procedures that they can use to systematically improve their creativity.

A Brief Background on Group Creativity

As described previously, creativity is an individual process and an individual input to a group or team. Creativity, however, "takes place in a social context" (Simonton, 2006, p. 493). In fact, Paulus, Nakui, and Putnam (2003) suggest that "a comparison between the groups literature and the individual creativity literature revealed that they were quite consistent" (p. 69). Paulus and Nijstad (2003) suggest that there are two additional, and very related, components to understanding group and team creativity that differ from what is necessary to understanding individual creativity, including:

1. Group and team members must understand their diverse pool of information; and
2. Group and team creativity requires the sharing of these unique ideas.

Although these additional requirements are seemingly simple, getting groups and teams to succeed in creative and innovative endeavors proves to be quite difficult.

One of the first to study and discuss group creativity was Alex Osborn in his book titled *Applied imagination*. Osborn recommended brainstorming as the method for improving creativity, and considerable research has examined the benefits and drawbacks of this since. As part of the book, Osborn (1963) recommended four rules to brainstorming. These rules included:

- *Focus on quantity*. Osborn recommended focusing on quantity rather than quality. He believed that quality, and hence unique and creative ideas, would only come through the generation of long lists from the group.
- *Withhold criticism*. Osborn understood the group pressure to fit in and withhold crazy and unique ideas that could occur when someone within the group criticized another member. Therefore, true brainstorming does not allow any criticism of members or their ideas.
- *Freewheeling is welcomed*. Freewheeling, according to Osborn, is when people recommend unique and unusual ideas. Osborn believed that this was where the power of creativity could start to be harnessed within a successful brainstorming group.
- *Seek combination and improvement*. Osborn's final rule was to combine ideas from different members and also to take what others have suggested and then build on and improve it. According to Osborn, this is where the group could truly gain synergy and begin to create a greater number of higher quality ideas.

Osborn's promise was that groups that used these brainstorming rules could produce more than twice as many ideas as well as ideas of a higher quality when compared to a corresponding set of individuals working alone (called a nominal group; a group in name only). Clearly, he was one of the first proponents of the concept of synergy.

The reality of brainstorming groups has not matched Osborn's promise. Many, many studies over the years have tested the success of brainstorming and have demonstrated that the typical brainstorming group is not nearly as effective as individuals working alone. In an excellent summary, Mullen, Johnson, and Salas (1991) reviewed and analyzed existing published data about brainstorming. Their study showed that "brainstorming groups are significantly less productive than nominal groups, in terms of both quantity and quality" (p. 3). Unfortunately, this occurs because the process losses found when members work together on a brainstorming task far outweigh any process gains that might occur through Osborn's expectations of success through freewheeling and the combination and improvement steps in brainstorming.

Diehl and Stroebe (1987) list the three theoretical explanations for why brainstorming groups have not yielded the success that Osborn predicted. These explanations included: production blocking, evaluation apprehension, and free riding. Production blocking is a procedural explanation. Production blocking is the social interference that occurs when one person is talking and then another cannot contribute (talk) at the same time. The second speaker must wait until the first speaker finishes. The second speaker then sometimes forgets what he or she was going to say; I'm sure most can remember a time when this has occurred to them. In addition, the conversation may move to another topic and then what the second speaker was going to say becomes moot, or for any other number of reasons, the second speaker may fail to contribute. A second explanation is evaluation apprehension, or the feeling that one might be negatively evaluated for coming up with an idea that is seen as "too" crazy and unusual. At some point, most of us have felt the pressure and discomfort that comes with saying something strange and unusual within a group. Finally, free riding is reduced social motivation that occurs when certain members decide to let the others contribute and choose not to fully participate. This is sometimes a conscious decision to avoid participation because others will do the work. Paulus and colleagues (2003) suggest an additional area of concern for groups and teams to consider when working on creative and innovative solutions, which are the social pressures that are created when some high performing members conform to low performance group norms from other members. In addition, Bolin and Neuman (2006) show that introverts dislike the group process required for brainstorming. Finally, Thompson (2003) includes social loafing, conformity, downward comparisons, and low norms for creativity as additional reasons for why the creative process suffers within teams. Although there is certainly research evidence for each of these explanations, Diehl and Stroebe find that the strongest evidence is for production blocking.

It is possible to overcome some of the process losses faced by brainstorming groups. Paulus and Dzindolet (1993), for example, find that informing members about the potential negative effects of brainstorming as well as setting high goals and allowing members to influence one another to meeting these goals can help improve brainstorming performance. Paulus and Yang (2000) find that allowing time for attention and idea incubation through a brainwriting session (an individual time for thinking when members individually write down ideas) can help to improve brainstorming performance. Baruah and Paulus (2008) find that "results indicate that training can increase both the quality and quantity of ideas generated in groups and that solitary idea generation prior to group brainstorming can be beneficial" (see also Bouchard, 1972; Talbot, 1993). Finally, computer-mediated brainstorming groups (Dennis & Valacich, 1993; this will be discussed further in Chapter 13) can help members to eliminate production blocking because the computer can accept multiple inputs at once. Computer-mediated brainstorming sessions often help to eliminate evaluation apprehension because the computer makes all contributions anonymous. With structured (and computer-mediated) procedures such as these, groups can overcome some of the process losses, though what remains unclear is whether brainstorming groups can regularly outperform individuals and yield the process gains that Osborn (1963) expected.

The literature clearly demonstrates that at a minimum groups and teams are no better than individuals at creative tasks and in fact may be far worse. This is because brainstorming groups have problems. Why, then, spend an entire chapter discussing creativity innovation? The answer is that there are valid reasons to use creative groups, even given the problems that occur during the social interaction required by the group creativity process. Four of these include (Paulus *et al.*, 2003):

1. Organizations will continue to use work teams anyway regardless of what the literature shows about the likely limited success of brainstorming groups. This is because of the false assumption that teams will reach synergy during brainstorming sessions and improve creativity beyond what might be expected of individuals;
2. Groups and teams can be a strong source of motivation for members, especially if goals and expectations for working together are high and groups are given the autonomy they require to succeed. People are social animals, and brainstorming with others is a much more satisfying, and hence a more motivating experience.
3. Groups and teams have a higher potential for success than individuals working alone because of the incredibly large and diverse set of information and ideas that members bring to the group.
4. Information exchange, social influence, conflict, and negation take place with others. Through these processes members can learn something new.

Hope remains for improving brainstorming and creativity. Landis, Jerris, and Braswell (2008) discuss how auditors are *required* by auditing standards to use brainstorming sessions to better understand causes of misstatements in financial reports. They conclude that through the use of clear, stepwise procedures, auditors can improve brainstorming outcomes beyond what the typical research study demonstrates.

Improving Group and Team Creativity

Chapter 1 reviewed the input-process-output model of group functioning. The IPO model shows that individual competencies are one input to group functioning. If members have the competencies to be creative, then groups with those members have a better chance at succeeding in creative and innovative endeavors than if the members do not have the competencies. Thus, interventions that are designed to improve group creativity can start by improving individual creativity.

The research about improving individual creativity shows definitively that creativity can improve through successful training. For example, in a review of 142 studies, Torrance (1972) found that about three-quarters of training programs that are designed to improve creativity in children actually improve individual creative functioning in adults as well. According to Baer and Kaufman (2006), there is unfortunately considerable variety in the training programs that are designed to improve individual creativity. So far, none of the reviews have found the single most important method. However, Baer and Kaufman suggest that most of the research demonstrates that procedures designed to both improve critical thinking and then support divergent thinking are necessary components of creativity training. Baer and Kaufman further suggest that although there is no one best curriculum in terms of success, the most well known creativity training program is the program developed by Parnes and colleagues (e.g., Parnes & Noller, 1972, 1973).

Improving individual creativity is only part of the requirement for improving group creativity. People working together on a creative or innovative project have greater potential because of the diversity of competencies and knowledge that the members bring. Groups and teams, however, also bring all of the additional issues around working together. Thus, improving group creativity requires additional interventions that also change group behavior beyond simply improving individual creativity. Thus, the interventions all provide guidance for members and groups.

A goal of many of the group and team interventions around creativity is to promote divergent thinking among members (e.g., Nijstad, Diehl, & Stroebe, 2003; Smith, 2003). Divergent thinking occurs when members consider a problem and the surrounding issues from multiple perspectives (Nemeth & Nemeth, 2003). And, divergent thinking within a group or team is helpful because it prevents fixation, which is when groups and teams get focused or even stuck on only one solution to a problem too early (Smith, 2003). Fixation results from the retrieval of well-learned material interfering with the creative process, when typical thinking causes groups and teams to only see the problem from within one paradigm, implicit assumptions causing groups to avoid considering new alternatives, and recent experiences creating a mental focus that forces groups and teams into one possible alternative. Avoiding fixation is only possible when a group has diversity of background and knowledge (West, Sacramento, & Fay, 2006) and then they are able to systematically avoid the typical process losses that are found in creativity and brainstorming situations (Diehl & Stroebe, 1987).

Smith and colleagues (Smith, Gerkens, Shah, & Vargas-Hernandez, 2006) modeled the process of group creativity, in part so that researchers can determine how creative groups work and avoid process losses. They suggest that a creative group functions in a way that is similar to an individual. The group, just like the individual, requires an understanding of the problem, an understanding of the possible solution, input from the environment, and retrieval from long-term memory to succeed. The group has greater potential because members can motivate each other as well as help each other to avoid fixation. Finally, according to Smith and colleagues, "the added potential that a group can have is that there are more resources on which to draw" (p. 12).

West and colleagues (2006) suggest four factors to help groups and teams to determine the level of possible group innovation that they may attain. These include: Task characteristics, group knowledge diversity and skills, external demands, and integrating group processes. Tasks that require a) interdependency, b) a group or team to complete the entire task, and c) allow the members to identify with the end product are better for groups working on creative endeavors. As described in the previous paragraph, groups with knowledge and skill diversity are more likely to succeed at creative tasks. External demands are the environment, both internal and external to organizations, that support a group in its innovation (or detract from it as well). Finally, groups that have shared objectives, participation, and norms that are supportive of innovation are more likely to succeed at creative problem solving. When the task does not support innovation, there is little background diversity, the environment does not reward creative endeavors, and the group process causes friction, creativity may be limited and these groups should avoid creative and innovative projects.

Three Interventions Designed to Improve Creativity

There is overwhelming evidence that group and team creativity can benefit from training and be improved. It is clear, however, that any improvement is not happenstance. Instead, it requires systematic effort to improve the processes that may contribute to losses. It is clear that improving creativity requires systematic intervention rather allowing unstructured groups to work on their own. Thompson (2003), for example, recommends 10 different strategies for building team creativity, including:

- *Diversify the team.* A team with members who have heterogenous backgrounds is more likely to succeed at creative tasks because they bring more diverse information to the process. This will help with divergent thinking.
- *Emphasize analogical reasoning.* Analogical reasoning is the ability to apply a concept from one domain to another. Teams often have the knowledge to make a creative decision, but they often converge on a decision too quickly. Thinking in terms of analogs (e.g., green is to go as red is to stop) can help groups and teams to think more creatively about a problem.
- *Use brainwriting.* Brainwriting is discussed in detail in this section, but the main idea is to have members write information down rather than say it aloud.
- *Use the Nominal Group Technique.* NGT is a decision-making technique that is first designed to constrain group process and then allow groups to make a decision. It is discussed in detail in the next chapter.
- *Create organizational memory.* According to Thompson, "one of the biggest drains on performance is the repetition of ideas and the forgetting of ideas" (p. 104). Using computer software to help record ideas and pass it on to future teams can help members to avoid this.
- *Train facilitators.* Trained, experienced facilitators can effectively help groups to focus on divergent thinking while preventing convergent thinking. This procedure, called Directed or Facilitated Brainstorming, is described in detail in this section.
- *Set high goals.* Stretch goals can improve performance. The Focus on Application in this section examines a case of Directed Brainstorming where the facilitator set a stretch goal, and the group surpassed it.

- *Change group membership.* One way to enhance creativity in a group that has started to suffer from convergent thinking or is stuck and unable to generate new ideas is to change some of the group's membership. Allowing one or two members to exit while providing opportunity for the same number of new members to join the group can help members to see different ideas.
- *Brainstorm electronically.* This has been shown to be a successful way to brainstorm, and is discussed in detail in Chapter 13, which discusses understanding and improving the virtual team.
- *Build a playground.* Change some spaces in an organization to create spaces where creativity and discussion is encouraged rather than discouraged. Thompson recommends creating brainstorming areas or "chill-out" zones that have unusual and inspiring paint jobs, such as surfboards and a beach theme or Technicolor hues, toys that encourage activity, such as soft basketballs and hoops, and supplies to help members to record creative ideas, such as white board, and flipcharts.

As can be seen, there are many different ways to intervene, most of which try to make creative teamwork a part of the culture rather than a necessary evil when making decisions (Thompson, 2003). Research has shown the success of many of these. The steps involved in three interventions are detailed here. The first two, brainwriting and facilitated brainstorming, are from scholars working within academia. The final one, improving group genius, is practitioner-based. All require groups and teams to follow a set of specific procedures that help members to work together to improve creativity and innovation. Regardless of whether the process was generated by scientists or practitioners, each provides a set of tools that can help groups and teams to be far more creative and innovative than the typical brainstorming group.

Brainwriting

Parnes and the Creative Studies Program (e.g., Parnes & Noller, 1972; Reese & Parnes, 1970; Reese, Parnes, Treffinger, & Kaltsounis, 1976) have been studying how to improve creativity for years – since Osborn's initial writing. The program started as a semester long course in creativity and has now developed into a complete graduate program designed to study and improve creative processes. It is easily the most well established training program for improving creativity, and has published countless articles and supported many different graduate thesis projects. In fact, the program seems to have worked to realize Osborn's (1963) goal for improving creative teams beyond what much of the past research has shown. Of course, Parnes and colleagues recommend far more training and a considerably more systematic approach than did Osborn (e.g., Parnes, Noller, & Biondi, 1977), but they have also been far more successful at generating creative outputs beyond what one might expect from reading a quick summary of the research about brainstorming.

One step that Parnes and colleagues recommend as a component of improving the creative process is brainwriting, which is also sometimes called ideawriting (e.g., Moore, 1987). Brainwriting is an individual brainstorming session that sometimes precedes brainstorming. It helps groups to avoid some of the process losses such as production blocking (when one person cannot talk because others are) because individuals are writing and evaluation apprehension because the ideas are seemingly more anonymous. There are many different versions of brainwriting, but most are similar in that they limit group discussion and instead require members to write their creative ideas and pass them to other members. A summary of the steps in brainwriting, adapted from Scholtes and colleagues (2003), is provided in Table 7.2.

A quiet brainwriting session is more effective than the typical brainstorming groups who are working aloud. The reasons it is more effective include a) it allows more time for silent thought, b) it mostly eliminates production blocking, c) members who might typically control the discussion are forced to remain silent, and d) it reduces (thought does not eliminate) evaluation apprehension because the ideas become less connected with any individual as the rounds continue. Several studies have shown the effectiveness of brainwriting, many of which demonstrate that brainwriting is as or more effective than nominal groups and that members like it better than working alone on an idea generation task (e.g., Paulus & Yang, 2000).

Directed brainstorming

Another way to generate ideas that seems to be more effective than the typical unstructured group working on a brainstorming task is to use directed or facilitated brainstorming. Directed or facilitated brainstorming is when a skilled facilitator works with a group to help members to create a larger set of unique ideas. It seems to help groups to generate more ideas because, like brainwriting, it reduces production blocking and it also, if used correctly can improve member motivation.

Santanen (2006) suggest using twenty different prompts to help groups generate more ideas as part of the process of directed brainstorming. Prompts can help groups to generate ideas because they force divergent thinking while the facilitator can, at the same time, work with members to freewheel and seek combination and improvement. The steps in a directed brainstorming session are detailed in Table 7.3.

As with brainwriting, directed or facilitated brainstorming is far more effective than are typical brainstorming groups. Osborn (1963) even discussed the possibility conducting brainstorming through facilitation, but most of the initial brainstorming studies used only his four steps without the addition of the two steps that included using a skilled facilitator to help groups to generate more ideas. Dennis and colleagues found that these brainstorming prompts (at least in an electronic environment) created divergence, which helped to generate a greater number of solutions that were judged by experts to be more creative. In addition to the work by Dennis and colleagues summarized previously, studies by Kramer and his colleagues (e.g., Kramer, Fleming, & Mannis, 2001; Offner, Kramer, & Winter, 1996) have provided evidence that groups using facilitated brainstorming can be as effective as (though not more effective than) nominal groups. Thus, facilitation, like brainwriting,

Table 7.2   A Summary of the Steps Involved in Brainwriting.

Step	Procedure

1. *Create the Brainwriting Form:* The form should include space for possible ideas (idea 1, idea 2, etc.) along the top of the form and rows along the side that represent the number of rounds in the columns.

Round	Idea 1	Idea 2	Idea 3	Idea 4
1				
2				
3				
4				
5				
6				

2. *Form groups.* Form groups of five to six people. Each person should start with a blank brainwriting form. The groups should sit at a table together and members should be close together.
3. *Introduce problem statement.* Discuss and clarify the problem (e.g., come up with a new name for a restaurant) that will be the focus of this brainwriting session. Write the topic of the brainwriting session on the top of each form.
4. *Individual idea generation.* Begin the individual idea generation session. Each person should take three–five minutes to write ideas on the first row of the form.
    a.   The sheets will be passed along to others, so write clearly so that others can read your ideas.
    b.   Make sure to provide enough information so that others will understand your ideas.
5. *Silent group idea generation.* Pass your form to the person on your right. Take two minutes with the new form that is in front of you.
    a.   Read the ideas in the first row.
    b.   Add three to four new ideas.
    c.   You may build on the other ideas, combine ideas from others, or come up with entirely new ideas.
    d.   If you run out of ideas, leave blanks (as the process continues, it is common to see more blanks).
6. *Continue silent group idea generation.* Continue with the process in Step 5 until every member has run out of ideas **and** every member has seen each form at least once.
7. *Group discussion period.* As a group, review the ideas.
    a.   Eliminate duplicates.
    b.   Combine ideas that are very similar.
    c.   Organize the ideas into categories.

Adapted from Scholtes, Joiner, and Streibel (2003).

Table 7.3 A Summary of the Steps Involved in Directed Brainstorming.

Step	Procedure

1.   *Facilitation Preparation*. The facilitator examines the problem ahead of time.

a. He or she works with one or more of those who will be in the brainstorming session and breaks the problem into four to five different problem-related areas.

b. For each problem area, the facilitator comes up with a list of four separate prompts.

c. Label the four prompts in the first area with A, in the second area with B, in the third area with C, in the fourth area with D, and of course, if there is a fifth problem area, label it with E. The twenty prompts they used with School of Business problem, for example, were as follows:

A. Suggest a solution that will solve the problems faced by the school of business.

A. Suggest another solution that will solve the problems.

A. Suggest a solution that will solve those problems that is different than any you see so far.

A. Suggest one more solution that will solve the problems of the school of business.

B. Suggest an inexpensive solution that will solve the problems in the school of business.

B. Suggest another solution that won't cost a lot to implement.

B. Suggest a solution that is cheap to implement that is different from any you have seen so far.

B. Suggest one more solution that is not costly that will solve the problems in the school of business.

C. Suggest a solution to the problems in the school of business that can be easily implemented.

C. Suggest another simple solution.

C. Suggest a solution that is easy to do that is different from any you see on your screen.

C. Suggest another simple solution that will solve the problems in the school of business.

D. Suggest a solution that can be implemented quickly.

D. Suggest another fast solution to the problems in the school of business.

D. Suggest another fast solution to these problems that is different than any you have seen so far.

D. Suggest one more solution that will quickly solve the problems faced by the school of business.

E. Suggest a solution that satisfies all of the different perspectives involved.

E. Suggest another solution that will be acceptable to each of the groups in the business school.

E. Suggest a different solution that will make everyone in the business school therapy.

E. Suggest one more solution that takes each of the different groups into the account.

(continued)

Table 7.3   (*cont'd*).

Step	Procedure
2.	*Brainstorming Session*. Start with the brainstorming session, which includes the facilitator as well as those performing the brainstorming task. a. The facilitator introduces the problem and begins the brainstorming session b. The facilitator starts with the first "A" prompt. Brainstorming participants then have two minutes to respond. c. After two minutes, the facilitator changes to the first B prompt and the process continues. d. The facilitator continues in this manner using a ABCDEABCDEABCDEABCDE design until she or he has completed all of the prompts.
3.	*Optional*. One reason that the ABCDEABCDEABCDEABCDE process described above helps groups to generate more creative ideas because it allows members to see the interconnectivity between the different parts of the problem. On the other hand, a process of AAAABBBBCCCCDDDDEEEE prompts is also effective at helping groups to generate creative ideas because it helps members to see depth in any one problem area.

Adapted from Santanen (2006).

is a process that members enjoy and does not suffer from process losses seen in the typical brainstorming group, but it also seems not to yield the process gains for which Osborn (1963) had hoped.

Group genius

Sawyer (2007) works with teams to enhance their creativity and innovation and reach as level that he calls group genius, a point at which group sand teams can reach "the unique power of collaboration to generate innovation" (p. xiii). Sawyer recommends seven rules that will help groups and teams to know before they start to work on a creative and innovative task. These include:

1. Do not use groups for additive tasks, or tasks where members can easily divide the parts and then simply put, or add, them back together at the end. Instead, use groups for complex tasks that require interaction and interdependence.
2. Keep groups working on creative and innovative projects small to minimize the problems due to the social nature of group work.
3. Make sure to use a skilled facilitator who understands the research about brainstorming, including its pitfalls and traps as well as ways to help make it succeed.
4. Reward the group.
5. Frequently switch between individual and group work, and make sure to allow sufficient time for breaks.

Table 7.4   A Summary of the Steps Involved in Creating Group Genius.

Step	Procedure
1.	*Consider the goal.* As described in Chapter 3, the goal needs to be one that all members understand and to which they remain committed.
2.	*Close listening.* All members need to be deeply engaged in and attentive to the work that the group is doing.
3.	*Complete concentration.* The hard work demanded of innovative and creative groups takes energy; when members are expending this energy, time moves quickly.
4.	*Being in control.* Groups need the autonomy to be innovative, make decisions, and then have those decisions be implemented.
5.	*Blending egos.* Members need to recognize that genius is created from blending all members into the performance of the entire group, not from the solo performance of any one of the individuals.
6.	*Equal participation.* For groups to achieve flow, all members have to be equal participants in the decision making. Power struggles and hierarchies should be left outside the room.
7.	*Familiarity.* Groups that achieve flow have a shared understanding of the knowledge, skills, abilities, as well as strengths and weaknesses, of the members of the group. This can help the members to communicate effectively.
8.	*Communication.* As described in Chapter 6, groups need to communicate well.
9.	*Moving it forward.* Groups achieve flow when members work together to build on each others' ideas.
10.	*The potential for failure.* A principle in my children's school is "Success is sweet, but failure is good food." Group flow is intended to produce the innovation and creativity that Sawyer calls group genius. However, it is important to recognize the potential for failure, and allow groups the chance to fail.

Adpated from Sawyer (2007).

6. Make sure the group has sufficient background/knowledge diversity.
7. Keep in mind that some members will enjoy the groupwork better and as a result perform better.

These seven considerations for group genius should be taken under consideration before the group starts working together. Groups that are focused on their goals and are working with a skilled facilitator, and meet Sawyer's other criteria, will be more likely to succeed at what Sawyer (2007) calls "group flow," or groups that begin to work together to and improvising "attain a collective state of mind" (p. 43). He recommends using 10 steps to help to create this group flow (see Table 7.4).

Sawyer's (2007) book, titled *Group genius,* includes more detail about how to create group flow. As is typical with practitioner-oriented books, there is little specific discussion of independent research to verify Sawyer's claims. However, the ideas that he recommends are consistent with the research about creativity and innovation. For example, he recommends that group goals help to create group genius. Chapter 3 has already detailed the importance of this. In addition, he recommends that group members have familiarity. Although the terminology is different, the concept is a common one in the groups literature, but is called shared mental models (Cannon-Bowers, Salas, & Converse, 1993) and transactive memory systems (Moreland, Argote, & Krishnan, 1996), and the research demonstrates how important this "familiarity" with member background and expertise is when creating effective groups (e.g., De Church & Mesmer-Magnus, 2010; Hollingshead & Brandon, 2003). The research is similarly clear about the effectiveness of Sawyer's other steps.

FOCUS ON APPLICATION

Improving creativity through directed brainstorming

The practitioner

Chris Comparetta is co-founder of Innovation Pathways an innovation capacity building firm. He has over 20 years of experience deploying organization effectiveness interventions and delivering leadership development programs. Chris has a Masters degree in Human Resource Development and a Graduate Certificate in Creativity and Change Leadership from the International Center for the Study of Creativity (previously the Creative Studies Program) in Buffalo, NY. Chris has a Bachelor of Arts in Computer Science and has eight patents for his computer engineering work. In addition to his consulting, he is adjunct faculty in the Graduate Organizational Learning and Human Resource Development program at St. John Fisher College.

The symptom

In a large product delivery corporation, the multi-year Six Sigma effort was producing successful results. However, on closer inspection, the manager of the Six Sigma support group had noticed a trend – the Six Sigma projects were producing solutions, but they were not the type of breakthrough, innovative solutions that would propel the company into new opportunities.

Assessing the problem

The first step was to explore the problem with the clients, through interviews and discussions with the manager of the Six Sigma support group and one of the staff members. As we explored the problem, we learned that there was an expectation that was causing the Black Belts responsible for the Six Sigma projects to produce 'achievable' rather than the expected 'wow' results.

Intervening: Using directed brainstorming

I suggested to the Six Sigma group manager that we could use the first step of the Creative Problem Solving process to explore the problem with experienced Black Belts. The use of the Creative Problem Solving process would provide the framework for gathering data about the problem in a short period of time. The Creative Problem Solving process effectively engages people in a group to work a problem, even when the members of the group have not worked together before or even know each other.

The intervention was set to run for 90 minutes and included six experienced Black Belts. There were varying levels of member familiarity; some of the Black Belts knew each other while some of the Black Belts knew of other members and some had no prior knowledge of the other members. An additional challenge was that one of the members was in Germany while the rest of the resource group was in the United States, so there was a virtual component to the process.

The Six Sigma manager started the meeting and introduced the problem – that Black Belt projects are not producing enough innovation – and asked for the support of the group. I introduced the participants to the Creative Problem Solving Process emphasizing the need to separate the divergent and convergent thinking phases.

As part of the introductions I took the group through an exercise so they could become familiar with a process called Stick'em Up Brainstorming and at the same time practice using virtual technology. Typically, Stick-em Up Brainstorming is conducted with Post-It Notes on flip charts or walls. In order to engage the member in Germany I chose to equalize by having all of the group members bring a lap top and connect up to the company intranet. Using Microsoft's Communicator (a chat tool) and sharing my laptop's screen using LiveMeeting, everyone was able to see what all the others were writing during our brainstorming sessions.

After the practice we began working on the problem. Our goal was to discover the contributing causes of the problem by generating at least 100 ideas that might be preventing the Black Belt projects from producing more innovation.

From conversations with the clients it was apparent that this was a multi-dimensional problem – that is there were multiple root causes. To tease out as many of the root causes, I designed the intervention to use four rounds of ideation (divergent thinking). Each round of ideation was prompted by a question:

1. When you think of a BB project what are the types of things that might be supporting creativity and innovation?
2. When you think of a BB project what are the types of things that might be preventing creativity and innovation?
3. What do you think could be done differently in or with the BB projects to promote creativity and innovation?
4. What do yo think could be done differently in or with the BB projects to prevent creativity and innovation?

Each round was three minutes in length. Including interval time between each round, the total amount of ideation was only 20 minutes. During this time the six members generated 138 ideas, exceeding our goal of 100. To close out the problem exploration phase, I asked the participants to group the 138 ideas into a Fishbone using the five P's of Creativity as the spines (Person, Press, Product, Process, and Persuasion).

Chapter Summary

This chapter examined creativity and innovation. A goal of many groups and teams has been to generate ideas. The concept of improved idea generation through teams is one that is very popular, yet flawed. Osborn (1963), for example, thought that group and teams could generate more than twice as many ideas as well as ideas of better quality than could a similar set of individuals who were working alone when they used his brainstorming procedures. However, this has not been the case. Process losses have caused groups and teams to be far less successful than expected, and in many cases they have been less successful at generating ideas than have a similar set of individuals working alone.

Regardless of the lack of success of brainstorming procedures as proposed by Osborn, scholars and practitioners have been working since the 1960s to understand and now improve the creative process. The most productive of these groups has been the Creative Studies Program, which has received continuous support from the Creative Education Foundation (for one of the best guides for improving creativity resulting from this program, see Noller, Parnes, & Biondi, 1976). These researchers, as well as many others, have shown that groups and teams can be far more successful at creative idea generation and creative problem solving than the initial research using Osborn's ideas showed. The basic premise is that groups and teams must use structured procedures and prompts to move from fixated and convergent thinking to open and divergent thinking. Groups and teams that are able to do this will succeed at creative idea generation and problem solving tasks and may even, in some conditions yield process gains rather than process losses.

Additional Resources

Isaksen, S. G., Dorval, K. B., & Treffinger, D. J. (1994). *Creative approaches to problem solving.* Dubuque, IA, Kendall/Hunt Publishing Company.

Moore, C. M. (1987). *Group techniques for idea building.* Thousand Oaks, CA: Sage Publications, Inc.

Mycoted. (2009). Creativity and Innovation Techniques – an A to Z: Retrieved February 4, 2010 from http://www.mycoted.com/Category:Creativity_Techniques.

Noller, R. B., Parnes, S. J., & Biondi, A. M. (1976). *Creative actionbook.* New York: Scribner.

Parnes, S. J., Noller, R. B., & Biondi, A. M. (1977). *Guide to creative action.* New York: Scribner.

Scholtes, P. R., Joiner, B. L., & Streibel, B. J. (2003). *The team handbook* (3rd ed.). Madison, WI: Oriel, Inc.

Thompson, L., & Choi, H. S. (2006). *Creativity and innovation in organizational teams.* Mahwah, NJ: Lawrence Erlbaum Associates, Inc.

Team Exercises

Exercise 7.1   Individuals versus interacting groups versus brainwriting groups

This exercise is designed to help people to understand the different levels of success of individuals, interacting groups, and brainwriting groups. In it, you will have some individuals and some groups come up with the number of uses for a paper clip. Then, compare individual (nominal group) performance to typical team performance and brainwriting performance.

Step	Procedure
1.	Break the larger group into several small groups of three to four people per group. It works best if the number of smaller groups can be divided by three.
2.	Give everyone a paper clip.
3.	Give one set of groups, the nominal groups, the instructions to sit with their backs to each other. Each person in those groups should work alone.
4.	Give another set of groups, the interacting groups, Osborn's four rules of brainstorming.
5.	Give the final set of groups, the brainwriting groups, the instructions in this book for brainwriting.

6.   Give all groups five minutes to work on the problem.
7.   Compare the performance of all groups.
8.   Discuss performance, the process losses in the interacting groups, how much people enjoyed each task, and the importance of using structured interventions to improve creativity.

Exercise 7.2   The impact of group goals on performance

One of the ideas is that the environment impacts creative performance by groups. In this exercise, you will have groups determine how many different uses there are for an ice tray. However, different groups will have different goals.

Step	Procedure
1.	Break the larger group into several small groups of three to four people per group. It works best if the number of smaller groups can be divided by three.
2.	Give one set of groups the instructions to determine "how many uses there are for an ice tray. Anything goes except for the obvious use. Given two minutes, the average number of uses that groups think up is 10. Your goal is to come up with 5 uses."
3.	Give another set of groups the instructions to determine "how many uses there are for an ice tray. Anything goes except for the obvious use. Given two minutes, the average number of uses that groups think up is 10. Your goal is to come up with 10 uses."
4.	Give the final set of groups the instructions to determine "how many uses there are for an ice tray. Anything goes except for the obvious use. Given two minutes, the average number of uses that groups think up is 10. Your goal is to come up with 20 uses."
5.	Compare performance on the groups with the low goal to those with the moderate or high goal.
6.	Discuss the importance of environmental constraints on idea generation.

Chapter 8

Improving Problem Solving and Decision Making

In 1998, the City of Rochester, NY, where I live, decided to begin a ferry service between Rochester and Toronto, Ontario, Canada. The idea was that the ferry would cross the lake and shuttle people between the two cities. People from Rochester would have an easy route to Toronto and those from Toronto would come down south to visit Rochester. A contract was issued to Canadian American Transportation Systems for the ferry service. CATS purchased a $42.5 million ferry, and the project was in part funded by city and state funding. Eventually, the gigantic ferry arrived. Although most people enjoyed the ferry ride, it proved not to be much faster than the three to four hour drive, yet considerably more expensive. Few Canadians made the trip south. The company, CATS, ended the ferry service.

Instead of ending ferry service there, the City bought the ferry and decided to operate the ferry itself. The results were similarly disastrous, and the City was left with considerable debt. With hindsight, buying the ferry was probably not a great decision. In addition, the key players involved probably did not conduct a thorough analysis of the problem which they were solving (it is, of course, always easier to criticize a decision after knowing the outcome).

One of the key responsibilities for many groups and teams is to solve problems and make decisions. The preceding chapter examined creativity, which is often a step in the problem-solving and decision-making process. This chapter expands on the content in the previous chapter to better understand how groups and teams solve problems and/or make decisions with creative outputs.

As you will see in this chapter, the problem-solving and decision-making literature are related. Often, teams have to find a set of creative solutions to a problem and then make a decision about which of the solutions to implement. These problems and

Group Dynamics and Team Interventions: Understanding and Improving Team Performance,
First Edition. Timothy M. Franz.

decisions can be as simple as a project team deciding on what to have for lunch to as complex as a medical team deciding how to best serve the needs of a terminally ill patient. The interventions in this chapter should help groups to improve their problem solving and decision making regardless of the importance of their decisions; however, groups making essential organizational decisions should be even more likely to consider using a structured intervention.

The first section of this chapter provides a brief background to the problem-solving and decision-making literature. The second section explains the key problems that you might identify during your assessment that might suggest when to use a decision-making intervention. The third section explains the details about how to use three common problem-solving and decision-making interventions that research has shown are effective.

Learning Goals for Chapter 8

- Better understand the interrelated processes of problem solving and decision making.
- Determine what assessment information might lead you to choose to use a structured problem-solving and/or decision-making intervention in your group.
- Intervene in your group using to improve problem solving and decision making.
- Find more information about many other structured interventions that are available to practitioners.

Assessing Problem Solving and Team Decision Making

Quality decision making requires good initial problem solving and information gathering, and then using as much of that information as necessary (given time constraints) to make the best decision possible. Janis and Mann (1977) described the typical process of decision making. In their book, they detail a number of problematic decision-making strategies that many people use. According to Janis and Mann, these typical decision-making strategies do not yield the best possible decisions, and these problems occur more often when making decision under stress.

Hollen (1994) used the concepts from Janis and Mann (1977) to create a scale that measures the quality of decision making. The scale has seven items that are based on the concepts that Janis and Mann found to be most important to quality decision making. These are provided in the assessment tool below. According to Hollen's research, these items provide a reliable and valid way to measure people's perception of whether they are reaching a quality decision. Although Janis and Mann's work, as well as Hollen's work that is based on it, was not designed to examine team decision making, the concepts easily generalize to team decision making as well. In fact, Janis (1982) used these same concepts when describing how to solve Groupthink, a faulty **group** decision-making process.

Table 8.1   Hollen's Assessment of Decision Making Quality.

	Not At All True	Not Very True	Somewhat True	Very True
How true do you think these statements are of your group's decision making?				
Thorough canvassing of alternatives	1	2	3	4
Thorough canvassing of objectives	1	2	3	4
Careful evaluation of consequences	1	2	3	4
Thorough search for information	1	2	3	4
Unbiased assimilation of new information	1	2	3	4
Careful re-evaluation of consequences	1	2	3	4
Thorough planning for implementation contingencies	1	2	3	4

Adapted from Hollen (1994).

Hollen's measure can be used by giving it to the members of a group and summing the responses of each member (Table 8.1). The possible range of summed scores is seven–28; scores closer to 28 mean that members perceive the group to be reaching high quality decisions while scores closer to seven mean that members perceive the group's decision to be of lower quality. Groups and teams can use this by examining the average score of members as well as examining the gaps between members (e.g., discussing why one member gives her or his group a low score while another member gives that same group a high score.

A Brief Background on Small Group Problem Solving and Decision Making

As you will see in this chapter, problem solving and decision making are interrelated processes. Often, groups and teams are required to progress from problem solving into decision making. Other times, groups and teams are also called to action for only part of the process. For example, a group or team may be called together to generate ideas (part of a problem solving). On the other hand, a group or team may be asked to make a decision about several solution alternatives for which they had no part in generating. As you can see, these processes are interrelated and overlapping. Thus, this chapter integrates the concepts and describes an overall process.

Bell, Raiffa, and Tversky (1988) describe three different views of the problem-solving and decision-making process, including descriptive and prescriptive. Descriptive approaches are those that describe what people *actually* do when solving problems and making decisions, including all the ways in which decisions go wrong. On the other hand, prescriptive and normative approaches (these are similar but not exactly the same) recommend what people *should* do or *ought* to do to make the best decision or solve the problem. Stanovich and West (1999) describe the gap between how people actually act and the performance that can be expected if they followed

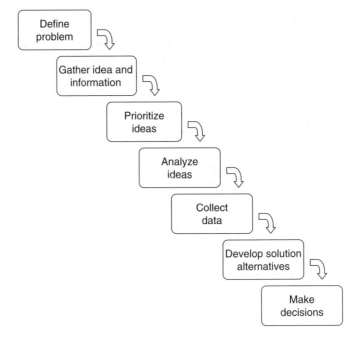

Figure 8.1   A Problem-Solving and Decision-Making Flowchart (adapted from Harrington-Mackin, 1994).

prescriptive approaches. It is important to note that this book includes a description of two of these components – the descriptive process about how groups and people act and then the prescriptive process about how to improve groups and teams who need support, intervention, and/or structure.

Harrington-Mackin (1994) recommends a stepwise approach to an integrated problem-solving and decision making process (see Andersen, 2007, for a far more detailed model). According to Harrington-Mackin there are six steps to the process. In addition to Harrington-Mackin's six steps, I have also included one more step at the beginning of the process – identifying the problem. These steps are summarized in Figure 8.1 and explained in detail in Table 8.2.

Problem solving is when groups and teams try to determine creative, unique, and effective solutions to problems they face. Decision making is the process through which groups move from inputs to a final decision. It is during this time that members of groups who have made the necessary preparations may potentially reach the process gains that were discussed earlier in this book. This is because when members are prepared for a group decision and are working on a complex task, they have the potential to best utilize the diverse knowledge, skills, and abilities of their members to choose a decision alternative that best responds to the issue.

Unfortunately, for the most part, groups fail to reach their possible process gains. In fact, because of process losses (Steiner, 1972), they often even fail to reach their potential. This is because members often get bogged down in the interpersonal and

Table 8.2   A Description of Problem Solving and Decision-Making Steps.

Problem Solving/Decision Making Step	Explanation
Identify the Problem	Similar to the first step in applied research, groups and teams must first clearly define the scope of the problem. Unfortunately, too many groups and teams skip this initial step and move into "Firefighting" mode (dealing with the symptoms) rather than focusing on the root cause (e.g., Preston, Inglis, & Horchner, 2001). This often causes them to generate solutions (the sixth step in this prescriptive process) that may not solve the problem. Many of the techniques designed for finding the root cause come from the literature and application about quality and continuous improvement.
Gather Information and Ideas	Once a group or team has defined the problem, the next step is to start to gather some background information and some ideas about what might be done to solve the problem. At this point, members should refrain from judgment or selection – these steps occur later in the process. The steps involved in improving group or team creativity (see Chapter 8) will be helpful as well.
Prioritize Ideas	After creating a complete list of possibilities, the next step is to prioritize the ideas. Groups and teams should do this so that they do not have to spend the time and energy analyzing every single idea; a number of good ones will likely be identifiable. One sub-step within this phase should include combination and improvement.
Analyze Ideas	Once the list of ideas has been narrowed, the next step is to analyze the subset of remaining ideas. At this time, there are many different methods of conducting this analysis, but the basic idea of each is to identify the problems and strengths of each idea and its impact on the initial problem.
Collect Data	Data collection is the next step, and this usually requires that the group or team reach out beyond itself to find out more information from others who may be more of an expert in the field than those working on the group or team.
Develop Solution Alternatives	The sixth step is to develop a list of solution alternatives using the evidence. This helps the group or team to generate true evidence-driven solutions rather than relying on anecdotal evidence that my not work.
Make Decisions	After generating the list of solutions, the final step is to make the decision about which of the solutions to use.

Adapted from Harrington-Mackin (1994).

structural, or task, problems with working in groups. Decision-making interventions provide a structure for the process that, in many ways, constrains the decision-making process, eliminates interpersonal barriers to effective decision making, and focuses members on the task steps required to improve the group decision. Structured decision-making processes are prescriptive by recommending how teams should solve problems and make decisions.

When to Use Interventions

After conducting your assessment of the group, you may identify one (or more) of five common problems that may be a factor in ineffective decision making. These include: Power differentials, poor or biased information sharing, group polarization, and groupthink. Although these are common problems in groups, any information in your assessment that identifies barriers in decision making from interpersonal issues or a failure to focus on the decision-making task should suggest the need for a structured intervention.

There are, of course, other possible concerns with poor decision making. The interventions suggested in this chapter, and the others that are referenced, should still help. Thus, you should consider training group members how to use these interventions if any information in your assessment that suggests faulty or problematic decision making. These interventions are designed specifically to improve group decision making without necessarily focusing on one specific problem. They are effective because they move groups from the typical, relatively unstructured environment to one that is much more structured and thus allows for more input from members.

Strong members/unequal power

One reason to use structured interventions in the decision making process is because of unequal power within the group or team. This is because an unreasonably strong group and team members who might capitalize on the situation to force his or her ideas on the group and undermine team effectiveness (Wageman & Mannix, 1998). This also makes it difficult for low-power members to carry out necessary and important group tasks (Brooks, 1994). Thus, members who have greater power than others have a higher likelihood of swaying any final decision with direct and/or indirect pressure as well as through the time they are allotted for discussion of information (e.g., Franz & Larson; Stasser, Stewart, & Wittenbaum, 1995).

Structured problem-solving and decision-making interventions can help groups and teams to minimize power differences because the structures imposed on a group actually limit the strong members while providing a voice for the less powerful members. This is because most structured problem-solving and decision-making interventions provide specific opportunities for each member to discuss relevant information such as ideas, facts, and underlying assumptions. In addition, many of the structured interventions impose some constraints on when the team leader can talk. Finally, the final decision-making processes provide for an equal weighting when voting.

Poor or biased information sharing

A second process that can impede the decision-making process is poor or biased information sharing. Information sharing among members is necessary for groups to make an informed decision. In fact, one of the main reasons that groups are used to make decisions is because of the unique information that each member brings to the group process. Unfortunately, it turns out that groups are quite inefficient information processors (Hinsz, Tindale, & Vollrath, 1997). In fact, groups tend to discuss a far greater proportion of the information that everyone knows rather than the unique information that only one or a few members know (e.g., Larson, Christensen, Franz, & Abbott, 1998; Stasser 1992). Surprisingly, research demonstrates that this problem with the failure to share unique information probably occurs regardless of whether the group is even quite functional.

Structured decision-making interventions can help groups to share more information because many of them have specific, prescribed steps that may help group members to recall information, increase their motivation to discuss that information, or provide the opportunities for them to bring that information out during discussion (Stasser, 1992). Groups using a structured decision-making intervention are more likely to use information better by increasing a) the probability of recall, b) member motivation, and c) opportunity to discuss all information.

Group polarization

Group polarization is a fourth process that your assessment may identify as a potential cause for why your group is less effective in its decision making. Group polarization was initially known of as the *risky shift* phenomenon because researchers noted that people working in groups tended to make riskier decisions than they would have if they were working alone. However, researchers soon identified that some groups also had a corresponding cautious shift as well. This seemingly contradictory research evidence was soon combined into one area which is now called group polarization (Moscovici & Zavalloni, 1969).

Group polarization is the tendency for groups to make decisions that are more extreme, or more polarized, after group discussion than those decision would be if the members would have made had they been working alone (Moscovici & Zavalloni, 1969). The basic idea behind group polarization is that groups move further along a continuum from caution to risk depending on where the members, on average, start. For example, if members, on average, are slightly cautious before meeting as a group (let's say they are at Point A on Figure 8.2), the group will be likely to move in an even more cautious direction after making its decision (to, for example, Point B on Figure 8.2). On the other hand, if the members' initial tendency is to be a little risky, on average (Point C), then they may likely make an even more risky decision after meeting as a group (Point D).

Figure 8.2   Group Polarization.

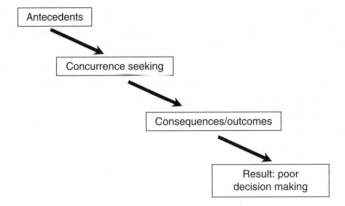

Figure 8.3   The Structure of the Groupthink Process.

Group polarization is of concern to groups because they may reach a decision where they either accept too much risk or fail to take on risk that may be necessary for a successful outcome. Structured interventions often allow for members to differ more in their opinions, and some even allow for groups to revisit decisions and potential problems with those decisions after an initial decision has been made. These varying choice alternatives should help groups to see the many options available to them, some of which are more risky and some of which are less.

Groupthink

Groupthink (Janis, 1982) is the final common problem discussed in this book that your assessment may identify as a possible issue that might cause poor decision making. This faulty decision-making process is perhaps the most widely known of the five reviewed here. Janis even convincingly suggests that groupthink was a distinct possibility for causing poor decisions ranging from the Bay of Pigs Fiasco in the Kennedy Administration to the Challenger Disaster in NASA, and there is more recent discussion that it possibly even may have caused the more recent problem that resulted in the Columbia shuttle breaking up over Texas (Ferraris & Carveth, 2003).

Groupthink is often misunderstood; it is **not** simply a group making a poor decision; as seen in the brief review in this chapter, there are many, many reasons that can cause a group to make a poor decision. Instead, Groupthink is a very specific faulty decision-making *process*, which is summarized in Figure 8.3, and which Irving Janis describes in depth in his book. In fact, Groupthink does not always produce a bad decision. Most of the time, groups and teams will struggle through their faults and problems and make an acceptable decision. But, when the decisions fail, they often fail spectacularly, like the Challenger Shuttle disaster highlighted at the very beginning of the book.

Janis first provides a list of five circumstances (termed antecedent conditions) that make the conditions ripe for the possibility of Groupthink to occur. When more of these antecedent conditions exist, group members are more likely to then emphasize one or more of eight possible concurrence seeking motives during group process rather than members focusing on fully reviewing the issue to make the best possible decision. The emphasis on concurrence seeking instead of effective decision making subsequently increases the possibility of the group facing one or more of seven poor consequences or outcomes that occur during decision making. These then each, or in combination, may cause the group to reach a poor decision. Table 8.3 provides more detail about the antecedent conditions, concurrence-seeking motives, and negative consequences and outcomes that are described by Janis.

There are certainly ways in which these negative consequences can be avoided. Janis (1982) provided nine different tools that arise from his review of high-profile, policy-making groups, some of which have successfully avoided the Groupthink process from occurring. These included:

- Assigning at least one member of the group, and possible more, the role of critical evaluator. This type of devil's advocacy may allow or even encourage members to speak out against the direction that the group may be heading and avoid the failure to reappraise and poor information search.

Table 8.3   A Summary of Groupthink Antecedents, Concurrence Seeking Motives, and Negative Consequences and Outcomes.

Antecedent Conditions	1.	A group with high **cohesiveness** is more likely to have Groupthink because members do not want to be ostracized from that group.
	2.	A group that is undergoing a **crisis or stressful situation** is more likely to have Groupthink because members do not have sufficient time to fully consider all decision alternatives.
	3.	A group that is **insulated** is more likely to have Groupthink because they fail to have access to resources outside of the group.
	4.	A group that **lacks impartial leadership** is more likely to have Groupthink because members are more likely to follow the suggestions of the group's leader rather than suggest alternatives of their own.
	5.	A group that **lacks specific decision making norms**, such as those that can be provided by using a structured decision-making intervention, is more likely to have Groupthink because the decision-making problem is unstructured.
Concurrence Seeking Motives	1.	First, Groupthink can cause an **illusion of invulnerability**, which is when groups feel their decisions cannot go wrong.
	2.	Second, Groupthink can cause an abnormally increased **sense of morality**, which is when groups feel that their goals and decisions are clearly better and more moral than those of others.

(continued)

Table 8.3 (*cont'd*).

	3. Third, Groupthink can cause groups to **discount warnings** provided by outsiders, because of their cohesiveness.
	4. Fourth, because of the illusion of invulnerability and the increase sense of morality, groups can **stereotype enemies** as unable, or unwilling.
	5. Fifth, the cohesiveness in groups can causes **self censorship**, which is when members fail to mention certain information or ideas for fear of ostracism.
	6. Sixth, self censorship creates a sense of **false consensus** so that some may not speak out even though there are others with similar views in the group.
	7. Seventh, when a member does speak out, there is direct **pressure to conform** to the will of the cohesive group.
	8. Finally, Groupthink sets up the possibility for **self-appointed mindguards**, which are individuals who enforce the stated view of the leader.
Consequences/ Outcomes	1. These groups have an **incomplete survey of their overall objectives**.
	2. These groups **fail to fully survey other possible choice alternatives** when making the decision.
	3. These groups **ignore risks of the preferred choice** when considering it.
	4. These groups **fail to reappraise** the situation after making a decision and instead trust the initial, poor decision.
	5. These groups have a **poor information search** because they ignore much of the information available to them.
	6. These groups have **biased information processing** because they are focused on information designed to support a choice rather than assumptions, what information supports the choice, and what facts fail to support the choice.
	7. These groups have **no contingency planning** because they neglect to see the faults in their preferred choice.

Adapted from Janis (1982).

- Having the leader of a group avoid stating her or his opinion at the outset, allowing a more unbiased discussion about the problem and potential solutions.
- Setting up multiple subgroups that solve a problem independently. Subgroups like this may come up with different, and perhaps competing, solutions to the problem, thus requiring an additional consideration of the issue.
- Allowing each member of a group to discuss the problem with a trusted associate who is not part of the group. This would help to prevent self-censorship and a false consensus.
- Bringing in an outside expert who can challenge the group's process and decision and provide a time to process more information, examine the risks of a decision, and reappraise if necessary.

- Paying attention to the potential risks of a decision and allowing time to create a realistic contingency plan. According to Janis (1982), this would "counteract members'; shared illusions of invulnerability and their tendency to ignore warning signals" (p. 269).
- Holding a "second chance meeting" where the "members are expected to express as vividly as they can all their residual doubts" (pp. 270–271).

As can be seen, these procedures set up structures and procedures in the group to help leaders and members to prevent Groupthink.

Although Groupthink is likely one of the most widely known concepts in the groups and teams literature, it is not without problems. Baron (2005) provides an excellent summary of the literature, and suggests that the Groupthink theory has failed to live up to many of the predictions. It is difficult to determine how common Groupthink is, because many of the research studies have been conducted using simulated laboratory groups which may not represent the level of cohesiveness that Janis expected in his conceptualization.

Three Interventions Designed to Improve Decision Making and Problem Solving

There are many structured group decision-making techniques that have been designed to improve the quality and hence the effectiveness of group decisions. The steps of three techniques are reviewed in detail in this chapter. These three structured techniques include the Nominal Group Technique, Dialectical Inquiry, and Multivoting. These three were chosen for inclusion in the text because they are common in the literature, are fairly easy to use, and the currently published research clearly demonstrates the effectiveness of each of these interventions at helping groups to reach better decisions.

The nominal group technique

The Nominal Group Technique (NGT; Van de Ven & Delbecq, 1974) is one of the most commonly used decision-making interventions. It was designed to solve many of the interpersonal problems associated with member behavior in face-to-face interacting groups. Some of these problems might include a leader pursuing a hidden or specific agenda, poor information sharing among group members, a strong member pushing his or her opinion, and/or the group rushing to quickly towards consensus and agreement. For example, it is all too common for one person, whether that member is a formal leader or a strong and outspoken group member, to immediately suggest his or her potential solution and then follow the suggestion by trying to gain agreement to it.

NGT helps to minimize the impact of these dysfunctional group processes on decision making by maximally constraining group discussion. The tight constraints imposed by the NGT structure allow a group to minimize the impact of one person, have more uniform information sharing by group members, and consider multiple possible solutions prior to advocating for any one of them.

Table 8.4 A Summary of the Steps Involved in the Nominal Group Technique.

Step	Procedure
1.	Members individually and silently generate ideas for solutions.
2.	Group members present and records their unique ideas through a round-robin listing of them.
3.	Group discusses ideas one at a time for clarification and evaluation.
4.	Group members silently vote on the ideas that were presented using a group decision rule upon which the group previously decided.

Adapted from Delbecq, Van de Ven, and Gustafson (1975) and Van de Ven and Delbecq (1974).

The steps for NGT are listed in Table 8.4. As can be seen, there are four steps. When using NGT, the first step is designed to improve the number of potential decision-making alternatives. During this step, members individually and silently generate a list of ideas for the decision. This step is completed individually to minimize member evaluation apprehension and group coordination problems that might otherwise result from group process.

The second step of the NGT process is for members to list their ideas. This is conducted in a round-robin format so that a) all ideas are listed, b) strong members cannot dominate, and c) every member has the opportunity to speak. The third step is the first where the technique opens up the possibilities to the group. At this point, the group goes through each idea. Members can ask questions that are focused on clarification and evaluation rather than critique; it is not the time to advocate for a specific choice alternative or against another. Finally, the group silently votes to make a decision based upon a common decision rule (e.g., consensus, majority rules, etc.; see Table 8.5) about which decision alternative the group should adopt.

A classic test of the effectiveness of NGT was conducted by Van de Ven and Delbecq (1974), the authors of the technique. They compared the effectiveness of NGT to a) another structured intervention called the Delphi technique and b) unstructured groups. Their results demonstrated that groups using NGT generated a larger number of decision alternatives than unstructured groups, and as many as groups using the Delphi technique. In addition, members remained satisfied with the group process.

Subsequent research has confirmed the success of this technique. For example, Rohrbaugh (1981) found that NGT groups generated decision alternatives that were equal in quality as those generated by groups using Social Judgment Analysis (Hammond & Brehmer, 1973). Stephenson, Michaelson, and Franklin (1982) found that NGT can be effectively used in real-world groups making decisions with complex tasks in long-range planning situations. Finally, Arunachalam and Dilla (1995) showed that NGT groups had higher judgment accuracy, higher outcomes, and more equal resource distribution than unstructured groups.

However, NGT is certainly no panacea to all issues; its success is limited to the tasks that match when it should be used. Because of the minimal group process, NGT is likely to be less useful when groups are working on a unitary task, or one that is not easily divided into subtasks (Forsyth, 2006). On the other hand, as one can imagine because of the way it divides members up, it is more useful when the task is divisible.

Table 8.5   A Summary of Group Decision Rules.

Decision Rule	Explanation
Consensus/ Unanimity	All members in the group must agree to gain support for a choice alternative.
Majority Rules	More than half of group members must agree to gain support for any one choice alternative.
Plurality	The group picks the choice alternative with the greatest support, regardless of whether it is more than half of the members; typically only useful if there are more than two choice alternatives.
Truth wins	The group picks a choice alternative if one member can identify the correct decision and then can explain the reasons for this to the other members (assumes that a correct decision can be identified).
Truth- supported wins	The group picks a choice alternative if one member can identify the correct decision, then can explain the reasons for this to the other members, and is supported by at least one other member (again, assumes that a correct decision can be identified).

Adapted from Miller (1989).

Dialectical inquiry

A second possible decision making intervention is called *Dialectical Inquiry* (Lourenco & Glidewell, 1975). Dialectical inquiry is based on the philosophy of Hegel, who suggested that conflict can be used for improvement. The steps involved in Dialectical Inquiry are summarized in Table 8.6. According to Lourenco and Glidewell (1975), the first step is to equally divide the main group into two subgroups. These subgroups become separate decision-making entities and will work separately until the end of the process. After breaking into subgroups, each group individually takes on the decision-making problem. Within the subgroup, subgroup members then decide on the important facts, assumptions, arguments, and potential solutions. Next, one of the subgroups recommends *in writing* a potential solution to the problem supported by facts and listing any assumptions they have made. Providing the solution in writing is a necessary component of the process because it properly focuses the conflict on solving the task rather than on allowing differences to create unnecessary and dysfunctional interpersonal conflict (Jehn, 1995).

After receiving the written recommendations, the other subgroup privately critiques the assumption and solution provided by the first subgroup and then, similar to the first group, provides *in writing* a counter recommendation along with a detailed list of the supporting facts, arguments, and any assumptions that they have made. At this point, each subgroup provides an oral summary, which then leads to a subsequent group discussion about the decision-making problem and allows for questions and clarification about each potential solution. When the two subgroups finally agree on the relevant facts, underlying arguments, and reasonable assumptions, they can then work together to find the best possible solution.

Table 8.6   A Summary of the Steps Involved in Dialectical Inquiry.

Step	Procedure
1.	Divide group members into two subgroups.
2.	Discuss case in subgroups and decide on the important facts, assumptions, arguments, and potential solutions.
3.	Subgroup 1 recommends initial solution in writing along with supporting facts and arguments.
4.	Subgroup 2 privately critiques the assumption and solution provided by subgroup 1.
5.	Subgroup 2 provides in writing a counter recommendation along with supporting facts and arguments.
6.	Subgroups 1 and 2 present recommendations orally.
7.	Subgroups 1 and 2 orally debate the assumptions, facts and proposed solutions until there is a final list of assumptions and facts.
8.	Using the final list of assumptions and facts, the entire group together develops a recommendation.

Adapted from Lourenco and Glidewell (1975) and Schweiger, Sandberg, and Ragan (1986).

Research testing the task effectiveness of Dialectical Inquiry has generally demonstrated it to be quite effective at improving group decisions when compared to unstructured groups or groups using a technique called consensus groups. Schweiger, Sandberg, and Ragan (1986), for example, found that dialectical inquiry strategic decision-making groups (MBA students) performed better than consensus groups. Other research by Schweiger, Sandberg, and Rechner (1989) and Schwenk and Valacich (1994) confirms these findings. Groups using Dialectical Inquiry have a more thorough analysis of the assumptions and create better recommendations.

However, research also demonstrates that people are often less satisfied with the decision-making process when they are using dialectical inquiry than when they are using a different intervention (usually consensus groups or an expert approach) that do not generate the conflict that dialectical inquiry does (e.g., Schweiger, Sandberg, & Ragan, 1986) and possibly lower acceptance of the decision by members than other techniques (Schweiger, Sandberg, & Rechner, 1989). Thus, one must be careful when using techniques that induce conflict within a group and may want to use these interventions minimally. This is because they may certainly improve decision making in the specific task in which they are being used, but may also harm future decision making in standing groups that will continue to interact in the future because the hostility they can possibly create among members, if not properly managed, may negatively affect group process.

Finally, there is considerable research that compares the dialectical inquiry to a similar technique termed devil's advocacy (e.g., Cosier & Rechner, 1985). At this point, the comparative effectiveness of which of these two techniques is more effective remains somewhat unclear. Currently, the most compelling evidence comes from a meta-analysis. Meta-analysis is a statistical tool that numerically compares the results of multiple research studies that have already been conducted. Schwenk (1990) conducted a meta-analysis using 16 past studies which each compared the effectiveness of the technique. His meta-analysis reveals that devil's advocacy might be a preferred approach.

Table 8.7   A Summary of the Steps Involved in Multivoting.

Step	Procedure
1.	After combining similar ideas, **all** ideas are listed on the wall using flipchart paper.
2.	Each person on the team votes for a certain number of ideas that he or she likes (the number of votes is determined ahead of time by a facilitator based on the number of ideas; larger overall numbers of ideas require more votes for each person while fewer ideas require fewer votes). He or she can use all of his or her votes on one idea of spread them out among many ideas. Votes can be placed on the flipchart paper using devices such as sticky dots, post it flags, or checkmarks with markers.
3.	The facilitator circles the ideas with the greatest number of votes are circled.
4.	The remaining ideas are again combined and consolidated, when possible.
5.	Each person votes again, but this time for only half the number of ideas that are circled.
6.	The multivoting process continues with Steps 2 through 5 until the list is down to at least three but no more than five ideas. This typically requires only one to three rounds.

Adapted from Nelson, Batalden, and Godfrey (2007) and Scholtes, Joiner, and Streibel (2003).

Multivoting

When conducting problem-solving and/or decision-making sessions, groups often generate a large number of good ideas, especially when using procedures such as facilitated brainstorming or brainwriting. Most groups and teams want to immediately progress to a thorough review and discussion of each idea. This may be useful to get at some of the important facts and assumptions underlying the ideas, but the discussion can be very time consuming and a group or team may spend considerable time reflecting on and evaluating choice alternatives that all (or even most) members will not consider reasonable. One intervention to help groups and teams with this is multivoting (Nelson, Bataldan, & Godfrey, 2007), which is summarized in Table 8.7.

Multivoting is a structured problem-solving procedure that is used to quickly narrow the number of items for consideration. This is helpful because after a multivoting process, members can immediately focus on evaluating a much smaller list of ideas that all or most members already value at least to some extent. Thus, multivoting is a time-saving technique because it focuses members on a short list of ideas to critique and evaluate rather than reflecting on the other ideas that most members would not consider anyway.

Multivoting is primarily a practitioner-based intervention, so there is very little research regarding its effectiveness. It is, however, found in many different practitioner handbooks designed to help groups and teams succeed in many different domains. For example, in *The team handbook*, Scholtes and colleagues (2003) advocate multivoting as a process to "select the most popular items with limited discussion and difficulty (pp. 3–20). Further, in *Quality by design*, Nelson, Batalden, and Godfrey (2007) recommend that multivoting be used to narrow a large set of ideas designed to make change. Finally, both sets of practitioners recommend that this follow a creativity-generating process such as brainstorming and then it should be followed by an intervention that evaluates and critiques the remaining ideas.

FOCUS ON APPLICATION

Using multivoting to improve problem solving and decision making

The practitioner

Todd Zyra is the Chief Operating Officer for Klein Steel Service Inc. He reports to the President and Chief Executive Officer and has previously held the positions of VP Operations, Plant Manager, and Processing Manager. At Klein Steel, Todd leads a team that encompasses Sales, Operations, Engineering, and Quality, providing a unified culture and infrastructure; coordination between personnel, structure, and the firm's strategic plan; necessary support for all company divisions; guidance to deliver on the corporate vision; and organizational business planning. He has earned a reputation for clear and consistent vision, keen analytical and strategic thinking skills, and igniting enthusiasm.

Todd received his bachelor's degree in Business Management at Niagara University in Niagara Falls NY. He then completed an MBA degree at Northeastern University in Boston MA. Todd makes time to be involved with community organizations. He has served on the Boards of the Rochester Regional Veteran's Business Council, the Metals Service Center Institute, and The Lakeside Health System Foundation.

The symptom: Reduced revenue in a field office

Klein Steel Service is a premier steel processing center headquartered in Rochester, NY with sales offices in several nearby cities. Klein Steel's 212 employees serve Upstate New York with a complete inventory of steel, stainless steel, aluminum, and fiberglass products, including specialty and hard-to-find items. In addition, Klein Steel Service provides a full range of cutting and processing services from one piece to multi-piece productions. All sales locations have both commercial and retail customers.

One of the sales offices is located approximately an hour away from the head office and had a team of eight employees. The team was facing a changing market as well as the introduction of several major competitors who moved into the area. As a result, sales revenue had dropped by 50% and the team's location was no longer profitable. It was clear that the old model of doing business no longer served this rapidly changing marketplace in this area.

Assessing the problem: Interviews and direct observations

We used multiple methods to assess what was happening in the sales office and this thorough analysis of the problem took us over six months to accomplish. First, we examined the financial history. A simple assessment of the finances alone might have suggested that we simply shut the sales office. However, we also directly observed what was occurring at the location and interviewed the key employees.

The observations were conducted for three to four hours twice a week for a period of two or three months. During this time, we observed employees' interactions with customers, counted the number of customers during each period, assessed nonverbal behavior of employees, and measured changes in inventory (including which inventory had the most dust on it). The observation and interview data provided many interesting findings. Most importantly, we learned that the majority of customers were individuals or from small companies who preferred to shop within the site.

Intervening: Using problem-solving and multivoting techniques

After collecting the data, we had a one-day team meeting to determine what do about the declining revenue and the office's profitability. During the meeting, we generated five reasonable options for how to improve the profitability within the sales office. These options included shutting the site down, expanding the region that the site serves, lowering prices to match the discounts the competitors were offering, changing the business model to better serve retail customers, and changing the location of the office.

We then conducted a thorough risk analysis of each of the five options. Next, we used a modification of the multivoting technique to select the single option that would best fit the future of Klein Steel Service. Within one month, we completely converted the business model in the sales office from one that focused on commercial delivery to a retail sales office that primarily emphasized walk-in customers.

Since making the change to the retail business model, the number of pounds of steel processed through that office has actually dropped by over 90% from its original rate because most commercial sales were moved from the sales office to the main office. But, the sales office has returned to profitability with almost no reduction in the number of employees who work on the team (the office now has seven team members rather than eight). This is primarily because of the increased retail sales. Further, Klein Steel Service better utilized resources by improving logistics, reducing inventory, and better serving the commercial customers from the head office in Rochester. Finally, the new sales office is now better suited to meet the future strategic goals of the organization.

Chapter Summary

Groups and teams that solve problems and emphasize high-quality decisions or those where group process has bogged down the interpersonal interactions involved in the decision-making process should consider using one of the structured interventions in this chapter, including: the Nominal Group Technique, Dialectical Inquiry, Multivoting, or one of the many other successful interventions that have been shown to improve group decision making. Most of these interventions are effective because they impose at least some restrictions on the typical unstructured group process. This can help groups to eliminate differences due to status and power, improve information sharing, and the rush to consensus that sometimes can occur in typical unstructured decision-making groups.

Additional Resources

There are many other structured problem-solving and decision-making interventions than this chapter could include; this area has received considerable attention. A few key references are below.

Dalkey, N. C. (1969). *The Delphi method: An experimental study of group opinion*. Santa Monica, CA: Rand.

Rogelberg, S. G., Barnes-Farrell, J. L., & Lowe, C. A. (1992). The stepladder technique: An alternative group structure facilitating effective group decision making. *Journal of Applied Psychology, 77*, 730–737.

Schweiger, D. M., Sandberg, W. R., & Ragan, J. W. (1986). Group approaches for improving strategic decision making: A comparative analysis of dialectical inquiry, devil's advocacy, and consensus. *Academy of Management Journal, 29*, 51–71.

Winquist, J. R., & Franz, T. M. (2008). Does the Stepladder Technique improve group decision making? A series of failed replications. *Group Dynamics: Theory, Research, and Practice, 12*, 255–267.

Team Exercises

Exercise 8.1   Structured problem solving

Using the structured problem-solving and decision-making procedures, solve the following problem and then make a group decision.

Organizational change requires in part, removing the supports for the previous values while at the same time providing rewards for the new values. Imagine that you have tried to change your organization into one that has a *high performing team culture*. How will you recognize and reward good work that is consistent with this vision on a limited budget?

Exercise 8.2   Making a decision

Step 1. Divide the group into two subgroups. One subgroup should complete the first task. The other subgroup should complete the second task.

Task 1: Which of the following is the best baseball team?
1.   Boston Red Sox
2.   Chicago Cubs
3.   Los Angeles Dodgers
4.   New York Yankees
5.   San Francisco Giants
6.   Colorado Rockies

Task 2: What is the mean and the sums of squares for the following set of numbers?
6, 8, 10
1. $M = 8, SS = 66.67$
2. $M = 8, SS = 2.67$
3. $M = 6, SS = 8$
4. $M = 8, SS = 8$
5. $M = 6, SS = 200$
6. $M = 8, SS = 200$

Step 2. Go over the answers that each group gave. More importantly, work with groups to reflect about the process through which they answered each question. Consider using the following questions:

What process did your group use to make its decision?
What decision rule did your group use?
What was different about the way you answered Question 1 versus Question 2?

Chapter 9

Understanding Cohesion and Collaboration

Imagine you had a choice of two new job offers. However, the group situations and behaviors were completely different between them, even though the job requirements were going to be almost identical. In the first job, the group in which you would be working is one where members want to be there working as part of that group. They prefer to work in groups rather than working alone. They feel close to the members with whom they are working. And, they believe that the group work is important and as a result, are committed to it. In the second job, the work group is completely different from the first. In fact, no one wants to be there. In this other group, members want to work alone, do not feel close to those with whom they are working, and believe that group work is a complete waste of their time. If you had to pick one of these two jobs, which of these two would you pick?

Almost all people would, of course, quickly accept the offer for the first job instead of the second. Many would even do so for somewhat less pay. This is because group members in the first hypothetical situation wish to remain a part of an exciting work group like that one for as long as they possibly can; they are members of a cohesive group. On the other hand, the second group lacks cohesion. Managers, leaders, and group and team members themselves are often searching for greater cohesion. This is no surprise. Cohesion is an important component of getting to synergy. The levels of cohesion in a group positively predict performance (e.g., Beal, Cohen, Burke, & McLendon, 2003; Gully, Devine, & Whitney, 1995; Mullen & Copper, 1994) As a result, cohesion is one of the commonly discussed concepts in the groups literature, and one of the common topics discussed by practitioners.

Group Dynamics and Team Interventions: Understanding and Improving Team Performance,
First Edition. Timothy M. Franz.
© 2012 Timothy M. Franz. Published 2012 by Blackwell Publishing Ltd.

Although there are certainly some people who are predisposed to liking group work than others and there are other individual characteristics that are predictors of group cohesion, cohesion is much more of a function of what happens during group process. Carron, Widmeyer, and Brawley (1985) define the predisposition for cohesion as individual attraction to group. But, it takes a group of individuals working together over time to develop actual cohesion. Thus, group cohesion does not occur only at the individual level; a person, for example, cannot be cohesive when working alone. As a result, Carron and colleagues, like many others, define the group-level concept as cohesion while the individual-level concept is attraction.

Cohesion is not only a popular concept, but it is also one that is widely misunderstood. The popular concept of cohesion is as a unitary concept that results from an emotional attachment to a group – more specifically, most talk about it solely as liking the members of a group (McPherson & Smith-Lovin, 2002). However, cohesion is in fact a multidimensional concept (Carron & Brawley, 2000). There are many different definitions of cohesion. Some emphasize, like the popular ideal of cohesion, attraction to and liking of group members while others emphasize attraction to the group task. In fact, there are some who even suggest that cohesion is synonymous with solidarity (Willer, Borch, & Willer, 2002).

Most recent definitions combine multiple concepts and, as a result, include some component of both task and social cohesion (e.g., Carron & Brawley, 2000). Myers and Anderson (2008), for example, differentiate task cohesion (called instrumental cohesion by others) from social cohesion (called interpersonal cohesion by others). Myers and Anderson define task cohesion as the degree to which members are committed to a group goal. On the other hand, they define social cohesion as positive affect (good feelings) towards members of a group. Overall, cohesion depends on the combination of task and social cohesion.

To contrast these different components of cohesion, imagine a presidential cabinet. Members of the cabinet might be fighting against other members for scarce resources and because of their diverse backgrounds and interests they might have considerably different viewpoints about what is important to carrying out policy decisions. However, it remains an important group to which those cabinet members want to belong. In fact, they may not even like each other – they were chosen for their role by the President, not because of their liking for the other cabinet members. But, because of their expertise, they remain a cohesive group because they want to be members; they are cohesive because of their commitment to a very important task.

For the purposes of this book, cohesion is defined as the "glue that makes the members of a group stick together" (Nelson & Quick, 2008, p. 295). This definition is broad enough to incorporate both task and social factors. I rely on this definition because it allows for cohesion to result from any and all factors that cause members to stay a part of that group. Cohesion and collaboration are considered together in this chapter because cohesion is a necessary precursor to collaboration. Groups that are cohesive can collaborate, and there are clear performance advantages that result from successful collaboration efforts.

Learning Goals for Chapter 9

- Define cohesion.
- Understand that cohesion includes attraction to the membership as well as attraction to the task and goals.
- Know the predictors of cohesion.
- Know the positive and negative outcomes of working in a cohesive group.
- Know what prevents cohesion from developing.
- Define collaboration.
- Know the importance of the relationship between collaboration and performance.
- Have a basic understanding of some tools that are designed to improve cohesion and collaboration.

Assessing Cohesion

Carless and De Paola (2000) created a 10-item scale to measure group cohesion that they call the Team Diagnostic Survey (Table 9.1). They modeled their Team Diagnostic Survey after the Group Environment Questionnaire (Carron & Brawley, 2000; Carron, Widmeyer, & Brawley, 1985), one of the most well-known measures

Table 9.1   Assessing the Organizational Environment: The Team Diagnostic Survey.

Work Cohesion Item	Strongly Disagree	Disagree	Neutral	Agree	Strongly Agree
1. Our team is united in trying to reach its goals for performance	1	2	3	4	5
2. I'm unhappy with my team's level of commitment to the task (R)	1	2	3	4	5
3. Our team members have conflicting aspirations for the team's performance (R)	1	2	3	4	5
4. This team does not give me enough opportunities to improve my personal performance (R)	1	2	3	4	5
5. Our team would like to spend time together outside of work hours	1	2	3	4	5
6. Members of our team do not stick together outside of work time (R)	1	2	3	4	5
7. Our team members rarely party together (R)	1	2	3	4	5
8. Members of our team would rather go out on their own than get together as a team (R)	1	2	3	4	5
9. For me this team is one of the most important social groups to which I belong	1	2	3	4	5
10. Some of my best friends are in this team	1	2	3	4	5

Adapted from Carless and De Paola (2000).

of cohesion, which was designed to measure cohesion in sports teams. The original Group Environment Questionnaire contains either 18 or 24 items, depending on the version. Carron and Brawley argue that the GEQ could be modified to use in other types of teams; this is exactly what Carless and De Paola accomplished by adapting the Group Environment Scale for use with work teams. The version presented here was developed by testing it on 120 employees of retail outlets in Australia. Although Carless and De Paola used a nine-point Likert response scale,I have modified it to a five-point response scale for ease of use by readers of this text.

When testing the effectiveness of the cohesion scale, Carless and De Paola's results showed that cohesion in work groups can be classified into three broad categories (statistically, this is the results of a factor analysis and is termed a three-factor solution): task cohesion, social cohesion, and interpersonal attraction to the group. These three categories are consistent with the way cohesion is defined and explained in this text. Items 1–4 measure task cohesion, Items 5–8 measure social cohesion, and Items 9–10 measure individual attraction to a group.

When measuring cohesion, a group's score is computed by averaging all of the member responses within a group using relevant reverse scoring (i.e., when there is an "R" behind the item, the item is worded in the opposite direction and the numbers need to be changed in the opposite direction so that a 1 becomes a 5, a 2 becomes a 4, etc.). Higher scores mean higher levels of cohesion, while lower scores mean lower cohesion. Teams with lower scores may need more assessment to understand the concerns about cohesion within the team and then intervention to improve group performance.

A Brief Background on Cohesion

Cohesion, as defined previously, is a group concept that results from attraction to a group and work within a group. There is an individual component that is from personal attraction to the group. There is also a group component that results in part from time spent working together and integrating ideas (Carron et al., 1985). Higher group cohesion results from contact because members of the group have increase their ties to one another (McPherson & Smith-Lovin, 2002; Schmidt, McGuire, Humphrey, Williams, & Grawer, 2005). In fact, cohesion is negatively related to high contact outside of the group (McPherson & Smith-Lovin, 2002).

What this means is that the more people are connected within their group and the less connected they are outside of it, the higher their cohesion. On the other hand, the less connected they are within the group and the more connected they are outside of the group, the lower their cohesion. One possible explanation of why contact is predictive of cohesion is because of contact increases information sharing and trust. Further, increased information sharing is tied to openness among members, and openness increases cohesion and trust (Mesmer-Magnus & DeChurch, 2009).

Simply being a member of a group, especially one who is powerful, can in and of itself create cohesion (Halevy, Bornstein, & Sagiv, 2008). Recall from Chapter 4 that people categorize themselves into ingroups and outgroups through process of social identity (Tajfel & Turner, 1986). As a quick summary, ingroups are the groups with which a person identifies. On the other hand, outgroups are those who are not among the ingroup but are members of other groups. Remember also that people prefer ingroup members to outgroup members. This ingroup bias can cause at least some minimal level of cohesion simply because of the categorization of members into groups (e.g., Hogg, 1996).

However, the ingroup bias and subsequent cohesion can be even stronger in powerful groups (Andreopoulou & Houston, 2002), because powerful groups are high status groups (Wahrman, 2010) and people want to be part of a high status and powerful group. The status and power of the group can strengthen something called collective esteem, which is how positively people feel about themselves as a result of being a member of that group, and this in turn improves individual self esteem (Crocker & Luhtanen, 1990).

The level of cohesion is also determined, in part, by comparing the power of one's group to that of other groups. If a group has high power relative to others, they are likely to be more cohesive because they want to be a part of that powerful group. However, the relationship is not so straightforward. Groups with high power relative to others as well as equal power among the members within the group are likely to have higher cohesion than high power groups that have substantial power differences among group members (Thye, Yoon, & Lawler, 2002).

Unfortunately, cohesion is not only related to within-group behavior and outside connections, it also is enhanced or hindered because of economic conditions that are outside of the group's control. Specifically, when group rewards are large, there is more cohesion and when rewards are low, there is less cohesion (Willer, Borch, & Willer, 2002). Taking from this, groups that are rewarded are more likely to be cohesive even when those rewards are driven by strong economic conditions and are unrelated to the group's behavior. On the other hand, if the group is not rewarded because the economy has soured, group cohesion suffers regardless of how much members have liked working together.

In addition, cohesion is related to group size. Carron and Spink (1995) tested cohesion within differently sized exercise groups using the Group Environment Questionnaire. To accomplish this, they conducted three studies where they gave the questionnaire to aerobics class members. Some of the classes were large (over 40 participants) while others were small (under 20 participants). Across all the studies, they found that smaller classes had higher task and social cohesion than larger classes. Their third study also demonstrated that this effect is stable over time. Similar results have also been found with even smaller groups comprised of three, six, and nine members (Widmeyer, Brawley, & Carron, 1990).

Finally, the task on which the group is working predicts cohesion. Hoogstraten and Vorst (1978) examined group versus individual tasks within three laboratory studies. The individual task focused participants on individual learning where individuals worked alone to learn and then report information. On the other hand, the group task focused participants on group learning where the group members worked together to learn and report the information. They found that when the task was oriented towards group learning, groups were more cohesive and had higher performance.

So far, this chapter has focused on what cohesion is and what predicts group cohesion. A question that remains is why cohesion is important. In one of the most comprehensive studies of the impact of cohesion to date, Carless and De Paola (2000) found that task and social cohesion were related to team morale, social support, communication, cooperation, workload sharing, participation in group process, preference for teamwork, work interdependence, job satisfaction, team performance, and team effectiveness. Interpersonal attraction to the group was moderately related to team morale, workload sharing and participation, and (not surprisingly) preference for teamwork. In addition, Cohen and Bailey (1997) suggest as a result of their research that cohesion is related to job satisfaction. Finally, cohesion is related to group identification and group identification improves trust among members (Kramer, Hanna, Su, & Wei, 2001). Not only do these studies demonstrate the importance of measuring the different components of cohesion, they are also indicative of the importance of creating a cohesive group.

As the very brief review demonstrates, cohesion is important to group work. As stated at the beginning of this chapter, there has been considerable research on the concept of cohesion, much of which has examined this relationship between cohesion and subsequent group performance. Much of the research has shown that creating cohesive groups can yield higher performance. However, not all of the research examining the link between cohesion and performance has been favorable, though. In fact, some have reviewed the literature and argued that when taking account of all of the research, there is no relationship between cohesion and performance (e.g., Stogdill, 1972).

As is the case with any research in the social or behavioral sciences, there are often some findings that are in one direction and some findings that are in the other direction. The research about cohesion is the perfect example of this – one set of researchers have shown that cohesion is important because cohesion improves group performance while on the other hand another set of researchers have shown that cohesion, while important for group functioning, is unrelated to performance. Historically, the only way to untie divergent findings such as those comparing cohesion to performance was for someone to sit down and read all of the literature and then make some qualitative judgments about what the set of research, taken together, implies. Many, like Stogdill in 1972, did so with the link between cohesion and performance and unfortunately even they reached somewhat different interpretations.

Thankfully, a new statistical tool called meta-analysis has become available to researchers during the past 30 years or so. Meta-analysis is used to statistically understand relationships across many studies, such as the one between cohesion and performance. In meta-analysis, a researcher calculates the size of the effect within a number of studies and then essentially computes an average effect size across multiple studies. Further, each study can be coded for different essential features, such as the type of cohesion that was measured or whether or not the task was one that was suited to groups. Then, the studies can be combined quantitatively (statistically) rather than qualitatively, and this analysis eliminates much of the judgment about the importance of any relationship.

Because of the vast literature examining the link between cohesion and group performance, Mullen and Copper (1994) conducted a meta-analysis. They identified 49 studies that met the criteria for their meta-analysis study. Their results showed definitively that cohesion in fact positively predicted group performance. At the time of their study, this finding was groundbreaking because of the mixed results in the literature up until that point. Further, they were able to identify the type of cohesion, and they found that cohesion resulting from commitment to the task was more predictive of performance than was cohesion that resulted from liking and interpersonal attraction to the group. In addition, they coded for the type of task, and provided some evidence, though weak, that the task was important when considering the relationship between cohesion and performance. Specifically, they showed that the link between cohesion and performance was likely stronger when the group tasks required more interdependence among members than when the task required members to act more independently, though they were not so confident about these final findings.

However, the meta-analysis by Mullen and Copper (1994) was only the first of several that have been conducted that examine the relationship between cohesion and group performance. Gully, Devine, and Whitney (1995) conducted a meta-analysis using 46 studies where they operationalized cohesion at a group level rather than an aggregate (usually an average) of individuals. They did this by examining the within group correlation of cohesion, a common technique for aggregating group level concepts (see James, Demaree, & Wolf, 1984, for a complete discussion about the importance of computing within-group correlations). What this means is that group cohesion is high in cases where group members all agree that there is high cohesion, and the more members who agree, the higher the measure of group-level cohesion.

Like Mullen and Copper, Gully and colleagues coded the studies for the level of task interdependence. What they found, in summary, is first that the previous studies about cohesion that averaged across individuals are likely to have underestimated the impact of the relationship between cohesion and task performance. Thus, not only is there a link between cohesion and group performance, but it is likely to be even more important than many past studies, even the meta-analysis by Mullen and Copper demonstrated. Second, they found definitive evidence that showed that the type of the task is important when trying to understand the relationship between cohesion and performance. Tasks that require interdependent group work have a stronger link between cohesion and performance. On the other hand, tasks that require little interdependence have a considerably weaker link between cohesion and performance. This should come as no surprise given the importance of the task in understanding group behavior that was described early in this book. The coordination, communication, and collaboration that occur within cohesive groups become considerably more important when the task requires members to work closely together.

Beal, Cohen, Burke, and McLendon (2003) conducted a meta-analysis where they again examined the link between cohesion and performance. This time, they were able to gather data from 64 different studies, some of which were unpublished. In addition, they were able to code for the different components of the concept of cohesion. The positive finding, not surprisingly, were that cohesion predicts interpersonal attraction among members, commitment to the task, and group pride. Surprisingly, they found that interpersonal attraction is the more important part of cohesion than cohesion resulting from commitment to the task. They found that the link between cohesion and performance is stronger when the task is suitable for a team. They sum up their results by concluding that cohesive groups are more efficient. Chiocchio and Essembre (2009) agree, but find more specifically that for project teams task cohesion improves performance on outcomes while social cohesion improves performance on behaviors.

Common Barriers to Cohesion

The previous section demonstrates that highly cohesive groups will likely perform better than ones that are not cohesive. The next question, then, is what gets in the way of creating a cohesive group? Just as working together, sharing information, and interacting builds cohesion, cohesion suffers in groups where there is a lack of interaction. Some of the barriers to creating a cohesive group are related to the type of group, such as working on a task that does not require interdependence or working virtually, and other barriers are related to the characteristics of the people within a group, including different personality types. These three barriers are discussed in detail in this section.

Task Type

There are several types of groups where interaction is difficult. First and foremost, if the task encourages members to divide up and separate the work only to add individual contributions back together again later (this is called an additive task), then members often fail to interact enough to generate the cohesion that might help them to succeed later as an interacting group. Consistent with this, cohesion is important for groups where members interact more as compared to those that have fewer interactions (Beal *et al.*, 2003). This is because in simple or additive tasks, members are focusing on individual work rather than group work. As I have argued in this book and as the literature about cohesion and performance demonstrates, groups should only be used on group tasks anyway.

Although Beal and colleagues (2003) were generally positive about the relationship between cohesion and performance, they also state that "there definitely were circumstances in which cohesive groups provided little help for performance" (p. 999). For example, they found that cohesion was predictive of performance-related behaviors, but it was not as predictive of actual team performance.

Virtual groups

Another type of group that does not have regular interactions among members is a virtual group. Virtual groups will be discussed at length later in this book, but the impact of virtual group work on cohesion is summarized here. There is mixed evidence about the impact of working virtually on cohesion. Conventional wisdom espoused by team leaders (e.g., Hambly, ONeill, & Kline, 2007), as well as limited research evidence (e.g., Piccoli & Ives, 2003), demonstrate that trust and cohesion likely suffer when working in virtual groups. This is because the face-to-face meetings are intended to help to "establish rapport, build trust, and get the team off to a good start" (Triana, Kirkman, & Garcia, 2009, p. 3). As a result, most people suggest that cohesion will be lower in virtual groups than in face-to-face interacting groups. Based on a summary of this and other research, Peters and Manz (2007) recommend that for virtual groups to succeed, they must focus on a) building trust, b) working towards developing deep relationships, and c) creating a shared under-standing about the goals and the direction of the team.

There is, however, some recent evidence that shows that at least under certain conditions cohesion may not suffer when working in a virtual group as much as many might predict. Triana, Kirkman, and Garcia (2009) find that computer-mediated teams may not always need a face-to-face meeting prior to working virtually. Specifically, Triana and colleagues find that minority members – in their case, women working in male-dominated groups – feel a greater sense of inclusion when the groups first meet virtually. According to their research, this occurs because the token women in male-dominated virtual teams feel more connected and stand out less than they would in a face-to-face group.

Diversity

Diversity was discussed in detail in Chapter 4 and to a lesser extent in Chapter 8. One specific finding that is common is that diversity is necessary to improve creativity. Unfortunately, diversity can be a double-edged sword. Though diversity is important for improving creativity and possibly improving group performance, it, at the same time, has the potential to reduce group cohesion (Shapcott, Carron, Burke, Bradshaw, & Estabrooks, 2006; Watson, Kumar, & Michaelsen, 1993).

One reason for this is that cohesion is at least partially related to liking. It is no surprise that people like those who are similar to themselves, a theory called the

Similarity-Attraction Hypothesis (Davison & Jones, 1976). Much of the research about similarity-attraction has found that people are more attracted to those who are demographically similar. What this means is that similarity increases attraction and liking, and this increases cohesion (Watson, Kumar, & Michaelsen, 1993), although not all agree with this finding (e.g., Webber & Donahue, 2001).

However, the relationship between diversity, cohesion, and group performance is even more complex than the previous two paragraphs suggest. Sargent and Sue-Chan (2001) examined the relationships among diversity, cohesion, and group performance. To do this, they studied group performance within 42 student project groups. What they found was that cohesion moderated the relationship between diversity and group performance. What this means is that for cohesive groups, diversity predicted high group performance because groups could tap into the diverse backgrounds and knowledge that they had. On the other hand, diversity did not predict performance for low cohesive groups; these groups had more trouble overcoming the differences among members. Interestingly, Sargent and Sue-Chan also found that groups that were low in cohesion and not diverse were the lowest performing, indicating the importance of creating at least some cohesion in all groups. Thus, groups that lack cohesion suffer from performance deficits regardless of whether they are diverse.

Personality differences

Most people have worked within a group or team where the personalities of certain members simply clash. As you can imagine, these personality differences are a final factor that reduce group and team cohesion. As a reminder, the five core factors of personality are extraversion, agreeableness, conscientiousness, emotional stability, and openness to experience. The personality of most people can be classified using these five areas.

Van Vianen and De Dreu (2001) examined how these five personality factors affect the way that members of groups and teams interact. First of all, they identified some positive effects from certain personality characteristics that occur in groups and teams. Specifically, social cohesion is stronger when members have high levels of extraversion and emotional stability. In addition, task cohesion is higher when members have higher levels of conscientiousness. Finally, performance is higher when members have high levels of conscientiousness.

However, Van Vianen and De Dreu found far more interesting results when examining how the personalities of different members fit together. Consistent with the literature about diversity, personality similarities among members of the group positively contribute to task cohesion. On the other hand, personality differences negatively contribute to task and social cohesion. What this means is that groups are more cohesive when people have similar personalities, and less cohesive when per-sonalities are more diverse. This is problematic, given that groups and teams are likely to become more diverse in the future.

So, are groups and teams destined to fail?

A quick interpretation of this section would suggest that many groups and teams are destined to fail because they are working on the wrong tasks or are composed of the wrong members and will never be cohesive. However, virtual groups, diverse groups, or teams where members have considerable variability in personality are certainly not doomed. As this chapter has argued, cohesion is an important part – maybe even an essential part – for group and team success. However, we also know that cohesion can be created. Thus, procedures to improve cohesion become even more important in many of the groups functioning in organizations today.

Schimdt and his colleagues (Schmidt, McGuire, Humphrey, Williams, & Grawer, 2005) argue that "building a team that gets along well, functions effectively, and performs well as individuals and as a group is the greatest challenge faced by the team's leaders" (p. 172). They suggest that cohesion is a necessary part of the formula for team success and it should be a constant effort for the team leaders to build cohesion within the team. Although their advice was designed to be for coaches of sports teams, it is certainly relevant because their goal is to a cohesive team that functions within a collaborative environment. Schmidt and his colleagues recommend specific activities to increase social attraction to the group when group members are getting to know one another (i.e., in the forming stage), building trust, and clearly defining goals and roles to avoid destructive conflict. This is what they call environmental engineering, and it requires strong leadership to help the team to succeed.

Engleberg and Wynn (2007, p. 189) also give guidance for improving cohesion. According to Engleberg and Wynn, there are four different methods of improving cohesion, including:

- *Establishing a group identity*: This requires creating group names, traditions, and using team language (we).
- *Emphasizing teamwork*: This is taking responsibility for individual efforts while at the same time taking pride in group work.
- *Recognizing and rewarding contributions*: This requires celebrating group successes and demonstrating appreciation for members' work. Constructive criticism, while important, does not help members to feel appreciated.
- *Respecting group members*: Respecting group members requires showing concern for interpersonal relationships and appreciate background and what members can contribute.

Some final warnings about cohesion

The law of unintended consequences suggests that there are always unexpected outcomes for any action. This is the case with the impact of group cohesion and performance. Although, in general, cohesion will typically benefit groups, there are certainly drawbacks with creating cohesive groups. Recall, for example, the groupthink process discussed in the previous chapter about problem solving and decision making. Cohesion is one of the antecedent conditions for groupthink to occur though certain research studies have been unable to identify this relationship (Flowers, 1977).

There are other concerns with groups that are too cohesive. First, cohesion increases the likelihood for groups to reach consensus, and consensus implies correctness (Stasser & Birchmeier, 2003). This means that cohesive groups may believe they are correct even when they are not. Second, cohesion leads to greater group polarization (Whitney & Smith, 1983). What this means is that cohesive groups may make decisions that are too risky or too conservative. Third, cohesive groups are less likely to assign responsibility to members for group failure (Schlenker & Miller, 1977). What this means is that cohesive groups may ignore the failures of members. Finally, cohesive groups can have low performance norms (Langfred, 1998). What this means is that if a cohesive group has expectations for low performance norm, group members will be more likely to guide the group to poor performance. Clearly, cohesion is not a panacea for solving problems and improving performance. Although cohesion will, in general, be a benefit, it is important to consider the drawbacks that also result from increasing cohesion within groups and teams.

Collaboration

The purpose of a cohesive group or team is so members will work well together – or collaborate better with one another. Collaboration is a process that can develop when groups and teams work together purposively to solve a problem or make a decision, and members take ownership of and responsibility for the work of the group (Liedtka, 1996; Schrage, 1990). According to Straus (2002) collaboration is a powerful experience that is energizing rather than draining. In addition, Straus states that when people are collaborating, they are participating in a process of working together to create meaningful outcomes. What this means is that groups and teams that can successfully collaborate are more likely to motivate members to work towards their common goal and enhance performance as well as satisfaction.

To increase collaboration, it is necessary to a) improve cohesion, b) have groups and teams working on tasks where there is an interdependent goal, c) provide the group with regular feedback, and d) give the group information about its performance. First, as I have argued many different times in this book, the task on which the group or team is working as well as its goal is important in guiding member behavior; the task must be one that requires at least some level of interaction and the goal must be a team goal. Tjosvold (1988) finds that goal interdependence improves both cohesion and collaboration, and as a result it increases member productivity. Creating a collaborative team can be a complicated process because not only the goals of all members need to be aligned, but also their concerns about the team and priorities about the team's focus. These priorities, concerns, and goals need to be integrated and discussed for the team to collaborate well (Nijhuis *et al.*, 2007).

Hackman (1987, p. 337) recommends asking the leaders the following two questions to help to allow their groups or teams to continue to successfully collaborate and possibly reach the elusive concept of synergy.

1. How can opportunities be provided for the group to renegotiate its design and context?
2. What process assistance can be provided to promote positive group synergy?

According to Hackman, carefully considered answers to these questions can help members to better collaborate and improve their process. For example, he suggests that the answers will help leaders and members to correct any process losses. In addition, the answers should help teams to find ways to improve team spirit. It is at this point that members should be able take advantage of some of the structures and interventions in this text and the many other interventions available to teams to help them to succeed.

In addition to task, goals, and context, other predictors of collaboration (Ellis, Porter, & Wolverton, 2008; Henley, 2009; Nijhuis *et al.*, 2007) include having a compelling purpose, having an organizational structure communicated, using positive decision-making processing, setting goals, creating a culture of trust, training team members, working to maintain continuity within membership, providing feedback, and having knowledge about group or team performance. In other words, collaboration can be increased by applying the concepts detailed within this book.

As suggested by Hackman, collaboration can move groups closer to, and possibly allow them to achieve, synergy. One of the main reasons that collaboration improves groups is because collaborative groups share more information, information sharing increases openness, and openness improves overall performance (Mesmer-Magnus & DeChurch, 2009). As a result of increased information sharing, groups and teams can improve their transactive memory systems (see Wegner, 1987, for a detailed description of transactive memory systems). A transactive memory system is when different members of a group take responsibility for different parts of the relevant knowledge base that is required for a successful decision-making or problem-solving situation. In addition, an important part of a transactive memory system is that different members not only have different knowledge, but they also know some details about what each of the members knows These transactive memory systems need to be developed over time, and when a group has an established transactive memory, it can process information much more efficiently and effectively. And, improving transactive memory systems can improve performance viability.

Although written specifically for librarians, Tucker, Billian, and Torrence (2003) go as far as to say "collaborate or die!" Their reasoning for this argument is that very few libraries have the resources available to succeed on their own. They face challenges such as increased costs for online resources and decreasing budgets with which to obtain those costs. In addition, libraries that collaborate have to take on more work to help other libraries – it's in any one library's best interest not to help others while at the same time receiving help. However, a library that fails to help others will not succeed in the long term (see the resource dilemmas section in the next chapter for more on this). Thus, academic libraries and will certainly not succeed and may even be unable to survive unless they willingly collaborate with other libraries.

Of course, Tucker and colleagues recommend improving collaboration with other libraries to improve each library's performance. And, this book makes many of the same points about working in groups and teams. Members are often faced with scarce resources. Members face conflicts between the goals of individual members with those of the team. Generalizing from Tucker and his colleagues, it is clear that collaboration can help cohesive groups and teams to succeed because the members are striving for unity rather than putting member needs in front of the needs of the group or team. Collaboration can also save resources, build relationships, strengthen the climate of the team. It is clear that a collaborative relationship increases its likelihood for success.

As is the case with any group, there are, of course, barriers to goal success that are working to offset any process gains. Lewin (1943) classified the forces that prevent a group from reaching its goal as hindering forces and also classified the forces that aid a group when reaching its goal as helping forces. According to Lewin, groups should conduct a force field analysis. As part of a force field analysis, members try to determine and classify the hindering and helping forces. Then, groups try to determine how to minimize the hindering forces while maximizing the helping forces.

In group collaboration, some of these hindering forces include failing to follow procedures, ignoring advice from within and outside of the group, neglecting to openly discuss opposing viewpoints, remaining indifferent to responsibility, and failing to communicate information (Tjosvold, 1995). As can be seen, most of these processes are simply in direct opposition to the earlier recommendations about improving collaboration. For example, one of the ways to improve collaboration is to share information and one of the barriers to collaboration is to fail to share information. Creating an environment for teamwork and improving structures that support teamwork should, of course, allow groups and teams to collaborate.

This section would be incomplete without a final warning about the potential drawbacks of collaboration. Royer (2004) uses two cases to illustrate what she calls "the seductive appeal of a collective belief" (p. 63). In both cases, large organizations moved forward with poor decisions – in one case, a decision to manufacture contact lenses that had no market, and in another case a decision to manufacture gypsum crystals to help create better paper when the evidence for whether it would actually work was weak. In both cases, groups successfully collaborated about a poor decision. Unfortunately, this is always a risk. According to Royer, both decisions occurred because of a false belief that became contagious within the project teams. Royer recommends 1) being wary of self-selected project teams that champion their own untested innovations, 2) creating a clear set of criteria a priori for evaluating project viability, and 3) appointing an "exit champion," or a person who questions the project and seeks objective evidence about the problems, in the same way that most project teams appoint a project champion.

Interventions to Improve Cohesion and Collaboration

The evidence in this chapter demonstrates that increasing cohesion and collaboration create positive benefits for group and team performance more often than they take away from performance. Thus, many groups and teams will want to improve their cooperation and collaboration. This section of the chapter summarizes the steps involved in three different interventions. The first intervention is a general team building intervention that details the steps that a leader, group, team, or consultant should go through to design and implement a team-building process. The second is an intervention that is specific to improving team goal setting, given the importance of common goals in supporting cohesion and collaboration. The final intervention is de Bono's (1999) *Six thinking hats*, which is a process that integrates creative thinking with coordination and collaboration procedures.

Team building

Voight and Callaghan (2001) provide an outline of a seven step team-building model that can be used to help determine where a team needs support (Table 9.2). Based on a review of the research, they recommend this approach because it can a) create a shared vision, b) improve collaboration, c) increase accountability, d) develop team identity, e) enhance cohesiveness, and f) encourage open and honest communication. They tested the model with Division I women's soccer teams. Coaches and team members rated the team-building intervention as successful. More importantly, both teams had some of their most successful seasons.

Klein and colleagues (2009; see also Salas, Rozell, Mullen, & Driskell, 1999) conducted a meta-analysis to examine the impact of team building interventions, like the one recommended by Voight and Callghan. Their "results are concouraging – they are suggestive of the idea that team building does improve team outcomes" (p. 212). Specifically, they found that the processes involved, such as role clarification, goal setting, improving interpersonal relations, and problem solving, are all moderately predictive of team outcomes, such as satisfaction and performance.

Table 9.2 A Summary of the Steps Involved in Creating a Team-Building Intervention.

Step	Procedure
1.	Conduct a Formal Needs Assessment. Voight and Callaghan recommend starting by asking leaders a question which is conceptually similar to one of the two recommended by Hackman (1987), or "What does the team need to be successful?"
2.	Create a Plan. As a second step, Voight and Callaghan recommend to plan an off-site team building meeting. The team-building session in their program lasted two days.
3.	Gather Team Input. During the meeting, Voight and Callaghan recommend first explaining the purpose of the meeting and going over a detailed agenda. Then, the next step is to gather team input about the needs of the team through a series of brainstorming sessions, or similar creative-thinking techniques and list them for the entire team.
4.	Prioritize Goals. For the fourth step, Voight and Callaghan recommend prioritizing the goals that the team listed in Step 3. After prioritizing the goals, the team then brainstorms ways to assess whether the goals have been met.
5.	Develop Action Plans. The fifth step is to create specific action plans around the goals listed in Step 3 and prioritized in Step 4. Action plans should be first be developed for goals with higher priorities.
6.	Conduct Follow-up Evaluation. As described in Chapter 2, follow-up evaluation is an important part of maintaining change. Voight and Callaghan recommend regular meetings to conduct follow-up to keep the team focused on its goals.
7.	Manage Conflict. Conflict is a common result of group interaction. Because of this, Voight and Callaghan recommend an optional seventh step that teams may need to use if necessary. They recommend calling relevant team members for additional meetings to determine the sources of the conflict and brainstorm ideas for how to resolve it.

Adapted from Voight and Callaghan (2001).

Team goal setting

As can be seen in the previous section, team building is a common tool for improving cohesion, especially among sports teams. Goal setting is one specific team building intervention. In fact, Voight and Callaghan learned that the group with which they were working needed to improve goal setting as part of its team-building intervention.

Unfortunately, general team-building activities are often unsuccessful because all too often the major focus is improving how members feel about one another (Senécal, Loughead, & Bloom, 2008) especially in non-work settings such as working together outside on completing a ropes course, or some other task that is unrelated to work behavior. These non-work activities can certainly be enjoyable for members,

Table 9.3   A Summary of the Steps Involved in Team Goal Setting.

Step	Procedure
1.	Select the team goals.
	a. Have the consultant provide an exhaustive list of possible performance indicators.
	b. Ask team members to individually identify the four most important indicators.
	c. Divide the team into subgroups of five members. Have each subgroup agree on the four most important indicators.
	d. Allow the entire to determine the four most important indicators.
2.	Establish the target for the team goals.
	a. Ask team members to individually identify targets for each of the four indicators.
	b. Divide the team into subgroups of five members. Have each subgroup agree on the targets.
	c. Allow the entire team to determine the four targets.
3.	Provide regular reminders of the performance indicators and their targets. Post them in locations that allow all team members to regularly see them.
4.	Establish a feedback loop. The consultant should provide regular feedback on whether the team is meeting its targets. As necessary, revisit and modify the performance indicators and targets.

Adapted from Senécal, Loughead, and Bloom (2008).

but it is questionable about whether group and team learning outside of the natural setting transfers to the actual setting. In fact, most research demonstrates that the skills learned in many of these outdoor experiential team-building interventions seldom transfer to improved skills back at work (e.g., Wagner & Roland, 1992). For many groups and teams, these so-called team-building interventions instead create lost time and wasted money because they do not build anything that can be used when the team returns to the office.

Senécal and colleagues (2008) designed a team-building intervention that did in fact help to improve cohesion. According to the literature reviewed by Senécal and colleagues, team building activities can in fact be successful at enhancing team cohesion when a) team members work together to set their own goals and targets, b) the team uses an external consultant to help facilitate the team goal setting, evaluation, and feedback process, and c) the team spends a considerable period of time focusing its efforts on enhancing task and social cohesion (see Table 9.3).

Senécal and colleagues conducted a study to test the effectiveness of team goal setting on cohesion in a sports team. They worked with eight high-school basketball teams; four of these teams used team goal setting while the other four served as a control. They assessed team cohesion at the beginning of the season and then tested it again at the end of the season. They found that athletes from the season-long goal-setting intervention had higher levels of cohesion than the athletes in the control condition.

It is likely that this team-building intervention worked because it focused on improving activities that were directly related to team success. In fact, there is considerable research that shows the success of interventions designed to improve goal setting. For example Whitney (1994) has also demonstrated that increase group goal commitment improves cohesiveness. In addition, the meta-analysis described previously by Klein and colleagues (2009) confirms that goal setting is one of the, if not the, most effective components of predicting team outcomes. Thus, the results of goal setting program on improving cohesion and collaboration by Senécal and colleagues should come as no surprise.

de Bono's six thinking hats

Just as cohesion can be improved in groups and teams through the use of structured interventions, so can collaboration. One technique that is designed to improve collaboration is de Bono's method of six thinking hats. In the six thinking hats intervention, members think about a problem differently depending on which hat they have been assigned to wear. According to de Bono, it improves collaboration through a process of parallel thinking, which focuses the energy, efforts, and thought processes of every member in the same direction. Further, one of the thinking processes, which de Bono titles "Blue Hat Thinking," requires members to focus their efforts on coordination of the group or team, thereby improving collaboration.

The six hats model is an intervention that is quite popular in practice. This is because "the six hats model provides a structure to facilitate a cooperative approach to thinking" (Culvenor & Else, 1997, pp. 200–201). In addition, Myers and Levin recommend using the six thinking hats method because the benefit is "the synergistic power of the experience and intellect of many people coming together to share ideas and insights [and] information flows more freely" (Myers & Levin, 2009, p. 7) and it can foster a sense of teamwork and open-mindedness" (p. 5). According to de Bono, the six thinking hats method helps groups because it minimizes arguments, eliminates power differentials, saves time, reduces the impact of strong members, focuses the energy of members in one direction. The steps involved in the six thinking method are detailed in Table 9.4.

Practitioners have detailed the results of success when using six thinking hats. For example, Myers and Levin (2009) find that when medical teams use the six thinking hats they are more likely to solve a clinical case. Peterson and Lunsford (1998) have used the six hats method with student groups in a management program. In a qualitative, informal assessment of their student groups, they find that group members "begin to appreciate the thinking skills of other members, thereby increasing the cohesiveness of the group" (p. 539). They also find that when their student groups

Table 9.4   A Summary of the Steps Involved in de Bono's Six Thinking Hats.

Step	Procedure
1.	Introduce the Process. A facilitator or team member should explain what each of the thinking hats means (for short descriptions of the hats, see also Dymer, 2004).
	a. Blue Hat Thinking focuses the group on control and organizing processes, and when to use the other hats.
	b. White Hat Thinking focuses the group on objective facts and figures that are necessary to solve a problem.
	c. Red Hat Thinking allows group members to provide their emotional views about an issue.
	d. Black Hat Thinking emphasizes caution and care, and is designed to identify the weaknesses of an idea.
	e. Yellow Hat Thinking focuses the group on the positive outcomes of a solution.
	f. Green Hat Thinking focuses the group on generating new ideas.
2.	Discuss the Rules.
	a. The group should always start with the blue hat.
	b. There are no specific guidelines for the sequence of the other hats; the only rule about the sequence of the other hats is that members should decide on the sequence ahead of time so that all member efforts are coordinated.
	c. The group should always end with the blue hat.
3.	Once members understand the hats and know the sequence, they work through a problem by using the approach described by the "hats." According to de Bono, members should be directed to think about the problem in a certain way (as described by a "hat,"), rather than describing what has already happened. Some of de Bono's (p. 5) recommendations for examples to help to remind other member to do this include: "Let's have some white hat thinking here," "I want your red hat on this," or "That is good black hat thinking; now let us switch to some yellow hat thinking."

Adapted from de Bono (1999).

use the six thinking hats method, they are more successful at solving survival simulations often used as teaching demonstrations. Finally, Culvenor and Else (1997) found that groups trained in the six thinking hats method were better at solving occupational safety problems than those who were not trained.

Although de Bono's process recommends using all six hats, others find this is not necessary. For example, Peterson and Lundsford (1998) recommend practicing the technique and then experimenting with alternative methods, such as skipping hats or rearranging the order. They also suggest using real hats so that group members have a tangible reminder of the thinking processes. They summarize by stating that "you can vary the technique as long as the variation focuses the thinking of the group and makes the thinking process more tangible" (p. 546).

FOCUS ON APPLICATION

Improving collaboration with the six thinking hats technique

The practitioner

Karen Barrow, MSOD, RODC is the owner and president of Baybridge Consulting, Inc. an Organization Development firm. She facilitates enterprise-wide change with executive groups in order to shape cultures that allow people to grow and thrive. She holds a Bachelors degree in Psychology from Nazareth College and a Masters degree in Organization Development from American University and is a "Registered Organization Development Consultant" from the Organization Development Institute in Chicago.

The symptom

Senior executives in a mid-size organization were tasked with the opportunity from their Board of Directors to become more innovative in order to remain competitive. This meant one thing to them – they had to change their culture. The engineering staff had an aversion to culture change as many efforts in the past had failed. Not only had changes been resisted, but outright sabotage from staff had been extraordinarily successful. The executives made the mistake of pushing the changes through the organization without buy-in. Without buy-in, staff saw any change from management as a program-of-the-month. Moreover, the executives tended to focus on the negative aspects of what was wrong rather than a more balanced approach; change was critical to improving the organization's overall health. As a result, I was invited in to work with the organization.

Assessing the problem

I spoke with as many staff as possible about the current culture. My objective was to learn what stories they were telling themselves and others so that I could assess values and deeply held assumptions. Most told me they were left out of critical conversations. To a person, they repeatedly stated that they heard from senior managers things were going to change when it came to innovation. While on one hand they understood the rational for this statement, on the other hand they truly did not understand what this would mean to improve their ability to collaborate with one another.

I also interviewed the senior staff. I quickly learned that they saw the engineering staff as unimaginative and uninspired about designing new products. They listed many reasons; not taking advantage of cutting edge resources, no willingness to part with pet projects, a group that had no motivation and as a whole, viewed their staff as unconcerned about the organization.

I shared the results of my interviews with the senior staff late on a Friday and gave them the weekend to give consideration to what they heard. On Monday, I facilitated another meeting with the executives to develop action plans. After much talk and disagreement they finally settled on a tentative approach. I suggested they take an idea for a product they wanted redesigned and give that to the engineers. The suggestion was to really test the senior staff's assumption that the engineers were lackluster and unmotivated. Although reluctant at first, the executives agreed that maybe the story they were telling themselves about the engineers was misguided. I decided on an intervention to improve their ability to collaborate around innovation.

Intervening: The six thinking hats technique

The following month, a group of senior, mid-level, and newly hired engineers gathered in a conference room. Their objective was to redesign one section of a complex machine and turn it into a new product – a project that required much collaboration and creativity. I used a technique that would generate a win-win for the executives and engineers – de Bono's Six Thinking Hats technique.

The model posits that when a new solution is required, one needs to, "deliberately explore the problem from a variety of perspectives" that are not necessarily one's own. The benefits of this creative approach are that it: allows one to say things without risk, highlights creative awareness that there multiple perspectives to be considered, encourages focused thinking, leads to improved communications, and leads to more creative out-of-the-box thinking. This process helped the engineers see that when they are redesigning products they can be innovative in ways that satisfy multiple constituents.

Once the product was redesigned, we again used the six hat technique to judge it, find its positive benefits, test the engineer's intuition and hunches about its viability, and develop new suggestions – each represented by a different color hat. Additionally, observers (white hat) focused on collecting objective facts and reflecting back to the group what it needed to do to move forward. The Six Thinking Hats technique clearly helped the engineers and executives to collaborate and develop the new product.

At the official product launch, I was invited back and learned how successful the new product was to the organization. First, the engineers decided to remain working as a team and became a product testing group where new ideas were filtered through this team to determine viability. Second, although this project was completed a little late, it came in under budget. Finally, the executives reported a notable change in their mindset and in the engineers' attitude and noted that the culture was in fact changing for the better so that everyone could work together more successfully.

Chapter Summary

Cohesion and collaboration are interrelated processes that develop as members work together; cohesion improves collaboration, collaboration improves cohesion. Together, they can improve performance. These interrelated processes typically contribute to group and team success.

Cohesion includes the task and social components that make up the glue that keep members together. It is improved by keeping members connecting, improving rewards, working on interdependent tasks, creating a team identity, and keeping groups small. As a result, cohesion improves other group process, such as communication, cooperation, and performance.

Collaborative groups, like cohesive groups, improve performance. Collaboration results from group work such as having a sense of purpose, communicating, having common goals, knowing about performance. It can help groups with performance through improving processes like decision making and problem solving, building relationships, and improving group memory.

A final warning is that cohesion and collaborative processes come with potential for improvement but also potential for problems. If cohesive groups make a poor decision, they are likely to stick with it longer. If cohesive groups prefer a risky or conservative strategy, they are likely to tolerate too much or too little risk, respectively. If cohesive groups have problems with accountability, they are less likely to assign blame. If cohesive groups have low performance norms, overall performance declines. Finally, collaborative and cohesive groups are likely to fall victim to faulty processes such as Groupthink.

Additional Resources

Harrington-Mackin, D. (1994). *The team building tool kit: Tips, tactics and rules for effective workplace teams.* New York: American Management Association.

Lencioni, P. (2005). Overcoming the five dysfunctions of a team: A field guide. San Francisco, CA: Jossey-Bass.

Locke, E. A., & Latham, G. P. (1990). *A theory of goal setting and task motivation.* Englewood Cliffs, NJ: Prentice-Hall.

Team Exercises

Exercise 9.1   Decide on a group name

One way to build a new team and create some initial cohesion in a new group is to ask the members to come up with a team name.

1. Ask members to sit together.
2. Members should share some personal and professional information about each other – about three to four minutes per member.
3. Using the background information in the second step, each member should individually brainstorm potential team names for two minutes. The team names should in some way represent the membership, task, background, or something similar for the group.
4. The group should report all information from the brainstorming session.
5. The group together should decide on a team name that represents the membership, task, background, or something similar for the group.

Exercise 9.2   Determine the team legacy

A legacy is what someone leaves behind. Usually, the term is used to describe the money or possessions a person leaves behind after death. But, teams also leave legacies, or thoughts, products, and processes, that can help future teams. A tool to get teams to start thinking about the end – what will their team legacy be? This exercise can be conducted at the beginning of a project, in the middle, or towards the end.

1. Members should spend 15 minutes to discuss the team goals.
2. Using the information from Step 1, the team should start to discuss what it intends to "leave behind." This can include:
    a. Outputs, such as project outcomes
    b. Organizational learning
    c. Processes
    d. Ways to work together better
    e. Advice for future teams
    f. Anything else that is relevant
3. The team should work together to present about its intended legacy.

Chapter 10

Reducing Dysfunctional Conflict and Improving Cooperation

A team of medical professionals at a hospital includes, among other specialties, a physician and a medical records specialist. Similar to most hospital systems, they have recently moved to an electronic records system, where medical records can be seen by all those with the necessary access. With this move to electronic forms, many members of the team are struggling to learn this new system and are, as a result, frustrated. When a returning patient shows up, the medical records specialist forwards a form to the physician and asks the physician to complete Page 2, detailing information about a past history with and predictors of diabetes. The physician returns the form to the specialist, knowing that the information is now available on the electronic record. She asks the specialist to complete the form. The specialist sends it back again asking the physician to complete it, leaving the form blank. The physician again sends it back, and now admittedly gets a little frustrated in her note to the specialist, and asks the specialist to complete the form again. The specialist returns the form, again asking for more information. This time, however most of the form is mostly complete, with only two questions highlighted. This is a common case of frustration with new technology, but also a conflict resulting from miscommunication and misperceptions. The physician had certain expectations from the medical records specialist and the medical records specialist had different expectations from the physician.

Thankfully, the event did not end leaving both frustrated; they did in fact resolve the conflict. A few days later the specialist initiated a dialogue about his concerns with the physician, and said that he felt disrespected by the physician because it is not his job to complete the physician's forms. The physician apologized, and said that she thought it was anyone's job on the team, including the one who had access

Group Dynamics and Team Interventions: Understanding and Improving Team Performance,
First Edition. Timothy M. Franz.

to the old information. In this short back and forth dialogue, both learned that they were frustrated by the other's behavior. Further, both learned how to work together better in the future. The conflict started between them because of the lack of information they had and the miscommunication about what each expected. Thankfully, it did not escalate to a point where it was unsolvable; the two involved in the conflict quickly improved their work together by communicating more clearly about their perceptions. I am confident that most of the readers can empathize with both sides in this conflict; in hindsight, it is easy to see the source of most conflicts. However, many conflicts do in fact escalate beyond this one because the group members involved fail to quickly resolve the conflict. This chapter is designed to help groups and teams prevent dysfunctional conflict and instead move groups towards functional behavior.

According to De Dreu and Gelfand (2008), conflict is "a process that begins when an individual or group perceives differences and opposition between itself and another individual or group about interests and resources, beliefs, values, or practices that matter to them" (p. 6). Their definition is purposefully broad so that it encompasses many different conflicts, including conflict between groups or conflict within groups as well as conflict among nations or conflict between two people in a close and intimate relationship. The definition includes conflict that is created from outside a group, such as that resulting from scarce resources, and conflict that is created from within with a group, such as that resulting from value differences. Finally, the definition describes the importance of interpersonal processes in creating and maintaining conflict.

This chapter purposefully follows Chapter 9 because the concepts, although covered in separate chapters, are completely interrelated. Cohesion, discussed at length in Chapter 9, is related to group identification. Of course, group identification improves trust. Trust typically improves cooperation, which decreases conflict (Kramer, Hann, Su, & Wei, 2001). Like cohesion and collaboration, the processes that cause cooperation or conflict are forces that may help and hinder a group or team. They are often seen, respectively, as opposite negative and positive forces affecting member functioning. Specifically, conflict is often perceived as a negative force while cooperation is perceived as a positive one. These forces are also perceived as two ends of a continuum where conflict is at one end of the continuum while cooperation is at the other side. What this means is that groups and teams are either on the conflict side or on the cooperative side. Deutsch (2006), for example, states that a lack of cooperation typically results from a source of conflict.

This is generally the case – to be more successful most groups want to move from dysfunctional conflict to cooperation so that members can cooperate to accomplish task-oriented goals. However, the impact of conflict and cooperation on performance is more nuanced than that simple (and artificial) continuum might suggest. In fact, conflict can be a positive force because it can create energy around sharing diverse information and viewpoints. This is called constructive conflict, and it can foster growth and improves decision making and problems solving. The Nineteenth

Century German philosopher Hegel, for example, claimed that conflict, through the dialectic process, could give rise to the perfect idea (Schiller, 1897). This philosophy focuses groups on using conflict or controversy to produce better ideas and have improved performance (e.g., Schultz-Hardt, Mojzisch, & Vogelgesang, 2008; Tjosvold, 1985). In addition to improving performance, conflict often helps groups and organizations to move towards necessary change (Rubin, Pruitt, & Kim, 1994). This concept of gaining synergy through the process of the dialectic is over 200 years old (recall the philosophy behind the decision making interventions of Dialectical Inquiry and Devil's Advocacy) and there is certainly plenty of recent research that demonstrates the potential benefit of conflict.

On the other side, we have destructive conflict, which includes the typical dysfunctional conflict that escalates and spirals out of control. Destructive conflict causes poor group performance (e.g., Gladstein, 1984; Sherif, 1954). It typically results from a pattern of negative relationship behaviors and increased emotionality that causes defensive behavior, inflexibility, contempt, and an unwillingness to work together. As you can see, the goal is to move groups from destructive to constructive conflict. For example, higher levels of cohesion are associated with constructive conflict, while lower levels of cohesion are associated with destructive conflict (Sullivan & Feltz, 2001).

There are times when sharing some emotions in groups can be effective, but too much of the sharing of emotions can lead to the unproductive and destructive conflict that most groups would appropriately like to avoid (Von Glinow, Shapiro, & Brett, 2004). The T-group, or sensitivity group, movement used this emotionality to improve work group productivity, and many within the T-group movement originally claimed that groups would be more effective if members shared emotion. In a T-group, "the focus is upon giving participants an opportunity to learn more about themselves and their impact on others, through small group session" and the "emphasis is therefore upon the feeling" (Miller, 1970, p. 296). Unfortunately, T-groups often did not work well in organizations in part because groups focused their energy on emotional conflict rather than task conflict, a distinction that is essential to understanding how to best manage conflict. According to Campbell and Dunnette (1968), "to sum up, the assumption that T-group training has positive utility for organizations must rest on shaky ground."

It is important to qualify the scope of this chapter before starting to explain the nature of conflict and cooperation. This chapter examines *intragroup* conflict, or conflict that occurs within a group or team. There is also an entire set of literature that examines *intergroup* conflict, or conflict that occurs across groups, teams, communities, societies, or nations. The main purpose of this book is to develop groups and teams so that they can reach synergy. Most of the literature about improving group and team performance that is devoted towards improvement focuses at the intragroup level. Further, there is considerable information about intergroup conflict that emphasizes large groups, communities, societies, or nations. Therefore, this book purposefully reviewed the literature about intragroup conflict because it is consistent with the purpose of the book, although there is certainly overlap between these two areas (e.g., Dovidio, Saguy, & Shnabel, 2009). Bornstein (2003) for example draws a parallel between the types of communication problems that cause intragroup and intergroup conflict. Dovidio, Saguy, and Shnabel (2009) discuss how intragroup and intergroup conflict are inter-related processes, and solving some intragroup conflict can occur as a result of resolving some intergroup (and intersubgroup) conflicts. For those interested in more information about intergroup conflict, see the additional resources section at the end of the chapter for more information. Further, some areas of conflict do pull important information from the intergroup conflict literature and apply it to the intragroup level.

Learning Goals for Chapter 10

- Be able to define cooperation, define conflict, and assess cooperation and conflict.
- Know the types of conflict – emotional versus task – and the impact of each.
- Know the causes of conflict.
- Know what brings about cooperation.
- Be able to recognize the difference between dysfunctional and functional conflict.
- Know the signs of dysfunctional cooperation.
- Have a list of possibilities that can potentially reduce dysfunctional conflict.
- Have a basic understanding of three intervention tools that are designed to help groups better manage conflict and cooperation.

To help understand the nature of conflict within groups, Cox (2004) developed a 16-item scale that she calls the Intragroup Conflict Scale (Table 10.1). To create the scale, she examined the antecedents of conflict, perceptions about behaviors related to conflict, and perceptions about affective states that result from conflict to create the items on the scale. She then developed a large set of items and tested them by giving the scale to 325 nurses at two sites: a community hospital located in the Mid-Atlantic region and an academic medical center in the Southeast. A factor analysis (a statistical technique that helps researchers to determine which items on a scale are conceptually related) revealed three different concepts in her scale: Opposition processes and negative emotion, trust and freedom of expression, and views about conflict. The items are detailed below.

After testing and developing the sixteen items for the scale, Cox compared the scores of the nurses who completed the measure to work satisfaction and team performance measures. She found that conflict, as measured by the Intragroup Conflict Scale, is negatively related to work satisfaction and team performance. What this means is that as conflict increases, work satisfaction and team performance decrease. This should come as no surprise to anyone who has been involved, either tangentially or directly, in a conflict.

Table 10.1   Assessing Conflict: The Intragroup Conflict Scale.

Instructions: Circle the appropriate number using the following scale: (1) = Strongly disagree, (2) = Disagree, (3) = Neither agree or disagree, (4) Agree, and (5) = Strongly agree.

Opposition Processes and Negative Emotion

1. Undercurrents of hostility make people feel uncomfortable.	1	2	3	4	5
2. Sometimes one party blocks the efforts of another.	1	2	3	4	5
3. Some parties become enraged at the slightest provocation.	1	2	3	4	5
4. Conflict interferes with the achievement of goals.	1	2	3	4	5
5. Negotiations are often shrouded in secrecy.	1	2	3	4	5
6. There is reluctance to express divergent points of view.	1	2	3	4	5

Trust and Freedom of Expression

7. There is mutual trust among parties.	1	2	3	4	5
8. Parties feel free to openly express feelings and opinions.	1	2	3	4	5
9. Parties feel free to express divergent views.	1	2	3	4	5
10. Communications among parties are honest.	1	2	3	4	5
11. Divergent views are valued.	1	2	3	4	5
12. Parties do not trust each other.	1	2	3	4	5
13. There is tolerance for disagreement.	1	2	3	4	5

Views of Conflict

14. Conflict is viewed as unhealthy.	1	2	3	4	5
15. Conflict is viewed as destructive.	1	2	3	4	5
16. Conflict is viewed as constructive.	1	2	3	4	5

Adapted from Cox (2004).

The nature of conflict

In what has become a classic paper about the nature of conflict, Jehn (1994; see also Jehn, 1995) defined two different types of conflict, including task conflict and relationship conflict. She defined task conflict as "disagreements among group members about the tasks being performed" and emotional conflict as "recognized interpersonal incompatibilities among group members" (p. 224). Task conflict focuses on the behaviors necessary for success while relationship conflict creates increased negative emotions. Using this distinction to better understand conflict has become the norm among those who study and understand conflict.

Jehn (1994) has been studying the different categories of conflict on group performance. In a groundbreaking study, she found that relationship conflict "was negatively associated with group performance and satisfaction, while task conflict was positively associated with group performance" (p. 223). In a follow-up study, Jehn (1995) found that the type of task mattered as well. Specifically, group performance is reduced when there is task conflict on a routine task because the conflict gets in the way of the normal functioning of the group. On the other hand, group performance can even be improved when there is task conflict on a novel task because the open discussions created an opportunity for critical evaluation of the group work.

In subsequent work, Jehn (1997) added a third category which she termed process conflict. Process conflict is when conflict occurs about how a task will be accomplished. It is somewhat similar in nature to task conflict. The difference is that task conflict is based on what will occur, while process conflict is based on how it will occur. For example, imagine a strategic planning group that is trying to determine whether to devote more resources to marketing or operations. A conflict that occurs about whether the group should use majority rules or consensus as a decision rule to make its decision about the strategy is process conflict. On the other hand, a conflict that occurs about whether the operations strategy or the marketing strategy is more important to the organization's success is task conflict. Finally, to complete the example, a conflict that occurs about the personal style and actions among two or more members is an example of relationship conflict. Process conflict has little to no impact in groups when they are early in their development and establishing their norms (whether formally or informally) but potentially may reduce performance when groups are subsequently trying to accomplish task work (Jehn & Mannix, 2001).

The importance of the impact of the different types of conflict on groups and teams is demonstrated in a meta-analysis which was conducted by De Dreu and Weingart (2003). They examined the impact of task and relationship conflict on team performance in 28 different studies. Surprisingly, the meta-analysis revealed that both task and relationship conflict can reduce team performance. However, the meta-analysis revealed findings that are generally consistent with the ideas described by Jehn and others (e.g., Jehn, Greer, Levine, & Szulanski, 2008). Specifically, relationship conflict has a larger impact on creating dysfunction and reducing performance than do task and process conflict. Thus, it seems that whether process and task conflict are actually beneficial to groups depends on the specific nature of the situation. Moderate amounts of process and task conflict may be beneficial (Martínez-Moreno, González-Navarro, Zornoza, & Ripoll, 2009). Relationship conflict and likely too much task conflict or task conflict based on routine tasks is definitely dysfunctional (Jehn, 1995), reduces trust (Rispens, Greer, & Jehn, 2007), creates dissatisfaction with and intentions to leave (Medina, Munduate, Dorado, Martínez, & Guerra, 2005), and reduces performance (Langfred, 2007; Martínez-Moreno, González-Navarro, Zornoza, & Ripoll, 2009).

Causes of Dysfunctional Conflict

Although there are many causes of conflict, four common causes are discussed here. These include a) dilemmas around individual versus group goals and resources, b) members who fail to perform their work within a team environment, c) miscommunication, misinformation, and misperception, and d) working with people who have different styles and values. Each of these areas creates friction in a group that can lead to process losses and prevent the group from reaching its true potential.

Social/resource dilemmas

Dawes (1980) explained that social dilemmas result when a person's self interest is potentially higher than the payoff for cooperative behavior. What this means is that self interests and group interests are in conflict. Imagine, for example, a poorly designed team reward system. Members are given individual rewards at the end of each year for their contributions to the organization. Further, they are not rewarded for cooperative behavior within the team, and there are no team rewards (recall from earlier in the text that these reward systems are quite common). Which behavior – team or individual – is each member going to emphasize? In this case, it is quite likely that members will focus more on individual behaviors rather than cooperative, team-based behaviors.

Dawes provides three different examples of social dilemmas – overpopulation, pollution, and resource depletion. The first example is the problem of overpopulation as a dilemma. In many communities it is better to have more children. This is because more children can help to support the family. However, the more children there are, the greater the drain on the overall resources in that community. The second example is pollution. It is easier for people (as well as organizations) to dump unwanted materials; it is less costly and takes less time. However, the more all people dump, the more the community as a whole suffers from the resources that it requires to deal with all of that pollution. The final example is resource depletion. For example, it is easier for me to drive my car and use a relatively small amount of gas rather than take my bike to the pharmacy. However, if all members of a society as a whole use gas to drive their cars on short trips, the gas is depleted at a higher rate and no fuel is saved for future generations. As you can see, social dilemmas are common in everyday behavior. Three common categories of dilemmas exist: the prisoner's dilemma, the commons dilemma (often called the tragedy of the commons), and the public goods dilemma.

One specific type of social dilemma, and the one that has received the greatest amount of research, is the prisoner's dilemma game. The prisoner's dilemma is the classic example of a mixed-motive dilemma, or a situation in which the motivation for individual work and group work are in conflict (like the reward example described previously). Dawes (1980, p. 182) succinctly describes the dilemma as follows.

> The dilemma is derived from an anecdote concerning two prisoners who have jointly committed a felony and who have been apprehended by a District Attorney who cannot prove their guilt. The District Attorney holds them incommunicado and offers each the chance to confess. If one confesses and the other doesn't, the one who confesses will go free while the other will receive a maximum sentence. If both confess they will both receive a moderate sentence, while if neither confesses both will receive a minimum sentence. In this situation, confession is a dominant strategy (If the other confesses, confession leads to a moderate sentence rather than to a maximum one; if the other doesn't, it leads to freedom rather than to a minimum sentence). But

confession leads to a deficient equilibrium, because dual confession results in moderate sentences, whereas a minimum sentence could be achieved by neither confessing. Hence, the dilemma.

This is the classic example of a mixed-motive dilemma, and many television programs and movies apply this concept, whether knowingly or unknowingly, when they portray the "good guys" trying to convince separate "bad guys" to confess. In mixed-motive dilemmas, like the prisoner's dilemma, the greater and more realistic the risk, the stronger the dilemma for those involved. Thus, even though much of the research has been conducted using simulations, real-world dilemmas are likely to even create more difficult conflicts to resolve.

The second type of mixed-motive dilemma is the commons dilemma (Dawes, 1980; van Dijk, Wit, Wilke, & de Kwaadsteniet, 2010), also called the tragedy of the commons, and is based on the consumption of resources. The commons dilemma is different than a prisoner's dilemma because it is based on the depletion of resources that make up a common good. The classic example of the commons dilemma is based on villages that make their living through herding. In many of these villages, there is a common area for grazing that many different herders may use. The mixed-motive results from what is best for the individual herder versus what is best for the community of herders. It is in each herder's best personal interest to let his or her herd spend as much time as possible grazing in the commons because the herd will get bigger and stronger. However if every herder allows the herd to graze like this, the commons will become overgrazed, and all herders will suffer as a result. The common good has been depleted because the herders are focused on individual self-interest rather than what is good for the village as a whole.

The final category of mixed-motive dilemmas is the public goods dilemma (Dawes, 1980; van Dijk, Wit, Wilke, & de Kwaadsteniet, 2010). The public goods dilemma differs from commons dilemma because it results from a decision about contributions to a public good rather than depleting a common resource. A common example of a public goods dilemma is the decision for any person to personally contribute to a local Public Television station. These stations can only survive if those who watch also contribute money. It is in each person's self interest to keep her or his money, but it is in the best interest of the community to fund Public Television programming so that the community resource can continue to operate. Again, the mixed-motive is created based on the difference between the individual self-interest, in this case maintaining wealth, versus the group's interest, in this case spending individual wealth.

The nature of conflict in these mixed-motive results from the dilemma creating competition between the individual and the other or the group, whether the competition results from competition between two prisoners or competition about whether to fund a community program. Competition is increased when communication is impaired, when those involved in the conflict lack a helpful attitude, with tasks that unable to easily be divided up into subunits, after repeated occasions of disagreement, when there has been continual rejection of ideas, when group members put forth efforts to enhance power and superiority rather than to work together, and finally when the parties involved feel that one side must win (Deutsch, 2000). These processes that improve competition can deepen and escalate a conflict.

Decreased trust in mixed-motive situations is also related to increased competition and conflict in teams (e.g., Bornstein, 2003). Negative or competitive behaviors directly decrease trust (Cook, Hardin, & Levi, 2005). And, the lack of trust reduces group cooperation (Kramer, 2010). Dilemmas that are caused by differences in perceptions about information reduce trust and create conflict. As the boundaries within and between groups get more restrictive and allow less information to flow, trust decreases and conflict increases even further (Zucker, Darby, Brewer, & Peng, 1996).

In addition, there are three factors of the organizational structure and group environment that can cause increased conflict, including incompatible goals, independent tasks, win-lose rewards, individual aspirations (Tjsosvold, 1986). First, incompatible goals should be avoided (clearly a theme in this book). Incompatible goals are caused when the group goals and individual goals are not in alignment. Second independent tasks should also be avoided. Tasks that can be completed individually are not group tasks. Third, win-lose rewards should be avoided. These are reward systems that pit one group member against another so that when one group member receives a reward, the others cannot. Finally, individual aspirations should also be avoided. Groups and teams work in an environment that is "we-oriented" (Rothwell, 2010) rather than one that is I-oriented.

Finally, threats can further escalate conflict. A classic study that tested the impact of threat in mixed-motive situations is the Acme-Bolt Trucking simulation (Deutsch, 1969). In the simulation, two participants carried loads from their trucking firm (Acme Trucking and Bolt Trucking) to their destination. To carry the loads, they had to either a) share a one-lane road or b) use a much longer alternate route. The goal in the game was for the participants to maximize their earnings, which they could do best by sharing the one lane road. When both participants had to share the road, they figured out ways to do so. However, in certain conditions, some of the participants were able to control a gate that prevented the other from using the one-lane road. Whenever there was a conflict about who would get to use the one-lane road, the participant who controlled the gate could threaten to close it and by doing so enhanced her or his earnings. However, these threats to close the gates also increased subsequent conflict. Finally, when both participants could each control the gates, overall threats increased, conflict increased, and neither participant was able to maximize earnings. According to Deutsch "the joint outcomes were best in the no-gate and worst in the twogate condition" (p. 1084). As can be seen through this classic simulation, threats increase competition and conflict and decrease performance.

Social loafing

Social loafing (Latané, Williams, & Harkins, 2006; Williams, Harkins, & Latané, 1981) is a second group process that can cause or escalate conflict. Social loafing is the "reduction in motivation and effort that occurs when individuals work together at a group task" (Stangor, 2004, p. 221). Virtually anyone who has worked in multiple groups can cite at least one example of social loafing by one or more group members. Among student groups at a minimum and likely among most work groups as well, social loafing is "highly prevalent" and possibly experienced by almost all people at one point (Jassawalla, Sashittal, & Malshe, 2009, p. 49). Social loafing is problematic because it causes reduced group output and performance because all members are not working at their potential. In addition, social loafing can cause reduced satisfaction with the process of participating in group work because at least some members feel that others are taking advantage of them.

There are many factors that contribute to social loafing, including structural ones such as working in large groups and cognitive ones such as free riding. For example, larger groups with more members may have more loafing than those with fewer members because some members feel more dispensable and therefore are less motivated (Kerr & Bruun, 1981). In addition, free riding suggests that members may feel de-motivated because they think that others may pick up the slack (Kerr & Bruun, 1983). As can be seen, the explanations regularly describe the underlying reasons why members lose motivation.

Social loafing creates conflict (Bornstein, 1992; Colman & Bexton, 1975) because the reduced effort creates problems with perceived fairness about the procedures (procedural justice) and then can increase relationship conflict (Zoghbi-Manrique-de-Lara, 2009), the type of conflict that is most associated with dysfunction group process. In addition, loafing results in negative reactions towards others on the team (Mulvey & Klein, 1998) because members who do not loaf feel that they have been taken advantage of. Bornstein (1992) even states that free riding is a paramount consideration in intergroup conflicts, especially if the loafing is tolerated by team leaders or managers.

Little research has been conducted about team leaders, supervisors, and managers who tolerate social loafing on their team and how that might even further exacerbate a conflict, although some logical claims can be made. Social loafing is one version of poor performance because members who loaf are not pulling their weight nor completing their tasks. We do know that supervisors who tolerate poor performance create even more conflict because poor performance causes tension as managers are generally reluctant to give negative performance feedback (Larson, 1989). The lack of feedback will continue the cycle of tension, conflict, and process losses. Although this is a concern that I have heard from managers and practitioners, it is clearly an area that deserves specific research attention.

Communication problems: Miscommunication, misinformation, and misperception

A third area that causes conflict is communication problems. Communication problems also cause conflict, and may even be the largest single cause of conflict. These communication problems can result from miscommunication, misinformation, and misperception. All three are related processes that cause the message that is sent to be different from the message that is received. Remember, conflict is caused by perceived differences, and communication breakdowns can be a major source of these perceived differences.

Miscommunication occurs when there are errors due to noise within a communication network. A good example of this is when I tell someone that I will be done with a project on Tuesday. Unbeknownst to me, they expect to receive it on Tuesday morning. I expect to deliver by Tuesday at 11:59 pm. The conflict occurs because the proper information about the time of delivery on that day was miscommunicated.

Misinformation is when people have the wrong information about a topic. A good example of this is a conflict about the safety of different cars when deciding which of two cars to buy. I might have heard that one type of car is safe in a rollover crash while the other person helping me to make the decision might have heard that the car is more dangerous in a two car collision. Neither of us has the actual information about overall safety, so the conflict is occurring based on a lack of information or even incorrect information. This conflict occurs because people have different information sources.

Finally, misperception, also known as pseudo-conflict (Beebe & Masterson, 2006), occurs because of different understandings or misinterpretations. Regardless of whether the perception is correct, misperception causes one member to see another member as untrustworthy, dishonest, unfriendly, selfish, and negative. A good example of this is I might ask about our dinner plans and another person in my family might assume that means that I expect the person to make the decision. The conflict in this final case occurs because both of us have different perceptions about the meaning of the question. All result from communication errors.

These three types of communication problems can be worsened because of the situation. Specifically, environmental uncertainty exacerbates communication problems and limits the amount of cooperation from those in conflict (van Dijk, Wit, Wilke, & de Kwaadsteniet, 2010). This means that when people are unsure about the situation, which is often the case during conflict, they are even more likely to be susceptible to the communication errors that cause conflict.

Personality and individual differences

Anyone who has heard about a group that has self destructed because members cannot get along certainly knows the impact of personality and other individual differences on conflict. There are many different speculations about how personality differences impact conflict, but the most well-known concept, and the one that has received the most attention, comes from Blake and Mouton (1964) and was then further defined and explained by Rubin, Pruitt, and Kim (1994). Blake and Mouton defined two different needs that group members might have, including concern for people versus concern for other. According to Blake and Mouton, the different needs cause friction and conflict. Rubin, Pruitt, and Kim followed up to later suggest a similar concept; they term it the party's aspirations versus the other's aspirations. As you can see, in both cases, there is a contrast between what one person wants and what another wants. If group members are concerned with the aspirations or needs of the other, then those people tend to want to work together and will likely have less conflict. On the other hand, if those involved in a group are more concerned with their needs and aspirations than those of the others involved, there is likely to be more conflict.

There are other personal behaviors that can increase conflict as well. According to Rubin, Pruitt, and Kim (1994), the behaviors fall into the category of contentious tactics. Contentious tactics are used to succeed at the expense of another. Some of these contentious tactics include ingratiation, gamesmanship, encouraging guilt trips, using forceful persuasive arguments, and making irrevocable commitments. Ingratiation is when one member tries to earn the favor of a second member. This can lower resistance to the conflict within the second member, but can increase conflict when the second member realizes what is happening. Gamesmanship is a process of feather ruffling that is designed to get another upset during a conflict. Like ingratiation, it works to lower resistance to conflict when another is unaware, and can increase conflict when that person becomes aware. Encouraging guilt trips occurs when a group member induces a guilt trip in another when he or she blames the entire problem on the other or tries to drag up past poor behavior. Forceful persuasive arguments are used to convince another person. However, persuasive arguments can be repeated too often, causing increased conflict. Finally, the strongest of the contentious tactics is making irrevocable commitments, and is designed to force the other to do something. They are similar to threats in that they are essentially if-then statements (e.g., if you don't mow the lawn then you will be grounded for a month!) and do not allow the group member who makes the irrevocable commitment to withdraw it. Using any or all of these contentions tactics can make a conflict even worse, and thus they should be avoided.

Personality differences are one source of conflict, but value differences also increase group conflict. In addition to increasing conflict, value differences decrease member satisfaction and member commitment to a team because these differences generally cause an increase in relationship rather than task conflict (Jehn, Northcraft, & Neale, 1999). In fact, value differences create far more conflict than do demographic differences (Hobman & Bordia, 2006), even though demographically diverse teams can, in fact, experience considerable conflict (King, Hebl, & Beal, 2009). This is because the type of diversity affects the nature of the conflict. If the differences in demographically diverse are based on competencies and skills, the conflict tends to be based on function rather then about personal relationships, and the conflict can be constructive and productive for the group. On the other hand, if the differences in demographically diverse teams are based on values, the conflict tends to be based on relationships and the increased conflict can be destructive for the group (see also Vodosek, 2007).

Reducing Dysfunctional Conflict and Building Cooperation

Conflict researchers and theorists examine the causes of conflict, but also discuss the ways to reduce dysfunctional conflict and make groups functional. Mixed motive dilemmas are improved through encouraging cooperative behavior. Social loafing is improved through structural and attitudinal changes in groups. Communication errors can be minimized through increased positive and structured communication processes. Finally, differences among personalities can be minimized through structured environments and training about the nature of differences and how they impact the group. Each of these is discussed in detail in the subsections below.

Improving cooperative behavior with limited resources

Deutsch is one of the foremost experts on cooperation and competition. According to Deutsch (2006), the following set of behaviors can help to minimize the negative impacts of destructive conflict.

- Reframe by focusing on it as a mutual problem resolved through cooperative efforts.
- Set norms for cooperation and respectful behavior.
- Search for common ground.
- Refrain from making personal attacks.
- Empathy; take other's perspective.
- Build on the ideas of others.
- Be responsive to other's legitimate needs.
- Empower one another.
- Remain honest, caring, and just.

According to Deutsch, the values underlying these behaviors that make them successful include reciprocity, equality and justice, a shared sense of community, nonviolence, and fallibility. Deutsch warns, however, that these behaviors cannot simply serve as a cookbook to practitioners – meaning that even well-intentioned practitioners who work to improve the practice of the behaviors may not be able to resolve every conflict. Instead, he implies that they are good guidelines for practitioners to follow when trying to minimize or resolve dysfunctional conflict.

In addition to the recommendations of Deutsch, emphasizing commonalities increases cooperation while emphasizing differences increases conflict (Van de Vliert & Janssen, 2001). The Robber's cave study is a classic example of the importance of commonalities (Sherif, 1954; Sherif & Sherif, 1953). In the Robber's Cave study, Sherif and colleagues studied conflict and cooperation in children in a summer camp. The group members had no established relationships prior to camp. Sherif then allowed the children to form their own friendships for three days. After the three days, they were randomly organized into groups; half of the children were put on the red team, while the other half were put on the blue team, thus splitting apart some of the early friendships that these children formed.

After the children were put into their groups, they were given functional relationships with games and camp duties that encouraged them to form group behaviors. Further, the groups were physically separated from one another. As you might imagine, the groups developed strong within-group loyalty and solidarity. They created their own group names (the Rattlers and the Eagles) and each group showed preference for different songs and activities. After a period of time working in each group, members started to denigrate those within the other group, including direct name calling and creating derogatory posters. The children in each group raided the other camp. There was, of course, a reversal of most of the (now) cross-group friendships that many children formed in the first three days. Finally, the conflict culminated with a fight at a joint lunch.

During this time, Sherif's graduate students worked as camp counselors and Sherif himself worked as the camp caretaker. They took the role of participant observers, and recorded their notes after boys went to sleep. Based on these reports, there was clearly considerable conflict that was caused by the competitive group environment.

The last phase of the study included attempts to reduce the conflict. To accomplish this, the counselors mixed the groups at the dining hall, organized joint birthday parties, included both groups at campfires, had individual rather than group competitions such as track meets, engaged in camp duties jointly, and organized a camp-wide softball game against another camp. These joint, cooperative activities where the groups had contact reduced some of the friction.

Although these cooperative activities requiring intergroup conflict reduced conflict, it was the final two tasks in the last phase the eliminated the conflict. In these tasks, Sherif established what he called a superordinate goal. A superordinate goal is a goal that brings the groups that are in conflict together to work towards a goal that cannot be accomplished by either group working alone. In one of these, the groups had to work together to pull a truck out of a rut that was purportedly carrying food for the camp. Working together on these superordinate goals effectively reduced the conflict. As a result of this and many other studies, Sherif and others recommend that "cooperation is developed by assigning people a common task, informing them that their role is to exchange information and ideas as they work on the task, rewarding them to the extent that the group successfully accomplishes its task" (Tjosvold, 1986, p. 25).

Some final ways to improve cooperation and reduce conflict include encouraging altruism, creating strong norms for cooperation, and working towards tit-for-tat behavior that is designed to reduce friction. These may work to reduce conflict because they are based on the norm of group reciprocity – if one member works to reduce conflict than the other member will likely do so as well (Kramer, 2010). Finally, group members can recognize that there are different ways to distribute limited resources, including need, equity, and equality (Deutsch, 1975). Need is distributing resources based on who needs it most. Equity is distributing resources based on who has put in the most effort. Finally, equality is distributing resources the exact same for all. Equality is often the norm because it is simple, effective, fair, and justifiable (van Dijk, Wit, Wilke, & de Kwaadsteniet, 2010), but moving to other ways may also help groups resolve conflict. Which distribution method is appropriate depends on the norms of the group and the situation, and unfortunately there are times that different members have different expectations about distribution rules. Thus, the rules should be explicit rather than implicit to help to avoid future conflict.

Reducing social loafing and increasing individual accountability to the group

Shepperd (1993) and Karau and Williams (1993) recommend ways to reduce social loafing. According to Shepperd, there are three broad categories of solutions. These correspond to the three causes of social loafing, including: (a) providing incentives for contributing, (b) making contributions indispensable, and (c) decreasing the cost of contributing. Karau & Williams (1993) give seven specific suggestions. The first is to providing individuals with feedback about their own performance. Second, provide members with feedback about the performance of their work group. Third, monitor individual performance or making such performance identifiable. Fourth, make sure to assign meaningful tasks. Fifth, make tasks unique such that individuals feel more responsibility for their work. Sixth, enhance the cohesiveness of work groups (using the techniques described in Chapter 9). Finally, work to make individuals feel that their contributions to the task are necessary.

Team leaders and managers can also help to reduce social loafing. First, rewards that include team and individual components lead to greater accountability and reduce loafing (Pearsall, Christian, & Ellis, 2010). Second, making sure to identify individual performance while still recognizing the importance of group performance will also help to reduce loafing (Karau & Williams, 2001). Third, team leaders and managers can ask for specific concessions – or actions – from those who are loafing that are designed to get them to perform equal to that of the other members (Tata, 2002). Finally, team leaders and managers can work to make sure that members feel that they are working on an important task, their rewards are meaningful to those involved, and less apprehensive about being evaluated as part of the group (Karau & Williams, 2001).

Minimizing Misperceptions and Improving Communication

Resolving conflict often requires increasing the level of communication. For example, in the real-life example at the beginning of the chapter, the physician and the medical records specialist resolved their conflict through dialogue. Lencioni (2005) says that communication and conflict are intertwined. Samuelson and Watrious-Rodriguez (2010) claim that "it is beyond empirical doubt that face-to-face group discussion increases cooperation" (p. 13). Tenbrunsel and Northcraft (2010) state that communication improves cooperation because it moves members to a group frame and when group members enter this group frame they are more likely to emphasize the collective rather than the individual, thus reducing conflict. Rubin, Pruitt, and Kim (1994) recommend contact and communication as part of the tools to resolve conflict. Tjosvold (1995) states that the exchange of information, discussion, and structured procedures that help communication processes improve cooperation. Moye and Langfred (2004) find that information sharing reduces task and relationship conflict. Dawes (1980) claims that increased communication improves cooperation by 72%. These few statements are only a very small sample of all of those who claim that open communication improves cooperation and reduces competition and conflict.

Scholtes, Joiner, and Streibel (2003) recommend six specific process-oriented tactics to improve the communication process to improve communication and reduce subsequent conflict. First, select neutral territory where one member does not feel more or less power. Second, keep the setting informal so that there can be open and frank discussion about the issues. Third, make sure that all appropriate people are present so that decisions can be made. Fourth, set ground rules for the conflict resolution process and stick to those rules. Fifth, make sure to manage the time so that there is slight time pressure to move the discussion along while at the same time there is enough time to get to resolution. Finally, use active listening processes.

Similarly, Runde, and Flanagan (2008) recommend five other communication and interpersonal tactics to create what they call a conflict competent team. First, work with members to create attitudes that conflict should be focused on the task to help groups come up with better ideas. Second, build trust so that members can risk being open and honest. Third, encourage a psychologically safe culture where members are open to risk taking. Fourth, build relationship skills so that members are able to recognize other member's needs and respond appropriately. Fifth, encourage a collaborative spirit. Groups and teams that use procedural and interpersonal tactics are more likely to be successful when working through conflict.

As can be seen in these two lists of tactics, there is little new information that has not been discussed in other areas of the book. For example, encouraging active listening, identifying effective team attitudes, building trust, creating the team culture, improving relationship skills, and encouraging collaboration were each reviewed in previous chapters. What this demonstrates is the inter-relationships among the concepts involved in improving group performance, whether it occurs through improving decision making or reducing conflict. As is the case with all of the behavioral sciences, any one intervention is likely to have multiple impacts that affect people in many different ways.

Understanding and managing different personalities

Thomas and Kilmann (Kilmann & Thomas, 1975, 1977; Thomas & Kilmann, 1978) used the information from Blake and Mouton's Managerial Grid (1964) as well as the theories about conflict from Rubin, Pruitt, and Kim (1994) to define the relationships

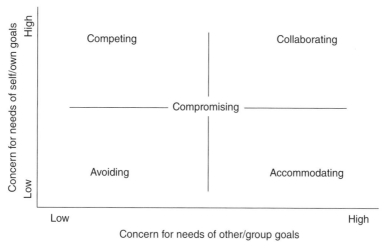

Figure 10.1   The Thomas-Kilmann Conflict Styles Grid.

among specific conflict styles (see Figure 10.1). They examined the concern for group goals (on the x-axis on the figure) and compared that for the concern for one's own goals (on the y-axis of the figure). Examining the figure, you can see that five different outcome categories occur.

The category of avoidance occurs when there is a low concern for one's own goal and a low concern for the group goal. As an example, imagine that both my wife and I decide to get a babysitter and go out and see a movie. As we talk, I learn that she would like to see the most recent romantic drama while I would like to see the most recent action movie. With avoidance, I am not concerned with seeing the movie myself and am not worried about whether my wife sees the movie. I don't call the sitter, we stay home, and do not talk about the situation. Avoidance can be a good short-term strategy when the outcome is of little importance. However, an undercurrent of dissatisfaction will occur if those avoiding the conflict continue to avoid it or the issues is one of high importance.

A second combination in Figure 10.1 is accommodation. In this case, there is high concern for the group goal while there is low concern for one's own goal. To continue the movie example, in this case I accommodate my wife and go see the romantic drama that she wants to see. Like avoidance, accommodation can be a good short-term strategy. It also works well if the parties involved are willing to accommodate one another in different situations (we see the action movie next week). However, dissatisfaction builds if one person continually accommodates and the other does not because one person will always lose.

A third combination is competition, which is when a person has high concern for one's own goal while there is low concern for the group goal. In the movie example, this is when I try to force my wife to see the action movie. Competition can create a power struggle, and like accommodation, it is a win-lose situation. If I win, that means my wife will lose.

A fourth combination is compromise. In compromise, both parties get something but at the same time both parties give up something. In the movie example, my wife and I might decide to see a science fiction movie instead. The movie may have some love interests, but not as strong as a romantic drama would. The movie may have some action, but not as much as the new action movie would. We both have gotten something while at the same time lost something. Thomas and Kilmann consider compromise a less then preferred situation.

The final combination is collaboration. In a collaborative situation, we meet our individual goals while still meeting the group goals. In the movie example, my wife and I might pick a third movie that both of us really wanted to see that we both forgot about. Through discussion, people are able to find a collaborative, win-win solution. This is the most preferred scenario because there are no losers in the conflict.

With the conflict grid, Thomas and Kilmann imply that the best solution is a collaborative or win-win one and that compromising is not succeeding. This is the case when there are unlimited resources or when there truly is a win-win solution. For example, if there is only one orange remaining in the house and I would like to make candied orange rinds and my wife would like fresh-squeezed orange juice, we can get to a collaborative agreement – I take the rind and she gets the juice. However, there are plenty of times that there is not a simple win-win solution, if there is one at all. Take the same situation; if there is only one orange remaining in the house but my wife and I both would like fresh-squeezed orange juice, there is not an immediate win-win solution unless one of us runs to the grocery store.

The conflict style of management is especially important because it affects the resultant level of conflict within that manager's team. DeChurch, Hamilton, and Haas (2007) examined the impact of conflict styles on relationship and task conflict in a laboratory study. They found that managers who used avoiding or competing conflict styles created higher perceptions of relationship conflict within their group. In addition, they found that competing conflict styles created higher perceptions of task-related conflict within the group. De Church and colleagues conclude by stating that collaborating, compromising, and accommodating styles create the lowest levels of relationship and task conflict.

The Thomas and Kilmann conflict style grid is quite popular among practitioners. One reason for this is that they have designed a measure that helps people understand their conflict styles. Two sample items from the Thomas and Kilmann measure of conflict style include: "I give up some points in exchange for others" and "I am more concerned with goals I believe to be important than with how others feel about things." As you can see, this measure attempts to measure the typical conflict style of a person whether it is a compromising style, as measured by the first sample item, or a competing style, as measured by the second sample item.

Thomas and Kilmann are not alone at recommending collaborative solutions. Desivilya and Yagil (2005), for example, find that collaborating reduces relationship conflict and improves group performance. Surprisingly, they also find that compromise similarly reduces relationship conflict and improves group performance. The reason for this is because in both situations there is no specific pattern of losses to one member that continues over time. In collaboration, both parties win, while in compromise, neither fully loses. The main idea with the work about Thomas and Kilmann conflict styles is that knowing the styles and potential outcomes can help those involved in a conflict to successfully move it from destructive to constructive.

Three final ways to improve collaborative efforts and reduce conflict include emphasizing the importance of justice, improving identification, and building bonds among team members. First, focusing the team on the importance of procedures and procedural justice minimizes the perceptions of value differences, improves efforts towards collaboration, and reduces conflicts (Tyler & Blader, 2003). Second, improving team identification moderates the impact of value differences on relationship conflict (Hobman & Bordia, 2005). Finally, improving the relationships and bonds among team members reduces the impact of task and relationship conflict (Rispens, Greer, & Jehn, 2007) when it does in fact occur.

Three Interventions to Reduce Conflict and Improve Cooperation

Reducing destructive conflict and stimulating constructive conflict may help groups, as long as if trust can be maintained (Simons & Peterson, 2000). There are many different conflict resolution processes designed to accomplish this. Tekleab, Quigley, and Tesluk (2009) find that extended work on conflict management can reduce conflict, improve cooperation, increase cohesion, and improve performance. Ross and Ward (1995) find that dispute resolution processes, among other things, remove the organizational barriers that restrict the flow of information that is caused by having too many people between those in conflict, and working through organizational politics.

Three different conflict resolution processes follow. The first is developing a conflict management procedure. The second is adopting a team design mentality. The final one is mediation and arbitration.

Developing a conflict management procedure

The Pfeiffer Book of Successful Team-Building Tools (Biech, 2001) is a compendium of theory-based interventions that practitioners use to improve team functioning. According to Biech, one of the characteristics of a successful team is managing conflict. Thus, one section of the book is devoted to interventions that are designed to improve conflict. As this chapter has argued, she states that conflict is an essential team process, but at times it must be managed. In the book, Porter (2001) provides the steps for one of the ways to develop procedures ahead of time to avoid and/or manage dysfunctional conflict (Table 10.2). The steps are detailed below.

There is plenty of advice about deciding a priori about how to deal with conflict when it does arise and how that improves conflict management within groups and teams. For example, a considerable portion of Runde and Flanagan's (2008) book, previously discussed, is devoted towards setting up procedures ahead of time so that

Table 10.2   A Summary of the Steps Involved in Developing a Conflict Management Procedure.

Step	Procedure
1.	The facilitator distributes copies of conflict management suggestions, including: a. Do not ignore something that is bothering you. b. Talk directly to the other group member involved in the conflict. c. Ask the human resources professional in your organization for advice on how to work with the other person. d. Get approval for any changes in work responsibilities. e. If someone approaches you with an issue, be ready and willing to work on it. f. If a person complains to you about another, encourage that person to talk directly with the other. g. If you have tried to work out the problem and have not succeeded, reach out for help from professionals.
2.	The facilitator reviews the conflict management suggestions.
3.	The team members assemble into subgroups where they create a draft set of conflict management guidelines. The information is recorded on a flipchart.
4.	The facilitator reconvenes the teams and asks each subgroup to present their ideas.
5.	The facilitator reviews the posted information and assists the entire team in achieving consensus about a set of guidelines. The final set can take one subgroup's set, the other subgroup's set, or use some combination of them.
6.	When the team members have reached consensus, they work together to record the final list of ideas on a flipchart.
7.	Before adjourning, the facilitator asks the team the following questions: a. What did you learn about managing conflict? b. What did you learn about developing procedures for the team to use: c. How can you ensure that the guidelines will be used? d. How will you ensure that the team will evaluate the guidelines you developed? e. What obstacles might get in the way of using the guidelines you developed?

Adapted from Porter (2001).

conflict can be avoided or managed. Further, Rubin, Pruitt, and Kim (1994) state that strong norms "regarding certain goals, rules of conduct, role definitions, procedures for decision making, and authority and status systems" (p. 21) discourage conflict from occurring. Thus, it is no surprise that Porter recommends that teams develop a specific and explicit plan for conflict management.

Adopting a team design mentality

Napier and Gershenfeld (1999) recommend using what they term a design mentality to resolve conflict (Table 10.3). A design mentality, according to Napier and

Table 10.3   A Summary of the Steps Involved in Adopting a Team Design Mentality.

Step	Procedure
1.	Focus the team on its goals.
2.	Ask members the following questions:
	a. What are the unresolved issues of the team?
	b. Which members are "in" and which are "out"? What is the impact of each member on the team's climate?
	c. Consider the physical setting. How does this affect the team? Should the team change the setting?
	d. Does the team have a clear understanding of its task? Has it evolved?
	e. Has the team established certain norms that inhibit its progress?
	f. What does the leader do that inhibits or facilitates the performance of the team?
	g. Are members able to openly and freely express opinions and ideas or are they prevented for some reason?
	h. Does the team need to change the time of day that it works to energize its members more?
	i. Do any personal or role issues inhibit the functioning of the team?
	j. What type of intervention might help the team move forward?
3.	Use these questions in a team meeting to plan developmental activities for the team.

Adapted from Napier and Gershenfeld (1999).

Gershenfeld, focuses team efforts on its goals rather than on the conflict by emphasizing the vision and design when deciding on how to work together rather than thinking in terms of individual needs. A facilitator guides this intervention. The purpose is for groups to determine the best way to design their teamwork processes so that they can set standards up front and avoid the typical conflict that occurs with many groups. The steps involved in adopting a design mentality follow.

Like most of the practitioner approaches, there is little direct evidence for whether Napier and Gershenfeld's Team Design Mentality will succeed. However, given the literature reviewed already in this text, there is no question that the steps they recommend are consistent with the literature. I have already discussed the importance of emphasizing team goals, creating a team climate, setting norms, and establishing roles on team performance. In this case, Napier and Gershenfeld recommend that these tools work because, in part, they reduce conflict.

Mediation/arbitration

In their classic book titled *Getting to yes*, Fisher, Ury, and Patton (1991) argue that negotiation is a fact of life; everyone is a negotiator. I think of this statement sometimes when trying to get one of my sons or my daughter to perform a chore.

We are clearly negotiating, and they have at a young age learned the beginnings of the art of negotiation. Pruitt and Carnevale (1993) identify five major strategies to negotiation, including, concession making, contending, problem solving, inaction, and withdrawal. Each of these processes creates a back and forth process of negotiation that is designed to resolve a conflict, whether they are used formally by experienced professional negotiators or informally by children who want to play rather than work.

As a reminder, this text is only discussing intragroup negotiation. There is a wealth of information about intergroup negotiation, such as the work on labor-management negotiations. Thompson and Fox (2001) divide the different types of negotiation processes into seven different levels, four of which are relevant to this book. According to Thompson and Fox, within-group negotiation can occur at the level of the dyad, which is one member negotiating with another member. It can also occur at the level of the polyad, which is negotiation involving more than two members, a situation that also allows for coalitions to form. The third category is intragroup, which is a negotiation process that considers all of the disparate interests among the members within a group. Finally, the fourth category is the intermediary, which is also called third party intervention.

One type of third party intervention is mediation. Mediation uses a skilled, neutral third-party facilitator to help with the negotiation that allows more tactics to search for common ground, such as less biased, skilled in problem solving strategies, promises for concessions, direct pressure, or inaction (Pruitt & Carnevale, 1993). The third-party intervention can be formal or informal, and the third party can be an outside facilitator, the group's leader, or a manager (Goldman, Croanzano, Stein, & Benson, 2008). In mediation, the third party has little real power, but works with those who are having the conflict to help them find a solution that works best for them. Arbitration is a second type of third party intervention. In this case, the third party listens to the member involved and then assigns a solution to which they have a priori said they will agree. In arbitration, the third party has power. A third type of third-party intervention is mediation/arbitration together, which is a process that combines these two third-party interventions.

The advantage of mediation/arbitration is that the third party facilitator first works as a mediator to find a solution that works best for those involved. However, if the group members involved in the conflict are unwilling or unable to find a solution, the mediator can move to arbitration and make the decision. This threat of decision making gives a mediator power even though he or she may not use it. The success of mediation/arbitration is in the possibility of the mediator turning into an arbitrator rather than the person actually making the decision. The steps involved in mediation/arbitration are summarized in Table 10.4.

Although mediation is not common in organizations, its success is well documented. McGillicuddy, Welton, and Pruitt (1987), for example, demonstrated that those involved in the conflict were less hostile and spent more time on problem solving than people who use straight mediation. In fact, third party interventions

Table 10.4   A Summary of the Steps Involved in Mediation/Arbitration.

Step	Procedure
1.	Identify a neutral third party who is comfortable working as a mediator/ arbitrator and is acceptable to those involved in the conflict (sometimes these may be identified through a referral agency).
2.	Bring the parties involved together.
3.	Set the ground rules. The third party will first work as a mediator. If the third party finds that mediation is unsuccessful, he or she will move the process to arbitration. Those involved in the conflict should sign up front saying that they will abide by the agreement.
4.	The parties start to work towards a mutually-acceptable agreement.
5.	If the parties strive to find a mutually-acceptable agreement, the third party writes the agreement and those involved in the conflict sign that they will agree to it.
6.	If the third party finds that there is a stalemate, he or she can threaten to use his or her power to arbitrate.
7.	If several threats to arbitrate do not force a mutually-acceptable agreement, the third party formally states that the process has now moved to arbitration.
8.	The third party allows each side to state their claims in turn. At this point, there should be no more talk between those involved in the conflict.
9.	The third party takes time to write the solution to which both parties have previously said they will agree.

Adapted from Rubin, Pruitt, and Kimm (1994).

such as mediation and arbitration are most effective in organizational contexts when there are perceptions of intentionality, more severe consequences resulting from the conflict, and significant power differences between those involved in the conflict (Arnold & Carnevale, 1997). Further, Sarat (1976) finds that people who have a past relationship as well as expectations of a future relationship are more likely to prefer third party interventions. Finally, Arnold and Carnevale (1997) find that preference for mediation and arbitration increases after disputants understand the purpose of third party intervention as well as learn details about its procedures.

Unfortunately, the evidence is not altogether positive. Richey, Bernardin, Tyler, and McKinney (2001), for example, found that job applicants are less likely to prefer organizations that use arbitration than those that use other grievance procedures. One possible reason for this is that arbitrators tend to use win-lose rather than integrative solutions during conflict resolution, even when trained to look for an integrative solution (Stuhlmacher & Halpert, 1998). Thus, it appears important to train team members in the methods of third-party intervention as well as how to generate an integrative solution to dysfunctional conflict.

FOCUS ON APPLICATION

Frank A. Cania, M.S.Emp.L., SPHR – CANIAHR, LLC

The practitioner

Frank A. Cania, M.S.Emp.L., SPHR is the president and CEO of CANIAHR, LLC, the company he founded in 2006. Recognized as a subject matter expert in employment law and regulatory compliance, Frank continues to provide consulting services to organizations in a variety of industries, including health care facilities, information technologies, manufacturing, retail sales, and construction. He earned an M.S. in Employment Law from the Shepard Broad Law Center at Nova Southeastern University and is certified by the HR Certification Institute as a Senior Professional in Human Resources (SPHR). Frank's community involvement includes active volunteer roles with the Society for Human Resource Management (SHRM) on the local, state, and national levels as well as serving as a member of the executive compensation and human resource committees for the YMCA of Greater Rochester.

The symptom

An electronic publishing company was experiencing several consecutive quarters of unprecedented growth after more than seven years of barely breaking even. One of the company's greatest assets from the very beginning was the operations manager, Brenda. Described as "the glue that held everyone and everything together," she was the go-to person for practically anything anyone needed. Brenda prided herself on being the first one in, and the last one to leave the office every day. But, with the company growing rapidly, even Brenda wasn't able to keep on top of everything.

When a new formal administrative structure was implemented, Brenda was promoted to director of operations and she hired Sarah from another position within the organization to fill the role of operations manager. However, within only a few weeks Brenda began micro-managing Sarah and finding fault in work that had been praised by other directors. Brenda also told Sarah that "she was getting a little too full of herself" and that the only opinion Sarah needed to be concerned about was Brenda's. Feeling angry and unappreciated, Sarah spoke to the president and offered her resignation. The president was concerned about what Sarah told him and felt it was appropriate to bring in a neutral third party to intervene.

Assessing the problem

My first step was to meet with Sarah and interview her so that I could hear for myself what she shared with the president. I also got get her perspectives on what she expected when she accepted the operations manager position, her initial impression of Brenda's management style, how that impression differed from what she was experiencing, and what she believed were the reasons for the disconnect. Although obviously frustrated, Sarah didn't attack Brenda. In fact she explained that working for Brenda was one of the biggest selling points of the position. Sarah had three requirements in her job search: 1. A strong growing company, 2. A position with practically unlimited growth potential, and 3. A mentor to help her grow professionally. Sarah thought she had hit the jackpot.

Next, I interviewed Brenda to get her perspectives on what Sarah had shared with me. Brenda was very cold and matter-of-fact as she explained that she felt it was necessary to micro-manage Sarah, the praise Sarah had received from the other directors was undeserved, and that Sarah *was* too full of herself and needed to hear it before all the false praise made her impossible to manage. Knowing that Brenda was responsible for hiring Sarah, the next question was simply "why did you hire her?" Strangely, this question caught Brenda off guard so it took her a few minutes before she could begin her answer. "Sarah reminded me of me when I first started with the company more than a dozen years ago; smart, motivated, and eager to make my mark on the company no matter what it took." Brenda explained that Sarah was too good, sometimes better than Brenda, and always looking for new challenges. "I can't keep up with her sometimes. It's like she's after my job every day! And soon she'll be able to do it better, so why would they keep me?"

I briefed the president on what I had discovered. He was astonished to learn about Brenda's fears of being replaced and upset that she hadn't come to him to share her fears. However, he did admit that he likely would have told her "that's crazy talk" and dismissed it.

Intervening: What did you do?

First I arranged and mediated a meeting between Sarah and Brenda. I asked Sarah to explain the three things that were most important to her when she accepted the operations manager position at the company working for

Brenda. Then I asked Brenda to explain what she saw in Sarah when she hired her. As they cleared the air in the structured session, the tension in the room was replaced with the acknowledgement of mutual respect. Brenda and Sarah pushed the reset button on their professional relationship that morning. They meet for five minutes each day to share yesterday's accomplishments and challenges and set today's priorities. They also meet for an hour each week to discuss important issues in greater detail.

The second meeting I arranged and mediated was between Brenda and the company president. After reviewing the meeting between Brenda and Sarah, the president reassured Brenda of her continued value to the company. Although starting in a different place, the reset button was also pushed on this professional relationship. Brenda also has daily five-minute meetings with the president as well as weekly one-on-one meetings to discuss plans, issues, and strategies. In addition, this communication model has been successfully implemented throughout the company. Based on quarterly follow-up calls, the company continues to grow and the operations department is the model of efficiency, effectiveness, and open communication for the entire company.

Chapter Summary

Conflict can be either constructive or destructive to groups. In constructive conflict, groups use the dialectic to improve problem solving and decision making and improve performance. In destructive conflict, groups suffer from dysfunctional conflict, usually based on values and relationships rather than on the characteristics of the task, that decreases group performance. These process losses from dysfunctional conflict can be quite severe.

Many of the causes of conflict can be categorized into four different themes: Conflict around resources and mixed-motive dilemmas, conflict from social loafers, conflict due to miscommunication, and conflict resulting from differences among people.

Because the impact of dysfunctional conflict on performance can reduce group performance, it is important to manage that conflict. Competitive mixed-motive environments can be changed to make them group members more cooperative. Social loafers can be identified and the free riding minimized. Communication problems can be corrected. Personal styles and behaviors can be measured and used to understand the sources of conflict. By assessing the causes of conflict and properly intervening, groups can move from low performance resulting from dysfunctional, destructive conflict to high performance groups that properly manage and use the conflict among members.

Additional Resources

De Dreu, C., & Van De Vliert, E. (1997). *Using conflict in organizations.* Thousand Oaks, CA: Sage Publications.

Lencioni, P. (2005). *Overcoming the five dysfunctions of a team: A field guide.* San Francisco, CA: Jossey-Bass.

Rubin, J. Z., Pruitt, D. G., & Kimm, S. H. (1994). *Social conflict: Escalation, stalemate, and settlement* (2nd ed.). NY: McGraw-Hill, Inc.

Team Exercises

Exercise 10.1   Resolving organizational conflict

Imagine that you are a consultant who was asked to assist the top management team of a large, multi-national organization that manufactures and distributes retail sports equipment. You are working with them to facilitate their strategic planning meeting to design a strategy for the next fiscal year. The budget decisions for the next year are being made in the meeting and the CEO has asked you to attend.

Prior to the meeting, the CEO and CFO have made it clear to all the officers who will be attending that resources will be very tight for the upcoming fiscal year. As a result, they will only fund one new initiative. You already know from your interviews of the top executives that two competing initiatives are going to be recommended by two different departments.

- The Vice President of Talent and Development is going to recommend a training initiative. Recent organizational research has shown that certain categories of people, such as women and minorities, are very underrepresented in the organization. As a result, the HR department wants $480,000 for a new management training program that will focus on training managers about how to recruit a diverse applicant pool. The program positively impacts the organization's ability to compete for some federal contracts.
- The Vice President of Sales and Marketing is going to recommend a new marketing campaign. Recently, a competitor was very successful at using a prosocial advertisement to improve their image. The marketing department would like $510,000 for a marketing campaign to increase and highlight the very high United Way contributions within the organization to improve overall image and regain some lost marketing share.

Both departments have defined how they will measure the outcomes to determine the impact of their initiatives, yet you know that it is unclear whether either will in fact succeed. You expect a fairly significant conflict between the leaders of the two departments. Given the content of this book, what steps would you recommend to help minimize and resolve this conflict?

Exercise 10.2   The prisoner's dilemma game

This is a variant of the original prisoner's dilemma game. It uses two rounds with 10 trials each.

1) A facilitator should pair people up with others whom they do not know well.
2) Provide each person with:
    - The prisoner's dilemma grid (below)
    - A large supply of candy, such as Starburst (make sure players know not to eat the Starburst yet!)
    - Index cards with the letters "A" or "B" printed in large letters on them.
    - A "kitty" with at least 10 Starburst in it.
3) Tell the players that the object of the first round of the game is to maximize each person's own Starburst.
4) Players play one round of 10 trials. In the first round, do NOT allow players to communicate at all.
    - Each player plays either the "A" or "B".
    - Payouts are determined using the grid.
    - After the 10 trials are done, have each person calculate her or his gains or losses and record it for Round 1.
5) Play a second round of 10 trials. This time, encourage communication and strategy. Again, record the gains or losses for each person.

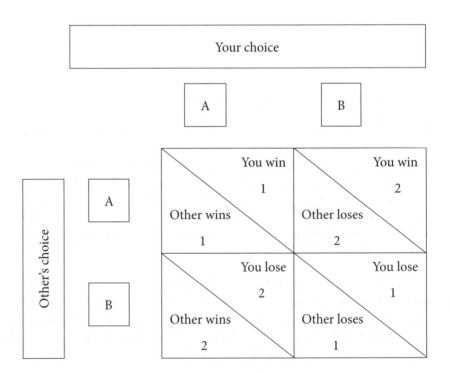

6) The facilitator should discuss the difference between the rounds as well as how and why play differed from dyad to dyad.

In other variations, the game can be played with fake money (such as Monopoly money), by using two-on-two players, or by playing with four to five players in one group against four to five players in another group.

Organize the class into dyads. Give out grid, and explain it.

Start PDG game. With each round, do 10 PDG trials. Change partners in the dyads between each round, using relevant instructions for that round.

Round	Communication	Goal
1	None	Maximize your income
2	Allowed	Maximize your income
3	Allowed	Maximize all income

Print the letters below to use for cards.

A   B

Exercise 10.3   Social dilemma

The game *Social Dilemma* is a modification of the prisoner's dilemma that is designed to work with small groups rather than dyads. To conduct the Social Dilemma game, follows these steps:

1) A facilitator should form groups, distribute the materials, and introduce the social dilemma game.
   - The object of the game is to gain as many points as possible.
   - This game works best with small groups of five to eight members.
   - Each member gets two small stacks of colored index cards. Any color combinations can be used, but for this example I will be using blue and white. The facilitator should keep an ample supply so that members can get new cards whenever they need them.
   - Members should be told that they are not allowed to talk during the game until directed to do so.
   - Members sit in a circle, choose which card to pass, and then pass their cards to the person to their right.
   - Members calculate points based on the combination of the color they send and the color they receive.

- ○ Give blue, get blue: 0 points
- ○ Give blue, receive white: 25 points
- ○ Give white, receive white: 10 points
- ○ Give white, receive blue: **lose** 15 points

2) Conduct 10 trials.
3) The facilitator should pause the game for five minutes while members are allowed to write messages to the other members but not talk.
4) Conduct 10 more trials.
5) The facilitator should pause the game for 10 minutes while all members openly discuss the game and strategies.
6) Conduct 10 more trials.
7) The facilitator should lead debriefing discussion with the larger group. Some opportunities for the facilitator include:
   - • Discussing strategies and what was best, who did well, and who did not.
   - • Discussing the difference between no communication, constrained communication, and open communication.

Note: Adapted from Harrod (1983).

Chapter 11

Influence, Power, and Leadership

What makes a great leader? There are many examples of great community leaders, such as Martin Luther King, Jr. He was able to take the reins of a grass-roots movement and then influence many people to follow his goals for civil rights. There are many examples of great spiritual leaders, such as Mother Teresa. She was a Nobel Peace Prize winner who was able to influence her followers to start hundreds of missions that serve the poor and disadvantaged. Finally, there are examples of great political leaders, such as John F. Kennedy. He was able to energize people in the United States, and his unfortunate assassination had a global impact. What is it that all these have in common and how do they influence people to follow them? This chapter examines the processes of power, influence, and leadership, especially within teams, that allow people to positively influence others.

Often, we think that effective leaders can influence followers to perform behaviors that they might otherwise not have done (Vroom & Jago, 2007). Let's carefully examine this premise. An example of a possible leader who fits this is Adolf Hitler. He was able to influence his followers to improve the infrastructure in Germany, reduce unemployment, and also to perform heinous acts, including the murder of millions, and likely tens of millions, of civilians in the name of country unity and racial purity. This leaves many unanswered questions, including was he a great leader? He influenced others, but is this the type influence we expect from a great leader? Then what does it mean to be a great leader and demonstrate great leadership? Consider what it means to be a leader while reflecting on what leadership is.

Group Dynamics and Team Interventions: Understanding and Improving Team Performance,
First Edition. Timothy M. Franz.
© 2012 Timothy M. Franz. Published 2012 by Blackwell Publishing Ltd.

The term leadership has been defined many different ways, including:

- Leadership encourages discretionary effort (i.e. performance over and above the minimum required performance) from organization members, Katz & Kahn, 1978).
- "Ultimately, leadership is a process of influence … a single thread uniting leadership researchers is their common interest in influence" (Lord & Brown, 2004, p. 7).
- Leadership is a relationship that requires a person to model the way, inspire a shared vision, challenge the process, enable others to act, and encourage the heart (Kouzes & Posner, 2000, 2007).
- Leadership is a "relationship of mutual stimulation and elevation that converts followers into leaders and may convert leaders into moral agents" (Burns, 1978, p. 4).

As you can see, there are different definitions of leadership, and many, many more than the small number of definitions that I have sampled here (see Yukl, 2010, for a summary of definitions or Winston & Patterson, 2006, for an integrative definition). Of all the definitions, I prefer the final one because it encompasses moral choices. According to this final definition, leadership includes the processes of influence, but it is also more than simply influencing people; it is influencing people to follow a leader towards moral goals, not just any goals. Thus, according to Burns, Hitler would not be considered by most people to be a great leader.

Leadership is a necessary component to effective teamwork. For better or worse, leaders are assigned either the credit or blame for team successes or failures, which Hackman (2005) calls the Leadership Attribution Error. Unfortunately, "the need to build effective teams is increasing, while the time available to build these teams is often decreasing" (Goldsmith & Morgan, 2000, p. 103), but too many leaders "preach effective teamwork, but often excuse themselves from its practice" (Goldsmith, 2000, p. 21). This is the case even though effective team leadership is strongly linked to organizational success because good leaders can motivate individual followers and enhance team success (Kaiser, Hogan, & Craig, 2008). What this means is that teams need good leadership more now than ever, but not all leaders seem to be taking their team leadership responsibilities seriously. This chapter should help team members to become better leaders, whether they serve as the team leader, a team facilitator, or the team uses a system of shared leadership.

Learning Goals for Chapter 11

- Be able to assess charismatic leadership.
- Know how to differentiate power, influence, and leadership.
- Learn how to positively influence people.
- Understand the history of leadership theories and their impact on those theories today.
- Know some current leadership theories.

- Know the competencies for team leadership.
- Be able to intervene to improve team leadership.

Leadership Assessment

Conger and Kanungo (1998) provide a list of charismatic leadership behaviors (Table 11.1). According to their work, there are five concepts necessary to be a charismatic leader, including having a strategic vision, sensitivity to the environment, sensitivity to member needs, personal risk, and unconventional behavior. Although all five are important, for brevity the two most relevant to team leadership are provided here. These include strategic vision and sensitivity to member needs.

Conger and Kanungo scored the items using a six-point scale from very uncharacteristic to very characteristic. They tested the scale in several studies with managers who worked in multiple corporations in multiple countries, and the participants in their studies had an average score of about 4.5. Scores on this scale predict charismatic leadership, team cohesion, trust in leadership, team satisfaction, reverence for leader, feelings of empowerment, and task efficacy. To score the

Table 11.1 Assessing Leadership: The Charismatic Leadership Scale.

Instructions: Circle the appropriate number using the following scale, where 1 = Very uncharacteristic of the leader while 6 = Very Characteristic.

Strategic Vision and Articulation of that Vision

1. Provides inspiring strategic and organizational goals.	1	2	3	4	5	6
2. Inspirational; able to motivate by articulating effectively the importance of what organizational members are doing.	1	2	3	4	5	6
3. Consistently generates new ideas for the future of the organization.	1	2	3	4	5	6
4. Exciting public speaker.	1	2	3	4	5	6
5. Has vision; often brings up ideas about possibilities for the future.	1	2	3	4	5	6
6. Entrepreneurial; seizes new opportunities in order to achieve goals.	1	2	3	4	5	6
7. Readily recognizes new environmental opportunities that may facilitate achievement of organizational objectives.	1	2	3	4	5	6

Sensitivity to Member Needs

8. Influences others by developing mutual liking and respect.	1	2	3	4	5	6
9. Shows sensitivity for the needs and feelings of the other members in the organization.	1	2	3	4	5	6
10. Often expresses personal concern for the needs and feelings of other members in the organization.	1	2	3	4	5	6

Adapted from Conger and Kanungo (1998).

scale, simply add the scores for each item. The range of possible values will be from 10 to 60. Scores closer to 10 represent a team leader who is not charismatic while scores closer to 60 represent a team leader who is charismatic.

Social Influence

Although leadership is more than influence, all the definitions of leadership have one theme in common: Leadership is, in part, about influencing others to perform. This section of the chapter examines the classic literature about influence.

One of the early classic studies of social influence was conducted by Norman Triplett (1898). Triplett was observing track bicycle racers at Indiana University. Some riders were riding alone against the clock, while others were riding for time and had another rider on the track. In all cases, the racers were trying to ride as fast as they could in order to get the best time. He realized that bicycle racers who were competing alone were typically a little slower than those who were competing against others, even though the goal was always the same. An experimental social psychologist, he moved from his real-world observations to the controlled environment of the psychology laboratory. In his experimental research, he compared people reeling in fishing reels. In some situations, he had the people reeling the fishing reels alone. In other situations, he had the people reeling in their fishing reels while competing against another person. In all cases, they were given the same goal: To reel as fast as they could. What he found was that when people were reeling against one another they were typically faster than when they reeled alone, a process he termed social facilitation. This was one of the first demonstrations of the power of social influence.

Another classic study was conducted by Muzafer Sherif (1935; this is the same Sherif as the Robber's Cave study). Sherif studied influence in an ambiguous task. In his study, he used the autokinetic effect (Adams, 1912) which is a perceptual illusion that occurs when a light is shone on the wall of a completely darkened room. People perceive movement of the light because the darkened room eliminates the visual cues that would typically help people to perceive stability (such as walls). The autokinetic effect occurs for all people, but the amount of movement they perceive differs. Sherif was interested in how much movement people would perceive when influenced by others. He measured the perceived movement when people were alone, and then again when people were working in groups. He found convergence in the perceptions as people worked together to judge the amount of movement, again strong evidence of social influence.

Solomon Asch (1951) carried the work by Sherif further. Asch's study (often referred to as the Asch paradigm), used a task based on line length. Each participant was given a test line and then was allowed to compare its length from across the room to three different lines; in all cases, the test line clearly matched the size of one of the three. When people were working alone, they were 100% correct in their judgments of which of the three lines matched the test line. Asch next put people together in groups. This time, however, all the people in the group except one were confederates, or part of the experiment, without the person knowing. In some trials, the confederates purposefully picked the wrong line. Asch showed that research participants picked the same line as the confederates, or the incorrect line, in approximately 25% to 33% of the trials. This demonstrates the impact of influence even when the task is ambiguous.

Asch's study inspired another classic study, this time by Stanley Milgram (1974), where Milgram studied obedience to authority. Milgram created a fictitious situation where one person would be a teacher and the other would be a learner. The teacher was supposed to teach the learner word pairs and was instructed by an experimenter to give increasingly severe shocks to the learner if the learner gave incorrect answers. In fact, the learner was a confederate of the experimenter and never received shocks. The learner gave many pre-programmed incorrect answers. As a result, the teacher was required to continually increase the shock voltage level by fifteen volt increments to very severe and dangerous levels (450 volts). If the teacher protested, the experimenter prompted him or her to continue. Milgram found that many participants gave dangerously high levels of shocks. The power of influence from an authority figure was far more powerful than anyone expected.

What all these studies have in common is the power of social influence, regardless of whether the task is ambiguous or unambiguous. Further, influence from an authority figure is even more powerful than influence from peers. Latané (1981) sums up the power of social influence in social impact theory. According to social impact theory, influence is a function of strength, immediacy, and number. Latané defines strength as the power or intensity of a given influence attempt, immediacy as closeness in space and time, and number as the number of attempts or people. Thus, influence attempts from a large number of powerful people are likely to be successful. On the other hand, influence attempts from one subordinate who is located across the country may not work at all.

Power in Leadership

Group members also may have substantial differences in power, whether the differences result from leadership, strong members, discrimination, or anything else. Power, however, is a multi-faceted concept. French and Raven (1959) provide a classic interpretation of the different sources of power. According to French and Raven, power can be classified into six types of power within two major categories. The first category is personal power, also called positive power. This category includes expert power, referent power, and information power. Expert power results from the belief that one holds credibility or expertise (e.g., an information technology expert in a group trying to roll out a new computer program). Referent power results from liking, respect, and admiration (e.g., a popular person in a group trying to determine how to run the next company picnic). Finally, information power results from access to specific information that may be necessary to the group (e.g., an administrative assistant who has access to the schedules of the executives).

The second category is positional power, also called negative power. This category includes legitimate power, reward power, and coercive power. Legitimate power is that which is externally validated (e.g., a manager of a group trying to make a decision). Reward power results from one's ability to offer rewards for behavior (e.g., senior management giving awards to a committee who coordinated a company picnic). Finally, coercive power results from one's ability to punish others to influence their behavior (e.g., a project manager on a cross-functional team who might complain to a team member's manager about the quality of work).

There is a definite contrast in the effectiveness of positive versus negative power. Unfortunately, negative power works. Rewards increase the likelihood of behavior. Threats also stop behavior. Legitimate power can be useful at changing behavior as well. It is easy to generate examples of these three from childhood times. For example, if a parent says "if you do your homework you can use the Internet," demonstrating reward power. A parent could also say "If you don't do your homework, you're grounded!" which is using coercive power. As a parent, my favorite is when I get to say "you do it because I'm your father" (and for some reason I always use the term father in these situations, not dad!). My children typically respond if I break down and use negative power. They don't do it because they want to, but instead because I have forced them. Using these sources of power comes along with problems, not the least of which is that the person who is targeted by the negative power may end up disliking the powerful person, because people feel forced to respond when using negative power.

On the other hand, positive power is when power is used in a way that makes people want to be influenced. People trust those who are experts, work with those who have information to share and are willing to share it, and want to perform for those whom they respect. I like it much better when my kids respond to my influence attempts because I have considerable expertise about skiing or bicycling, can help to teach them about mathematical or statistical information, or because they like me. As you can see, positive power is much more, well, positive. As a result, people respond much more positively when influenced using these methods.

The problem with the impact of power on the decision making process is that powerful members can easily sway the group even though they are not always the ones who have the most information or who can make the best decision. Power, whether resulting from legitimate authority or the impact of admiration, can easily affect the behavior and decisions of the other group members (Tyler, 1998). If, for example, a powerful group leader, strong member, or high status person initiates the discussion about one decision alternative and then strongly advocates for it, a group is likely to follow along with that member (Janis, 1982).

As the previous paragraph demonstrates, misuses of power can be detrimental to team functioning. Wageman and Mannix (1998) argue that these misuses of power fall into three major categories. First, they argue that dictating the specific values and norms of a group or team is a misuse of power. This is because groups and teams should be motivated because they are setting their own norms and goals. Second, they argue that it is a misuse of power to try to influence the collective motivation of a team because groups and teams that are setting their own norms and working together on a task should be motivated by their own involvement in the task processes. Finally, they argue that it is a misuse of power to take on any of the behaviors that are collectively the responsibility of the group or team, because this takes away members' ability to function on their own.

Although misuses of power can occur, using power properly certainly has its place in organizations. Wageman and Mannix (1998) argue that power is useful because it helps groups and teams to monitor their performance, set strategies, properly promote and then manage conflict, discuss organizational values, and manage the perceptions of those external to the group or team. Using power in each of these areas is functional because it allows someone who has power or authority to promote the team and make sure that the team is headed in a direction that is consistent with the goals of the organization. As Scanlan and Atherton (1981) state, "the key to successful use of both power and participation is knowing when and how to use them effectively" (p. 702).

A Brief Background on Theories of Leadership

A considerable amount of the writing about group and team leadership finds its foundations in the traditional theories of the general principles of leadership. There have been almost as many theories of leadership as there have been definitions of what leadership is. These theories follow an historical progression where the success and failures of early theories led to newer theories. Like others, I categorize the historical progression of theories in terms of whether they predicted that leaders would be successful in every situation, called universal theories, or only successful in situations that matched their competencies, called contingency theories. I also classify them in terms of whether they emphasized internal characteristics that were immutable (traits) or sets behaviors that could be learned (behaviors). The progression of philosophies is summarized in Table 11.2. I provide this summary so that readers who have never read the leadership literature have an understanding of foundational leadership philosophies as well as know some examples of some specific theories explaining possible causes of effective leadership.

The earliest theories of leadership were ones that predicted that certain traits created great leaders, and these traits were universal. This means that the traits would make someone a great leader regardless of the situation. These theories were popular for many years and then formalized in the early 1900s (e.g., the idea of royalty is based on being born into a family with certain characteristics that make a person ready to be a king or queen). Many people lump all these theories into one category termed the "Great Man" theories, arguing that most of the people who followed this philosophy of leadership examined great men and then tried to determine the set of

Table 11.2   An Historic Progression of Leadership Theories.

		Trait	Behaviors
Universal		Timing: – Oldest set of theories about leadership – Popular until about 1940	Timing: – Followed the trait theories of leadership – Popular from about 1940 until 1960
		Core Assumptions: – Leaders are born and not made – People must already have the "right" set of traits for them to be great leaders Example: – "Great Man" set of theories	Core Assumptions: – Leaders are made and not born – People must act in the "right" way for them to be great leaders Example: – Ohio State University studies/ LBDQ – University of Michigan studies
Contingency		Timing: – Followed universal situation theories – Popular from about 1950 to 1970 Core Assumptions: – Leaders are born and not made – The "right" set of traits is necessary for people to be great leaders, but the traits have to be matched to the correct types of followers to succeed. Example: – Fiedler's LPC model	Timing: – Followed the contingency trait theories – Popular from about 1960 until 1980 Core Assumptions: – Leaders are made and not born – The "right" behaviors are necessary for people to act as great leaders, and people can be trained to act in ways that match the situation. Example: – Vroom & Yetton's Normative model

characteristics from studying them. They were by their very nature sexist theories; the assumption at the time was that being male was one of the necessary characteristics for being a great leader. Most of the remaining characteristics also focused on physical features, such as height, appearance, age, and so on. (Den Hartog & Koopman, 2001). Unfortunately, very few researchers could identify a clear set of traits that defined what it took to be a great leader in all situations.

As a result, researchers moved to the next philosophical ideal of what it meant to be a great leader. Because nobody could identify the traits that defined great leaders across situations, the second set of theories examined the styles, or behaviors, that were necessary for great leadership. They were different because traits are characteristics which, for the most part, are the result of genetic predispositions.

Behaviors, however, may be enacted by many different people. Like the previous theories, these theories were assuming universality, meaning that the behaviors would work across situational contexts.

A good example of a specific theory that was based on universal behaviors was the Ohio State studies that resulted in the Leadership Behavior Description Questionnaire (LBDQ; it is free to use without any required permission – see the Ohio State University website for more information). The LBDQ resulted from many studies of leadership by scholars at the Ohio State University Personnel Research Board. The researchers identified two different sets of behaviors that were related to leadership. They termed these sets of behaviors which they termed initiating structure and consideration. Initiating structure is a leader's task oriented behavior while consideration is his or her socio-emotional behavior (see Leadership Behavior Description Questionnaire Manual, 1957; 1962). The LBDQ is an excellent tool for measuring differences in initiating structure versus consideration behaviors for leaders. This means there is certainly some validity in using the scale when considering these as part of what it means to be a leader (Judge, Piccolo, & Ilies, 2004). Unfortunately, the scale cannot be easily used to determine which of the two categories of behaviors actually made for effective leadership (Den Hartog & Koopman, 2001).

After the failures of the universal theories, scholars began to turn to contingency theories. Hackman and Wageman (2007) put this succinctly by saying that we should not be examining "the traits of leaders, but how do leaders' personal attributes interact with situational outcomes to shape outcomes" (p. 44). Contingency theories recognize that good leadership depends on the situation, which may account for as much as three times the variance in what explains effective leadership as do the theories that focus on individual characteristics (Vroom & Jago, 2007). The first contingency theories examined which traits made for successful theories when properly matched to the situation. A classic example of a theory that is based on traits that are contingent on the situation is Fiedler's Contingency Model (e.g., Fiedler & Garcia, 1987). Fiedler's contingency model uses a measure of the leader termed the Least Preferred Coworker scale. The measure asks the leader to define her or his least preferred coworker, and uses that information to define whether the leader has a tendency towards a task orientation or human relations orientation (similar to the concepts of initiating structure and consideration, respectively, as defined by the Ohio State studies). But, the Contingency Model goes further by defining the situation in terms of the followers. It classifies followers' task and social needs. The major difference between this and the previous model is a major philosophical one – according to Fiedler, it is not a matter of changing leader behaviors but instead it is necessary to match the leader to the situation. This requires selecting the correct types of followers or changing the leader. Fiedler's Contingency Model was not without its failings, such as the measure of LPC may not be stable over time (Yukl, 1970), but it was the first theory of leadership that was successful in identifying characteristics that were related to great leadership.

The final core historical philosophy was also one that defined contingencies, but it reverted to behaviors rather than traits that were contingent on the situation. In these types of theories (e.g., House, 1996), leadership scholars examined which behaviors would make a successful leader and how those behaviors might depend on the situation. A classic example of this is Vroom and Yetton's (1973) decision tree. According to Vroom and Yetton, leaders can act in ways that range from completely autocratic when the leader him or herself makes a decision to completely group when the leader allows the group to make a decision. The difference depends on what the situation demands. Vroom and Yetton provide a detailed decision tree that is designed to help leaders to ask the correct questions so they know whether to make an autocratic decision, a democratic decision, or to let the group itself decide. Two example questions include "How important is subordinate commitment to the decision" and "Do you (the leader) have sufficient information to make a high quality decision on your own?" As you can see, this implies that the leader's behavior should depend on the situation. Like Fiedler's Contingency Model, it was far more successful at predicting effective leadership than the universal theories.

More recent theories often apply some of the best ideas from the theories of the past. Hersey and Blanchard's (1977) Situational Leadership Model, for example, has done this and has been one of the most commercially successful theories. According to Hersey and Blanchard, great leadership depends on the situation. Thus, it is a contingency theory. Unlike the previous theories, however, Hersey and Blanchard recognize that different people have different natural tendencies (they do not specifically term these tendencies traits but recognize that people tend to act in certain ways). They also recognize that people can change their behavior depending on the situation. Thus, the Situational Leadership Model accounts for internal characteristics and behavior change at the same time.

In the Situational Leadership Model Hersey and Blanchard define four different categories of leadership, including: telling, selling, participating, and delegating (listed in decreasing order of directiveness and increasing order of participation). Like Fiedler, Hersey and Blanchard define the situation in terms of the followers. According to Hersey and Blanchard, followers can fall into one of four categories based on abilities and willingness, including: they do not have the skills and are unwilling, they have the skills but are unwilling, they do not have the skills but are willing, and they have the skills and abilities. And, like Fiedler, Hersey and Blanchard explain that great leadership can occur when there is a match between the leadership tendencies and the follower's needs. Followers, for example, who are willing and able work well with a leader who tends to delegate. Where Hersey and Blanchard differ from Fiedler is in their assumption that leader's can also change their behavior. For example, if a leader's tendency is to delegate while his or her follower's need a leader who will tell, there is a mismatch that needs to be corrected through changing the behavior of the leader, changing the behavior of the leader, changing the leader, or changing the follower. Although the academic research about the success of the Situational Leadership Model is limited and somewhat mixed (Vecchio, 1987; Yukl, 2010), it has been a very successful leadership development tool and has certainly made contributions to our understanding of effective leadership.

Leadership Theories Today

The previous theories represent an historical progression that ends in the 1970s, but the thoughts about what it means to be a great leader have continued to grow and develop from these foundations. Many theories today try to include some of the ideals of charismatic (Conger & Kanungo, 1998) or transformational leadership (Burns, 1978) when understanding what it means to be a great leader (it is important to note that some theorists view these two terms as essentially equivalent concepts while others view them as different concepts – Yukl (2010), provides a nice summary of these arguments. For the purposes of this brief summary, the terms are used as essentially the same). These theories are in contrast to leadership theories that emphasize a transactional relationship. Bass and Avolio (1993) provide a thorough summary describing the differences between charismatic or transformational leadership and transactional leadership. According to Bass and Avolio, transformational leadership is involved in change while transactional leadership is involved in rewards, management, and performing action. The core components of transformational leadership include: having charisma, being inspiring, being intellectually stimulating, and the ability to work with individuals. There is no doubt that the three leaders listed in the first paragraph of this chapter are truly transformational leaders – it is the transformational leaders who are at the heart of making positive change in organizations and communities.

The contrast between the transformational and transactional distinction has its roots in McGregor's Theory X and Theory Y (McGregor, 2002). According to McGregor, a Theory X manager is one who assumes that workers are basically lazy. As a result, managers who believe this way motivate people through rewards and punishments. On the other hand, a Theory Y manager is one who assumes that workers are ambitious and self-motivated. As a result, managers who believe this way motivate people through providing the conditions for their success while utilizing their talents. Burns further developed this distinction to explain the difference between transactional leaders (like Theory X managers) and transformational leaders (like Theory Y managers). Although both transformational and transactional leadership can help teams to succeed, transformational leadership behaviors have a higher correlation with performance than transactional leadership ones (Judge & Piccolo, 2004).

Conger and Kanungo (1998) built on the foundation of transformational leadership and examined what they called charismatic leadership, which is a continuation of Burns' concept of transformational leadership. According to Conger and Kanungo, charismatic leadership is based on a constellation of behaviors, including: Vision, inspiration, meaning-making, empowerment, setting high expectations, and fostering a collective identity. Charismatic leaders govern in an egalitarian manner and actively empower followers. They understand the nature of the status quo and shortcomings, provide a vision of the future, and can even express a plan for achieving that vision. Like transformational leaders, charismatic leaders are change agents (Conger, 1989). Unfortunately, charismatic leadership (as well as transformational leadership) often comes with some drawbacks. Conger and Kanungo find that charismatic leaders may be authoritarian and narcissistic, have a high need for power, disregard legitimate authority, and seek unquestioning obedience.

Another recent theory of leadership is Functional Leadership Theory (Hackman & Walton, 1986). Functional leadership theory is different from the previous theories in that it recommends that leaders do whatever is necessary to create success among followers, and are more taxonomies of how leaders should behave than theories of why they behave the way they do (e.g., Morgeson, DeRue, & Karam, 2010). As a result, functional leadership is more of a recommendation for actions rather than an overarching philosophy of what it means to be a great leader. According to Morgeson (2005; Morgeson, De Rue, & Karam, 2010), few of the more noticeable actions recommended by functional leadership theorists include:

- Leaders attend to the internal and external needs of the group.
    - Knowing about group performance compared to a benchmark.
    - Collect relevant information about group performance.
    - Knowing about group goals.
    - Interpreting the external environment and forecasting changes in the environment.
- Leaders intervene to improve group functioning, including:
    - Supporting a team's self management.
    - Providing information to members about their performance.
    - Providing a method of communicating information within the team.
    - Coaching team members.

As you can see, functional team leadership has a much different emphasis by providing leaders with practical and research-tested recommendations for actions that will improve group and team performance.

Finally, "trait" theories of leadership have, made a resurgence recently. However, these theories and the corresponding research tend to focus more on common personality characteristics, so they are quite unrelated to the typical trait theories that were common at the turn of the century. For example, Judge, Bono, Ilies, and Gerhardt (2002) reported that some traits such as extraversion, openness to experience, and conscientiousness are positive predictors of leadership while others such as neuroticism was negatively related to leadership. Hofmann and Jones (2005; see also Judge & Bono, 2000 and Lim & Ployhart, 2004) found that openness, agreeableness, conscientiousness, and extraversion within a group are related to transformational leadership. Finally, a meta-analysis by Lord and his colleagues (Lord, De Vader, & Alliger, 1986) demonstrates that the characteristics of intelligence, masculinity, and dominance are related to perceptions of leadership performance. To summarize this more recent work, Zaccaro (2007) argues that the trait-based approaches were rejected too quickly and that certain traits are predictive of leadership performance independent of the situations though they certainly do not explain all (or even half) of effective leadership.

Gender and leadership

Although the number of women in leadership positions has increased dramatically during the last decades, women still make up a much smaller percentage of leaders, especially at the higher levels of leadership (Eagly & Sczesny, 2009). Some argue that woman do not break through the glass ceiling because of true differences in leadership behaviors of men and women while others argue that the difficulty in breaking through the glass ceiling results mainly from prejudices about women leaders. The gender bias that exists in leadership likely exists because men are assumed to be more assertive, a characteristic that is perceived to be a part of effective leadership, while women are assumed to be more compassionate (see Eagly & Carli, 2007).

The research about gender differences in leadership behaviors clarifies this. What the research demonstrates is that in general, there are few differences in the behaviors of women and men and most authors find that there are no "pervasive sex differences in effectiveness" (Eagly, Karau, & Makhijani, 1995, p. 125). Eagly and colleagues identified 96 different studies that tested the leadership effectiveness of men and women. Their findings demonstrated that when averaging across all situations, women and men are equally effective as leaders.

However, Eagly and her colleagues also identified several situational variables that do make a difference in determining whether men or women are good leaders. Thus, certain situational conditions favor women as leaders while other situations favor men as leaders. First, when the leadership role was defined in masculine terms (or one in which men tended to report that they would be more interested in working) it favored men. On the other hand, when the leadership role was defined in feminine terms (or one in which women tended to report that they would be more interested in working) it favored women. Second, if the leadership role was dominated with other men, men tended to be more effective leaders. On the other hand, if the leadership role was dominated with women, women tended to be more effective leaders. Finally, the type of organization had an impact. Military organizations tended to favor male leaders while on the other hand businesses, governments, and social service organizations tended to slightly favor female leaders, although, these differences between the effectiveness of men and women in leadership are small. Eagly and colleagues argue that gender differences will become even less important as women become more common in leadership positions.

Another gender difference in leadership occurs in the tendency for women and men to act as transformational versus transactional leaders. Eagly and colleagues (Eagly, Johannesen-Schmidt, & Engen, 2003) conducted a different meta analysis where they examined 45 studies that tested gender and leadership style. This second meta analysis revealed that women tend to act in more transformational ways as leaders while men tend to act in more transactional ways. Specifically, men engaged in more reward-contingent behaviors as leaders than do women, suggesting that men are more likely to offer rewards to influence their followers. This is surprising given the importance that most organizations place on transformational leadership.

Team Leadership

At a most basic level, leadership in teams requires the same set of skills, behaviors, and characteristics as those defined by the general leadership theories. For example, transformational leadership in teams is related to higher team performance (Lim & Ployhart, 2004). Team leadership uses these traditional ideas, but also requires different skills as well (Stewart & Manz, 1995). Where the leadership processes differ is that effective team leadership also requires additional skills including facilitation (Zaccaro & Klimoski, 2002), a willingness to share power, a willingness to share or abdicate leadership as the situation dictates, especially in self-directed work teams, an emphasis on member learning, and team building (Stewart & Manz, 1995). When a team leader provides an enabling structure, a compelling direction, a supportive organizational context, and proper coaching, it can lead to effective teamwork (Hackman, 2002) and synergy (Bennis, Parikh, & Lessem, 1994).

Zaccaro, Heinen, and Shuffler (2009) break the type of team leadership into three broad categories. The first of their categories is when there is an internal leader. An internal leader is one who is a full, participating member of the team. This type of leadership will likely require the largest amount of shared power between the leader and other members. The second category of team leadership is when there is an external leader. An external leader gives direction to the team and is involved in supervising day-to-day operations. This type of leadership would likely require less sharing of power between the leader and the other members, but would mean that within the team, members have to take on a small proportion of the group management functions. The third category is what they term an executive coordinator. According to Zaccaro and colleagues, executive coordinators give broad strategic direction but give little input on day-to-day operations. Executive coordinators would share little power with group or team members because they would set direction and then step away. However, in this case the members themselves would likely have to share a large proportion of the management and leadership functions.

In a detailed review of the literature, Stagl, Salas, and Burke (2007) list the practices of team leadership that best create team effectiveness. According to their review, team leaders should perform the following functions:

- Ensure that the goals, task, and feedback are all suited to group work while providing members with direction towards an overall collective mission.

- Explicitly define accountability for a group.
- Clarify the structure, including the level of authority as well as the decisions for which the team is responsible.
- Work to keep membership stable while maintaining the right people for the task and developing member skills.
- Promote team goal setting, team reward structures, and processes designed to improve team learning.
- Ensure that the group has the information it needs to complete its task and get the information if necessary.

Yukl (2010) and Zaccaro and colleagues (Zaccaro, Rittman, & Marks, 2001) also recommend using many of these same leadership behaviors when working with teams. Yukl further suggests that the type of behavior depends, in part, on the type of team. For example, groups and teams working to make change within an organization require more transformational behaviors from their leader. Zenger and colleagues (Zenger, Musselwhite, Hurson, & Perrin, 1991) also add that the goals of team leaders' should include anticipating change as well as championing cross-functional efforts, both of which would also improve the transformational leadership of team leader.

Leaders also must be sensitive to changes in groups and teams over time. In project teams, for example, social behaviors (e.g., consideration) are more necessary during the first half of the project while task-related behaviors (e.g., initiating structure) are more important during the second half (Bowling, Bergman, & Bergman, 2009). In addition, it appears to be more important for leaders to use transformational behaviors early during group and team development (Sivasubramaniam, Murry, Avolio, & Jung, 2002).

According to Stewart and Manz (1995), the major goal in leading teams is to move them from traditional leadership behaviors to behaviors that emphasize power building and empowerment. Team leaders who are secure in their roles and want to create effective teams should work to develop a team culture, guide and encourage members, reinforce positive team behavior, model the behaviors that allow a team to regulate themselves, link the team with the rest of the organization, and assist the team in developing relationships with other teams. Teams can be more successful parts of an organization when a team leader works to build power in the team in this way.

Shared team leadership and management functions

Sharing leadership is becoming more common when working with or in groups or teams. According to Yukl (2010), there are many different terms that essentially represent this same concept, such as participative leadership, empowerment, power sharing decentralization, consultation, joint decision making, and democratic leadership. Participative processes benefit groups and teams because they often result in higher quality decisions, greater decision acceptance, higher member engagement, and better skill development (Yukl, 2010).

Teams also require a combination of management and leadership functions. Managers focus on the day to day activities while leaders focus on long-term objectives. Managers supervise people and match their performance to preset standards while leaders bring about change. Managers administer policies while leaders innovate within the organization. Managers act within the culture while leaders change culture. Finally managers typically use transactional processes while leaders instead use transformational ones (Conger & Kanungo, 1998). Effective team leadership requires a proper mix of these management and leadership functions. If team leaders spend the bulk of their time managing their group rather than leading, members may not have a clear vision and as a result they cannot effect change. On the other hand, if team leaders spend the bulk of their time leading their group and not managing it, members may neglect day-to-day activities and processes.

Unlike organizational leaders, team leaders need to be focused on the inputs, processes, and outputs of their teams. They must know how to share leadership and manage collective efforts (Zaccaro, Heinen, & Shuffler, 2009). When choosing team leaders, some of the most important characteristics and skills include having above average intelligence, knowing about the task, having emotional maturity, and demonstrating personal courage (Hackman, 2005). In addition, a leader who has skills providing feedback to team members and, as important, following through on the recommendations of the feedback can also improve team effectiveness (Goldsmith & Morgan, 2000).

All team members must participate and share in team leadership, even when there is a formal team leader (Hackman, 2002). Zaccaro and colleagues suggest that what teams really need is collectively shared leadership skills across the members of a team rather than the traditional view of leadership where the formal leadership function and the requisite leadership skills fall within one member. These team leadership functions can positively affect team interactions, including development and group process, and then improve performance, team viability, member adaptability. Some leadership functions that can be shared include setting direction, managing operations, developing future leadership, and setting goals. Zaccaro and colleagues imply that the more members who have expertise in these areas, the more likely it is that the team will succeed. In fact, Hackman (2005) argues that "the richer the set of leadership skills held by team members, the greater the number of options available" for enabling team success (p. 134). Recent research shows that, at least under certain conditions, this might be true (Mehra, Smith, Dixon, & Robertson, 2006).

Group and team leadership may also be a group-level phenomenon that is distributed among members, requires interdependencies within the group or team, and is embedded in processes of social interaction (Fletcher & Kaufer, 2003). Seers, Keller, and Wilkerson (2003) nicely summarize the processes that will help to facilitate shared leadership as well as the barriers to creating a strong sense of shared leadership. These are summarized in Table 11.3. As can be seen in the table, when

Table 11.3   The Facilitators of and Barriers to Shared Leadership.

Facilitators of Shared Leadership	Barriers to Shared Leadership
Task requires role differentiation and multiple exchange relationships. When there are multiple roles and the communication networks are open, shared leadership will likely be more successful.	*People do not like the idea.* If there is strong organizational resistance or resistance among group members, it will not succeed.
Larger group size, up to the point where coordination requires formalization. When there are many members, creating group roles and routines can help a group to succeed, and there is a larger likelihood for successfully sharing leadership.	*Evidence of strong status differentials.* If there are traditional status hierarchies that are difficult to avoid then it will struggle.
Higher ratings of each other's abilities to contribute toward a goal. If members trust that their peers can successfully complete their tasks, shared leadership is more likely to succeed.	*One or two leaders usually emerge in leaderless groups.* The status differentials as well as other individual behavior may create a situation where one or two strong members emerge as leaders.
High interpersonal attraction. When members like one another and enjoy working together, they are more likely to trust one another and jointly share leadership, power, and influence.	*Individual differences in status seeking.* Along with the perceptions of status differences, certain individuals see a relationship between leadership and status and may seek a leadership role to improve their own status.
Generalized exchange norms. Theories of social exchange predict that interpersonal relationships are a function of the natural giving and taking that occurs as part of exchange relationships. When there are strong norms for social exchange, sharing leadership is more successful.	*Implicit leadership theories.* Most members have an implicit expectation that leadership applies to individuals and not the multiple members of a group or a team. *Demographic composition of group.* Demographic diversity can create perceived differences among members, and these differences may reduce the ability for low-status members to fully participate in shared leadership processes.

Adapted from Seers, Keller, and Wilkerson (2003).

there is an appropriate culture within the organization, the right type of tasks, common goals, high cohesion, and strong norms for working collectively, the organizational system will likely support shared leadership. On the other hand, if there is a culture that supports traditional leadership, status and role hierarchies, people who are seeking to enhance their power, or strong value differences, the organization may want to avoid attempts at using shared leadership.

Groups and teams that share leadership are more successful. In fact, shared leadership can:

- Improve performance (Avolio, Jung, Murry, & Sivasubramaniam, 1996; Carson, Tesluk, & Marrone, 2007; O'Connell, Doverspike, & Cober, 2002).
- Improve the effectiveness of work with customers (Carson, Tesluk, & Marrone, 2007).
- Create perceptions of group efficacy (Avolio, Jung, Murry, & Sivasubramaniam, 1996).
- Improve quality (O'Connell, Doverspike, & Cober, 2002).
- facilitate organizational change (Olson, Olson, & Murphy, 1998); and
- Build trust (Avolio, Jung, Murry, & Sivasubramaniam, 1996).

Clearly, effective shared leadership processes can help organizations to succeed.

Although shared leadership only implies that "members have significant authority to chart the team's forward path" (Cox, Pearce, & Perry, 2003, p. 53), the possibility exists for teams to eliminate all but a token leader. These are called self-managed (or self-directed) work teams (Manz & Sims, 1987), and the importance of these teams in creating high performance work groups has been discussed by scholars since the early 1900s (Tubbs, 1994). A self-managed work team is "an intact group of employees who are responsible for a whole work process … [where] members work together to improve their operations, handle day-to-day problems, and plan and control their work. In other words, they are responsible not only for getting work done but also for managing themselves" (Wellins, Byham, & Wilson, 1991, p. 3). According to Pearce & Conger (2003), "members can, and do, take on roles that were previously reserved for management" (p. 11). The "central principle behind self-managing teams is that the teams themselves, rather than managers, take responsibility for their work, monitor their own performance, and alter their performance strategies as needed to solve problems and adapt to changing conditions" (Wageman, 1997, p. 49). Self-managed teams are intact groups, perform a complete task over an extended period of time, have high contributions that result from the unique skills and abilities of members, and exercise discretion over their methods, schedules, feedback, and rewards (Polley & Van Dyne, 1994). Self-managed work teams are quite common at the executive level but can also be effective, process-oriented teams at lower levels of an organization where members are responsible for their own management functions (Kline, 2003).

Wageman (1997) argues that the steps necessary to create successful self-managed teams are in the design. These processes are similar to those required to create effective teams, including: setting an engaging direction, making sure that the team is working on an interdependent task, empowering the team with the authority to complete the task, verifying that the team has the necessary skills or knows where to get them, making sure that the people in the team are in the correct jobs and have the skills to complete the task, and working to create stable team membership. Although the proper design of the self-managed team does not guarantee its success, self-directed teams with more of these design features are more likely to succeed than those that are improperly designed (Cohen, 1994).

If self-managed work teams work within an organization, they can be an asset. They improve some member inputs, including creating a stronger sense of collective efficacy (Solansky, 2008) and providing an atmosphere of innovation Muthusamy, Wheeler, & Simmons, 2005). They improve group process, including providing groups with a stronger transactive memory system (Solansky, 2008), improving knowledge transfer (Zárraga & Bonache, 2005), building participation, improving communication (Kauffeld, 2006), and enhancing within-team helping (Duimering & Robinson, 2007). Members of self-managed work teams have greater outputs, including a greater sense of effectiveness (Tata & Prasad, 2004), and they may even have higher satisfaction and perform a greater number of organizational citizenship behaviors (Foote & Tang, 2008).

Self-managed work teams pose a difficult problem for organizational leaders: If they are truly self-managed, they should have no leader. However, organizational structures often require one person who is accountable. According to Sims and Manz (1994), there is a "gap between the theoretical conceptualization of self-managed work teams (e.g., absence of formal hierarchical leadership and the reality of this work system in practice. In actuality, self-managed work teams are usually located somewhere along an evolutionary continuum from external dependence to complete self-managing autonomy" (p. 189). Sims and Manz provide advice for the leaders of self-managed work teams, including shifting their evaluation to the team, letting the team solve problems on its own, serving primarily as a team resource and advocate, and providing training about organizational philosophy and culture. If team leaders can serve as these external resources and facilitators, self-managed work teams are more likely to thrive.

However, self-managed work teams do come with potential organizational drawbacks. First, members of self-managed work teams can be co-dependent (Cook & Goff, 2002). What this means is that when there is a poor performing member, the other team members may hold onto that member and support him or her longer than if that team had a formal leader. Second, self-managed work teams can fail when there is low commitment to collective efforts (Foote & Tang, 2008). Third, self-managed work teams are often unsuccessful when members are unable to tolerate uncertainty (Polley & Van Dyne, 1994). Finally, there is considerable evidence that true self-managed work teams are rare. In fact, in most cases there is considerable resistance (O'Toole, Galbraith, & Lawler, 2002), some type of external leader who fails to share power and actively intervenes instead of allowing the team to manage itself (Stewart & Manz, 1995), or one member emerges as a strong internal leader (Sims & Manz, 1994). Wageman (1997) provides case study evidence of many of these problems and discusses how to overcome them using the procedure discussed earlier in this section.

Improving followership in teams

The leadership literature often leaves a vacuum between the leader and group or team performance. However, leadership assumes, and requires, followership. Leaders have more power and influence, both formal and informal. Followers, on the other hand, are defined by their subordinate status and their behavior – they typically go along with someone else's influence attempts (Kellerman, 2008). Further, leaders and followers are part of an interrelated process. For the leader to succeed, the followers must follow and for the followers to follow, there must be a leader (Chaleff, 2008). However, followers do in fact have choice; they sometimes follow while other times do not follow their leader. There are many examples of this, such as acts of civil disobedience. Kellerman says that the reasons for following include creating a sense of stability and security, it is part of the social nature of human behavior, it provide groups with organizing structure, and it helps groups to achieve goals.

Kellerman defines five categories of followers: isolates, bystanders, participants, activists, and diehards. Though classified by Kellerman as followers, isolates are those who are truly detached from the group and prefer to work alone. Bystanders are those who observe but do not actively participate. Participants would like to have an impact on the organization, and as a result actively participate. However, their level of participation depends on how much they agree with the leader. If they agree, they will participate while if they disagree they will not. Activists are energetic and engaged. They feel strongly about the organization and its leaders. Finally diehards are completely dedicated. Once they become attached to a leader, they will follow that person regardless of the cause.

Leadership is effective when it impacts a person's self concept (Lord & Brown, 2004). The success of leaders in part can be attributed to the impact on their followers. Charismatic leaders, for example strongly improve team members' sense of self worth (Conger & Kanungo, 1998). Thus, diehards must first be convinced about the importance of a cause by their leader. Once convinced, they are easy to lead because they feel a sense of worth when the leader, and by default, his or her followers, succeed. On the other hand, isolates do not judge their worth from collective efforts. Thus, it will be very difficult for leaders to convince them to follow. Successful leaders can surround themselves with the followers that are necessary for success.

Three Interventions to Improve Leadership and Influence

Three interventions that are designed to improve shared leadership include empowerment, coaching, and reinforcing candor. According to Bennis and colleagues (1994), group synergy can only be reached by empowering the members of that group. Thus, the first intervention is one that is designed to help leaders to empower others. One of the take-home messages from this chapter is that leading groups and teams requires additional skills that many who are effective leaders in other situations may not have. Thus, the second intervention is coaching so that leaders may improve their team facilitation skills. Finally, feedback and trust are interrelated concepts that are necessary for team leaders to succeed. As a result, the third intervention recommends how a leader may improve trust among her or his followers through allowing straightforward and honest feedback.

Empowerment

According to Lloyd (2000), leadership and power are all too often intertwined. Unfortunately, many team leaders have trouble differentiating power from leading by empowering others. In fact, Lloyd argues that effective team leaders should work to move from a position of power to one of empowerment. Specifically, the goal of effective leadership is to, over time, shift the proportions of responsibility from leaders to their team so that the team members themselves may define what leadership means within their team and eventually the team leader is an active, participating member of the team.

Lloyd provides team leaders with a stepwise approach designed to help teams implement a structure that encourages leaders to empower team members (Table 11.4). Lloyd recognizes that, in many organizations, a shift from power at the level of the leadership team to appropriately sharing leadership and power among teams at all organizational levels is a significant shift in culture. Thus, he starts the intervention with work at the level of leadership, including working on the importance of the need for change (see Kotter, 1996). Consistent with the simple model of change that is presented in this book, the next step that Lloyd recommends is to design the intervention in a way that is tailored to the organization, implement the intervention, and then finally check to verify what is working and what needs to be modified to further improve empowerment and performance within a team.

There is no shortage of evidence that demonstrates the success of team empowerment interventions; only a small sample of the studies demonstrating that empowerment leads to performance gains is reviewed here. Kirkman and Rosen (1999) demonstrate that, overall, empowerment improves performance in face-to-face teams. Empowering virtual teams can also improve performance, especially if the virtual teams meet face-to-face at least some of the time (Kirkman, Rosen, Tesluk, & Gibson, 2004). Lambe, Webb, and Ishida (2009) demonstrated that empowerment improves sales team performance. Chen, Kirkman, Kanfer, Allen, and Rosen (2007) showed that the combination of individual empowerment and team empowerment together also improve team performance. Srivistava, Bartol, and Locke (2006) demonstrated that empowerment is related to knowledge sharing and team efficacy, and these two together improve team performance. According to Mathieu, Gilson, and Ruddy (2006), the reason that empowerment improves performance is because empowering a team improves the underlying team process, such as communication, creating a vision, taking action. Finally, Seibert, Silver, and Randolph (2004) show that empowered work groups perform better and, in addition, members of empowered groups have higher overall job satisfaction, which may make them stay in their jobs longer.

Coaching for team leaders

Coaching team leaders has become a common development tool because it is a way to help leaders improve the performance of their group by focusing on the people and allow members to flourish (Goldsmith, Lyons, & Freas, 2000). In fact, "coaching

Table 11.4 A Summary of the Steps Involved in Empowering a Self-Managed Work Team.

Step	Procedure
1.	Implement a new vision within senior management. In an intervention that is as significant as changing the power structure within an organization, the first step is to work with the senior leadership to change the culture of the organization. According to Lloyd, there are four steps at the leadership level that are required to empower teams, including: a. create a need for change to self-managed work teams; b. work with the leadership to help them to clarify their vision around sharing power; c. work with leaders to set overall goals and objectives for the implementation; and d. involve all of the other stakeholders in the organization to appropriately modify the goals and objectives.
2.	The second major step in changing organizational culture to one that shares power within teams is to design the intervention. a. Lloyd first recommends a gap analysis, which involves assessing the current state of power sharing in the organization and then compare that current state to what is the stated vision. b. During the gap analysis, Lloyd emphasizes that it is as important to consider the social analysis – thinking in terms of how team members will react to the change – as well as the technical analysis. c. The third step is to create a tentative team design. d. Fourth, Lloyd recommends changing the organizational support system so that it encourages teamwork rather than individual work. e. Fifth, the design phase is the time to not only agree on the process for rolling out the change but also the metrics involved in examining whether the change was successful. f. Lloyd's final step is to develop a final action plan for the roll out of empowered, self-managed teams throughout the organization.
3.	Implementation. The third major step is to intervene using the strategies that were created during the action planning phase. a. According to Lloyd, the first part of implementation is to communicate the roll out for the plan. b. The second part of implementation that Lloyd recommends is training all members of the organization about how to empower others, especially those in leadership positions. c. Finally, Lloyd discusses the importance of reevaluation and necessary change during the implementation phase.
4.	The fourth major phase of an empowerment intervention is to monitor the success of the program. a. First, similar to the steps described by the research feedback loop in Chapter 2, it is necessary to evaluate the success of the intervention as attitudes and awareness. b. Second, the information gathered through the evaluation will likely not only show what is working but also what could be improved, and this should lead to an appropriate redesign as necessary.

Adapted from Lloyd (2000).

Table 11.5   A Summary of the Steps Involved in Coaching Team Leaders.

Step	Procedure
1.	Identify attributes for the leader you are coaching.
2.	Determine who can provide meaningful feedback about that leader.
3.	Collect that feedback using surveys, focus groups, and/or interviews.
4.	Analyze the feedback results using either quantitative or qualitative methods, depending on the data that you collected.
5.	Develop an action plan for the competencies that the leader needs to develop. Focus on those competencies when working with the leader.
6.	Work with the team leader to have her or him respond to the stakeholders about the changes in leadership behavior.
7.	Work with the team leader to develop an ongoing follow-up process with his or her team.
8.	Review results from the ongoing follow-up and start again.

Adapted from Goldsmith (2000).

often provides the necessary impetus for building and motivating teams" (Lyons, 2000, p. 9). There are several reasons for this. First, coaching helps team leaders to change behavior (Goldsmith, 2000). This is because leaders can identify, through research, the competencies that they need to develop and then work in a confidential one-on-one situation about how to change the requisite behaviors. Second, coaching requires most managers to change their mindset to that of leaders (Crane, 2000). Finally, effective coaching can bring about deep change and improved self concepts (Smither & Reilly, 2001). Goldsmith (2000) provides the following steps designed to provide leadership coaches with a framework for improving team leadership (Table 11.5).

Coaching processes such as this one work because they are focused, provide feedback, and allow specific time for follow-up (Goldsmith & Morgan, 2000). Hackman and Wageman (2005) review the literature about team leadership and coaching. They summarize several different methods (e.g., process consultation) and list a selection of research demonstrating the importance of coaching for improving effectiveness. They conclude by saying that coaching is an important part of team leadership processes.

Reinforcing candor to build trust in leadership

Trust in leadership is important and necessary. Whipple (2009) claims that trust is like a bank account; leaders can "deposit" into the bank account by performing actions that increase trust and then "withdraw" from that same account when it is necessary to take action to initiate a change. This is somewhat similar to Hollander's (1958) concept of idiosyncrasy credits. Hollander suggests that leaders earn credits through enacting positive behaviors and then burn the credits when performing idiosyncratic behavior. Whipple applies this same idea specifically to a conceptual account that is limited to trust. As one way to build trust, Whipple recommends a three step process designed to increase candor within a group or team; this allows a leader to make "deposits" into the trust account. These steps are summarized in Table 11.6.

As is the case for most of the interventions designed by practitioners, there is no specific research about using the specific steps recommended by Whipple (2009). However, there is certainly considerable research that demonstrates that a) communication by a team leader improves trust (e.g., de Vries, Bakker-Pieper, & Oostenveld, 2010), b) feedback from a leader improves trust (e.g., Geister, Konradt, & Hertel, 2006), and c) trust in leadership is necessary for leaders to succeed (e.g., Roussin, 2008). In addition, there is evidence that leaders build or burn credit (Hollander, 1958) depending on performance (Howell, Lederman, Owen, & Solomon, 1978). Thus, it is likely that the steps recommended by Whipple will improve trust in leadership and, as a result, leaders will work in more effective group and team environments.

Table 11.6   A Summary of the Steps Involved in Building Trust in Team Leaders.

Step	Procedure
1.	*Place the Table Stakes.* According to Whipple, building trust is like placing the table stakes in a card game. To build integrity, a team leader must ante up table stakes to play. In this case, though, the stakes are not financial. Instead, they are values such as honesty, openness, positive communication, consistency, and being ethical.
2.	*Follow with Enabling Actions.* After a team leader puts up the "table stakes," then he or she must follow with specific actions that are consistent with the stated goals. Whipple provides some examples, such as following up, advocating well, being fair, and admitting mistakes. When a team leader behaves with these actions, it enables the leader to tolerate situations that happen as a result of ill-advised decisions or unfortunate circumstances. Whipple states that putting up the table stakes and then following with enabling actions are necessary but insufficient conditions for trust to endure.
3.	*Reinforce Candor from Others.* The final step for Whipple is when team leaders spending time reinforcing the candor of those on the team, which is the ability for team members to speak up and continue to feel positive about their team leader even when expressing concern with that leader's behavior. When a team leader reinforces the candor of team members, it builds trust because people are typically punished for expressing a concern rather than reinforced for it. This creates a sense of transparency and, in Whipple's terms, creates a large trust deposit.

Adapted from Whipple (2009).

FOCUS ON APPLICATION

Improving leadership by reinforcing candor and building trust

The practitioner

Robert T. Whipple is CEO of Leadergrow Inc., an organization dedicated to the development of leaders. As a leadership coach and business consultant, he works with individual clients and large organizations such as the Rochester Business Alliance.

A highly successful leader at Eastman Kodak Company for over 30 years, Mr. Whipple accomplished revolutionary change while leading a division of over 2,000 people through the application of outstanding "people" skills. He holds a Bachelors Degree in Mechanical Engineering from Union College, a Masters Degree in Chemical Engineering from Syracuse University, and a Masters of Business Administration from The Simon School at the University of Rochester.

The symptom

This organization was in a state of flux. The entire group had just merged with a similar unit in a different city, resulting in significant organizational turmoil and uncertainty. For example, the Division Operations Manager of the unit had been fired, and the VP to whom he was reporting was then demoted to Operations Manager.

Several other staff realignments were also occurring. Morale was low because the perception was that this unit had been "taken over" during the merger. Leadership training seemed to provide some stabilizing concepts to prevent an even further destabilization. Several of the supervisors were newly appointed to their position and had never been in a management role prior that time. For example, two of the supervisors were on their first day in the new position when we started the training.

Assessing the problem

A leadership development instrument was used to assess which areas needed emphasis in training. Participants responded using a four point scale (0 = no need to 3 = Urgent need) with over 40 areas of leadership development.

The assessment included a contrast of the perceived needs at different levels in the organization. For example, for the item "selecting the right people for key positions" The Supervisor group rated it 2.88 out of a possible 3.0 (absolutely critical training need) while the Management group rated the same item 2.2 (important, but not critical). In another example, the item "handling your mistakes" scored "important" to the Supervisors, but "low need" to the managers. Looking at the variation of items between groups gave good insight into how the different levels saw development needs. This information was factored into the course design.

I then conducted focus groups to better understand the numerical analysis. These sessions gave qualitative data to further inform the quantitative analysis. Finally, I met with management to ascertain the interpersonal dynamics of the groups.

Following the analysis, I developed a program plan that contained details of the trust and candor intervention. As a result of the up-front analysis, the training activities were laser-focused on the specific needs and showed an excellent chance for a good return on investment.

Intervening: Trust and candor

I gave eight managers and thirteen supervisors a series of five half-day sessions highlighting the methods of building candor and improving trust within their organization. Specifically, I

1. Generated training materials customized for the need areas and in the language of the organization. All case studies were generated for the particular business sector.
2. Conducted the training sessions. There were six sessions at four hours each. The goal was to have the training sessions focused on andragogy rather than pedagogy. Participants were to be actively involved rather than passively listening at least 40% of the time.
3. Divided sessions into appropriate themes, including: 1. Key Leadership Concepts, 2. Creating a Plan, 3. Customer Service, 4. Creating a Culture of Trust, 5. Communication and Corporate Skills, 6. Putting It All In Focus.
4. Used pretest and posttest surveys about leader attitude about the training as well as a self-graded leadership skill inventory. These data allowed for a statement of progress accomplished by the training.
5. Conducted a debrief meeting for management, and information was disseminated throughout the population.
6. Provided the organization with recommendations for follow up work.

I conducted much of the steps involved in the intervention as one large group, although there were times when I separated the leaders into managers and supervisors for some of their breakout sessions and small group work.

The results showed a significant improvement in trust and interpersonal skills when measured by a pre and post survey of individual perceptions. Specifically, ratings on the organization's annual survey showed a 28% increase in commitment to improving leadership. The number of hours per week spent trying to resolve employee issues went from 11.6 to 13.6, which was a 17% increase. Further, people were happier to invest the time in this leadership training effort at the end than before, and were more satisfied with the tools and equipment to do their job. One vice president even commented that "after working with Leadergrow, our managers and supervisors are communicating better, and there is a higher bond of trust within the organization. I was particularly pleased to see that our leaders feel a higher level of support as a result of the training."

Chapter Summary

Leadership has been one of the most widely studied topics in organizational science. This is because leaders can be an avenue for team success as well as a tool for team failure. This chapter examined the historical progression of leadership from the simplistic "Great Man" theories to the practical Functional Leadership Model. Each theory contributes in part what it means to our conception of what a great leader is. Team leadership, however, is a specific function of leadership. Team leadership requires a level of sharing of power that is not typically required of the transformational and charismatic leaders that often become case examples of what it means to be a great leader. Further team leadership requires the skills of a facilitator in addition to those of a leader. Finally, team leadership may even rotate, and there is the possibility (though it seems to be uncommon in practice) of leaderless teams. Improving leadership through the three interventions described here or by using others can help to improve a team's chances for reaching its goals.

Additional Resources

Conger, J. A., & Riggio, R. E. (2007). *The practice of leadership: Developing the next generation of leaders*. San Francisco: Jossey-Bass.

Pearce C. L., & Conger J. A. (2003). *Shared leadership: Reframing the hows and whys of leadership*. Thousand Oaks, CA: Sage Publications, Inc.

Wageman, R. (1997). Critical success factors for creating superb self-managing teams. *Organizational Dynamics, 26*, 49–61.

Yukl, G. (2010). *Leadership in organizations* (7th ed.). Upper Saddle River, NJ: Prentice Hall.

Team Exercises

Exercise 11.1   Lead like a marine

The United States Marine Corps has spent countless hours working to improve how they develop leaders. As a result of their research, they created a set of 11 leadership principles, which they consider goals, and 14 leadership traits, which they consider qualities for thought and action.

1. As a group, review the principles and traits below.
2. Consider how they are relevant to leadership in your group or team.

Marine corps leadership principles

- Know yourself and seek improvement.
- Be technically and tactically proficient.
- Know your Marines and look out for their welfare.
- Keep your Marines informed.
- Set the example.
- Ensure the task is understood, supervised, and accomplished.
- Train your Marines as a team.
- Make sound and timely decisions.
- Develop a sense of responsibility among your subordinates.
- Employ your command in accordance with its capabilities.

Marine corps leadership traits

- Justice
- Judgment
- Dependability
- Initiative
- Decisiveness
- Tact
- Integrity
- Enthusiasm
- Bearing
- Unselfishness
- Courage
- Knowledge
- Loyalty
- Endurance

Exercise 11.2   Leadership gap analysis

One way to develop leadership is through a self-assessment of where people currently stand in their leadership skills and comparing that to where they should be. The following sheet provides a list of leadership behaviors across many leadership theories, including functional and transformational theories. Print out the form. Cut along the line that is above "How competent" and fold that section back. Then, have team leaders take the checklist about the importance of leadership areas, rating themselves on a 1–5 scale where 1 = not very important while 5 = very important.

After team leaders complete their ratings of the importance. Have them fold the sheet back and then rate their level of competence from 1 = not very competent while 5 = very competent.. In each team leader, look for the largest gaps between the importance column and the competent column. These are the areas where that team leader may want to spend some energy further developing competencies.

Leadership Gap Analysis

Below is a list of the requirements of a leader. Please answer the questions to the best of your ability on a scale of 1–5, where 1 = not at all and 5 = very.

	How important is this area to your leadership?		How competent are you in this area?
Skills and Abilities			
Initiate ideas	_____	....	_____
Informally interact	_____	....	_____
Support subordinates	_____	....	_____
Take responsibility	_____	....	_____
Develop group atmosphere	_____	....	_____
Organize/structure work	_____	....	_____
Communicate formally	_____	....	_____
Reward and punish	_____	....	_____
Set goals	_____	....	_____
Make decisions	_____	....	_____
Train and develop others	_____	....	_____
Solve problems	_____	....	_____
Generate enthusiasm	_____	....	_____
Job Requirements			
Organizing	_____	....	_____
Analyzing	_____	....	_____
Planning	_____	....	_____
Communication	_____	....	_____
Delegation	_____	....	_____
High-quality work	_____	....	_____
Carefulness	_____	....	_____
Interpersonal skills	_____	....	_____
Job knowledge	_____	....	_____
Organizational knowledge	_____	....	_____

Toughness	————	··········	————
Integrity	————	··········	————
Develop others	————	··········	————
Listening	————	··········	————

Transformational Leadership

Develop a clear and appealing vision	————	··········	————
Develop a strategy	————	··········	————
Articulate and promote the vision	————	··········	————
Act confident and optimistic	————	··········	————
Express confidence in followers	————	··········	————
Use early success to build on	————	··········	————
Celebrate successes	————	··········	————
Use dramatic, symbolic actions	————	··········	————
Lead by example	————	··········	————
Create and/or change symbols, slogans and ceremonies	————	··········	————

Chapter 12

Working in Virtual Teams

A project manager leads a team of scientists who are involved in remediating a site with contaminated ground water. To help him maintain a meaningful work-family balance and tap into the expertise of others within his organization who are located in other national and international offices, his organization supports his work at home several days each week. He can still succeed with his projects because he can avoid a long commute in a major metropolitan area while still actively participating in meetings with his team members, who are located in various cities across the country at times that are mutually convenient for them all. He achieves this by using computer-mediated communication software, a cellular phone, electronic mail, instant messaging, a phone with a landline, social networking software, a home facsimile machine, and video conferencing software.

Twenty years ago a virtual team like this one was rare because the technology to support such teams was not readily and easily available to most team members, especially when working within a home office. Now, however, group and team members typically have powerful desktop computers, high-speed internet, and almost free or completely free and easy-to-use programs such as Skype for video conferences, WebEx for online presentations, Google Groups for file storage and discussion boards, and Facebook to provide social interaction (to name just a very small number of readily available possibilities, many of which are freeware). The question is no longer the simple black and white dichotomy of whether a team is virtual or not, but instead how virtual is the team. Even as recently as 2003, scholars and practitioners wondered somewhat rhetorically about whether virtual teams are with us to stay (Wageman, 2003). It is clear now that almost all teams work virtually

Group Dynamics and Team Interventions: Understanding and Improving Team Performance,
First Edition. Timothy M. Franz.
© 2012 Timothy M. Franz. Published 2012 by Blackwell Publishing Ltd.

Figure 12.1   Dilbert Reflects about Virtual Teams. DILBERT © (2007) Scott Adams. Used By permission of UNIVERSAL UCLICK.

to at least some extent regardless of whether they work in offices that are located next door to one another or they are located in different countries and time zones.

Certainly, working virtually can allow members who are separated by time and distance to continue to succeed together, as Dilbert tries to do in the cartoon in this chapter (Figure 12.1). Unfortunately, like any team process, working virtually as a team comes with some trade-offs. In the earlier example of the project manager: During one virtual meeting, he had to drive approximately 40 miles to a different location where there was a physical office because of unexpectedly spotty and poor cellular phone service. At another virtual meeting, he neglected to turn his phone on mute when his two-year old twins came running into his home office – his team-mates enjoyed a one-minute discussion in "babytalk" prior to reminding him to mute his phone. A third example is when he neglected to tell his team that he walked away from the phone for a bathroom and coffee break during a phone conference just as they asked him for some advice; he was, of course, not there to provide it. These are just a few of the many problems that can occur when working together virtually.

On one hand, many of the processes and interventions described and recommended in this book are certainly relevant for helping virtual as well as face-to-face teams to succeed. According to Richard Hackman (as quoted in Coutu & Beschloss, 2009), "Virtual teams have really come into their own in the past decade, but I don't believe they differ fundamentally from traditional teams." On the other hand, there do seem to be meaningful differences between working virtually in a team versus working solely in a face-to-face environment. As Kirkman and Mathieu (2005) argue, it is important to understand the level of virtuality of teams to determine "(a) what is trying to be accomplished through virtual means, (b) what competencies are required to execute the virtual processes, and (c) who needs to be trained" (p. 714). This chapter empha-sizes only the ways in which virtual teams have different processes from face-to-face ones while recognizing that there are far more similarities than differences.

Table 12.1   Measuring the Level of Team Virtuality.

Instructions: Circle the appropriate number using the following scale: (1) = Strongly disagree, (2) = Disagree, (3) = Neither agree or disagree, (4) Agree, and (5) = Strongly agree.					
1. Most of the day-to-day communication between team members was face-to-face (reverse coded).	**1**	**2**	**3**	**4**	**5**
2. Most of the day-to-day communication between team members was through computer or telephone interaction.	**1**	**2**	**3**	**4**	**5**
3. Our project team was considered a virtual project team, that is, we primarily interacted through computer and telecommunications technologies.	**1**	**2**	**3**	**4**	**5**

Adapted from Bierly, Stark, and Kessler (2009) and Stark and Bierly (2009).

Learning Goals for Chapter 12

- Learn how to assess the virtuality of a team.
- Understand the different types of virtuality.
- Know how to make a virtual team succeed.
- Know some of the drawbacks of virtual team work.
- Understand the processes that might cause a virtual team to fail.
- Learn to match the communication medium to the task and the team.
- Know how to intervene to help a virtual team to succeed.

Assessing Virtual Teams

Martins, Gilson, and Maynard (2004) reviewed the research about virtual teams. One of the many contributions from their review was to more clearly define what it means to be virtual. According to Martins and colleagues, virtuality results when "team members use technology to varying degrees in working across locational, temporal, and relational boundaries to accomplish an interdependent task" (p. 808). Kirkman and Mathieu (2005) also suggest three similar categories, including a) contextual features, b) task-member-media compatibility, and c) temporal characteristics. Contextual features are made up of the number of boundaries crossed including time space culture, division, and so on. (more than 30 meters), the proportion of co-located members, and team size. Task-member-media compatibility is made up of task complexity and team member competencies. Finally, temporal characteristics are made up of time available for task completion, team evolution and maturation, and the rhythms of team processes (more likely in action rather than transition phases).

Using the theories and ideas developed by Martins and colleagues, Stark and Bierly (2009; Bierly, Stark, & Kessler, 2009) created three items to assess the level of virtuality (Table 12.1). The items measure the location, temporal, and relational boundaries that make up the virtual interactions of teams in organizations today.

The first item in this measure is reverse-scored. Thus, to determine the level of team virtuality, first subtract the score for item one from six. Next, add that difference to the scores for items two and three, and divide by three to create an average perceived level of virtualness. According to Bierly and his colleagues (2009; Stark & Bierly, 2009), this scale better tests the nuances in the level of virtuality than many of the previous measures that considered virtual teams as an all-or-none phenomenon, where teams that met face-to-face even once were not considered to be virtual. Using this measure, Bierly and colleagues find that virtual teams have more difficulty than face-to-face teams with trust, collaboration (Bierly et al., 2009), and managing conflict (Stark & Bierly, 2009). Staples and Webster (2008) provide a more detailed measure of virtuality that, unlike Bierly and colleagues, is based on objective measures rather than the perception of virtuality that Bierly and colleagues used and is based on number of sites, level of isolation of members, the spread across zones, stability of the virtual team, language diversity, and how often the team actually meets face-to-face. However, it is more difficult to calculate and is not easily used as a self-assessment tool, like the ones in this book.

A Brief Background on Virtual Groups and Teams

I have included a chapter about working the impact of virtuality on working in groups and teams because members of virtual groups and teams have a different – and in many cases less well defined – sense of what it means to be a member. And, organizations have barely even started learning about the problems with virtual communication media yet. Scholars and practitioners are just beginning to figure out how to use social networking sites, tweeting, podcasts, video feeds, and many of the other technologies that are made up of what is being called Web2.0 (Iverson & Vukotich, 2009). It is likely that even more virtual communication technologies are being developed now, and the nature of computer-mediated communication will change even more in the near future.

As described at the beginning of this book, an expectation of "groupness" is that people see themselves as part of the group and others also see them as part of that group. The distinction about whether or not a person is actually in a group is not altogether clear in virtual teams. This is especially true for groups and teams where all but one member is co-located. But, do virtual members even think of themselves as an integral contributor to the group? Do others outside the group see them as members? These distinctions impact group process and performance and as you will see, group process and performance are impacted when technology mediates group members' working relationships (Driskell & Salas, 2006).

The purpose for using virtual teams is not simply to exploit the available technology but when virtuality is necessary for accomplishing necessary group or team tasks. Specifically, a virtual team is "a group of geographically dispersed employees who are assembled using a combination of telecommunication and information technologies for the purpose of accomplishing an organizational task" (Shin, 2005, p. 331). Many teams today work within at least some level of virtuality (Martins et al., 2004).

Even or group and team members who are typically co-located, at any one point in time, one team member may be at home, another may be in the office, a third may be working in another office, while a final member may be on a business or family trip. Like Driskell, Radtke, and Salas (2003), This book uses "the term virtual team to refer to a team or group whose members are mediated by time, distance, or technology. Other closely related terms that have been used to describe this type of environment include computer-mediated communications and computer-supported cooperative work" (p. 297). Scott (1999) provides even more terms that can be added to this list of virtual group arrangements, such as groupware, group communication technology, and electronic meeting systems.

People who work virtually must have additional skills and abilities to be successful group or team members than those required when working in face-to-face teams (Orvis & Zaccaro, 2008). Hertel, Konradt, and Voss (2008) suggest that members working virtually need the same taskwork and teamwork skills and abilities, but also need what they term telecooperation skills as well. According to Hertel and colleagues, these telecooperation skills and abilities include self management (made up of independence, persistence, creativity, and motivation to learn), interpersonal trust, and intercultural abilities. In their initial research, they developed a measure to identify the necessary telecooperation skills and abilities, which showed that these additional telecooperation skills may predict success above and beyond the task and teamwork skills necessary for working virtually.

There are advantages to working virtually, the most significant of which are explained here. First, group and team members no longer must be co-located. In fact, they can be in many different times and places, as is the example at the beginning of the chapter. Second, virtual work provides members with a level of anonymity that face-to-face communications do not provide. In brainstorming and other creativity tasks, this can benefit the team because people feel less likely to be evaluated, and are more likely to share truly creative ideas. Finally, working virtually in a group or team may allow members to maintain a healthy work-life balance. A working parent may continue to work if, for example, a sick child is required to stay home from school. Bell and Kozlowski (2002) suggest, in general, that the purpose of virtual groups and teams is to create more flexibility in working relationships. Thus, organizations have less downtime from missing group or team members, an impact that is especially important when a meeting would have to be canceled if that member missed it. Unfortunately, this is not always a benefit to employees because working virtually also allows work to bleed into family time, which is a benefit for the organization but not necessarily for the group or team member.

Virtual group work certainly brings advantages. However, it also comes with disadvantages. The most commonly discussed disadvantage from working virtually is the loss of nonverbal cues that occurs in many different computer-mediated communication mediums (Potter & Balthazard, 2002). In many, and maybe even all, virtual environments, people no longer have eye contact, lose information about tone, cannot easily judge facial expressions, do not clearly see body posture, and fail to get many of the other nonverbal and verbal contextual cues that help people to make sense of discussion. This dramatically restricts the amount of information passed back and forth in the communication process. Communication is necessary in groups and teams, and the communication process changes when mediated by computer technology (Potter & Balthazard, 2002). This is even more difficult given that the computer systems that we use were designed for computations rather than for communication (Scott, 1999).

At least some of these communication disadvantages in groups and teams that work virtually can be mitigated to some extent by the type of communication system used by the group or team. Computer-mediated communication systems can be classified as creating rich versus sparse environments, whether it is a rich environment due to the number of nonverbal cues that can be identified within the virtual environment (Daft & Lengel, 1986). Impoverished or sparse environments are ones where the person communicating information gets little to no acknowledgement or feedback about understanding from the receiver (Driskell, Radtke, & Salas, 2003). In face-to-face communication, feedback that shows that a receiver is misunderstanding information can take the form of puzzled looks, dozing off, lack of eye contact, or a loss of the typical "uh-huhs" that serve as part of the active listening process. Email is an example of a sparse environment – groups have few of the nonverbal cues and as a result messages passed through email can sometimes be misinterpreted. On the other hand, rich virtual environments are ones that allow for the communication of these cues. Rich environments, such as videoconferencing, are much closer in nature to face-to-face communication. These environments allow for better communication of nonverbal information and result in less miscommunication resulting from the computer-mediated environment; rich environments are those that are more similar to face-to-face communication.

Although losing nonverbal cues during communication is often listed as the major disadvantage of working virtually, it is certainly not the only one. A second disadvantage of virtual group work results from the greater potential for technology issues to arise. A computer or system can fail, lines can lose connection, or users can accidentally disconnect. A third disadvantage is that there is the greater potential for social loafing that may result from the lack of accountability. All who have worked virtually can tell stories of at least one member who has failed to answer a question (or can probably report the number of times that that they were reading unrelated email or checking a social networking site during a meeting). Fourth, group process may be required to slow down. Many of the subtle (or not so subtle) norms and restrictions that control the flow of communication, such as a raised eyebrow or confused look, are lost when working virtually (Baltes, Dickson, Sherman, Bauer, & LaGanke, 2002). Fifth, virtual teamwork creates leadership challenges (Bell & Kozlowski, 2002), especially around the difficulties with monitoring behavior, coaching, and performance management. Negative feedback specifically is very difficult to give virtually. Finally, there is a gap between typing speed and thinking speed. Often, virtual environments slow the communication process down. Many of these disadvantages seem to be tempered over time, so that groups that work virtually together for long periods of time can minimize or eliminate the problems caused by the disadvantages (Walther, 1992).

Table 12.2 Examples of Different Communication Mediums.

Category	Example	Media Richness	When to Use
Synchronous: Use these when dialogue is required	Face-to-Face	Very Rich	For collocated members To manage conflict During difficult, challenging, or uncomfortable conversations
	Video conference	Rich	For members who are located in different places but who are, more or less, working at similar times When nonverbal cues are necessary When virtual team members need face time
	Telephone/ Teleconferencing	Moderate	When members may want to avoid having a detailed record of a sensitive discussion
	Chat room	Sparse	When a discussion requires a written record and/or the technology cannot support videoconferencing
Asynchronous: Use these when passing along information	Email	Sparse	When a written record is required To pass along important documents
	Voicemail	Sparse	When leaving information where nuance (e.g., voice tone) is important to understanding a message
	Texting	Sparse	When a short amount of information needs to be delivered quickly.
	Blog, Wiki, or Discussion Board	Sparse	When keeping records of a discussion that occurs over a long period of time.

There are different types of computer-mediated communication environments, and each serves a purpose. A selection of these different environments and when each should be used is detailed in Table 12.2. The first and most cursory distinction is whether the environment is synchronous or asynchronous. Synchronous means at the same time, and these mediums allow people to "meet" even if not face-to-face, and have a dialogue. The synchronous systems allow members to have a dialogue about issues that require at least some back and forth conversation. Systems allowing for synchronous communication can be effective tools for decision making, resolving conflict, and discussing sensitive issues.

Examples of four different synchronous environments are included in Table 12.2. The first is a face-to-face environment, which is often the benchmark for all other environments. Face-to-face communication is the most rich; members have all of the nonverbal cues that help to improve communication processes (McGrath & Berdahl, 1998). Because of this, face-to-face conversations are often best if there is considerable conflict or the conversation is one that is sensitive. A second example of a synchronous environment is a video conference. Video conferences, like face-to-face conversations, provide a considerable amount of information and are also quite rich. These environments suit teams that need to dialogue and need some "face time" but for budgetary or other reasons are not collocated. A third synchronous environment is a phone conference. With phone conferences, users can hear some of the nonverbal, such as voice tone and inflection, but lose the visual cues. Thus, though not as sparse as other environments, phone conferences are richer than text-based communication mediums and can be used for somewhat sensitive conversations where the members do not want a detailed record of the conversation. A final synchronous method of communication listed in the table is a chat room, which allows members to dialogue while at the same time failing to provide a rich environment. These should be reserved for discussions where members need to dialogue and may need a record, but do not expect the discussion to be one that is sensitive in nature.

The second major category includes computer-mediated environments that are asynchronous. These are systems where members do not meet at the same time. The asynchronous systems are typically better for processes involving detailed information exchange, though the effectiveness of the information exchange depends on the fluidity and fluency of members to use the medium (McGrath & Berdahl, 1998). Email, voicemail, texting, and discussion boards/wikis/blogs are examples of asynchronous systems. Each of these tools allows group members to communicate virtually, but members do not have to be working on the system at the same time. First, email is an excellent virtual tool for small groups to communicate because it provides direct access to only those members and allows for (somewhat) confidential transmission of information. Second, voicemail can be a virtual tool for communicating confidential information between two members. However, it usually does not easily allow for long-term storage of those messages. Third, texting (a virtual tool that has components of synchronous and asynchronous communication, depending on how it is used) allows quick access to members when available, but is most efficient at passing along small amounts of information among two or three members; many groups may be far too large to use texting efficiently. Finally, discussion boards, blogs, and wikis can provide excellent tools for large groups to keep track of information. These tools are best managed by a few members and can quickly become cumbersome if a large number of members is contributing.

The Relationship between Virtuality and Group/Team Outcomes

Surprisingly, the impact of the level of virtuality on group and team performance remains unclear. The reason for this is because there simply is not yet enough research about virtual group and team outcomes – the detailed study of this area is just beginning (Kirkman & Mathieu, 2005). This is a definitely a case in which practitioners have quickly moved their practice well beyond what scholars have studied (Bell & Kozlowski, 2002). As a result, there are plenty of practical claims about how to improve virtual teams, but scant research evidence demonstrating whether these claims actually work as predicted.

Scott (1999) completed a thorough, albeit now dated, review of the research literature about the performance of computer-mediated groups and teams. Unfortunately, the only clear outcome was that the findings were unclear. According to Scott, it is likely that computer-mediation can potentially lead to higher performing groups, but only when very specific conditions for success have been met. Some of those conditions are listed here.

First, computer-mediated groups must find ways to compensate for the loss of nonverbal information (Potter & Balthazard, 2002). Wageman (2003) suggests that virtual teams have at least the possibility for gains with proper coaching about the causes of losses in effort as well as the coordination problems that are exacerbated when working in a computer-mediated environment. She says to look for these opportunities for coaching during team launch and then again during critical break points in task behavior, such as when the team is struggling. Third, McGrath and Berdahl (1998) find that computer-mediated teams, although not as successful as face-to-face communication at first, do fine after working together for a period of time. In addition, they find that members of computer-mediated groups must work harder because they have to overcome some of the barriers to communication caused by the medium.

On the other hand, Fjermestad (2004) reviewed the literature and finds that computer-mediated groups are as or more successful than face-face groups. First, Fjermestad says that the evidence "shows an overwhelming tendency to find 'no significant differences between unsupported face-to-face modes and the types of group support systems that have been studied thus far'" (p. 252). Also, he finds that rich environments are better for most tasks and groups can succeed when using a rich environment. Finally, he finds that virtual groups, even though somewhat less efficient, have fewer process losses and more process gains than face-to-face groups because the computer-mediated environment minimizes some of the typical personality and interpersonal conflicts and group process issues that decrease performance in face-to-face groups.

To some extent, this may be true. Electronic brainstorming groups definitely eliminate production blocking, a major cause of process losses in face-to-face brainstorming groups. They do this by providing group members with more communication channels as well as an unlimited opportunity to provide information to discussion (Dennis & Valacich, 1993; Gallupe, Bastianutti, & Cooper, 1991). As a result, these electronic brainstorming groups show performance above that of both traditional brainstorming and nominal groups (Dennis & Valacich, 1993; Gallupe, Bastianutti, & Cooper, 1991).

Another positive outcome of working virtually is improved member participation. A meta-analysis by Rains (2005) revealed that in virtual teams

a) members have more equal participation, b) the group shares more unique information, c) members have more equal influence, and d) members have more equal
influence, at least for computer-mediated systems where members are anonymous.
Unfortunately Rains also found that this did not increase overall participation
rates. In fact, there was less total communication in virtual teams when compared
to face-to-face teams.

Finally, there may be gender differences in participation rates as well.
Specifically, women feel more included in predominantly male virtual teams than
they do in predominantly male face-to-face teams (Triana, Kirkman, & Garcia,
2009). The women in the study by Triana and colleagues report that they no
longer feel like tokens in male-only groups because "social categorization may be
lessened" (p. 32) and the typical status cues that result from face-to-face interaction are missing (Driskell, Radtke, & Salas, 2003). Traina and colleagues state that
the biases potentially resulting from demographic diversity have less of an impact
within virtual teams – at least those that do not have an initial face-to-face meeting and hold few face-to-face meetings in general. If members do not know the
demographic information that face-to-face meetings provide, they cannot hold
the same biases against members of certain groups that are traditionally
discriminated against.

Regardless of whether there are overall performance benefits when working in a
virtual group, the evidence reveals that, for the most part, members of virtual teams
struggle with the affective outcomes associated with group functioning. First, computer-mediated groups are less cohesive than face-to-face groups (Warkentin,
Sayeed, & Hightower, 1997). Second, members generally have lower satisfaction
(Graebner, Offermann, Basu, & Wirtz, 2009; Redman & Sankar, 2003), however this
depends on the levels of participation. When members participate more they are
satisfied with their group efforts. On the other hand, if there is more competition
and less participation, members are less satisfied. It is likely the problems that are
caused by communication technology are the cause of the dissatisfaction (Whitman
et al., 2005).

One final point is that virtual groups must have a good fit between person, task,
and technology, as detailed in Figure 12.2. However, this "fit between task and technology is dynamic, not static" (McGrath & Berdahl, 1998, p. 221), so the members
(and leaders) of virtual groups must recognize how it changes over time. Specifically,
some virtual technologies may work better for certain people and specific tasks at
one time, while other technologies may work better for other people and tasks at
another time. The reality is that no team should be expecting to use just one virtual
medium to communicate over the life of that group.

According to Kirkman and Mathieu (2005; Bell & Kozlowski, 2002) the major
task characteristic that drives success and defines whether groups should work
virtually is task complexity, discussed earlier in this book. Structured tasks which
only require pooled interdependence require less rich environments while complex tasks that require reciprocal interdependence require richer environments.
In addition, Kirkman and Mathieu suggest that tasks which require intensive

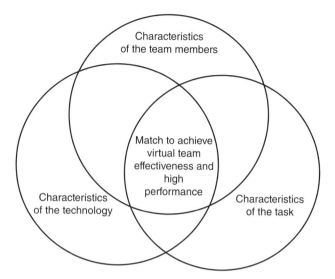

Figure 12.2   Getting to Virtual Team Effectiveness: Matching the People with the Task and Communication Medium.

interdependence should be avoided by virtual groups. The reason for this is that less complex tasks require less communication and coordination while more complex tasks, especially those which require considerable interdependencies, require far more communication and coordination (see also Staples & Webster, 2008).

A second implication of the match is that members must be proficient in using the technology (McGrath & Berdahl, 1998). Clearly, all group members must have the technical competencies to perform virtually, but they may also require training in the interpersonal competencies that a virtual environment requires. Finally, they must have the willingness to succeed in a virtual environment, which changes over time. As a result, virtual groups may succeed only when the communication medium matches the needs of the person and the type of task on which the group is working.

Potential Pitfalls to Success in Virtual Groups and Teams

As described previously, there is considerable evidence that there is reduced effort, whether actual or perceived, in virtual teams (Wageman, 2003). In addition to the potential problems with technological competencies described previously (see also Peters & Manz, 2007), trust, conflict, counternormative behavior, and problems with leadership may cause these reduced efforts. With knowledge and training in virtual competencies, group and team members who work virtually can likely minimize, or even eliminate, these problems.

Trust is necessary for all groups and teams to succeed, and may even be more important in virtual groups and teams than it is in face-to-face teams. This is because members work from a distance and often do not have the social interaction that members working in face-to-face situations have (Peters & Manz, 2007; Bierly *et al.*, 2009; Staples & Webster, 2008). The lack of social interaction reduces the ability for members to get to know one another.

Unfortunately, even though trust may be more important when working virtually, there are concerns about reduced trust in virtual groups and teams (Shin, 2005). Virtuality, though, does not seem to affect cognitive-based trust (Sanchez, Olson-Buchanan, Schmidkte, & Bradley, 2009), which is the type of trust that is based on keeping to task-related commitments and tends to affect performance outcomes.

Because of the lack of trust, virtual groups and teams may experience increased task-related conflict when compared to those that interact face-to-face. According to Shin (2005), this occurs because of the spatial, temporal, cultural, and organizational dispersion under which virtual groups and teams typically function. The multiple levels of dispersion may cause ambiguity about who is responsible, a lack of task clarity, role conflict, a greater potential for members to lack an understanding of the differing values of other members, and a weak group identity. These result in a greater likelihood of lower group cohesiveness when working virtually than when working in typical face-to-face situations.

For many groups and teams, the electronic communication medium is replacing at least some of the face-to-face communication process and team members must learn how to work together in this computer-mediated environment (Peters & Manz, 2007). Unfortunately, as these members start to work together and move further along the continuum of virtuality, many of them fail to establish virtual norms. As a result, there is a greater potential for flaming or other uninhibited and counternormative behavior that results from the partial anonymity and deindividuation provided by a virtual environment (Peters & Manz, 2007). Driskell, Radtke, and Salas (2003) review the literature and conclude that, although this does occur, it is not as common as many think. They conclude that flaming and counternormative behavior likely occurs under certain specific conditions of group tension and are especially high when those groups and teams have not established additional norms necessary for their virtual work.

As a result of the potential for lower trust, increased conflict, and increased counternormative behavior in virtual groups and teams, many have suggested that teams should start with a face-to-face meeting (Hambley, O'Neill, & Kline, 2007). In this initial meeting, members should get to know one another, establish norms, define tasks, clarify roles, and discuss cultural differences. In addition, virtual groups and teams may want to consider ongoing and regular face-to-face meetings, especially during times when the group or team is facing a difficult and complex task, the potential for conflict, or when critical (and potentially negative) feedback is possible.

Finally, virtual groups and teams face leadership problems because members are distributed across time and space (Braga, 2008). In addition, leaders must manage and facilitate groups and teams in which members may have lower trust and cohesion (Braga, 2008). This becomes a more difficult task, especially for new leaders or ones who are not a part of the everyday work of the group or team. Thus, leaders are required to focus more on establishing a group identity, building trust, managing the communication medium, motivating people, coordinating group efforts, and developing member potential (O'Neill, Lewis, & Hambley, 2008) than they might when members are working in a typical face-to-face group or team.

Three Interventions to Improve Performance in Virtual Teams

Most of the resources for improving virtual teams are from practitioners because they have been at the forefront of making change and creating improvement for virtual teams. As discussed previously in this chapter (Staples & Webster, 2008), virtual teams also need general teamwork skills. Thus, many of the books about improving virtual teams also discuss, in general, how to improve teams. For example, Lipnack and Stamps (2000) detail a seven-step model for improving virtual teams. The first six steps of their model are almost identical to any other team development model that is designed for face-to-face teams and include creating a team identity, determining the mission of the team, determining milestones, setting goals, identifying who should be on the team, membership, and establish relationships among team members. Their seventh step is the only one that is specific to improving teams that are mediated by technology. A more recent book Brown, Huettner, and James-Tanny (2007) is conceptually similar to the book by Lipnack and Stamps. Brown and colleagues detail general group improvement in their first eight chapters, and then discuss how groups and teams may incorporate virtual tools to improve their group work throughout the remainder of their book.

Because of this practitioner focus, many of the interventions with virtual teams are designed with the basic procedures involved for team training as their backbone. The overarching goal of the bulk of these virtual team training programs is to create deeper personal and/or work relationships among members that are spread across time and distance so that members have a better shared understanding of the competencies of the other members and teams can build trust as a result (Baan & Maznevski, 2008; Peters & Manz, 2008). The three programs described here include virtual team training, virtual mediation, and a structure for setting up virtual teams for success.

Virtual Team Training

Thompson and Coovert (2006) summarize recent literature about methods to improve the performance of virtual teams. Based on their review, they recommend

Table 12.3   A Summary of the Steps Involved in Virtual Team Training.

Step	Procedure
1.	*Provide Training on Groupware.* Thompson and Coovert recommend moving beyond the standard team training and instead focus also on training that is specific to the virtual tools that the team will be using. Many of the tools have powerful options that a casual user may not know.
2.	*Open and Honest Conversation.* Thompson and Coovert also recommend that facilitators or leaders encourage reflection and open conversations about the difficulties of the computer-mediated environment. Reflection about what works as well as what does not can help teams to learn and move to a higher level of performance.
3.	*Training about Virtual Information Needs.* Thompson and covert suggest that teams need training about the informational needs within virtual teams. Specifically, they recommend that team members learn to share information about situational constraints that are more difficult to identify in virtual teams than they would be in face-to-face teams. For example, concepts about goals, activities, progress, and similar areas that may be explicit in face-to-face teams are often implicit in computer-mediated teams.
4.	*Continuous Communication.* Communication is an important component in any situation, and virtual work only increases the problems with communication. The amount of communication within virtual teams must increase dramatically over what is expected of typical face-to-face teams. Because members do not have the benefit of brief or informal face-to- face discussions and, in part, to overcome the lack of nonverbal information, virtual team members need to be trained in how to continuously communicate.
5.	*Training about Lack of Cohesion.* Virtual teams typically have lower cohesion than face-to-face teams. Because cohesion is linked to group and team performance, virtual teams must be trained about any additional difficulties the members may face in group process and performance due to this lack of cohesion.
6.	*Training about Biases.* Members of any group are at risk for utilizing heuristics and biases such as the Fundamental Attribution Error (just a reminder: this is the tendency for people to attribute another person's behavior to personality factors rather than the situation). Because of the reduced interaction and lower cohesion, virtual teamwork increases this risk. Teams where members receive training about how to minimize the impact of these biases on their work are more likely to succeed than those where the members do not receive this training.

Adapted from Thompson and Coovert (2006).

six specific steps that organizations may use to better prepare teams for their virtual work. These steps are beyond the recommendations that many have about improving groups and instead are targeting the problems that virtual groups and teams may have that differ from the standard face-to-face groups. Table 12.3 summarizes the additional training needs for virtual groups and teams.

Thompson and Coovert make these six recommendations based on a literature review but provide specific empirical evidence about whether they improve group and team performance. Freeman, Haimson, Diedrich, and Paley (2006) trained virtual teams in the Air Force. Although they did not use the exact steps described by Thompson and Coovert, many of the concepts in their training program were conceptually similar to those that Thompson and Coovert recommend. First, their primary emphasis about the training was information exchange, method of delivery, and discussions of priority of information needs. Their results were of no surprise: They found that virtual team training dramatically improved the performance of Air Force teams. The most significant finding, however, was that they found an increase in overall communication and, more importantly, there were considerably fewer communication errors after training.

Creating a Virtual Mediation System

Almost all teams will eventually face some level of conflict. As discussed in the chapter on conflict, establishing processes to manage conflict ahead of time can help groups to be more successful when it occurs. Shin (2005) developed a plan for virtual conflict resolution, which he calls a Virtual Mediation System. The concept is similar to face-to-face mediation. However, Shin defines what is necessary for the virtual component of the mediation system. The steps involved in creating a Virtual Mediation System are summarized in Table 12.4.

Shin (2005) claims that virtual mediation environments in chat rooms can be even more effective than face-to-face mediation because the "text-based conversations used in the Virtual Mediation System can help disputers de-escalate their negative emotions and feelings and be honest to each other" (p. 338). Although Shin provides anecdotal evidence from organizations that have successfully used virtual mediation systems, there is not yet any published empirical research that uses these four steps. The Virtual Mediation System is definitely an interesting concept – especially whether it is more successful than face-to-face mediation.

Table 12.4   A Summary of the Steps Involved in Creating a Virtual Mediation System.

Step	Procedure
1.	*Setting up the Mediation*. According to Shin, teams need to create an online mediation system using a chat room so that all parties involved, including the impartial, third-party mediator, can be in the "room" at the same time.
2.	Defining the Needs and Issues.
3.	Facilitate Perspective Taking.
4.	Move to Problem-solving and Agreement.

Adapted from Shin (2005).

Clearly, there is a need for additional research about conflict resolution in virtual environments.

Setting Virtual Teams Up for Success

DeRosa and Lepsinger (2010) recognized the importance of virtual teams to organizations. In addition, they recognized that most organizations had no plan or guide to help them to develop a system for helping virtual teams to succeed. As a result, they developed a practical guide to helping virtual teams succeed. They divide their recommendations into tasks that must be completed before launching the team, tasks that need to be completed at launch, and finally tasks that must be completed after launch. Many of the steps in their process are the standard group steps but they integrate the necessary steps for succeeding virtually into a typical team development process. These steps are summarized in Table 12.5.

De Rosa and Lepsinger's stepwise approach is so recent that there is little specific research using these steps yet. Her consulting firm's research demonstrates the success of their approach to improving virtual teams (De Rosa 2009a, 2009b). In addition, the steps described in the book are consistent with the research reviewed in this chapter as well as the general research about improving the success of groups and teams.

Table 12.5   A Summary of the Steps Involved in Setting Virtual Teams Up for Success.

Step	Procedure
1.	*Before Launch.*
	a) Determine who should be on the team, but make sure the team is not too large
	b) Make sure teams have the right mix of virtual skills as well as technical skills
	c) Select the virtual communication technologies
	d) Determine how to recognize and reward team and virtual team performance
2.	*Launch.*
	a) Hold a great kick-off meeting
	b) Create a sense of purpose for the virtual team
	c) Clarify goals and roles, including the roles that are virtual
	d) Develop a communication plan that includes virtual and face-to-face communication, as necessary
	e) Work together to develop the virtual skills of all team members
3.	*After Launch.*
	a) Monitor and assess team task performance
	b) Monitor and assess team virtual performance

Adapted from De Rosa and Lepsinger (2010).

FOCUS ON APPLICATION

Matching the task to the technology to the group members

The practitioner

Eric Williams is the Chief Executive Officer of Frontier Renewal, a real estate re-development firm specializing in re-positioning urban real estate properties that have significant environmental challenges. Frontier Renewal is comprised of experts in real estate, environmental cleanup, and public and private finance, and combines this unique blend of in-house expertise with capital to solve complex real-estate problems. Key to the company's success is the ability to effectively and efficiently communicate with teams in multiple locations in a highly professional manner.

He has almost 30 years of consulting and management experience in the field of environmental cleanup as well as in the brownfield redevelopment industry. As a nationally-recognized expert in brownfields, his experience and expertise in the brownfield business includes all aspects of redevelopment: identification and qualification of potential brownfield projects, determining best use, environmental risk management, land use planning, entitlements, public incentive programs, public and private financing, and overall deal structuring. Finally, he provides strategic direction, leads the Board of Directors and translates board direction into organizational action.

The symptom

Frontier Renewal is a real estate firm headquartered in Denver, Colorado. As part of its ongoing operations, the organization was putting together a large real estate deal. The deal involved a team spread across multiple locations across the country – Frontier Renewal and its attorneys in two offices in Denver; Board members in two offices in Austin, Texas; investors in Houston, Texas and Seattle, Washington; a bank and partner in two offices in Spokane, Washington; and finally an old-school property owner in Seattle who was the linchpin to the entire deal; a total of nine groups in nine offices in five cities.

The deal was complex and involved over $50,000,000 changing hands as part of the brownfield redevelopment project. To further complicate matters, the group needed to be able to share and immediately access large data files. And lastly, time was of the essence in completing this extraordinarily complex environmental clean up and real-estate transaction.

Assessing the problem

We quickly realized that we would need to find a way to improve virtual communication across a very complex group. Frontier Renewal's assessment of the transaction needs first involved determining what types of traditional communication tools would need to be discarded for this group – email attachments would be too large, sending CDs or hard copies too slow and environmentally wasteful, and conference calls were inadequate to communicate large amounts of visual information. The second phase of assessment included identifying each of the communication and information needs of each individual within the group (and subgroups) involved in the transaction – large electronic file sharing for some, "live" dynamic, online presentations for others, and highly professional and organized communication for the entire group. To accomplish this, we interviewed, via email and phone calls, the members of the group to learn about their communication preferences and the technology that their organization had readily available. Based on the assessment, Frontier Renewal, as leader of the transaction team, quickly recognized that a single communication tool would be inadequate to meet the needs of the team. In addition, it quickly became clear that many of the group members had different abilities and some of their organizations did not have the capabilities to communicate virtual Therefore, we developed and implemented a multi-media communication plan.

Intervening

The communication plan involved a combination of technology mediating the communication which we mixed with ongoing face-to-face human interaction. For groups needing to access large data files, we created a secured, shared access site on Frontier Renewal's servers. With an access address and a password provided by Frontier Renewal, access was granted to those who needed it. Universal access to all data wasn't needed or desired, so a file structure was developed so that secured access could be customized by each member of the group. Those who needed data could get it without seeing information not designed for all group members to see.

A live, web-based information sharing tool, GoTo Meeting, was used extensively to communicate dynamic concepts. For example, a virtual Google Earth tour of properties could be given to several groups in several locations simultaneously, without the related travel costs or logistical challenges. Using the same tool, a dynamic power point presentation could be given virtually to multiple parties with nothing more than internet access.

Finally, video conferencing was used when delicate communications were needed. The best application of video conferencing was when Frontier Renewal executives needed to convince investors to place millions of dollars into the project. Time and money didn't always allow for a personal visit, so video conferencing allowed the face-to-face interaction necessary for the situation. And the property owner who was the linchpin for the entire deal? Frontier Renewal's CEO flew to Seattle and sat across his mahogany desk to negotiate the deal in person, old-school style. Twice.

Based on no small part to well-planned and implemented the multimedia communication program that included face-to-face interaction as necessary, the $52,000,000 deal closed and Frontier Renewal earned the reputation for being a highly professional and efficient communicator.

Chapter Summary

Virtual teamwork is no longer something limited to a few technologically savvy people spread across long distances. Instead, almost all teams will spend at least some of their time working virtually, even when members work in the same hallway. These teams not only face the same group dynamics problems faced by all groups and teams but also additional concerns that are unique to the virtual environment. Some off the concerns that these groups and teams may face, some of which include:

* less nonverbal information in the communication system, which may contribute to an increase in other group dynamics problems, such as conflict;
* lower cohesion;
* potential for increased time to reach decisions.

Groups and teams can avoid the process losses associated with working virtually by leveraging some of the benefits of virtual work, such as:

* knowing when to use synchronous versus asynchronous methods;
* having a record of the conversation that some virtual environments allow;

- providing anonymity for member contributions which may improve creativity; and
- eliminating the perceived or actual power and status differences that naturally occur.

Finally, these groups need to make decisions about the virtual environments in which they work. They will have to make decisions about the importance of face-to-face meetings and when to have them. Second, they will have to determine the specific

Table 12.6   A Summary of the Steps Involved in Creating a Virtual Session.

Step	Procedure
1.	*Prepare the Environment.*
	a. *Identify the virtual tools.* Identify two virtual environments to which all group or team members have access, one of which is asynchronous (a discussion board) and the other of which is synchronous (i.e., a chat room). There are many of these systems available for free online, and many organizations have these systems available today.
	b. *Get logins.* Make certain that all members have login information for the system.
	c. *Create a decision making task.* Create a simple decision-making task that can be used for a synchronous discussion. Some simple tasks are to have groups pick 10 items for a time capsule that will be opened 100 years later or brainstorm a new name for a restaurant or building.
	d. *Design a discussion board.* Create five questions to spark discussion, such as:
	i. The virtual environment is better for groups.
	ii. Our performance was better because of the virtual environment.
	iii. The virtual environment created problems that we could not overcome.
	iv. I like working in virtual groups better than face-to-face groups.
	v. I felt like I was part of a group when working together virtually.
2.	*Define a Virtual Meeting Time.* Pick a one and one-half hour session that will be the virtual meeting time for the group. Make sure all members are available. They should put signs on their door indicating that they are in a virtual meeting.
3.	*Have a Virtual Meeting in Real-Time.* Use the chat room to make a decision. Give groups about one-half hour to make their decision. A facilitator should monitor the chat rooms so that she or he can facilitate a subsequent discussion.
4.	*Have an Asynchronous Virtual Discussion.* After the allotted time, close the chat rooms and have all members move to the discussion board. The facilitator should monitor this transition and remind members to move over. A five-minute warning is sometimes helpful.
5.	*Debrief.* The facilitator should compare responses from the asynchronous discussion to the what actually occurred in the synchronous discussion. This is an opportunity for a skilled facilitator to create a discussion about what works and what does not, including how to improve the virtual skills of members.

Adapted from Franz and Vicker (2010).

training they need to succeed. Last, they will have to make decisions about how to match the task on which they are working to the computer-mediated program and the virtual competencies of the members who are working on those tasks. When they can leverage the benefits and make informed decisions about the necessary virtual tools, they may be able to reach synergy within a computer-mediated environment.

Additional Resources

Bowers, C., Salas, E., & Jentsch, F. (2006). *Creating high-tech teams: Practical guidance on work performance and technology.* Washington, D.C.: American Psychological Association.

Brown, M. K., Huettner, B., & James-Tanny, C. (2007). *Managing virtual teams: Getting the most from wikis, blogs, and other collaborative tools.* Plano, TX: Wordware Publishing, Inc.

Lipnack, J., & Stamps, J. (2000). *Virtual teams: People working across boundaries with technology.* NY: John Wiley & Sons, Inc.

Nemiro, J., Beyerlein, M., Bradley, L., & Beyerlein, S. (2008). *The handbook of high-performance virtual teams: A toolkit for collaborating across boundaries.* San Francisco: John Wiley & Sons, Inc.

Team Exercises

Exercise 12.1   Creating an understanding of virtual teamwork

Some groups and teams that work in face-to-face environments are transitioning to virtual environments. Other times, new group or team members may not be used to a virtual environment already used by existing members. In these situations, an introductory training program can help members to better understand the nature of the virtual environment (Table 12.6).

Part IV

Outputs

Chapter 13

Searching for Synergy: Creating a High-Performing Team

This book is intended to help people within organizations understand and then improve work teams and potentially reach synergy. As a reminder, synergy is when groups and teams create outputs that are beyond what can be explained by individual work alone. Whether teams can truly achieve synergy is unclear. Teams definitely have the potential for process gains through processes such as increased member motivation, diversity of knowledge, enhanced information sharing, improved creativity, and/or better idea generation. These gains can improve the team's productivity beyond what would be expected by examining the group's potential with a simple statistical combination of individual inputs.

Steiner provides a well-known formula to understand group behavior, summarized in Figure 13.1. In the formula, Steiner recognizes the difference between a group's potential (potential productivity) and its reality (actual productivity). A group's potential is based on the resources and inputs to the group. Unfortunately, most groups and teams are faced with losses due to problems resulting from poor coordination, dysfunctional conflict, and any of the other problems discussed in this book. Once these process losses are removed from the group's potential, actual productivity is reduced below the group's potential.

Process gains were actually added later (see Dennis & Williams, 2003, for a review) to at least account for the possibility that synergy could occur (Collins & Guetzkow, 1964). If a group suffers no losses, then, according to Steiner's original formula, a group's actual productivity would equal its potential. If it is possible to reach synergy, then the original formula could not account for it. Thus, adding gains to potential productivity can yield synergy, as long as the gains outweigh any process losses.

Group Dynamics and Team Interventions: Understanding and Improving Team Performance,
First Edition. Timothy M. Franz.
© 2012 Timothy M. Franz. Published 2012 by Blackwell Publishing Ltd.

Figure 13.1   Steiner's Formula for Group Productivity.

In fact, synergy is a difficult goal to attain because of the losses that so many groups face. Losses occur through group processes such as unclear roles, interpersonal conflict, social loafing, and/or miscommunication. These losses more often than not cause actual productivity to be lower than what is expected by examining the group's potential. As a result, reaching synergy is quite difficult. Regardless of whether groups and teams can actually achieve synergy, what is definitely clear, though, is that, through practice with structured interventions, teams can be far more successful than they would otherwise be without using those structures and procedures. An understanding of where groups and teams fall short of expectations along with a toolbox of interventions, such as those found within this text, can help to yield performance above what might be expected of the typical unstructured and untrained group.

Imagine the following situation: Four different four-person groups are working together on a five-item quiz. Each person takes the quiz first as an individual and then again as a group. We can see the scores of their individual quizzes and their group scores, but they do not know how well they did (thus they cannot just share correct answers). Imagine further that in all of the groups, the first member gets the correct answer for Item 1, the second member gets Item 2 correct, the third member gets Item 3 correct, and the fourth member gets Item 4 correct. As you can see, each member earned a 20% on her or his individual quiz. After taking the quiz individually, they next meet as a group and dialogue, discuss, and debate all possible answers; remember at this point they do not know who is correct, so they cannot simply pick the "correct" answers (as is the case for most real-life groups!). After group discussion, they complete one group quiz, which is also scored for accuracy (for a thorough discussion of these issues, see Michaelsen, Watson, & Black, 1989; Tindale & Larson, 1992a, 1992b).

Now take the differences that we might see among the four group accuracy scores. The members of Group 1 debate and each try to convince one another of the answers. But, only one member convinces others of the right answer; the rest instead convince the others of the wrong answers. Their group only scores a 20%, which is lower than their potential. They have faced process losses due to undue influence. The members of Group 2 discuss and debate the answers. Three members convince the others of the correct answers, but one member convinces the others about the wrong answers. They have scored a 60%, exceeding the members but not reaching their potential of 80%; if only they knew who was correct they could have performed better. Thus, they still face some process losses, though are certainly not in the same position as Group 1. The members of Group 3 succeed through discussion and dialogue in identifying who has the correct answers and gets an 80% on the group quiz. To some, they have reached synergy because the group outperformed the members. However, they have not outperformed their potential. According to Steiner's formula, they have only avoided any process losses. The final group spends a considerable portion of its time dialoguing about the logic behind each of the questions. They pull together, and score a 100% on the group quiz, moving beyond their group potential of 80%. This is the example of true synergy, where the group has had process gains as a result of the processes through which members worked together.

To help fully understand the concept synergy, Larson (2010) differentiates weak from strong synergy. Larson explains that synergy is "a gain in performance that is attributable in some way to group interaction" when a group "is able to accomplish collectively something that could not reasonably have been achieved by any simple combination of individual member efforts" (p. 4). According to Larson, weak synergy is "group performance that exceeds the performance of the typical group member when working alone" (p. 6). On the other hand, strong synergy is "group performance that exceeds the solo performance of even the best group member" (p. 7).

As can be seen in the examples, the concept of what is actually group synergy is more complicated than determining whether a group simply outperformed its members. Instead, to fully understand whether a group achieves synergy can be determined by asking how to identify which member is the best and/or whether the group outperformed its potential, depending on the task that the group or team is completing. As you may now see, it is rare, though possible, for a group to move beyond the potential defined by the competencies of its individual members, though some may achieve it. There are groups that reach weak or strong synergy when they can minimize process losses. Unfortunately, many groups do not even perform as well as the average member because of the process losses they face.

Whether groups and teams can actually achieve weak synergy or maybe even reach strong synergy after facing the long list of potential process losses is unclear. Most people can provide ample evidence of their groups and teams that have struggled through losses. What is clear, however, is that through training and practice with structured interventions, teams can develop their skills and as a result be far more successful than they would otherwise be without using those structures and procedures. An understanding of where groups and teams fall short of expectations along with a toolbox of interventions, such as those found within this text, can help to yield performance above what might be expected of the typical unstructured and untrained group.

There are, in fact, many examples of high performance teams that have likely reached some level of synergy. In fact, Harvard Business Review devoted one of their article compendiums, titled *Teams that Succeed*, to the methods and procedures involved in creating these high performing teams. The concepts that appear in the monograph range from team learning through decision making and communication. Some of the high performing teams that the authors discuss include a team that is cross-training team members at Hewlett-Packard (Druskat & Wolff, 2004), cardiac surgery teams (Edmondson, Bohmer, & Pisano, 1994), and President Kennedy's cabinet when responding to the Cuban missile crisis (Garvin & Roberto, 2001). Given the brief descriptions about the teams, it is unclear whether they have achieved strong or weak synergy. Regardless, they have performed above that of the typical work team. Hopefully, the chapters in this book can also help groups and teams to reduce some of the process losses and create at least some process gains that may help to groups and teams to reach synergy.

Learning Goals for Chapter 13

- Define and understand the different components of synergy, including process losses and process gains.
- Learn how to assess the process losses that might be preventing synergy.
- Recognize the key recommendations in the literature about how to improve the chances of a group or team reaching synergy.
- Know what team outputs are important to organizations, teams, and team members.
- Recognize the importance of intervening to improve teams.

Assessing for High Performance: Indentifying Team Blockages

Before working with members to eliminate losses, improve performance, and possibly reach synergy, it is necessary to assess the group or team's current state to determine where to focus intervention efforts. One way to do this is through a Team Blockage Questionnaire. Woodcock and Francis (2005), known for their work on the Blockage Questionnaire (Woodcock & Francis, 1979) developed the Team Blockage Questionnaire to help teams determine what is stopping them from achieving their highest level of performance. The complete Team Blockage Questionnaire, published in their book titled *Team Metrics,* has 50 items that tap different team processes are designed so that teams get an overall idea for the various process losses that groups and teams may be facing. For the purposes of this text, I only show the first 10 items, from Section 1. These items are shown in Table 13.1.

For this book the scale has been modified to a five-choice Likert-type response scale from strongly disagree to strongly agree. To use the Team Blockage Questionnaire, examine the scores on each question because they test 10 different areas of team performance. Item 1 examines the appropriateness of leadership, Item 2 asks about team membership, Item 3 asks about the organization's team climate, Item 4 is a test about objectives, Item 5 tests the team's standards, Item 6 gets at ineffective work methods, Item 7 asks about the openness within the team. Item 8 taps into team development. Item 9 measures innovation. Finally, Item 10 measures social relationships. In the full measure, there are four more items for each area, creating

Table 13.1   Assessing Team Blockages.

Instructions: Circle the appropriate number using the following scale: (1) = Strongly disagree, (2) = Disagree, (3) = Neither agree or disagree, (4) Agree, and (5) = Strongly agree. Our team would be strengthened if:

1.	*Appropriateness of Leadership:* Our team leader was more dominant.	1	2	3	4	5
2.	*Team membership:* We had a greater variety of personalities on the team.	1	2	3	4	5
3.	*Team Climate:* Team members were fully committed to team success.	1	2	3	4	5
4.	*Objectives:* We were 100% clear about what we have to achieve.	1	2	3	4	5
5.	*Team Standards:* We set high standards for individual performance.	1	2	3	4	5
6.	*Ineffective Team Behaviors:* Team meetings were more effective.	1	2	3	4	5
7.	*Openness:* Team members were more fully open with one another.	1	2	3	4	5
8.	*Team Development:* Individuals felt that their needs were being met by being members of the team.	1	2	3	4	5
9.	*Team innovation:* We used team interaction more often to develop our creative ideas.	1	2	3	4	5
10.	*Social Relationships:* There was greater cooperation between our team and other parts of this organization.	1	2	3	4	5

Adapted from Woodcock and Francis (2005).

an even more stable measure that can be used with teams to help them to identify areas where they need to focus interventions.

Reaching High Performance: A Summary of Literature about How to Succeed

I am, of course, certainly not the first author who has recommended ways to intervene to improve groups and teams. In this section, I provide brief reviews of what some other well-known authors have to say about improving groups and teams so that they might reach synergy. To maintain the scientist-practitioner focus of this text, the first three books are by authors whose primary responsibility is science (see Table 13.2.a) while the second three books are by authors whose primary responsibility is practice (see Table 13.2.b). Each of these authors' brief professional biography is described below.

The three books with academic authors include Alvin Zander, J. Richard Hackman, and Carl Larson/Frank La Fasto. Zander, the first of the academic authors, was a pioneer in the field of group dynamics. He worked with Kurt Lewin and was one of the early members of the Research Center for Group Dynamics (now part of the Institute

Table 13.2a Major Themes for Creating Effective Groups and Teams by Academics.

I-P-O Category	Major Theme for Group/Team Improvement	Zander: Making Groups Effective	Larson & La Fasto: Teamwork	Hackman: Groups that Work
Inputs	Clarify tasks, goals, and roles	– Establish Group Standards – Set Clear Goals	– Clear, elevating goals and competent team members	– Guarantee the Task is Appropriate – Give Clear Goals and Set Deadlines – Develop Member Skill Sets – Set Group on Path to Success
	Define group culture	– Strengthen Desire for Group Success	– A results-oriented structure	
	Garner organizational support	– Create a Supportive Organizational Environment	– Organizational support and recognition	– Provide Necessary Organizational Support
Processes	Improve trust and communication	– Improve Communication and Participation	– An environment of trust and collaboration	
	Emphasize creativity and innovation			
	Improve problem solving and decision making	– Improve Decision-Making and Problem-Solving Processes		
	Improve cohesion and collaboration	– Improve Cohesiveness	– Unified in commitment to the team and pressure to meet high standards	
	Eliminate dysfunctional conflict	– Manage Conflict		
	Improve influence, power, and leadership	– Become an Influential Member – Cope with Power	– Principled leadership	– Provide Stable Leadership and Coaching – Manage Authority

Table 13.2b Major Themes for Creating Effective Groups and Teams by Practitioners.

I-P-O Category	Major Theme for Group/Team Improvement	Robbins & Finley: Why Teams Don't Work	Lencioni: Five Dysfunctions of a Team	Eckes: Six Sigma Team Dynamics
Inputs	Clarify tasks, goals, and roles	Unclear goals and objectives and role ambiguity No vision		Don't establish roles and responsibilities, set goals and objectives, or manage meeting time No ground rules or norms No accountability for poor team performance
	Define group culture			
	Garner organizational support	Organizational policies, reward systems, and cultures that don't support teams		
Processes	Improve trust and communication	Lack of trust, no feedback	Foster trust and create meaningful dialogue	
	Emphasize creativity and innovation	Too few tools to promote creativity		Do not use tools to enhance quality
	Improve problem solving and decision making	Poor decision making processes		Fail to determine ways to reach agreement on decisions Waste time
	Improve cohesion & collaboration		Members hold each other accountable to results	
	Eliminate dysfunctional conflict	Personality conflicts	Create productive conflict	
	Improve influence, power, and leadership	Leadership problems		No clear leader

for Social Research), which moved from MIT, where it was founded by Lewin, to the University of Michigan. He has written a classic book titled *Making groups effective* (1982; 1994). In his book he provides advice and recommendations for improving groups. The second academic author is Hackman, who edited a popular book titled *Groups that work (and those that don't*; 1990). Hackman is the Edgar Pierce Professor of Social and Organizational Psychology at Harvard University. His area of scholarship is team dynamics and performance and is one of the foremost scholars about improving groups and teams. The final book is by Larson and La Fasto, who worked as an academic/practitioner team. Larson is a professor of communications and LaFasto a corporate Vice President. Together, they authored a bestselling teams book, titled *Teamwork: What must go right, what can go wrong* (1989). It was designed for those working in teams in management, and is a book that, though the first author was an academic, was definitely written for practitioners interested in improving groups and teams. The major concepts that groups and teams need to understand so that they succeed from these three books are summarized in Table 13.2.a.

The three books with practitioner authors include Harvey Robbins/Michael Finley, Patrick Lencioni, and George Eckes. Harvey Robbins, who trained as a clinical psychologist, is a president of Robbins & Robbins, Inc and a practicing business psychologist while Michael Finley is a syndicated business columnist and writer. Together, they authored a book titled *Why teams don't work: What went wrong & how to make it right* (1997). The second practitioner, Patrick Lencioni, is president of the Table Group, a consulting group that specializes in team development. He wrote a *Business Week* bestselling book titled *The five dysfunctions of a team*. In it, he provides a fictional story about a team that runs into considerable trouble when trying to work together. As a result of his work, he recommends five common problems that teams face and gives recommendations for teams to avoid each of those problems. The final practitioner is George Eckes, president and founder of a consulting firm that applies Six Sigma principles to workplace. He is author of the book *Six sigma team dynamics* (2002). The book applies Six Sigma Principles to improving work teams. The major concepts that groups and teams need to understand so that they succeed from these three books are summarized in Table 13.2.b.

The main themes within many of these books, whether they are classic texts or more recent popular-press business books or whether they are authored by academics or practitioners, are in fact quite similar. There are many consistencies across the books in what authors define as the causes of process losses. A summary of some of these key themes include:

- Groups and teams often fail to clearly establish roles and goals.
- Groups and teams often fail to clarify a vision and create a group culture.
- Groups and teams often work in organizations that have not learned how to support teamwork.
- Groups and teams sometimes struggle with distrust and miscommunication.
- Groups and teams often do not know how to access their creative potential.
- Groups and teams tend struggle with problem solving and decision making.

- Groups and teams often fail to properly manage conflict.
- Groups and teams often do not have leaders who support teamwork.

In addition, some of the key themes here are that to make groups and teams more successful, members, leaders, and/or facilitators should:

- Set them up for success up front by working to create goals, define roles, and clarify roles.
- Create a group culture so that all members feel like they are a part of the team.
- Work to change organizational structures so that teamwork is supported rather than discouraged.
- Train groups and teams on how to communicate and then work with them to build trust.
- Provide groups and teams with the tools they need to improve creativity and generate innovation.
- Work with groups and teams to teach them problem-solving and decision-making structures that will help them to succeed rather than get embroiled in conflict.
- Be prepared to intervene when dysfunctional conflict occurs so that a group or team can quickly move forward.
- Develop leaders who understand the importance of groups and teams within the organization and know how to lead those teams.

As you can see, there is a surprising amount of similarity between books by academics, books by practitioners, and the themes in this text.

Understanding Team Outputs: More than Team Performance

This book is organized around the input-process-output model of group functioning. When discussing outputs, we often focus on creating synergy in task-specific behaviors – meaning there is a typically an emphasis on improving performance, productivity, efficiency, or effectiveness (all these terms overlap some in their meaning) as well as improving quality and reducing the number of errors and mistakes. All of these are a part of task-related outcomes. For all organizations, improving task-related performance is essential because groups and teams are typically called to do something specific for an organization.

However, task-related behavior is not the only output that results from successful and effective team processes. Other team outputs from successful group and team processes include:

- *Increased organizational citizenship behaviors.* Organizational Citizenship is, in summary, going above and beyond for an organization when not actually being rewarded for it (see Organ, 1988). Van Dyne, Kossek, and Lobel (2007) linked improvements to group process to a greater level of group-level OCBs.

- *Increased commitment to the organization.* Organizational commitment is a person's psychological attachment to an organization (Meyer & Allen, 1991). It has components that are affective ("I stay because I like it"), normative ("I stay because I should"), and continuance (I stay because I have no other choice"). Members who are more satisfied with group process are more committed to the team and organization, especially for affective commitment (Caballer, Gracia, & Peiró, 2005).

- *Improved job satisfaction.* Job satisfaction reflects the thoughts and feelings people have about their job (Saari & Judge, 2004). Team members who are satisfied with team process are also satisfied with their work (Schippers, Den Hartog, Koopman, & Wienk, 2003).

- *Reduced absenteeism and tardiness.* Absenteeism and tardiness are outcomes that have direct impact on an organization's bottom line. In other words, teams are less effective when members are out or late. Manz and Neck (1995) reviewed the literature and found that improved team processes are linked to reduced absenteeism. In addition, Sagie, Koslowsky, and Hamburger (2003) linked group-level processes to lateness behavior.

- *Improved organizational communication.* Communication is both a process and an output. Organizations often intervene to improve communication so that overall work outputs can flow better. Interventions that target group process also improve organizational communication (Gurtner, Tschan, Semmer, & Nägele, 2007).

- *Improved social benefits for members.* People are social animals and belong to groups and teams not only for organizational but also social reasons. Groups and teams, for example, make people feel better about themselves. How a group or team works together affects how members feel about their group identity (i.e., their collective esteem), and collective esteem is related to their individual self-esteem (Marmarosh & Corazzini, 1997).

- *Increased affective reactions towards other team members.* Finally, people like to be liked, and like others who like them. Groups that emphasize process are more likely to have members who like one another (Kline, 2003).

As you can see, there are other outcomes besides task-related behavior that result from improving group process. Groups and teams that work well together can improve many other areas of organizational functioning. Further, there is ample research to link each of these areas, either directly or indirectly, to increased productivity, improved quality, or reduced costs from lower turnover, absenteeism, and/or direct sabotage.

Interventions to Improve Team Performance: A Final Word

Although some groups and teams may have all the right stuff to reach synergy, most will need some level of support to improve. Intervening can help many of these teams to reduce the process losses and reach some process gains, even if they don't reach synergy. Intervention and training is a means to an end, or a process involved in group and team improvement, not simply an end in and of itself. When intervening, it is important to remember some of the major themes involved in the process, including:

- Intervening first requires knowing about where the team currently stands – as defined in the book, this is a process of assessment. Each chapter in this book lists one specific assessment that may be used to help understand where a group or team currently stands. However, there are many more. A search of the literature, including recommendations by academics and practitioners, will yield far more possible assessment tools. Some are free for students, academics, and practitioners to use, while others require a nominal fee (and whether they cost sometimes depends on their use). Some require professionals to administer the assessment tool, such as an Industrial-Organizational Psychologist or Organizational Development specialist, while others may be used and interpreted by a practitioner with only limited knowledge of testing and measurement issues.

- Once the issues with which a team is dealing have been identified, the next step is to plan an intervention. The results of the assessment should always be the guide as to what interventions are necessary. In each chapter, there is only one assessment tool listed. In many cases, however, it may be best for an organization to conduct a multi-mode, multi-method assessment to better understand what is happening in the groups and teams within that organization. Multi-mode means that the applied researcher should use multiple assessment tools, while multi-method means that the applied researcher should use multiple assessment methods (e.g., questionnaires and focus groups). Multi-mode and multi-method applied research procedures may help the practitioner to better pinpoint the issues where intervention is necessary.

- This book provides summaries of a handful of assessment and intervention tools as well as the references so that readers can find more information about each of them. It is important to remember that these are only summaries, and further reading is typically necessary for any applied researcher to fully understand the nature of the assessments and interventions so that the tools can be used properly.

- After intervening, follow-up evaluation is the necessary next step to determine the effectiveness of each part of the intervention. Many people fail to conduct proper evaluations because they, unfortunately, see evaluation as a threat. Their false view is that the evaluation will show a dichotomous outcome that proves either the success or failure of an intervention (and if the intervention is a failure their job may be at risk!). However, this follow-up evaluation will almost never provide the simple black and white outcomes such as success and failure, but instead demonstrate which parts of an intervention that have been successful while at the same time finding other components of an intervention that need to be improved – in fact leading to more work! This is because the findings of any evaluation can be used to define the next assessment or they can, in and of themselves, be used as the next assessment and help to determine what intervention to plan next.

- All the interventions have been summarized as they were described by the original author(s) of the intervention. However, I believe that there is no one solution to improving groups and teams. Each of these interventions can and should be tailored for the specific situation required by groups and teams. Further, with practice with the interventions and follow-up evaluation, most will start to learn how to change each for the situation. If there is one thing that industrial and organizational psychologists can agree on, it is that the answer is always "it depends."

- In addition, I recommend combining interventions as necessary. In the world of research, where many of group and team interventions have been designed and tested, it is always important to test the impact of one intervention at a time to determine effectiveness of that intervention. This is done in order to control the environment so that we can be confident about determining the impact of one change on whatever outcome(s) we are measuring (this is often called experimental control and/or rigor of research design). In the real world, however, practitioners are often unconcerned with which specific intervention is working when things are going wrong. Instead, they just want things to improve and are less concerned with understanding the why. An example for this comes from medicine. Physicians are often quite good at this multi-method intervention when working with patients. They may recommend three treatments at the same time to solve a patient's health problem. For example, if a patient went to an orthopaedic specialist with a foot problem (which I did), the physician may at the same time recommend a drug (e.g., a cortisone shot), physical therapy (e.g., strengthening and balance exercises), and steps to improve flexibility (e.g., using a stretcher board). At the moment of intervention, the physician is quite unconcerned with which of the three interventions work but instead how to make this person's foot better as soon as possible. It may be that the cortisone shot was completely ineffective and instead the stretching and exercise worked. What is most important, however, is that at least one of the three interventions worked.

- Further, many of the interventions are designed to be used in an integrative way. For example, during a three-day strategic planning session, a team meeting facilitator should at one point be intervening to generate a greater number of creative outputs, at another point be working with the group to develop a procedure to solve a problem, and at some point should be using a procedure to allow the group to get to decision. During this time, the facilitator may also be intervening to resolve a conflict or working with the group to set some norms and goals. And, the facilitator should also have some quick assessments handy so that the group can conduct team process checks to determine whether members are working together as well as they could.

Concluding Comments: The Future of Group Work

As group work continues to develop and improve, scientists and practitioners should continue to develop their practices in the following three areas:

- *Virtuality*. Virtuality is becoming an integral part of teamwork. One of the major points in Chapter 12 is that the question is no longer whether groups and teams work virtually but how much virtual teamwork the members will be doing. Our understanding of virtual work is still in its infancy. This is an area that needs considerably more attention.

- *Globalization*. Friedman (2005) wrote a compelling, and popular, book about the globalization of the world economy. Because of the electronic "flattening" of our world, global teamwork is becoming far more common. This will require an even greater understanding of how to work in groups and teams that have value and cultural differences.

- *Intervention*. By using this book, groups and teams may be able to intervene so that they may avoid some of the process losses that the typical group faces. With practice, these same groups and teams may get closer to synergy, and maybe some of them will even attain it. As anyone in today's work world knows, groups and teams are here to stay. In fact, organizations are relying on them even more. Group work is not going to go away.

FOCUS ON APPLICATION

A multi-method intervention to improve team and organization performance

The practitioner

Paul M. Mastrangelo, PhD specializes in the transformation of employee data into insightful pathways to change. He has over 20 years of experience in psychological assessment, organization development, and adult education. Paul works as a Senior Consultant and Director of New Service Development at CLC-Genesee, where he has designed, implemented, and analyzed employee surveys for companies such as Johnson & Johnson, Hewlett Packard, Cisco Systems, Raytheon, Lyondell, Polaroid, and Columbus McKinnon. Paul has over 20 original publications and is a regular presenter at the Society for Industrial and Organizational Psychology's annual conference. Paul received his PhD in Industrial/Organizational Psychology from Ohio University.

The symptom

Often our clients work with us to develop a survey as a general monitoring device rather than calling us to diagnose a specific problem. This client (110,000+ employees worldwide) created its survey to have employees evaluate the extent to which the company is living up to its deeply rooted value system. When we issued reports, the HR director at one operating unit contacted me because their scores had dropped so dramatically, she thought there must be a mistake. This was a reasonable question to ask, but there was no mistake. Looking back on this project, I realize that management's questioning the validity of the survey results was in itself a symptom of the underlying issue.

Assessing the problem

To be clear, we interpreted the survey data by comparing this unit's scores with their previous results and with the company's internal normative data, and we had sophisticated statistical models that indicated which survey topics were most related to key outcomes. However, the heart of the matter did not become clear until we began meeting with groups of employees at off-site locations for half-day sessions. After assuring their anonymity, we held up one graph showing the decline in scores over the course of one year, and we asked "what's going on?" The answers, which we eventually summarized and shared with the management team, suggested that a series of isolated events had woven themselves together to create a frustrated workforce.

In essence, employees' high commitment to the company created high standards of customer service, which were no longer being met, to the point where employees were losing sleep, becoming ill, and wondering why they were not leaving for the competition. We saw tears, we received pages of hand-written background information, and we listened to hour-long phone calls from those unable to attend group sessions. What could make such a passionate group of employees so distraught? Was it recent upheavals on the executive team, including a new president? Was it increased competition for an aging product line? Was it an unfortunate flaw in their product packaging that led to their main revenue source being temporarily pulled from the market? Was it abrupt changes to their marketing and sales processes? Was it recent job cuts, perceived by some as unfair or even as retribution for publically criticizing leaders? Was it the company's culture regarding time management (described as "Wait. Wait … I need it now!") that was destroying work-life balance?

We concluded it was all of these factors, but what made matters worse is that employees felt that management just "didn't get it." Those who approached executives about these issues felt that they, the messengers, were blamed. Others remarked that even when leaders asked for feedback, they did not listen. When one employee heard that management was surprised by the survey results, he called their reaction "insulting." When we were called in, employees no longer trusted their leaders. They were demanding change and threatening to leave the jobs that they loved. Yet, many disavowed themselves from being a part of the solution. How do you create engagement within such a reluctant workforce?

Intervening

First, we took advantage of a sales meeting (where 95% of employees would be in attendance) to present a summary of what they had told us and what we had told their senior leaders. The president acknowledged the findings, and then facilitated a two hour session where breakout groups suggested "Monday Morning Actions" – initial plans to either start or stop behaviors in order to begin fixing problems without the delays required to acquire a budget or undergo planning. One suggestion that the president immediately approved was to put a three month moratorium on all surveys within the company! While this response did not dissolve all concerns over time-consuming activities, it did get a round of applause in what had been a very tense atmosphere.

Next, Tim Franz and I outlined an intervention process that we now call the Enchangement Template, a play on words to highlight that employee engagement doesn't require a "gauge" so much as it requires "change." We worked with managers to create a cross-functional, cross-level response team that had representation across regions. Members were nominated by their peers and selected (with our guidance) to meet our criteria for representativeness. Before selected employees agreed to join, they had to meet with their supervisors to assure that they could create time to meet at least once a month in initial stages. Unlike processes that call for volunteers or announce a hand-picked champion, the peer nomination system identified people who were already respected as formal or informal leaders – what Peter Senge calls "network leaders." Thus, the team had pre-established credibility and would be motivated to maintain that credibility. To their credit, everyone who was asked to serve agreed to do so. Peer nomination, it seems, created a sense of responsibility.

Nominated members were joined by the unit president and the HR director to assure that the team would create realistic action plans for which leaders would be held accountable. The formation of the team itself was considered to be action plan number one. Their task was to prioritize and address the problems that we had identified, starting with relatively easy changes and progressing to more complex changes. In other words, each business problem would be addressed by a series of iterative action plans, where early actions could be publicized as proof that management was serious about making improvements. The team, relying on the informal communities who nominated members, had the responsibility of gathering feedback and making adjustments. Through their efforts, employees could be certain that management now "got" the message.

Of course, there was really an intervention within the intervention: Even though all members knew each other, this group was initially a team only in the nominal sense. We used a two-day, off-site retreat at a conference center for their first meeting together. Our agenda was designed to share our assessment of the situation and to initiate their work, but we allotted nearly half of our time together to have them define their team, choose their method of governance, define how decisions would be made, agree to the confidentiality of any sensitive or tumultuous conversations, and so forth. As trust was established, different sides of the same story were told and heard. We did not accomplish as much as we had hoped in those two days, but in some ways the team benefitted from going slowly. As important as their destination was (and is), this team's journey could not be rushed.

Indeed, it is too soon to judge the intervention as a success, but early indications suggest that they have reversed their slide. After just one year, this unit's survey scores have made a modest but significant improvement, while the division in which they operate saw a sizeable decrease in scores. Their hard work underscores the value of establishing intervention teams from members throughout the organizational chart.

Chapter Summary

One of the main expectations of working together is so members of a group or team can create something that is beyond what would be expected by those same people when working alone, a process called synergy. Synergy is a process that results from taking the potential of team, minimizing any process losses, and leveraging the possible process gains. Synergy, however, is an elusive concept for most groups and teams. Strong synergy is when a group accomplishes something that is beyond what could be expected by combining member efforts. Weak synergy is group performance that exceeds the best member but is not beyond what could be expected by combining member efforts. An assessment of the process losses can help groups and team to determine where they are blocked.

There are many recommendations for improving group and team processes found in the academic and practitioner literature. These can be categorized into eight main themes. First, create goals and roles. Second, create a group culture. Third, establish an organizational structure that supports teams. Fourth, train members how to communicate and work with them to build trust. Fifth, provide tools to improve creativity and innovation. Sixth, use problem-solving and decision-making structures that can help to avoid losses. Seventh, have a conflict management plan. Finally, develop effective team leaders, empower members, and share leadership whenever possible. If teams are properly supported, organizations should see improvements in performance, productivity, organizational citizenship, job satisfaction, and social connections as well as reductions in absenteeism and tardiness.

Additional Resources

Eckes, G. (2003). *Six sigma team dynamics: The elusive key to project success*. Hoboken, NJ: John Wiley & Sons, Inc.

Hackman, J. R. (1990). *Groups that work (and those that don't): Creating conditions for effective teamwork*. San Francisco: Jossey-Bass Publishers.

Larson, F., & La Fasto, C. (1989). *Teamwork: What must go right/What can go wrong*. Thousand Oaks, CA: Sage Publications.

Lencioni, P. (2002). *The five dysfunctions of a team: A leadership fable*. San Francisco: Jossey-Bass Publishers.

Robbins, H., & Finley, M. (1995). *Why teams don't work: What went wrong and how to make it right*. Princeton, NJ: Peterson's/Pacesetter Books.

Zander, A. (1983). *Making groups effective*. San Francisco: Jossey-Bass Publishers.

Appendix

Improving Team Meetings

Like most people, I once had the worst meeting I think I could ever experience. I was at a meeting of all of the faculty members at an institution (not the one I'm at now!). There was a policy in that university that stated that all faculty members had to submit grades within 24 hours of the final examination session. This was a reasonable expectation when faculty members gave objective final examinations, such as ones that include multiple choice questions. However, it was an unattainable goal for faculty members when they gave subjective examinations, such as essay examinations or final papers.

To end this confusion, a committee made a motion that stated that "Faculty members will inform the Registrar's Office if they cannot meet the deadline" (what I would call a common sense policy anyway, but I will save that complaint for another day). There was an argument on the floor about the word "inform." Two faculty members who were almost always at odds debated whether it was too weak and had enough teeth in it or, on the other hand, it was just fine. I left the meeting after almost 20 minutes, as did another faculty member. When we left, the group lost its quorum – the number of people required to have a vote about policy – and the motion died. There were about 120 faculty members in that room, and the two bickering members had just wasted 40 person-hours of productive work time.

In this appendix, I briefly summarize some ideas about how to improve group and team meetings, including how to prepare the environment, prepare the facilitator, and prepare other members for the meeting. I am confident that anyone reading this appendix has had a similar experience with bad meetings, as described by Wally in the Dilbert cartoon below.

Group Dynamics and Team Interventions: Understanding and Improving Team Performance,
First Edition. Timothy M. Franz.
© 2012 Timothy M. Franz. Published 2012 by Blackwell Publishing Ltd.

Figure A.1   Wally Describing a Bad Experience with Meetings. DILBERT © (1995) Scott Adams. Used By permission of UNIVERSAL UCLICK.

Even though I can easily remember the worst meetings I've been in, it is difficult to remember really great meetings. I don't think I have ever had a "fist-pumping" experience where I left a meeting as if I just completed the Tour de France! – this is usually not the intent of most meetings. But I have been in many good meetings, leading to the question: What is a good meeting? Good meetings are often defined by the outcomes; there are results and/or a path to get to some desired outcomes. This includes having goals, resolutions, clear objectives, knowledge about how to execute plan, guidance for follow through activities, and major questions answered. Good meetings also come with an emotional response. People who have attended a good meeting feel more energized, inspired, engaged, have a sense of fulfillment (or relief), feel a sense of accomplishment, and are motivated to complete their assigned tasks. According to Kayser (2011), making meetings effective is a result of PDoRA: having a sense of **p**urpose, knowing the **d**esired **o**utcomes, assigning **r**oles for the meeting, and having a structured **a**genda.

Appendix Learning Goals

- Learn how to plan for a meeting structure.
- Know the components of a structured agenda.
- Understand the skills necessary for facilitating a meeting.
- Know how to prepare the other team members.

Assessing Past Meetings

Just like any group or team behavior or activity, meetings can be assessed and improved. Engleberg and Wynn (2007) provide their readers with a post meeting reaction form. This form was adapted below, for use as a general meeting assessment. It can also be used with minor modifications to evaluate specific meetings (Table A.1).

According to Engleberg and Wynn, all group and team members should complete the meeting assessment, including the team leader. Then, members should tally the

Table A.1   Assessing Past Meetings.

Instructions: Circle the appropriate number using the following scale: (1) = Strongly disagree, (2) = Disagree, (3) = Neither agree or disagree, (4) Agree, and (5) = Strongly agree.

1. The goals of our meetings are clear.	1	2	3	4	5
2. Meeting agendas are useful.	1	2	3	4	5
3. The meeting room is comfortable.	1	2	3	4	5
4. Members are prepared for meetings.	1	2	3	4	5
5. Everyone has an equal opportunity to participate in the discussions.	1	2	3	4	5
6. Members listen effectively and consider different points of view.	1	2	3	4	5
7. There is a friendly environment in our meetings.	1	2	3	4	5
8. Assignments and deadlines are clear at the end of our meetings.	1	2	3	4	5
9. Overall, our meetings are productive.	1	2	3	4	5

Adapted from Engleberg and Wynn (2007).

results and examine the lowest scoring areas. During this discussion, members can determine the different meeting issues and use the information as necessary to make change. This group-level assessment is a development tool that can help members to improve meeting behavior and meeting effectiveness.

Preparing the Environment

The first step in creating effective meetings is to define a structured agenda. The agenda should clearly define the purpose of the meeting. A structured agenda should include the goals, topics to be covered, overall time for the meeting, anticipated time for each topic on the agenda, a brief biography or background for any meeting guest, any relevant background information that is necessary to process the information in the meeting, minutes or a summary from past meetings that includes who was present, who was excused, and who could not attend. The agenda as well as this other information should be sent to those attending the meeting with enough time so that they can prepare for the meeting.

The recommendations for ordering the information items versus discussion points on an agenda differ slightly depending on the source. According to Engleberg and Wynn (2007), meeting agendas should be arranged so that they start with simple items and points of information. Difficult and important items should be reserved for the middle of the agenda, and finally, easy discussion items should be scheduled for the last third of the meeting. They find that this order provides those attending with a sense of accomplishment before tacking difficult issues and then the members also end the meeting on a positive note.

Table A.2   A Sample Agenda.

Performance Management System Review Meeting			

Purpose: To finalize the revisions to the simplified performance management system
Room: Building A, Room 103
Attending: Elizabeth (primary facilitator), George (scribe), Aaron (recorder), Linda (secondary facilitator)
Excused: John

Action Item	Time	Desired Outcome(s)	Leading Discussion
I. Welcome	8:00–8:05	Welcome and bagels	Elizabeth
II. Information: Revisiting the Targeted Outcomes	8:05–8:10	a. Simplify Performance appraisal document b. Review performance management process and determine whether to eliminate steps	Elizabeth
III. Discussion: Advantages and Disadvantages	8:10–8:40	Determine what will be eliminated	Entire Group
IV. Discussion: Steps in Performance Management Process	8:40–9:20	a. Advantages and disadvantages of current system b. Eliminate unnecessary steps	Elizabeth
V. Action Items	9:20–9:25	Review list of action items for each person	Elizabeth
VI. Closure	9:25–9:30	a. Questions b. Meeting evaluation	Elizabeth

Similarly, Kayser (2011) recommends starting the meeting with information sharing items. These should be given little time on the agenda, Kayser's recommendations differ slightly from those by Engleberg and Wynn for the next sections. Kayser recommends that the second group of agenda items should be what he calls information discussion items, which are items where there may be questions, but any outcome is unlikely to change. Kayser recommends keeping to a specified time frame on the agenda for these items. Kayser recommends putting what he calls information processing items last, similar to the information that Engleberg and Wynn suggest placing in the middle of the meeting. He recommends this because it allows the agenda to use a more flexible time frame, allowing as much or as little discussion on these difficult or challenging items. A sample structured meeting agenda is included in Table A.2.

The second part of preparing for a meeting requires creating an environment that is conducive to meetings. According to Eller (2004) this includes knowing how to welcome people, having an icebreaker ready if necessary, deciding on the time of day for the meeting, preparing for meals if necessary, knowing how to deal with those who show up late, having an understanding of interpersonal dynamics, and appropriately reserving and arranging the room.

The room should be large enough so that there is ample space for members to move around as necessary. Chairs should be arranged so that attendees are not facing windows or hallways that may create a distraction. In addition, there should be one or more flipcharts so that the group can write important information in a way that all can see. Finally, the room should have tables and chairs arranged in a way that is appropriate for the meeting. If the agenda consists primarily of presentation items, the chairs should be arranged in traditional lecture format. If the agenda consists primarily of information discussion items (information sharing with questions and answers), then the room should be arranged with the facilitator in front and the chairs and tables in a "U." Finally if the agenda consists primarily of information processing information, the room should be set up in a circle (or "board") format, or with subgroups around small tables if breakout groups will be used as part of the information processing session.

Preparing the Facilitator

Groups and teams that determine ahead of time who should facilitate the meeting. The person who is facilitating the meeting can either create or minimize problems, depending on the facilitator's level of preparation. The facilitator need to understand the tasks involved, know how to suspend personal opinion and needs, be able to observe and diagnose how the group meeting is working, make sure to monitor the energy level of participants, know when to press toward task completion, be prepared adapt to changing situations (Eller, 2004).

According to Kayser (2011), a facilitator is "a person who helps a group free itself from internal obstacles or difficulties so that the meeting's desired outcomes can be pursued more efficiently and effectively" (p. 29). Kayser explains that there are seven fundamental behaviors required for facilitation. These include:

- Focusing on defining and accomplishing desired outcomes.
- Creating an efficient communication process.
- Creating opportunities for group decision making.
- Establishing procedures for efficient decisions.
- Creating a supportive and open group atmosphere.
- Keeping the group on track and focused on important tasks.
- Fostering the discovery of alternative solutions while protecting less vocal or powerful members.

Kayser recommends appointing an outside facilitator when possible, though he also gives recommendations for how facilitation may rotate through team member or even be conducted by the group manager. However, he also emphasizes that facilitation is a shared responsibility. Although one person in the group may serve for a time as a facilitator, all members present must serve as secondary facilitators.

Engleberg and Wynn (2007) break the facilitator's tasks into pre-meeting activities, activities that occur during the meeting, and post-meeting activities. The pre-meeting activities include notifying members about the meeting, distributing materials, reminding members about their tasks and responsibilities, and preparing for discussion. During the meeting, the activities include beginning on time, delegating the minutes to a recorder, following the agenda, facilitating the actual discussions, and providing a sense of closure for the meeting. Finally, the post-meeting responsibilities are evaluating the meeting, distributing the minutes, and monitoring the tasks that each member

Preparing the Team Members

Not only do team leaders and/or facilitators needs to prepare, but they must also help the other meeting participants to prepare. First, team leaders should be monitoring progress on any tasks that need to be completed by other participants prior to the meeting. They should be defining specifically what is expected by members so that when members attend the meeting there is no question about what is required.

The second requirement to prepare other members includes defining roles that will need to be completed during each meeting. Depending on the topic, a team leader may want to bring in an outside facilitator or appoint another team member to facilitate. The team leader or facilitator should also appoint a time keeper, a recorder/notetaker, and a scribe. The time keeper's responsibility is to keep the meeting as close as possible to the times written on the agenda. The recorder/notetaker's responsibility is to keep notes so that there is information for the meeting minutes. When completed, the meeting minutes should focus on the outcomes and responsibilities, not what was included in all discussions and debates. Finally, all of these roles should rotate through members so that each person carries out each role across different meetings. Thus, members must be aware of and/or trained in the responsibilities for each role so that they can carry them out when appropriate.

Running the Meeting

Eller (2004), Englberg and Wynn (2007), and Kayser all give similar recommendations for how to run a meeting. These are summarized below:

1) Only call meetings that are necessary and make sure to only invite those who need to be there.
2) Allow time for socialization at the beginning of the meeting. It is likely going to happen, and should be accounted for so that the formal part of the meeting does not start late.

3) Make sure to set norms and ground rules, especially for groups that are meeting for the first time.
4) Separate presentations from discussion items, and use subgroups as necessary for processing information.
5) Finally, firmly but fairly deal with disruptive members
6) Include a time for wrap up and closure, so that participants know what has been accomplished and where to go next.

Summary

This appendix includes a brief summary describing how to improve group and team meetings. In addition to structuring the meeting time, effective meetings require preparing the environment, preparing the facilitator, and preparing other members for the meeting. Preparing the environment is the first phase. To prepare the environment, create a structured agenda, and consider the physical setting of the meeting. Meeting facilitators need to understand what it means to be a facilitator. Finally, other members need to become secondary facilitators as well as have the time to prepare. When running the meeting, make sure to allow time for socialization, set ground rules as necessary, and provide a sense of closure that includes what was accomplished and what the next steps are.

Additional Resources

Eller, J. (2004). *Effective group facilitation in education: How to energize meetings and manage difficult groups*. Thousand Oaks, CA: Corwin Press, a Sage Publications Company.

Engleberg, I. N., & Wynn, D. R. (2007). *Working in groups: Communication principles and strategies* (4th ed.). Boston: Houghton Mifflin Company.

Kayser, T. A. (2011). *Mining group gold: How to cash in on the collaborative brainpower of a team for innovation and results*. New York: McGraw-Hill.

The Official Robert's Rules of Order Web Site (n.d.). http://www.robertsrules.com/.

References

Adams, H. F. (1912). Autokinetic sensations. *Psychological Monographs, 14*, 1–45.

Adams, S. (2008). Making all your teams into A-teams by Steve Adams, *Training Journal,* August, 44–47.

Adams, S. (2009). The four stages of effective team-building. *Training & Management Development Methods, 23*, 317–320.

Agency for Healthcare Research and Quality (n.d.). *TeamSTEPPS Teamwork Attitudes Questionnaire (T-TAQ).* U.S. Department of Health & Human Services. Retrieved from http://teamstepps.ahrq.gov/.

Aime, F., Meyer, C. J., & Humphrey, S. E. (2009). Legitimacy of team rewards: Analyzing legitimacy as a condition for the effectiveness of team incentive designs. *Journal of Business Research, 63*(1), 60–66.

Amodeo, A., Baker, D., & Krokos, K. (2009). Assessing teamwork attitudes in healthcare: TeamSTEPPS teamwork attitudes questionnaire development. Paper presented at the 2009 Annual Conference of the Society for Industrial and Organizational Psychology.

Ancona, D. S., & Caldwell, D. F. (1988). Beyond task and maintenance: Determining external functions in groups. *Group and Organization Studies 13*, 468–494.

Andersen, B. (2007). *Business process improvement toolbox* (2nd ed.). Milwaukee, WI; ASQ Quality Press.

Anderson, N. R., & West, M. A. (1994). *The Team Climate Inventory: Manual & Users' Guide.* Windsor, U,K.: Assessment Services for Employment, NFER-Nelson.

Anderson, N. R., & West, M. A. (1998, May). Measuring climate for work group innovation: development and validation of the team climate inventory. *Journal of Organizational Behavior, 19*, 235–258.

Andreopoulou, A. & Houston, D. M. (2002). The impact of collective self-esteem on intergroup evaluation: Self-protection and self-enhancement. *Current Research in Social Psychology, 7*(14), 243–256.

Argyris, C., & Schön, D. (1978). *Organizational learning: A theory of action perspective.* Reading, MA: Addison-Wesley.

Arnold, J., & Carnevale, P. J. (1997). Preference for dispute resolution procedures as a function of intentionality, consequences, and power. *Journal of Applied Social Psychology, 27,* 371–398.

Arrow, H., McGrath, J. E., & Berdahl, J. L. (2000). *Small groups as complex systems: formation, coordination, development, and adaptation.* Thousand Oaks, CA: Sage Publications, Inc.

Arthur, W., Edwards, B. D., Bell, S. T., Villado, A. J., & Bennet, W. (2005). Team task analysis: identifying tasks and jobs that are team based. *Human Factors, 47*(3), 654–669.

Arunachalam, V., & Dilla, W. N. (1995). Judgment accuracy and outcomes in negotiation: A causal modeling analysis of decision-aiding effects. *Organizational Behavior and Human Decision Processes, 61,* 289–304.

Asch, S. E. (1951). Effects of group pressure upon the modification and distortion of judgment. In H. Guetzkow (ed.) *Groups, leadership and men.* Pittsburgh, PA: Carnegie Press.

Atkinson, P., & Coffey, A. (2002). Revisiting the relationship between participant observation and interviewing. In J. F. Gubrium, & J. A. Holstein (Eds.), *Handbook of interview research: Context & method* (pp. 801–813). Thousand Oaks: Sage Publications, Inc.

Atwater, L., Brett, J. F., & Charles, A. C. (2007). Multisource feedback: Lessons learned and implications for practice. *Human Resource Management, 46,* 285–307.

Avolio, B. J., Jung, D. I., Murry, W. D., & Sivasubramaniam, N. (1996). Building highly developed teams: Focusing on shared leadership processes, efficacy, trust, and performance. *Advances in Interdisciplinary Studies of Work Teams, 3,* 173–209.

Baan, A., & Maznevski, M. (2008). Training for virtual collaboration: Beyond technology competencies. In J. Nemiro,, M. Beyerlein, L. Bradley, & S. Beyerlein (Eds.), *The handbook of high-performance virtual teams: A toolkit for collaborating across boundaries.* San Francisco: John Wiley & Sons, Inc.

Bader, G. E., Bloom, A. E., & Chang, R. Y. (1994). *Measuring team performance: A practical guide to tracking team success.* San Francisco: Pfeiffer.

Baer, J., & Kaufman, J. C. (2006). In J. C. Kaufman, & R. J. Sternberg (Eds.). *The international handbook of creativity.* Cambridge: Cambridge University Press.

Baker D. P., Amodeo A. M., Krokos K. J., Slonim A., & Herrera H. (2010). Assessing team-work attitudes in healthcare: development of the TeamSTEPPS teamwork attitudes questionnaire. *Quality and Safety in Health Care, 19,* 49–52.

Baltes, B. B., Dickson, M. W., Sherman, M. P., Bauer, C. C., & La Ganke, S. (2002). Computer-mediated communication and group decision-making: A meta-analysis. *Organizational Behavior and Human Decision Processes, 87,* 156–179.

Baron, R. S. (2005). So right it's wrong: Groupthink and the ubiquitous nature of polarized group decision making. *Advances in Experimental Social Psychology, 37,* 219–253.

Baron, R. S., & Kerr, N. L. (2003). *Group process, group decision, group action. Mapping social psychology.* Buckingham, England: Open University Press.

Baron, R. S., Kerr, N. L., & Miller N. (1992). *Group process, group decision, group action.* Pacific Grove, CA: Brooks/Cole.

Baruah, J., & Paulus, P. B. (2008). Effects of training on idea generation in groups. *Small Group Research, 39*(5), 523–541.

Baskett, G. D. (1973). Interview Decisions as Determined by Competency and Attitude Similarity. *Journal of Applied Psychology, 57,* 343–345.

Bass, B. M., & Avolio, B. (1993). Transformational leadership: A response to critiques. In M. M. Chemers, & R. Ayman (Eds.), *Leadership theory and research: Perspectives and directions.* NY: Academic Press.

Bavelas, A. (1950). Communication patterns in task oriented groups. *Journal of the Acoustical Society of America, 57*, 271–282.

Beal, D. J., Cohen, R. R., Burke, M. J., & McLendon, C. L. (2003). Cohesion and performance in groups: A meta-analytic clarification of construct relations. *Journal of Applied Psychology, 88*(6), 989–1004.

Beebe, S. A., & Masterson, J. T. (2006). *Communicating in Small Groups Principles and Practices* (8th ed.). Boston: Pearson Education, Inc.

Bell, B. S., & Kozlowski, S. W. J. (2002). A typology of virtual teams: Implications for effective leadership. *Group and Organization Management, 27*(1), 14–49.

Bell, D. E., Raiffa, H., & Tversky, A. [Eds.] (1988). *Decision Making: Descriptive, Normative and Prescriptive Interactions.* Cambridge, UK: Cambridge University Press.

Benne, K. D., & Sheats, P. (1948). Functional roles of group members. *Journal of Social Issues, 4*(2), 41–49.

Bennis, W., Parikh, J., & Lessem, R. (1994). *Beyond leadership: Balancing economics, ethics, and ecology.* Cambridge, MA: Blackwell Publishers.

Bavelas, A. (1948). A mathematical model for small group structures. *Human Organization, 7*, 16–30.

Bavelas, A. (1950). Communication patterns in task oriented groups. *Journal of the Acoustical Society of America, 22*, 271–282.

Biech, E. (2001). *The Pfeiffer book of successful team-building tools.* San Francisco: Jossey-Bass/Pfeiffer.

Bienvenu Sr., M. J. (1971). An interpersonal communication inventory. *Journal of Communication, 21*(4), 381–388.

Bierly, P. E., Stark, E. M., & Kessler, E. H. (2009). The moderating effects of virtuality on the antecedents and outcome of NPD team trust. *Journal of Product Innovation Management, 26*, 551–565.

Bies, R. J., & Tripp, T. M. (1996). Beyond distrust: "Getting even" and the need for revenge. In R. M. Kramer, & T. R. Tyler (Eds.), *Trust in organizations: Frontiers of theory and research* (pp. 246–260). Thousand Oaks, CA: Sage Publications.

Blake, R. R., & Mouton, J. S. (1964). *The managerial grid.* Houston, TX: Gulf.

Bolin, A. U., & Neuman, G. A. (2006). Personality, process, and performance in interactive brainstorming groups. *Journal of Business and Psychology, 20*(4), 565–585.

Bolman, L. G., & Deal, T. E. (2003). *Reframing organizations: Artistry, choice, and leadership.* Hoboken, NJ: Jossey-Bass.

Borgatti, S. P. (1997). *Communication structure and its effect on task performance.* Retrieved from http://www.analytictech.com/networks/commstruc.htm.

Bornstein, G. (1992). The free-rider problem in intergroup conflicts over step-level and continuous public goods. *Journal of Personality and Social Psychology, 62*, 597–606.

Bornstein, G. (2003). Intergroup conflict: Individual, group, and collective interests. *Personality and Social Psychology Review, 7*(2), 129–145.

Bouchard, T. J. (1972). Training, motivation, and personality as determinants of the effectiveness of brainstorming groups and individuals. *Journal of Applied Psychology, 56*, 324–331.

Bowers, C., Salas, E., & Jentsch, F. (2006). *Creating high-tech teams: Practical guidance on work performance and technology.* Washington, D.C.: American Psychological Association.

Bowling, J. J., Bergman, J. Z., & Bergman, S. (April, 2009). *Leadership in teams: Emergent leadership and the punctuated equilibrium model.* Paper presented at the 24th Society for Industrial Organizational Psychology Annual Conference, New Orleans, LA.

Boyd, D. (2007). A structured, facilitated team approach to innovation. *Organization Development Journal 25*(3), 119–122.

Braga, D. (2008). Transformational leadership attributes for virtual team leaders. In J. Nemiro, M. Beyerlein, L. Bradley, & S. Beyerlein (Eds.) *The handbook of high-performance virtual teams: A toolkit for collaborating across boundaries*. San Francisco: John Wiley & Sons, Inc.

Brannick, M. T., Salas, E., & Prince, C. (1997). *Team performance, assessment, and measurement: Theory, methods, and applications*. Mahwah, NJ: LEA.

Brewer, M. (1995). Managing diversity: The role of social identities. In S. E. Jackson, & M. N. Ruderman (Eds.), *Diversity in work teams: Research paradigms for a changing workplace*. Washington, DC: American Psychological Association.

Brooks, A. K. (1994). Power and the production of knowledge: Collective team learning in work organizations. *Human Resource Development Quarterly, 5*, 21–235.

Brown, M. K., Huettner, B., & James-Tanny, C. (2007). *Managing virtual teams: Getting the most from wikis, blogs, and other collaborative tools*. Plano, TX: Wordware Publishing, Inc.

Brunsson, N. (1989). *The organization of hypocrisy: talk, decisions and actions in organizations*. New York: John Wiley & Sons, Inc.

Buckham, R. H. (1987). Training trends: Applying role analysis in the workplace. *Personnel, 64*(2), 63–65.

Burgoon, J. K., & Burgoon, M. (1974). Unwillingness to communicate, anomia-alienation, and communication apprehension as predictors of small group communication. *Journal of Psychology: Interdisciplinary and Applied, 88*(1), 31–38.

Burke, W. W. (1994). *Organization development: A process of learning and changing*. Reading, MA: Addison Wesley Publishing Co.

Burns, J. M. (1978). *Leadership*. New York. Harper & Row.

Buros Institute. *Mental measurements yearbook*.

Bushe, G. R. (1998). Appreciative inquiry with teams. *Organization Development Journal, 16*(3), 41–50.

Bushe, G. R., & Kassam, A. (2005). When is appreciative inquiry transformational? A meta-case analysis. *Journal of Applied Behavioral Science, 41*, 161–181.

Caballer, A., Gracia, F., & Peiró, J. M. (2005). Affective responses to work process and outcomes in virtual teams: Effects of communication media and time pressure. *Journal of Managerial Psychology, 20*(3–4), 245–260.

Campbell, D. T. (1958). Common Fate, Similarity, and Other Indices of the Status of Aggregates of Persons as Social Entities. *Behavioral Science, 3*, 14–25.

Campbell, J. P., & Dunnette, M. D. (1968). Effectiveness of T-group experiences in managerial training and development, *Psychological Bulletin, 70*, 73–104.

Campion, M. A., Papper, E. M., & Medsker, G. J. (1996). Relations between work team characteristics and effectiveness: A replication and extension. *Personnel Psychology, 49*, 429–452.

Cannon-Bowers, J. A., Salas, E., & Converse, S. A. (1993). Shared mental models in expert team decision making. In N. J. Castellan, Jr. (Ed.), *Individual and group decision making: Current issues* (pp. 221–246). Hillsdale, NJ: Erlbaum.

Cannon-Bowers, J. A., & Salas, E. (1997). Teamwork competencies: The interaction of team member knowledge, skills, and attitudes. In O'Neil Jr., & Harold F. (Eds.), *Workforce readiness: Competencies and assessment* (pp. 151–174). Mahwah, NJ: Lawrence Erlbaum Associates Publishers.

Carless, S. A., & De Paola, C. (2000). A measurement of cohesion in work teams. *Small Group Research*, *31*(71), 71–88. doi: 10.1177/104649640003100104.

Carron, A. V., & Brawley, L. R. (2000). Cohesion: Conceptual and measurement issues. *Small Group Research*, *31*(1), 89–106. doi: 10:1177/104649640003100105.

Carron, A. V., & Spink, K. S. (1995). The group size-cohesion relationship in minimal groups. *Small Group Research, 26*(1), 86–105.

Carron, A. V., Widbeyer, W. N., & Brawley, L. R. (1985). The development of an instrument to assess cohesion in sport teams: The group environment questionnaire. *Journal of Sport Psychology, 7*, 244–266.

Carson, J. B., Tesluk, P. E., & Marrone, J. A. (2007). Shared leadership in teams: An investigation of antecedent conditions and performance. *Academy of Management Journal, 50*(5), 1217–1234.

Case Western Reserve University (n.d.). *The Appreciative Inquiry Commons*. Retrieved from: http://appreciativeinquiry.case.edu/.

Costa, A. C. (2003). Work team trust and effectiveness, *Personnel Review, 32*, 605–622.

Chaleff. I. (2008). Creating new ways of following. In R.E. Riggio, I. Chaleff, & J. Limpan-Blumen (Eds.), *The art of followership: How great followers create great leaders and organizations*. San Francisco: Jossey-Bass.

Chen, G., Kirkman, B. L., Kanfer, R., Allen, D., & Rosen, B. (2007). A multilevel study of leadership, empowerment, and performance in teams. *Journal of Applied Psychology*, *92*(2), 331–346.

Chiocchio, F., & Essembre, H. (2009). Cohesion and performance: A meta-analutic review of disparities between Project Teams, Production Teams and Service Teams. *Small Group Research, 40*, 382–421.

Clutterbuck, D. (2008). Are you a goal junkie? *Training Journal,* 43–46.

Cohen, D. S. (2005). *The heart of change field guide: Tools and tactics for leading change in your organization*. Boston: Harvard Business School Press.

Cohen, S., & Bailey, D. E. (1997). What makes teams work: Group effectiveness research from the shop floor to the executive suite. *Journal of Management, 23*, 239–290.

Cohen, S. G. (1994). Designing effective self-managing work teams. In M. M. Beyerlein, & D. A. Johnson (Eds.), *Advances in interdisciplinary studies of work teams: Theories of self-managing work teams*. Greenwich, CT: JAI Press Inc.

Collins, B. E., & Guetzkow, H. (1964). *A social psychology of group processes for decision-making*. New York: John Wiley & Sons, Inc.

Coleman, J. (1990). *Foundations of social theory*. Cambridge, MA: Harvard University Press.

Colman, A. D., & Bexton, W. H. (1975). *Group relations reader*. Sausalito, CA: GREX.

Comadena, M. E. (1984). Brainstorming groups: Ambiguity tolerance, communication apprehension, task attraction, and individual productivity. *Small Group Behavior, 15*(2), 251–264.

Comer, L. B., & Drollenger, T. (1999). Active empathetic listening and selling success: A conceptual framework. *Journal of Personal Selling & Sales Management, 19*(1), 15–29.

Conger, J. A. (1989). *The charismatic leader: Behind the mystique of exceptional leadership*. San Francisco: Jossey-Bass.

Conger, J. A., & Fulmer, R. M. (2003). Developing your leadership pipeline. *Harvard Business Review, 81*(12), 76–84.

Conger, J. A., & Kanungo, R. N. (1998). *Charismatic leadership in organizations*. Thousand Oaks, CA: Sage Publications, Inc.

Conger, J. A., & Riggio, R. E. (2007). *The practice of leadership: Developing the next generation of leaders.* San Francisco: Jossey-Bass.

Cook, K. S., & Cooper, R. M. (2003). Experimental Studies of Cooperation, Trust, and Social Exchange. In E. Ostrom, & J. Walker (Eds.), *Trust and reciprocity.* New York: Russell Sage, 209–244.

Cook, K. S., Hardin, R., & Levi, M. (2005). *Cooperation without trust?* NY: Russell Sage Foundation.

Cook, R. A., & Goff, J. L. (2002). Coming of age with self-managed teams: Dealing with a problem employee. *Journal of Business and Psychology, 16*(3), 485–496.

Cooper, D. R., & Schindler, P. S. (2006). *Business research methods* (9th ed.). Boston: McGraw Hill.

Cooperrider, D. L. (1998). *Appreciative inquiry: A positive revolution in change.* Presentation retrieved August 20, 2009 from http://appreciativeinquiry.case.edu/practice/toolsMod elsPPTsDetail.cfm?coid=183.

Cooperrider, D. L., & Srivastva, S. (1987). Appreciative inquiry in organizational Life. In W. Pasmore, & R. Woodman (Eds.), *Research in organization change and development* (Vol. 1, pp. 129–169). Greenwich, CT: JAI Press.

Cooperrider, D. L., & Whitney, D. (n.d.). What is Appreciative Inquiry? *Appreciative Inquiry Commons.* Retrieved August 20, 2009 from: http://appreciativeinquiry.case.edu/intro/ whatisai.cfm

Cosier, R. A., & Rechner, P. L. (1985). Inquiry method effects on performance in a simulated business environment. *Organizational Behavior and Human Decision Processes, 36,* 79–95.

Costa, A. C. (2003). Work team trust and effectiveness. *Personnel Review, 32,* 605–622.

Coutu, D., & Beschloss, M. (2009). Why teams don't work: an interview with J. Richard Hackman. *Harvard Business Review, 87*(5), 98–105.

Cox, K. B. (2004). The intragroup conflict scale: Development and psychometric properties. *Journal of Nursing Measurement, 12*(2), 133–146.

Cox, J. F., Pearce, C. L., & Perry, M. L. (2003). Toward a model of shared leadership and distributed influence in the innovation process: How shared leadership can enhance new product development team dynamics and effectiveness. In C. L. Pearce, & J. A. Conger (Eds.) *Shared leadership: Reframing the hows and whys of leadership* (pp. 48–76). Thousand Oaks, CA: Sage Publications. .

Crane, T. G. (2000). Becoming a coach for the teams you lead. In M. Goldsmith, L. Lyons, & A. Freas, (Eds.), *Coaching for leadership: How the world's greatest coaches help leaders learn.* San Francisco: Jossey-Bass/Pfeiffer.

Creed, W. E. D., & Miles, R. E. (1996). Trust in organizations: A conceptual framework linking organizational forms, managerial philosophies, and the opportunity costs of controls. In R. M. Kramer, & T. R. Tyler (Eds.), *Trust in organizations: Frontiers of theory and research* (pp. 16–38). Thousand Oaks, CA: Sage Publications.

Crocker, J., & Luhtanen, R. (1990). Collective self-esteem and ingroup bias. *Journal of Personality & Social Psychology, 58,* 60–70.

Culvenor, J., & Else, D. (1997). Finding occupational injury solutions: The impact of training in creative thinking. *Safety Science, 25*(1–3), 187–205.

Curtis, E. F., & Dreachslin, J. L. (2008). Diversity management interventions and organizational performance: A synthesis of current literature. *Human Resource Development Review, 7,* 107–134.

Daft, R. L., & Lengel, R. H. (1986). Organizational information requirements, media richness and structural design. *Management Science, 32*, 554–571.

Dalkey, N. C. (1969). *The Delphi method: An experimental study of group opinion*. Santa Monica, CA: Rand.

Darley, J. M., & Gross, P. H. (1983). A hypothesis-confirming bias in labeling effects. *Journal of Personality and Social Psychology, 44*(1), 20–33.

Davidson, E. J. (2005). *Evaluation methodology basics: The nuts and bolts of sound evaluation*. Thousand Oaks, CA: Sage.

Davison, M. L., & Jones, L. E. (1976). A similarity-attraction model for predicting sociometric choice from perceived group structure. *Journal of Personality and Social Psychology, 33*(5), 601–612.

Dawes, R. M. (1980). Social dilemmas. *Annual Review of Psychology, 31*, 169–193.

De Bono, E. (1999). *Six thinking hats*. New York: Back Bay Books.

De Church, L. A., Hamilton, K. L., & Haas, C. (2007). Effects of conflict management strategies on perceptions on intragroup conflict. *Group Dynamics: Theory, Research, and Practice, 11*(1), 66–78.

De Church, L. A., & Mesmer-Magnus, J. R. (2010). The cognitive underpinnings of effective teamwork: A meta-analysis. *Journal of Applied Psychology, 95*(1), 32–53.

De Dreu, C. K. W., & Gelfand, M. J. (2008). Conflict in the workplace: Sources, functions, and dynamics across multiple levels of analysis. In C. K. W. De Dreu, & M. J. Gelfand (Eds.), *The psychology of conflict and conflict management in organizations*. NY: Lawrence Erlbaum Associates.

De Dreu, C., & Van De Vliert, E. (1997). *Using conflict in organizations*. Thousand Oaks, CA: Sage Publications.

De Dreu, C. K. W., & Weingart, L. R. (2003). Task versus relationship conflict, team performance, and team member satisfaction: A meta-analysis. *Journal of Applied Psychology, 88*(4), 741–749.

Delbecq, A. L., Van de Ven, A. H., & Gustafson, D. H. (1975). *Group Techniques for Program Planning*. Glenview, Ill.: Scott, Foresman.

De Leon, L. (2001). Accountability for individuating behaviors in self-managing teams. *Organization Development Journal, 19*(4), 7–19.

Den Hartog, D. N., & Koopman, P. L. (2001). Leadership in organizations. In N. Anderson, D. S. Ones, H. K. Inangil, & C. Viswesvaran (Eds.), *Handbook of industrial, work, and organizational psychology, Vol. 2: Organizational psychology*. Thousand Oaks, CA: Sage Publications.

Dennis, A. R., Garfield, M., & Reinicke, B. (2008). Towards an integrative model of group development, Indiana University, USA. *Sprouts: Working Papers on Information Systems, 8*(3). http://sprouts.aisnet.org/8-3

Dennis, A. R., & Valacich, J. S. (1993). Computer brainstorms: More heads are better than one. *Journal of Applied Psychology, 78*(4), 531–537.

Dennis, A. R., Valacich, J. S., Carte, T. A., Garfield, M. J., Haley, B. J., & Aronson, J. E. (1997). Research report: The effectiveness of multiple dialogues in electronic brainstorming. *Information Systems Research, 8*, 203–211.

Dennis, A. R., & Williams, M. L. (2003). Electronic brainstorming: Theory, research, and future directions. In P. B. Paulus, & B. A. Nijstad (Eds.), *Group creativity: Innovation through collaboration*. Oxford: Oxford University Press.

De Rosa, D., & Lepsinger, R. (2010). *Virtual team success: A practical guide for working and leading from a distance*. San Francisco: Jossey-Bass, a Wiley Imprint.

De Rosa, D. (2009b). In Focus/Virtual Teams – Improving performance by emulating the best. *Leadership in Action, 29*(2), 17–19.

De Rosa, D. (2009b). Virtual success: The keys to effectiveness in leading from a distance. *Leadership in Action, 28*(6), 9–11.

De Shon, R. P., Kozlowski, S. W. J., Schmidt, A. M., Milner, K. R., & Wiechmann, D. (2004). A multiple-goal, multilevel model of feedback effects on the regulation of individual and team performance. *Journal of Applied Psychology, 89*(6), 1035–1056.

Desivilya, H. S., & Yagil, D. (2005). The role of emotions in conflict management: The case of work teams. *The International Journal of Conflict Management, 16*(1), 55–69.

Deutsch, M. (1969). Socially relevant science: Reflections on some studies of interpersonal conflict. *American Psychologist, 24*, 1076–1092.

Deutsch, M. (1975). Equity, equality, and need: What determines which value will be used as the basis of distributive justice? *Journal of Social Issues, 31*(3), 137–149.

Deutsch, M. (2000). *The handbook of conflict resolution.* San Francisco, CA: Jossey-Bass.

Deutsch, M. (2006). Cooperation and competition. In M. Deutsch, P. T. Coleman, & E. C. Marcus (Eds.), *The handbook of conflict resolution: Theory and practice* (2nd ed., pp. 23–42). Hoboken, NJ, US: Wiley Publishing.

Devine, D. J., Clayton, L. D., Phillips, J. L., Dunford, B. B., & Melner, S. B. (1999). Teams in organizations: prevalence, characteristics, and effectiveness. *Small Group Research, 30*, 678–711. Retrieved May 31, 2007.

De Vries, R. E., Bakker-Pieper, A., & Oostenveld, W. (2010). Leadership = communication? The relations of leaders' communication styles with leadership styles, knowledge sharing and leadership outcomes. *Journal of Business and Psychology, 25*(3), 367–380.

Dick, B. (2005). Grounded theory: a thumbnail sketch. Available at: http://www.scu.edu.au/schools/gcm/ar/arp/grounded.html.

Dickens, L., & Watkins, K. (1999). Action research: Rethinking Lewin. *Management Learning. 30*(2), 127–140.

Diehl, M., & Stroebe, W. (1987). Productivity loss in brainstorming groups: Toward the solution of a riddle. *Journal of Personality and Social Psychology, 53*(3), 497–509.

Di Tomaso, N., Cordero, R., & Farris, G. F. (1996). Effects of group diversity on perceptions of group and self among scientists and engineers. In M. Ruderman, M. Hughes-James, & S. Jackson (Eds.), *Selected research on work team diversity* (pp. 99–119). Greensboro, NC: Center for Creative Leadership and Washington DC: American Psychological Association.

Dovidio, J. F., Saguy, T., & Shnabel, N. (2009). Cooperation and conflict within groups: Bridging intragoup and intergroup processes. *Journal of Social Issues, 65*(2), 429–449.

Driskell, J. E., Radtke, P. H., & Salas, E. (2003). Virtual teams: Effects of technological mediation on team performance. *Group Dynamics: Theory, Research, and Practice, 7*(4), 297–323.

Driskell, J. E., & Salas, E. (2006). Groupware, group dynamics, and team performance. In C. Bowers, E. Salas, & F. Jentsch (Eds.) *Creating high-tech teams: Practical guidance on work performance and technology.* Washington, D.C.: American Psychological Association.

Druskat, V. U., & Wolff, S. B. (2004). Building the emotional intelligence of groups. In *Harvard Business Review on teams that succeed.* Boston: Harvard Business School Press.

Duimering, P. R., & Robinson, R. B. (2007). Situational influences on team helping norms: Case study of a self-directed team. *Journal of Behavioral and Applied Management, 9*(1), 62–87.

Duke Corporate Education. (2005). *Building effective teams.* Chicago: Dearborn Trade Publishing: A Kaplan Professional Company.

Dwyer, K. K. (2000). The multidimensional model: Teaching students to self-manage high communication apprehension by self-selecting treatments. *Communication Education, 49*(1), 72–81.

Dymer, C. (2004). Six hats to manage your next meeting. *Successful Meetings, 53*(9), 30–31.

Eagly, A. H., Johannesen-Schmidt, M. C., & Engen, M. L. (2003). Transformational, transactional, and laissez-faire leadership styles: A meta-analysis comparing women and men. *Psychological Bulletin, 129*, 569–591.

Eagly, A. H., & Carli, L. L. (2007). *Through the labyrinth: The truth about how women become leaders.* Boston: Harvard Business School Press.

Eagly, A. H., Karau, S. J., & Makhijani, M.G. (1995). Gender and the effectiveness of leaders: A meta-analysis. *Psychological Bulletin, 117*(1), 125–145.

Eagly, A. H., & Sczesny, S. (2009). Stereotypes about women, men, and leaders: Have times changed?. In M. Barreto, M. K. Ryan, & M. T. Schmitt (Eds), (2009). *The glass ceiling in the 21st century: Understanding barriers to gender equality* (pp. 21–47). Washington, DC: American Psychological Association.

Eckes, G. (2003). *Six sigma team dynamics: The elusive key to project success.* Hoboken, NJ: John Wiley & Sons, Inc.

Edmuondson, A., Bohmer, R., & Pisano, G. (2004). Speeding up team learning. In *Harvard Business Review on teams that succeed.* Boston: Harvard Business School Press.

Eller, J. (2004). *Effective group facilitation in education: How to energize meetings and manage difficult groups.* Thousand Oaks, CA: Corwin Press, a Sage Publications Company.

Ellis, A. P. J., Porter, C. O. L. H., & Wolverton, S. A. (2008). Learning to work together: An examination of transactive memory system development in teams. In V. L. Sessa, & M. London (Eds.), *Work group learning: Understanding, improving, and assessing how groups learn in organizations.* NY: Lawrence Erlbaum Associates.

Engleberg, I. N., & Wynn, D. R. (2007). *Working in groups: Communication principles and strategies* (4th ed.). Boston: Houghton Mifflin Company.

Eys, M. A., Hardy, J., & Patterson, M. M. (2006). Group norms and their relationship to cohesion in an exercise environment. *International Journal of Sport and Exercise Psychology, 4*(1), 43–56.

Feldhusen, J. F. (1993). A conception of creative thinking and creativity training. In S. G. Isaksen, M. C. Murdock, R. L. Firestein, & D. J. Treffinger (Eds.), *Nurturing and developing creativity: The emergence of a discipline.* Norwood, NJ: Ablex Publishing Corporation.

Fernandez-Ballesteros, R. (2003). *Encyclopedia of psychological assessment.* Thousand Oaks, CA: Sage.

Ferraris, C., & Carveth, R. (2003). NASA and the Columbia disaster: Decision making by Groupthink? *Proceeding of the 2003 Association for Business Communication Annual Convention.*

Fiedler, F. E., & Garcia, J. E. (1987). *New approaches to leadership, cognitive resources and organizational performance,* New York: John Wiley and Sons, Inc.

Fields, D. L. (2002). *Taking the measure of work: a guide to validated scales for organizational research and diagnosis.* Thousand Oaks, CA: Sage.

Fink, A. (2003). *The survey kit* (2nd ed.). Thousand Oaks, CA: Sage.

Fisher, R., Ury, W., & Patton, B. (1991). *Getting to yes: Negotiating agreement without giving in.* Boston: Houghton Mifflin Company.

Fiske, J. (1982). *Introduction to communication studies*. London: Methuen.

Fjermestad, J. (2004). An analysis of communication mode in group support systems research. *Decision Support Systems, 37*, 239–263.

Fletcher, J. K., & Käufer, K. (2003). Shared leadership: Paradox and possibility. In C. L. Pearce, & J. A. Conger (Eds.). *Shared leadership: Reframing the hows and whys of leadership*. Thousand Oaks, CA: Sage Publications, Inc.

Flowers, M. L. (1977). A laboratory test of some implications of Janis's groupthink hypothesis. *Journal of Personality and Social Psychology, 35*(12), 888–896.

Foote, D. A., & Tang, T. L. (2008). Job satisfaction and organizational citizenship behavior (OCB): Does team commitment make a difference in self-directed teams? *Management Decision, 46*(6), 933–947.

Forsyth, D. R. (2006). *Group dynamics*. Belmont, CA: Wadsworth.

Franklin, M. (2006). *Performance gap analysis*. Alexandria, VA: American Society for Training & Development.

Franz, T. M., & Larson, Jr., J. R. (2002). The impact of experts on information sharing during group discussion. *Small Group Research, 33*(4), 383–411.

Franz, T. M., & Vicker, L. A. (2010). Using a virtual class to demonstrate computer-mediated group dynamics concepts. *Teaching of Psychology, 37*(2), 124–128.

Freeman, J., Haimson, C., Diedrich, F. J., & Paley, M. (2006). Training teamwork with synthetic teams. In C. Bowers, E. Salas, & F. Jentsch (Eds.), *Creating high-tech teams: Practical guidance on work performance and technology*. Washington, D.C.: American Psychological Association.

French, J. R. P., & Raven, B. (1959). Bases of social power. In D. Cartwright, & A. Zander (Eds.), *Group dynamics*. New York: Harper & Row.

French, W. L., & Bell, C. H. (1984). *Organization development*. Upper Saddle River, NJ: Prentice-Hall.

Friedman, T. L. (2005). *The world is flat: A brief history of the twentieth-first century*. NY: Farrar, Straus and Giroux.

Gabel, M., & Brunner, H. (2003). *Global Inc.: An atlas of the multinational corporation*. New York: New Press.

Gallupe, R. B., Bastianutti, L. M., & Cooper, W. H. (1991). Unblocking brainstorms. *Journal of Applied Psychology, 76*, 137–142.

Garvin, D. A., & Roberto, M. A. (2001). What you don't know about making decisions. In *Harvard Business Review on teams that succeed*. Boston: Harvard Business School Press.

Geister, S., Konradt, U., & Hertel, G. (2006). Effects of process feedback on motivation, satisfaction, and performance in virtual teams. *Small Group Research, 37*(5), 459–489.

Gersick, J. G. (1988). Time and transition in work teams: Toward a new model of group development. *Academy of Management Journal, 31*(1), 9–41.

Gladstein, D. L. (1984). Groups in context: A model of task group effectiveness. *Administrative Science Quarterly, 29*, 499–517.

Goldhaber, G. M. (1974). *Organizational communication*. Dubuque, IA: WM. C. Brown Company.

Goldman, B. M., Cropanzano, R., Stein, J., & Benson, L. III. (2008). The role of third parties/ mediation in managing conflict in organizations. In C. K. W. DeDreu, & M. J. Gelfand (Eds.), *The psychology of conflict and conflict management in organizations*. NY: Lawrence Erlbaum Associates.

Goldman, B. A., Mitchell, D. F., & Egelson, P. E. (1996). *Directory of unpublished experimental mental measures*. Washington DC: American Psychological Association.

Goldsmith, M. (2000). Coaching for behavioral change. In M. Goldsmith, L. Lyons, & A. Freas, (Eds.), *Coaching for leadership: How the world's greatest coaches help leaders learn*. San Francisco: Jossey-Bass/Pfeiffer.

Goldsmith, M., Lyons, L., & Freas, A. (2000). *Coaching for leadership: How the world's greatest coaches help leaders learn*. San Francisco: Jossey-Bass/Pfeiffer.

Goldsmith, M., & Morgan, H. (2000). Team building without time wasting. In M. Goldsmith, L. Lyons, & A. Freas, (Eds.), *Coaching for leadership: How the world's greatest coaches help leaders learn*. San Francisco: Jossey-Bass/Pfeiffer.

Golembiewski, R. T., & McConkie, M. (1975). The centrality of interpersonal trust in group processes (pp. 131–185). In Cooper, G. L. (Ed.), *Theories of group processes*: London: John Wiley & Sons, Ltd.

Graebner, R., Offerman, L., Basu, S., & Wirtz, P. (April, 2009). *Virtual teams: Group process and satisfaction with virtual interactions*. Poster presented at 24th Society for Industrial Organizational Psychology Annual Conference, New Orleans, L.A.

Graen, G. (1976). Role making processes within complex organizations. In M. D. Dunnette (Ed.), *The handbook of industrial and organizational psychology* (pp. 1201–1245). Chicago: Rand McNally.

Guion, R. M. (1998). *Assessment, measurement, and prediction for personnel decisions*. Mahwah, NJ. LEA.

Gully, S. M., Devine, D. J., & Whitney, D. J. (1995). A Meta-Analysis of Cohesion and Performance: Effects of Level of Analysis and Task Interdependence. *Small Group Research, 26*, 497–520.

Gurtner, A., Tschan, F., Semmer, N.K. & Nägele, C. (2007). Getting groups to develop good strategies: Effects of reflexivity interventions on team process, team performance, and shared mental models. *Organizational Behavior and Human Decision Processes, 102*(2), 127–142.

Guzzo R. A., Jette R. D., & Katzell R. A. (1985). The effects of psychologically based intervention programs on worker productivity: A meta-analysis. *Personnel Psychology, 38*, 275–292.

Guzzo, R. A., & Shea, G. P. (1992). Group performance and intergroup relations in organizations. In M. D. Dunnette, & L. M. Hough (Eds.), *Handbook of industrial and organizational psychology, 3* (2nd ed.) (pp. 269–313). Palo Alto, CA: Consulting Psychologists Press.

Hackman, J. R. (1987). The design of work teams. In J. W. Lorsch (Ed.), *Handbook of organizational behavior*. Englewood Cliffs, NJ: Prentice-Hall. (pp. 315–342).

Hackman, J. R., & Morris, C. G. (1975). Group tasks, group interaction process, and group performance effectiveness: A review and proposed integration. In L. Berkowit (Ed.), *Advances in experimental social psychology*, 1–99. New York, Academic Press.

Hackman, J. R., & Wageman, R. (2007). Asking the right questions about leadership: Discussion and conclusions. *American Psychologist, 62*, 43–47.

Hackman, J. R., & Walton, R. E. (1986). Leading groups in organizations. In P. S. Goodman (Ed.), *Designing effective work groups* (pp. 72–119). San Francisco: Jossey-Bass.

Hackman, J. R. (1987). The design of work teams. In J. Lorsch (Ed.), *Handbook of organizational behavior* (pp. 315–342). New York: Prentice Hall.

Hackman, J. R. (1990). *Groups that work (and those that don't): Creating conditions for effective teamwork*. San Francisco: Jossey-Bass Publishers.

Hackman, J. R. (2002). *Leading teams: Setting the stage for great performances*. Boston: Harvard Business School Press.

Hackman, J. R. (2005). Rethinking team leadership or team leaders are not music directors. In D. M. Messick, & R. M. Kramer (Eds.), *The psychology of leadership: New perspectives and research*. Mahwah, NJ: Lawrence Erlbaum Associates, Inc.

Hackman, J. R., & Wageman, R. (2005). A theory of team coaching. *The Academy of Management Review, 30*(2), 269–287.

Hackman, J. R., & Wageman, R. (2007). Asking the right questions about leadership. *American Psychologist, 62*, 43–47.

Halevy, N., Bornstein, G., & Sagiv, L. (2008). "In-group love" and "out-group hate" as motives for individual participation in intergroup conflict: A new game paradigm. *Psychological Science, 19*(4), 405–411.

Halfhill, T., Nielsen, T. M., & Sundstorm, E. (2008). The ASA framework: A field study of group personality composition and group performance in military action teams. *Small Group Research, 39*, 616–635.

Halpern, D. F. (1998). Teaching critical thinking for transfer across domains. Dispositions, skills, structure. *American Psychologist, 53*, 449–455.

Hambly, L. A., O'Neill, T. A., & Kline, T. J. B. (2007). Virtual team leadership: Perspectives from the field. *International Journal of e-Collaboration, 3*, 40–64.

Hamilton, D. L., & Gifford, R. K. (1976). Illusory correlation in interpersonal perception: A cognitive basis of stereotypical judgment. *Journal of Experimental Social Psychology, 12*, 392–407.

Hammond, K. R., & Brehmer, B. (1973). Quasi-rationality and distrust: Implications for international conflict. In L. Rappoport, & D. Summers (Eds.), *Human judgment and social interactions*. New York: Holt, Rineholt, & Winston.

Harrington-Mackin, D. (1994). *The team building tool kit: Tips, tactics and rules for effective workplace teams*. New York: American Management Association.

Harris, L. C., & Ogbonna, E. (1998). Employee responses to culture change efforts. *Human Resource Management Journal, 8*(2), 78–92.

Harrod, W. J. (1983). Social Dilemma: A Teaching Game. *Teaching Sociology, 10*, 266–274.

Harvey, D. F., & Brown, D. R. (2001). *An experiential approach to organization development*. Upper Saddle River, NJ; Prentice Hall.

Henley, D. (2009). Power of Collaboration. *Leadership Excellence, 26*(8), 4.

Hersey, P. and Blanchard, K. H. (1977). *Management of Organizational Behavior: Utilizing Human Resources* (3rd ed.) New Jersey/Prentice Hall.

Hersen, M. (2003). *Comprehensive Handbook of Psychological Assessment*. Hoboken, NJ: John Wiley & Sons, Inc.

Hertel, G., Konradt, U., & Voss, K. (2008). Competencies for virtual teamwork: Development and validation of a web-based selection tool for members of distributed teams. *European Journal of Work and Organizational Psychology, 15*, 477–504.

Hewlett, S. A. (2009). *Top talent: Keeping performance up when business is down*. Boston: Harvard Business Press.

Hill, G. W. (1982). Group versus individual performance: are N + 1 heads better than one? *Psychological Bulletin, 91*(3), 517–539.

Hinsz, V. B., Tindale, R. S., & Vollrath, D. A. (1997). The emerging conception of groups as information processors. *Psychological Bulletin, 121*, 43–64.

Hobman, E. V., & Bordia, P. (2006). The role of team identification in the dissimilarity-conflict relationship. *Group Processes & Intergroup Relations, 9*(4), 483–507.

Hofman, D. A., & Jones, L. M. (2005). Leadership, collective personality, and performance. *Journal of Applied Psychology, 90*, 509–522.

Hofstede, G. (2001). *Culture's consequences: Comparing values, behaviors, institutions, and organizations across nations* (2nd ed.). Thousand Oaks, CA: Sage Publications.

Hogg, M. A. (1996). Social identity, self-categorization, and the small group. In E. H. Witte, & J. H. Davis (Eds.), *Understanding group behavior* (pp. 227–253): *Vol. 2. Small group processes and interpersonal relations*. Hillsdale, NJ, England: Lawrence Erlbaum Associates, Inc.

Hollander, E. P. (1958). Conformity, status, and idiosyncrasy credit. *Psychological Review, 65*(2), 117–127.

Hollen, P. J. (1994). Psychometric properties of two instruments to measure quality decision making. *Research in Nursing & Health, 17*(2), 137–148.

Hollenbeck, J. R. (2000). A structural approach to external and internal person-team fit. *Applied Psychology: An International Review, 49*(3), 534–549.

Hollingshead, A. B., & Brandon, D. P. (2003). Potential benefits of communication in transactive memory systems. *Human Communication Research, 29*(4), 607–615.

Homan, A. C., van Knippenberg, D., Van Kleef, G. A., & De Dreu, C. K. W. (2007). Bridging faultlines by valuing diversity: Diversity beliefs, information elaboration, and performance in diverse work groups. *Journal of Applied Psychology, 92*, 1189–1199.

Hoogstraten, J., & Vorst, H. C. (1978). Group cohesion, task performance, and the experimenter expectancy effect. *Human Relations, 31*(11), 939–956.

Hopf, T., & Colby, N. (1992). The relationship between interpersonal communication apprehension and self-efficacy. *Communication Research Reports, 9*(2), 131–135.

House, R. J. (1996). Path-goal theory of leadership: Lessons, legacy, and a reformulated theory. *Leadership Quarterly, 7*, 323–352.

Houston, J. A., & White, J. T. (1997). Building bridges: How the power of the pen can drive quality improvement. *Quality Progress, 30*(6), 128.

Howell, S., Lederman, C., Owen, V., & Solomon, L. Z. (1978). Compliance as a function of status. *The Journal of Social Psychology, 106*(2), 291–292.

Ilgen, D. R., Hollenbeck, J. R., Johnson, M., & Jundt, D (2005). Teams in organizations: From IPO models to IMOI models. *Annual Review of Psychology, 56*, 517–544.

Isaksen, S. G., Dorval, K. B., & Treffinger, D. J. (1994). *Creative approaches to problem solving.* Dubuque, IA: Kendall/Hunt Publishing Company.

Iverson, K., & Vukotich, G. (2009). OD 2.0: Shifting from disruptive to innovative technology. *OD Practitioner, 41*(2), 43–49.

Izard, C. (1960). Personality similarity, positive affect, and interpersonal attraction. *Journal of Abnormal and Social Psychology, 61*, 484–485.

Jablin, F. M., & Sias, P. M. (2001). The effects of group proportions on group dynamics. In F. M. Jablin, & L. L. Putnam (Eds.), *The new handbook of organizational communication: Advances in theory, research and methods* (pp. 819–862). Thousand Oaks, CA: Sage.

Jackson, S. E., & Ruderman, M. N. (1995). *Diversity in work teams: Research paradigms for a changing workplace.* Washington, DC: American Psychological Association.

Jackson, S. E., & Ruderman, M. N. (1995). Introduction: Perspectives for understanding diverse work teams. In S. E. Jackson, & M. N. Ruderman (Eds.), *Diversity in work teams: Research paradigms for a changing workplace.* Washington, DC: American Psychological Association.

Jackson, S. E., Brett, J. F., Sessa, V. I., Cooper, D. M., Julin, J. A., & Peyronnin, K. (1991). Some differences make a difference: Individual dissimilarity and group heterogeneity as correlates of recruitment, promotions, and turnover. *Journal of Applied Psychology, 76*(5), 675–689.

James, L. R., Demaree, R. G., & Wolf, G. (1984). Estimating within-group interrater reliability with and without response bias. *Journal of Applied Psychology, 69*, 85–98.

Janis, I. L. (1982). *Groupthink: Psychological studies of policy decisions and fiascoes* (2nd ed.). New York: Houghton Mifflin.

Janis, I. L., & Mann, L. (1977). *Decision making: A psychological analysis of conflict, choice, and commitment.* New York, NY: Free Press.

Jassawalla, A., Sashittal, H., & Malshe, A. (2009). Students' perceptions of social loafing: Its antecedents and consequences in undergraduate business classroom teams. *Academy of Management Learning & Education, 8*, 42–54.

Jehn, K. A. (1994). Enhancing effectiveness: An investigation of advantages and disadvantages of value-based intragroup conflict. *The International Journal of Conflict Management, 5*(3), 223–238.

Jehn, K. A. (1995). A multimethod examination of the benefits and detriments of intragroup conflict. *Administrative Science Quarterly, 40*(2), 256–282.

Jehn, K.A. (1997). A qualitative analysis of conflict types and dimensions in organizational groups. *Administrative Science Quarterly, 42*, 530–557.

Jehn, K. A., Greer, L., Levine, S., & Szulanski, G. (2008). The effects of conflict types, dimensions, and emergent states on group outcomes. *Group Decision and Negotiation, 17*, 465–495.

Jehn, K. A., & Mannix, E. A. (2001). The dynamic nature of conflict: A longitudinal study of intra-group conflict and group performance. *Academy of Management Journal, 44*(2), 238–251.

Jehn, K. A., Northcraft, G. B., & Neale, M. A. (1999). Why differences make a difference: A field study of diversity, conflict, and performance in workgroups. *Administrative Science Quarterly, 44*(4), 741–763.

Johnston, M. K., Reed, K., Lawrence, K., & Onken, M. (2007). The link between communication and financial performance in simulated organizational teams. *Journal of Managerial Issues, 19*(4), 536–553.

Jones, E. E., & Harris, V. A. (1967). The attribution of attitudes. *Journal of Experimental Social Psychology, 3*, 1–24.

Judge, T. A., & Bono, J. E. (2000). Five-factor model of personality and transformational leadership. *Journal of Applied Psychology, 85*, 751–765.

Judge, T. A., Bono, J. E., Ilies, R., & Gerhardt, M. W. (2002). Personality and leadership: A qualitative and quantitative review. *Journal of Applied Psychology, 87*, 765–780.

Judge, T. A., Piccolo, R. F., & Ilies, R. (2004). The forgotten ones? The validity of consideration and initiating structure in leadership research. *Journal of Applied Psychology, 89*, 36–51.

Judge, T. A., & Piccolo, R. F. (2004). Transformational and transactional leadership: A meta-analytic test of their relative validity. *Journal of Applied Psychology, 89*, 755–768.

Kaiser, R. B., Hogan, R., & Craig, S. B. (2008). Leadership and the Fate of Organizations. *American Psychologist, 63*, 96–110.

Karau S. J., & Williams, K. D. (1993). Social loafing: A meta-analytic review and theoretical integration. *Journal of Personality and Social Psychology, 65*, 681–706.

Karau, S. J., & Williams, K. D. (2001). Understanding individual motivation in groups: The collective effort model. In M. E. Turner (Ed.) *Groups at work: Theory and research.* Mahwah, NJ: Lawrence Erlbaum Associates.

Karriker, J. H. (2005). Cyclical Group Development and Interaction-based Leadership Emergence in Autonomous Teams: An Integrated Model. *Journal of Leadership & Organizational Studies, 11*, 54–64.

Katz, N. (2001). Getting the most out of your team. *Harvard Business Review, 79*(8), p. 22.

Katz, D., & Kahn, R. (1978). *The social psychology of organizations* (2nd ed.). New York: John Wiley & Sons, Inc.

Katzenbach, J. R., & Smith, D. K. (1993). *The wisdom of teams: Creating the high-performance organization.* Boston: Harvard Business School.

Katzenbach, J. R., & Smith, D. K. (2005). The discipline of teams. *Harvard Business Review, 83*(7/8), 162–171.

Kauffeld, S. (2006). Self-directed work groups and team competence. *Journal of Occupational and Organizational Psychology, 79*(1), 1–21.

Kaufman, G. (1993). The logical structure of creativity concepts: A conceptual argument for creativity as a coherent discipline. In S. G. Isaksen, M. C. Murdock, R. L. Firestein, & D. J. Treffinger (Eds.), *Understanding and recognizing creativity: The emergence of a discipline.* Norwood, NJ: Ablex Publishing Corporation.

Kayser, T. A. (2011). *Mining Group Gold: How to Cash in on the Collaborative Brain Power of a Group* (3rd. ed.). New York: McGraw-Hill.

Kellerman, B. (2008). *Followership: How followers are creating change and changing leaders.* Boston: Harvard Business School Press.

Kerr, N. L., & Bruun, S. E. (1981). Ringelmann revisited: Alternative explanations for the social loafing effect. *Personality and Social Psychology Bulletin, 7*, 224–231.

Kerr, N. L., & Bruun, S. E. (1983). Dispensability of member effort and group motivation losses: Free-rider effects. *Journal of Personality and Social Psychology, 44*, 78–94.

Keyser, D., & Sweetland, R. (1991; 1994; 2004). *Test Critiques.* Austin, TX: Pro-ed.

Kilmann, R. H., & Thomas, K. W. (1975). Interpersonal conflict-handling behavior as reflection of Jungian personality dimensions. *Psychological Reports, 37*(3, Pt 1), 971–980.

Kilmann, R. H., & Thomas, K. W. (1977). Developing a forced-choice measure of conflict-handling behavior. The "MODE" instrument. *Educational and Psychological Measurement, 37*(2), 309–325.

King, E. B., Hebl, M. R., & Beal, D. J. (2009). Conflict and cooperation in diverse workgroups. *Journal of Social Issues, 65*, 261–285.

Kiozlowski, S. W. J., & Ilgen, D. R. (2006). Enhancing the effectiveness of work groups and teams. *Psychological Science in the Public Interest, 7*, 77–124.

Kirkman, B. L., & Mathieu, J.E. (2005). The dimensions and antecedents of team virtuality. *Journal of Management, 31*(5), 700–718.

Kirkman, B. L., & Rosen, B. (1999). Beyond self-management: The antecedents and consequences of team empowerment. *Academy of Management Journal, 42*, 58–74.

Kirkman, B. L., Rosen, B., Tesluk, P. E., & Gibson, C. B. (2004). The impact of team empowerment on virtual team performance: The moderating role of face-to-face inter-action. *Academy of Management Journal, 47*(2), 175–192.

Kirkpatrick, D. L. (1994). *Evaluating training programs: The four levels* (2nd ed.). San Francisco: Berrett-Koehler Publishers, Inc.

Klein, C., Diaz Granados, D., Salas, E., Le, H., Burke, C. S., Lyons, R., & Goodwin, G. F. (2009). Does team building work? *Small Group Research, 40*(2), 181–222.

Klimoski, R., & Jones, R. G. (1995). Staffing for effective group decision making: Key issues in matching people and teams (pp. 291–332). In R. A. Guzzo, E. Salas, & Associates (Eds.), *Team effectiveness and decision making In organizations.* San Francisco: Jossey-Bass Publishers.

Kline, D. A. (2005). Intuitive team decision making. In H. Montgomery, R. Lipshitz, & B. Brehmer (Eds.), *How professionals make decisions. Expertise: Research and applications.* (pp. 171–182). Mahwah, NJ: Lawrence Erlbaum Associates Publishers.

Kline, T. J. B. (2003). *Teams that lead: A matter of market strategy, leadership skills, and executive strength.* Mahwah, NJ: Lawrence Erlbaum Associates, Inc.

Knippen, J. T., & Green, T. B. (1994). How the manager can use active listening. *Public Personnel Management, 23,* 357–359.

Kossek, E., Zonia, S. C., & Young, W. (1996). The limitations of the power of organizational demography: Can diversity climate be enhanced in the absence of teamwork? In M. Ruderman, M. Hughes-James, & S. Jackson (Eds.), *Selected research on work team diversity* (pp. 121–152). Greensboro, NC: Center for Creative Leadership and Washington DC: American Psychological Association.

Kotter, J. P., & Cohen, D. S. (2002). *The heart of change: Real-life stories of how people change their organizations.* Boston: Harvard Business School Press.

Kotter, J. P. (1996). *Leading change.* Boston: Harvard Business School Press.

Kouzes, J. M., & Posner, B. Z. (2000). In M. Goldsmith, L. Lyons, & A. Freas, (Eds.), *Coaching for leadership: How the world's greatest coaches help leaders learn.* San Francisco: Jossey-Bass/Pfeiffer.

Kouzes, J. M., & Posner, B. Z. (2007). *The leadership challenge* (4th ed.). San Francisco: Jossey-Bass.

Kozlowski, S. W. J., & Ilgen, D. R. (2006). Enhancing the effectiveness of work groups and teams. *Psychological Science in the Public Interest, 7*(3), 77–124.

Kramer, R. M. (2010). Dilemmas and doubts: How decision-makers cope with interdependence and uncertainty. In R. M. Kramer, A. E. Tenbrunsel, & M. H. Bazerman (Eds.), *Social decision making: Social dilemmas, social values, and ethical judgments.* NY: Psychology Press.

Kramer, R. M., Hanna, B. A., Su, S., & Wei, J. (2001). Collective identity, collective trust, and social capital: Linking group identification and group cooperation. In. M. E. Turner (Ed.), *Groups at work: Theory and research.* Mahwah, NJ: Lawrence Erlbaum Associates.

Kramer, T. J., Fleming, G. P., & Mannis, S. M. (2001). Improving face-to-face brainstorming through modeling and facilitation. *Small Group Research, 32*(5), 533–557.

Krueger, R. A., & Casey, M. A. (2000). *Focus groups: A practical guide for applied research* (3rd ed.). Thousand Oaks, CA: Sage.

Kristof, A. L. (1996). Person-organization fit: An integrative review of its conceptualizations, measurement, and implications. *Personnel Psychology, 49,* 1–49.

Lambe, C. J., Webb, K. L., & Ishida, C. (2009). Self-managing selling teams and team performance: The complementary roles of empowerment and control. *Industrial Marketing Management, 38*(1), 5–16.

Landis, M., Jerris, S. I., & Braswell, M. (2008). Better brainstorming. *Journal of Accountancy, 206*(4), 70–73.

Langfred, C. W. (1998). Is group cohesiveness a double-edged sword? An investigation of the effects of cohesiveness on performance. *Small Group Research, 29*(1), 124–143.

Langfred, C. W. (2007). The downside of self-management: A longitudinal study of the effects of conflict on trust, autonomy, and task interdependence in self-managing teams. *Academy of Management Journal, 50*(4), 885–900.

Larson, F., & La Fasto, C. (1989). *Teamwork: What must go right/What can go wrong.* Thousand Oaks, CA: Sage Publications.

Larson, J. R., Jr. (1986). Supervisors' performance feedback to subordinates: The impact of subordinate performance valence and outcome dependence. *Organizational Behavior and Human Decision Processes, 37*, 391–408.

Larson, J. R., Jr. (1989). The dynamic interplay between employees' feedback-seeking strategies and supervisors' delivery of performance feedback. *Academy of Management Review, 14*, 408–422.

Larson, J. R., Jr. (2010). *In search of synergy in small group performance*. New York, NY, US: Psychology Press.

Larson, J. R., Jr., & Christensen, C. (1993). Groups as problem-solving units: Toward a new meaning of social cognition. *British Journal of Social Psychology, 32*, 5–30.

Larson, J. R., Jr., Christensen, C., Franz, T. M.., & Abbott, A.S. (1998). Diagnosing groups: The pooling, management, and impact of shared and unshared case information in team-based medical decision making. *Journal of Personality and Social Psychology, 75*, 93–108.

Latané, B. (1981). The psychology of social impact. *American Psychologist, 36*, 343–356.

Latané, B., Williams, K., & Harkins, S. (2006). Many Hands Make Light the Work: The Causes and Consequences of Social Loafing. In J. M. Levine, & R. L. Moreland (Eds.), *Small groups. Key readings in social psychology*. (pp. 297–308). New York: Psychology Press.

Latham, G. P., & Locke, E. A. (2007). New developments in and directions for goal-setting research. *European Psychologist, 12*(4), 290–300.

Lau, D. C., & Liden, R. C. (2008). Antecedents of coworker trust: Leaders' blessings. *Journal of Applied Psychology, 93*, 1130–1138.

Leadership Behavior Description Questionnaire Manual. (1957.1962). Retrieved 6/12/2010 From https://fisher.osu.edu/offices/fiscal/lbdq/.

Leavitt, H. J. (1951). Some effects of certain communication patterns on group performance. *Journal of Abnormal and Social Psychology, 46*, 38–50.

Lee, T. W. (2003). *Using qualitative methods in organizations*. Thousand Oaks, CA: Sage Publishers.

Lencioni, P. (2002). *The five dysfunctions of a team: A leadership fable*. San Francisco: Jossey-Bass.

Lencioni, P. (2005). *Overcoming the five dysfunctions of a team: A field guide*. San Francisco, CA: Jossey-Bass.

Levine, J. M., & Moreland, R. L. (1990). Progress in small group research. *Annual Review of Psychology, 41*, 585–634.

Lewicki, R. J., & Bunker, B. B. (1996). Developing and maintaining trust in work relationships. In R. M. Kramer, & T. R. Tyler (Eds.), *Trust in organizations: Frontiers of theory and research* (pp. 114–139). Thousand Oaks, CA: Sage Publications.

Lewicki, R. J., & Bunker, B. B. (1996). Developing and maintaining trust in work relationships. In R. M. Kramer, & T. R. Tyler (Eds.), *Trust in organizations: Frontiers of theory and research* (pp. 114–139). Thousand Oaks, CA: Sage Publications.

Lewin K. (1943). Defining the "Field at a Given Time." *Psychological Review, 50*, 292–310.

Lewin, K. (1946/1948). Action research and minority problems. In G. Lewin (Ed.), *Resolving social conflicts* (pp. 201–216). NY: Harper & Row Publishers.

Lewis, J. P. (2004). *Team-based project management*. Washington, DC: Beard Books/AMACOM.

Liedtka, J. M. (1996). Collaborating across lines of business for competitive advantage. *Academy of Management Executive, 10*, 20–34.

Lim, B., & Ployhart, R.E. (2004). Transformational leadership: Relations to the five-factor-model and team performance in typical and maximum contexts. *Journal of Applied Psychology, 89,* 610–621.

Lipnack, J., & Stamps, J. (2000). *Virtual teams: People working across boundaries with technology.* NY: John Wiley & Sons, Inc.

Littlepage, G. E., Schmidt, G. W., Whisler, E. W., & Frost, A. G. (1995). An input-process-output analysis of influence and performance in problem-solving groups. *Journal of Personality and Social Psychology, 69,* 877–889.

Liu, C., Pirola-Merlo, A., Yang, C., & Huang, C. (2009). Disseminating the functions of team coaching regarding research and development team effectiveness: Evidence from high-tech industries in Taiwan. *Social Behavior and Personality, 37,* 41–58.

Lloyd, B. (2000). Leadership and power: Where responsibility makes the difference. In M. Goldsmith, L. Lyons, & A. Freas, (Eds.), *Coaching for leadership: How the world's greatest coaches help leaders learn.* San Francisco: Jossey-Bass/Pfeiffer.

Locke, E. A., & Latham, G. P. (1990). *A theory of goal setting and task motivation.* Englewood Cliffs, NJ: Prentice-Hall.

Loden, M. (1996). *Implementing diversity.* Burr Ridge, IL: Mc-Graw Hill Publishing.

Lord, R. G., De Vader, C. L., & Alliger, G. M. (1986). A meta-analysis of the relation between personality traits and leadership perceptions: An application of validity generalization procedures. *Journal of Applied Psychology, 71,* 402–410.

Lord, R. G., & Brown, D. J. (2004). *Leadership processes and follower self-identity.* Mahwah, NJ: Lawrence Erlbaum Associates, Inc.

Loughry, M. L., Ohland, M. W., & Moore, D. D. (2007). Development of a Theory-Based Assessment of Team Member Effectiveness. *Educational and Psychological Measurement, 67,* 505–524.

Lourenco, S.V., & Glidewell, J.C. (1975). A dialectical analysis of organizational conflict. *Administrative Science Quarterly, 20,* 489–508.

Luijters, K., van der Zee, K. I., & Otten, S. (2008). Cultural diversity in organizations: Enhancing identification by valuing differences. *International Journal of Intercultural Relations, 32,* 154–163.

Lyons, L. S. (2000). Coaching at the heart of strategy. In M. Goldsmith, L. Lyons, & A. Freas, (Eds.), *Coaching for leadership: How the world's greatest coaches help leaders learn.* San Francisco: Jossey-Bass/Pfeiffer.

Maddox. T. (2003). Tests: *A comprehenseive reference for assessments in psychology, education, and business.* Austin, TX: Pro-ed.

Major, D. A., Kozlowski, S. W., Chao, G. T., & Gardener, P. D. (1995). A longitudinal investigation of newcomer expectations, early socialization outcomes, and the moderating effects of role development factors. *Journal of Applied Psychology, 80*(3), 418–431.

Mannix, E., & Neale, M. A. (2005, October). What differences make a difference? The promise and reality of diverse teams in organizations. *Psychological Science in the Public Interest, 6*(2), 31–55.

Manstead, A. S. R., & Hewstone, M. (1996). *The Blackwell Encyclopedia of Social Psychology.* NY: Wiley-Blackwell.

Manz, C. C., & Sims, H. P. (1987). Leading workers to lead themselves: the external leadership of self-managing work teams. *Administrative Science Quarterly, 32,* 106–129.

Manz, C. C., & Neck, C. P. (1995). Teamthink: Beyond the groupthink syndrome in self-managing work teams. *Journal of Managerial Psychology, 10*(1), 7–15.

Maras, S. (2001). Beyond the transmission model: Shannon, Weaver, and the critique of sender/message/receiver. *Communication Abstracts, 24*(4), 443–588.

Maras, S. (2008). On Transmission: A Metamethodological Analysis (after Régis Debray). *Fibreculture, 12*. Retrieved September 30, 2009 from http://journal.fibreculture.org/issue12/issue12_maras.html.

Marmarosh, C. L., & Corazzini, J. G. (1997). Putting the group in your pocket: Using collective identity to enhance personal and collective self-esteem. *Group Dynamics: Theory, Research, and Practice, 1*(1), 65–74.

Martinez-Moreno, E., Gonzalez-Navarro, P., Zornoza, A., & Ripoll, P. (2009). Relationships, task and process conflicts on team performance: The moderating role of communication media. *International Journal of Conflict Management, 20*(3), 251–268.

Martins, L. L., Gilson, L. L., & Maynard, M. T. (2004). Virtual teams: What do we know and where do we go from here? *Journal of Management, 30*(6), 805–835.

Mastrangelo, P. M. (2008). Designing a global survey process to realize engagement and alignment. In M. I. Finney (Ed.), *Building high-performance people and organizations: Volume 1. The new employer-employee relationship* Westport, CT: Praeger.

Mathieu, J. E., Gilson, L. L., & Ruddy, T. M. (2006). Empowerment and team effectiveness: An empirical test of an integrated model. *Journal of Applied Psychology, 91*(1), 97–108.

Mathieu, J. E., & Rapp, T. L. (2009). Laying the foundation for successful team performance trajectories: The roles of team charters and performance strategies. *Journal of Applied Psychology, 94*, 90–103.

Mayer, R. C., Davis, J. H., & Schoorman, F. D. (1995). An integration model of organizational trust. Academy of Management. *Academy of Management Review, 20*, 709–734.

Maynard, R. (1997, September). Sharing the wealth – of information. *Nation's Business, 85*(9), 14.

McAllister, D. J. (1995). Affect- and cognition-based trust as foundations for interpersonal cooperation in organizations. *Academy of Management Journal, 38*, 24–59.

McCracken, G. (1988). *The long interview: Qualitative research methods series vol. 13.* Thousand Oaks, CA: Sage.

McCroskey, J. C. (1977). Oral communication apprehension: A summary of recent theory and research. *Human Communication Research, 4*, 78–96.

McGillicuddy, N. B., Welton, G. L., & Pruitt, D. G. (1987). Third-party intervention: A field experiment comparing three different models. *Journal of Personality and Social Psychology, 53*(1), 104–112.

McGrath, J. E. (1984). *Groups: Interaction and performance.* Englewood Cliffs, NJ: Prentice Hall.

McGrath, J. E., & Berdahl, J. L. (1998). Groups, technology, and time; Use of computers for collaborative work. *Social psychological applications to social issues*, 205–228.

McGrath, J. E., Berdahl, J. L., & Arrow, H. (1995). Traits, expectations, culture, and clout: The dynamics of diversity in work groups. In S. E. Jackson, & M. N. Ruderman (Eds.), *Diversity in work teams: Research paradigms for a changing workplace.* Washington DC: American Psychological Association.

McGregor, D. (2002). Theory x and theory y. *Workforce, 81*(1), 32.

Mackenzie, K. (1966). Structural centrality in communications in social networks. *Psychometrika, 31*, 17–25.

McPherson, M., & Smith-Lovin, L. (2002). Cohesion and membership duration: Linking groups, relations, and individuals in an ecology of affiliation. In S. R. Thye, & E. J. Lawler (Eds.), *Group cohesion, trust, and solidarity.* NY: Elsevier Science.

Medina, F. J., Munduate, L., Dorado, M. A., Martinez, I., & Guerra, J. M. (2005). Types of intragroup conflict and affective reactions. *Journal of Managerial Psychology, 20*(3/4), 219–230.

Mehra, A., Smith, B. R., Dixon, A. L., & Robertson, B. (2006). Distributed leadership in teams: The network of leadership perceptions and team performance. *The Leadership Quarterly, 17*, 232–245.

Mellott, R. N., & Mehr, S. L. (2007, February). Reaffirming the role of the scientist-practitioner model of training in psychology. *American Behavioral Scientist, 50*(6), 842–845.

Mental measures. Washington, DC: American Psychological Association.

Mertler, C. A., & Vannatta, R. A. (2010). *Advanced and multivariate statistical methods* (4th ed.). Glendale, CA: Pyrczak Publishing.

Mesmer-Magnus, J. R., & De Church, L. A. (2009). Information sharing and team performance: A meta-analysis. *Journal of Applied Psychology, 94*(2), 535–546.

Meyer, J. P., & Allen, N. J. (1991). A three-component conceptualization of organizational commitment: Some methodological considerations. *Human Resource Management Review, 1*, 61–98.

Michaelsen, L. D., Watson, W. E., & Black, R. H. (1989). A realistic test of individual versus group consensus decision making. *Journal of Applied Psychology, 74*(5), 834–839.

Michaelsen, L. K., Watson, W. E., Schwartzkopf, A., & Black, R. H. (1992). Group decision making: How you frame the question determines what you find. *Journal of Applied Psychology, 77*(1), 106–108.

Milgram, S. (1974). *Obedience to authority.* NY: Harper Colophon Books.

Miller, E. G. (1970). The impact of T-groups on managerial behavior. *Public Administration Review, 30*, 296–297.

Miller, C. E. (1989). The social psychological effects of group decision rules (pp. 327–355). In P. B. Paulus (Ed.) *Psychology of group influence* (2nd ed.). Hillsdale, NJ: Lawrence Erlbaum Associates, Inc.

Mishra, A. K. (1996). Organization responses too crisis: The centrality of trust. In R. M. Kramer, & T. R. Tyler (Eds.), *Trust in organizations: Frontiers of theory and research* (pp. 261–287). Thousand Oaks, CA: Sage Publications.

Mohrman, S. A., & Quam, K. F. (2000). Consulting to team-based organizations: An organizational design and learning approach. *Consulting Psychology Journal: Practice & Research, 52*(1), 20–35.

Moore, C. M. (1987). *Group techniques for idea building.* Thousand Oaks, CA: Sage Publications, Inc.

Moreland, R. L., Argote, L., & Krishnan, R. (1996). Socially shared cognition at work: Transactive memory and group performance. In J. L. Nye, & A. M. Brower (Eds.), *What's social about social cognition? Research on socially shared cognition in small groups* (pp. 57–84). Thousand Oaks, CA: Sage.

Morgan, D. L., & Krueger, R. A. (1997). *The focus group kit* (Vol 1–6). Thousand Oaks, CA: Sage.

Morgan, B. B., Salas, E., & Glickman, A. S. (1993). An analysis of team evolution and maturation. *The Journal of General Psychology, 120*(3), 277–291.

Morgeson, F. P. (2005). The external leadership of self-managing teams: Intervening in the context of novel and disruptive events. *Journal of Applied Psychology, 90*(3), 497–508.

Morgeson, F. P., DeRue, D. S., & Karam, E. P. (2010). Leadership in teams: A functional approach to understanding leadership structures and processes. *Journal of Management, 36*, 5–39.

Morgeson, F. P., Mumford, T. V., & Campion, M. A. (2005). Coming full circle: Using research and practice to address 27 questions about 360-degree feedback programs. *Consulting Psychology Journal: Practice and Research, 57*(3), 196–209.

Moscovici, S., & Zavalloni, M. (1969). The group as a polarizer of attitudes. *Journal of Personality and Social Psychology, 12*, 125–135.

Moye, N. A., & Langfred, C. W. (2004). Information sharing and group conflict: Going beyond decision making to understand the effects of information sharing on group performance. *The International Journal of Conflict Management, 15*(4), 381–410.

Muchinsky, P. M. (2009). *Psychology applied to work* (9th ed.). Summerfield, NC: Hypergraphic Press.

Mullen, B., & Copper, C. (1994). The relations between group cohesiveness and performance: An integration. *Psychological Bulletin, 115*, 210–227.

Mullen, B., Johnson, C., & Salas, E. (1991). Productivity loss in brainstorming groups: A Meta-analytic integration. *Basic and Applied Social Psychology, 72*(1), 3–23.

Mulvey, P. W., & Klein, H. J. (1998). The impact of perceived loafing and collective efficacy in group goal processes and group performance. *Organizational Behavior and Human Decision Processes, 74*, 62–87.

Muthusamy, S. K., Wheeler, J. V., & Simmons, B. L. (2005). Self-managing work teams: Enhancing organizational innovativeness. *Organization Development Journal, 23*(3), 53–66.

Mycoted. (2009). *Creativity and Innovation Techniques – an A to Z*: Retrieved February 4, 2010 from http://www.mycoted.com/Category:Creativity_Techniques.

Myers, S. (1996). *Team building for diverse work groups: A practical guide to gaining and sustaining performance in diverse teams.* Lake Forest, CA: Richard Chang Associates.

Myers, G., & Levin, R. F. (2009). Explore clinical problems by wearing different hats. *Research and Theory for Nursing Practice: An International Journal, 23*(1), 5–7.

Myers, S. A., & Anderson, C. M. (2008). *The fundamentals of small group communication.* Thousand Oaks, CA: Sage Publications.

Nandhakumar, J., & Baskerville, R. (2006). Durability of online team working: Patterns of trust. *Information Technology & People, 19*(4), 371–399.

Napier, R. W., & Gershenfeld, M.K. (1999). *Groups: theory and experience* (6th ed.). Boston: Houghton Mifflin.

Nelson, D. L., & Quick, J. C. (2008). *Understanding Organizational Behavior* (3rd ed.). Florence, KY: Cengage Learning, Inc.

Nelson, E. C., Batalden, P. B., & Godfrey, M. M. (Eds.). (2007). *Quality by design: A clinical microsystems approach* (pp. 321–330). San Francisco, CA: Jossey-Bass.

Nemeth, C. J., & Nemet, B. (2003). Better than individuals? The potential benefits of dissent and diversity. In P. B. Paulus, & B. A. Nijstad (Eds.), *Group creativity: Innovation through collaboration.* Oxford: Oxford University Press.

Nemiro, J., Beyerlein, M., Bradley, L., & Beyerlein, S. (2008). *The handbook of high-performance virtual teams: A toolkit for collaborating across boundaries.* San Francisco: John Wiley & Sons, Inc.

Nichols, M. P. (2009). *The lost art of listening: How learning to listen can improve relationships.* New York: Guilford Press.

Nichols, R. G. (1960). *The Supervisor's Notebook, 22*(1). Chicago: Scott, Foresman & Co.

Nichols, R. G., & Stevens, L. A. (1957). *Are you listening?* New York, McGraw-Hill.

Nijhuis, B. J. G., Reinders-Messelink, H. A., de Blecourt, A. C. E., Olijve, W. G., Groothoff, J. W., Nakken, H., & Postema, K. (2007). A review of salient elements defining team collaboration in pediatric rehabilitation. *Clinical Rehabilitation, 21*(3), 195–211.

Nijstad, B. A., Diehl, M., & Stroebe, W. (2003). Cognitive stimulation and interference for idea-generating groups. In P. B. Paulus, & B. A. Nijstad (Eds.), *Group creativity: Innovation through collaboration*. Oxford: Oxford University Press.

Noller, R. B., Parnes, S. J., & Biondi, A. M. (1976). *Creative actionbook*. New York: Scribner.

O'Connell, M. S., Doverspike, D., & Cober, A. B. (2002). Leadership and semiautonomous work team performance: A field study. *Group and Organization Management, 27*, 50–65.

Offner, A. K., Kramer, T. J., & Winter, J. P. (1996). The effects of facilitation, recording, and pauses on group brainstorming. *Small Group Research, 27*(2), 283–298.

Oishi, S. M. (2002). *The survey kit, vol. 5: How to conduct in-person interviews for surveys*, (2nd ed.). Thousand Oaks, CA: Sage.

Olson, P. D., Olson, J., & Murphy, C. J. (1998). Empowering teams to promote change: The leadership challenge. *Proceedings of the Academy of Educational Leadership, 3*, 35–39.

O'Neill, T. A., Lewis, R. J., & Hambley, L. A. (2008). Leading virtual teams: Potential problems and simple solutions. In J. Nemiro, J., M. Beyerlein, L. Bradley, & S. Beyerlein (Eds.), *The handbook of high-performance virtual teams: A toolkit for collaborating across boundaries*. San Francisco: John Wiley & Sons, Inc.

O'Reilly, C. A., Chatman, J., & Caldwell, D. F. (1991). People and organizational culture: A profile comparison approach to assessing person-organization fit. *Academy of Management Journal, 34*, 487–516.

Organ, D. W. (1988). *Organizational Citizenship behavior: The good soldier syndrome*. Lexington, MA: Lexington Books.

Örtqvist, D., & Wincent, J. (2006). Prominent consequences of role stress: A meta-analytic review. *International Journal of Stress Management, 13*(4), 399–422.

Orvis, K. L., & Zaccaro, S. J. (2008). Team composition and member selection: Optimizing teams for virtual collaboration. In J. Nemiro, M. Beyerlein, L. Bradley, & S. Beyerlein (Eds.), *The handbook of high-performance virtual teams: A toolkit for collaborating across boundaries*. San Francisco: John Wiley & Sons, Inc.

Osborn, A. F. (1963). *Applied imagination: Principles and procedures of creative problem solving* (3rd ed.). New York, NY: Charles Scribner's Sons.

O'Toole, J., Galbraith, J., & Lawler, E. E. (2002). When two (or more) heads are better than one: The promise and pitfalls of shared leadership. *California Management Review, 13*, 110–126.

Parks, C., & Sanna, L. (1999). *Group performance and interaction*. Boulder: Westview Press.

Parnes, S. J., & Noller, R. B. (1972). Applied creativity: The creative studies project: II. Results of the two-year program. *Journal of Creative Behavior, 6*(3), 164–186.

Parnes, S. J., & Noller, R. B. (1973). Applied creativity: The creative studies project: IV. Personality findings and conclusions. *Journal of Creative Behavior, 7*(1), 15–36.

Parnes, S. J., Noller, R. B., & Biondi, A. M. (1977). *Guide to creative action*. New York, NY: Scribner.

Paulus, P. B., & Dzindolet, M. T. (1993). Social influence processes in group brainstorming. *Journal of Personality and Social Psychology, 64*, 575–586.

Paulus, P. B., & Nijstad, B. (2003). Group creativity: An introduction. In P. B. Paulus, & B. Nijstad (Eds.), *Group creativity: Innovation and collaboration in groups* (pp. 3–14). New York: Oxford University Press.

Paulus, P. B., Nakui, T., & Putnam, V. L. (2003). Group brainstorming and teamwork: Some rules for the road to innovation. In Thompson, L. and Choi, H-S. (2006). *Creativity* and innovation in organizational *teams* (pp. 69–86). Mahwah, NJ: Lawrence Erlbaum.

Paulus, P. B., & Yang, H. C. (2000). Idea Generation in Groups: A Basis for Creativity in Organizations. *Organizational Behavior and Human Decision Processes. 82*, 76–87.

Pearce C. L., & Conger J. A. (2003). All those years ago: The historical underpinnings of shared leadership. In C. L. Pearce, & J. A. Conger (Eds.), *Shared leadership: Reframing the hows and whys of leadership*. Thousand Oaks, CA: Sage Publications, Inc.

Pearsall, M. J., Christian, M. S., & Ellis, A. P. J. (2010). Motivating interdependent teams: Individual rewards, shared rewards, or something in between? *Journal of Applied Psychology, 95*, 183–191.

Penley, L. E., Alexander, E. R., Jernigan, E. I., & Henwood, C. I. (1991). Communication abilities of managers: The relationship to performance. *Journal of Management, 17*(1), 57–76.

Peters, L. M., & Manz, C. C. (2007). Identifying antecedents of virtual team collaboration. *Team Performance Management, 13*(3/4), 117–129.

Peterson, T. O., & Lunsford D. A. (1998). Parallel Thinking: A Technique for Group Interaction and Problem Solving. *Journal of Management Education, 22*, 537–554.

Piccoli, G., & Ives, B. (2003). Trust and the unintended effects of behavior control in virtual teams. *MIS Quarterly, 27*, 365–376.

Politis, J. D. (2003). The connection between trust and knowledge management: What are its implications for team performance. *Journal of Knowledge Management, 7*(5), 55–66.

Polley, D., & Van Dyne, L. (1994). The limits and liabilities of self-managing work teams. In M. M. Beyerlein, & D. A. Johnson (Eds.), *Advances in interdisciplinary studies of work teams: Theories of self-managing work teams*. Greenwich, CT: JAI Press Inc.

Polzer, J. T. (2008). Making diverse teams click. *Harvard Business Review, 86*(7/8), 20–21.

Ponterotto, J. G. (1996). Designing surveys and questionnaires for research. In F. T. L Leong, & J. T. Austin (Eds.), *The psychology research handbook: A guide for graduate students and research assistants* (pp. 72–84). Thousand Oaks, ca: Sage.

Porter, G. (1997). Trust in teams: Member perceptions and the added concern of cross-cultural interpretations. In M. M. Beyerlein, & D. A. Johnson (Eds.), *Advances in inter-disciplinary studies of work teams* (Vol. 4, pp. 45–77). Stamford, CT: JAI Press.

Porter, L. C. (2001). Conflict management: Developing a procedure. In E. Biech (ed.) *The Pfeiffer book of successful team-building tools*. San Francisco: Jossey-Bass/Pfeiffer.

Porter, L. W., & Steers, R. M. (1973). Organizational, work, and personal factors in employee turnover and absenteeism. *Psychological Bulletin, 80*, 151–176.

Postmes, T., Spears, R., & Cihangir, S. (2001). Quality of decision making and group norms. *Journal of Personality and Social Psychology, 80*(6), 918–930.

Potter, R. E., & Balthazard, P. A. (2002). Virtual team interaction styles: Assessment and effects. *Int. J. Human-Computer Studies, 56*, 423–443.

Preston, A. P., Inglis, S. M., & Horchner, P. (2001). Creating an applied learning infrastructure for management decisions. *Journal of Workplace Learning, 13*(6), 228–238.

Pritchard, R. D., Jones, S. E., Roth, P. L., Stuebing, K. K., & Ekeberg, S. E. (1988). The effects of feedback, goal setting and incentives on organizational productivity. *Journal of Applied Psychology, 73*, 337–358.

Pruitt, D. G., & Carnevale, P. J. (1993). *Negotiation in social conflict*. Pacific Grove: Brooks/ Cole Publishing.

Puchta, C., & Potter, J. (2004). *Focus group practice*. Thousand Oaks, CA: Sage.

Raghurman, S., & Garud, R. (1996). Vicious and virtuous facets of workface diversity. In M. Ruderman, M. Hughes-James, & S. Jackson (Eds.), *Selected research on work team* (pp. 155–178). Greensboro, NC: Center for Creative Leadership and Washington, DC: American Psychological Association.

Rains, S. A. (2005). Leveling the organizational playing field virtually: A meta-analysis of experimental research assessing the impact of group support system use on member influence behaviors. *Communication Research, 32*(2), 193–234.

Randel, A. E., & Earley, C. P. (2009). Organizational culture and similarity among team members' salience of multiple diversity characteristics. *Journal of Applied Social Psychology, 39*, 804–833.

Reddy, W. B. (1994). *Intervention skills: Process consultation for small groups and teams*. San Diego, CA: Pfeiffer & Company.

Reddy, W. B. (1996). *Group-level team assessment: A 10-step sequence to a committed team*. San Diego: Pfeiffer & Company.

Redman, C. A., & Sankar, C. S. (2003). Results of an experiment comparing the analysis of Chick-Fil-A case study by virtual teams versus face-to-face teams. *Journal of SMET Education: Innovations and Research, 4*(1/2), 55–61.

Reed, T., & Francis, L. M. (2003). *Infoline: Using consulting systems*. Alexandria, VA: ASTD Press.

Reese, H. W., & Parnes, S. K. (1970). Programming creative behavior. *Child Development, 41*, 413–423.

Reese, H. W., Parnes, S. J., Treffinger, D. J., & Kaltsounis, G. (1976). Effects of a creative studies program on structure of intellect factors. *Journal of Educational Psychology, 68*, 401–410.

Rentsch, J. R., & Hall, R. J. (1994). Members of great teams think alike: A model of team effectiveness and schema similarity among team members. *Advances in the Interdisciplinary Studies of Work Teams, 1*, 223–261.

Richey, B., Bernardin, H. J., Tyler, C. L., & McKinney, N. (2001). The effect of arbitration program characteristics on applicants' intentions toward potential employers. *Journal of Applied Psychology, 86*(5), 1006–1013.

Rispens, S., Greer, L. L., & Jehn, K. A. (2007). It could be worse: A study on the alleviating roles of trust and connectedness in intragroup conflicts. *International Journal of Conflict Management, 18*(4), 325–344.

Robbins, H., & Finley, M. (1995). *Why teams don't work: What went wrong and how to make it right*. Princeton, NJ: Peterson's/Pacesetter Books.

Rogelberg, S. G., Barnes-Farrell, J. L., & Lowe, C. A. (1992) The stepladder technique: An alternative group structure facilitating effective group decision making. *Journal of Applied Psychology, 77*, 730–737.

Rohrbaugh, J. (1981). Improving the quality of group judgment: Social judgment analysis and the nominal group technique. *Organizational Behavior and Human Performance, 28*, 278–288.

Rosenthal, R., & Jacobson, L. (1966). Teachers' expectancies: Determinants of pupils' IQ gains. *Psychological Reports, 19*, 115–118.

Ross, L., & Ward, A. (1995). Psychological barriers to dispute resolution. *Advances in experimental social psychology, 27*, 255–304.

Rothwell, W. J. (2005). *Practicing organization development: A guide for consultants*. San Francisco: Pfeiffer.

Rothwell, J. D. (2010). *In mixed company: Communicating in small groups and teams*. Boston: Wadsworth.

Rothwell, W. J., & Sullivan, R. L. (2005). Models for change (pp. 39–80). In W. J. Rothwell, & R. L. Sullivan (Eds.) *Practicing organization development: A guide for consultants* (2nd ed.). San Francisco, John Wiley & Sons, Inc.

Roussin, C. J. (2008). Increasing trust, psychological safety, and team performance through dyadic leadership discovery. *Small Group Research, 39*(2), 224–248.

Royer, I. (2004). *Why bad projects are so hard to kill. In Harvard Business Review on Teams that Succeed*. Boston: Harvard Business School Publishing Corporation.

Runde, C. E., & Flanagan, T. A. (2008). *Building conflict competent teams*. San Francisco: Jossey-Bass Publishers.

Rubin, J. Z., Pruitt, D. G., & Kim, S. H. (1994). *Social conflict: Escalation, stalemate, and settlement* (2nd ed.). NY: McGraw-Hill, Inc.

Saari, L. M., & Judge, T. A. (2004). Employees attitudes and job satisfaction. *Human Resource Management, 43*(4), 395–407.

Saavedra, R. P., Barley, C., & Van Dyne, L. (1993). Complex interdependence in task-performing groups. *Journal of Applied Psychology, 78*(1), 61–72.

Sagie, A., Koslowsky, M., & Hamburger, Y.A. (2002). Antecedents of employee lateness: A multiple-level model (pp. 1–20). In M. Koslowsky, & M. Krausz, (Eds.), *Voluntary employee withdrawal and inattendance: A current perspective*. New York: Kluwer Academic/Plenum Publishers.

Salas, E., Rozell, D., Mullen, B., & Driskell, J. E. (1999). The effect of team building on performance. *Small Group Research, 30*, 309–330.

Samuelson, C. D., & Watrous-Rodriguez, K. (2009). Group discussion and cooperation in social dilemmas: Does the medium matter? In R.M. Kramer, M. Bazerman, & A. Tenbrunsel (Eds.), *Social decision making: Social dilemmas, social values, and ethical judgments*. New York: Routledge.

Sanchez, R. J., Olsen-Buchanan, J. B., Schmidtke, J. M., & Bradley, J. A. (April, 2009). *It's just business: Affective and cognitive trust in virtual teams*. Paper presented at the 24th Society for Industrial Organization Psychology Annual Conference, New Orleans, L.A.

Sanger, J. (1996). *Compleat observer: A field research guide to observation* (Qualitative Studies Series). NY: Routledge.

Santanen, E. L. (2006). Opening the black box of creativity: Causal effects in creative solution generation. In L. Thompson, & H-S. Choi (Eds.), *Creativity and Innovation in Organizational Teams*. Mahwah, NJ: Lawrence Erlbaum Associates, Inc.

Sarat, A. (1976). Alternatives in dispute processing: Litigation in small claims court. *Law & Society Review, 10*, 339–375.

Sargent, L. D., & Sue-Chan, C. (2001). Does diversity affect group efficacy? The intervening role of cohesion and task interdependence. *Small Group Research, 32*(4), 426–450.

Sawyer, K. (2007). *Group genius: The creative power of collaboration*. New York: Basic Books.

Scanlan, B. K., & Atherton, R. M. (1981). Participation and the effective use of authority. *Personnel Journal, 60*, 697–703.

Schein, E. H. (1990). Organizational culture. *American Psychologist, 45*, 109–119.

Schein, E. H. (2004). *Organizational culture and leadership* (3rd ed.), San Francisco, CA: Jossey-Bass.

Schiller, F. C. S. (1897). Review of Studies in the Hegelian Dialectic. *Psychological Review, 4*, 193–196.

Schippers, M. C., Den, H., Deanne N., Koopman, P. L., & Wienk, J. A. (2003). Diversity and team outcomes: the moderating effects of outcome interdependence and group longevity and the mediating effect of reflexivity. *Journal of Organizational Behavior, 24*(6), 779–802.

Schlenker, B. R., & Miller, R. S. (1977). Group cohesiveness as a determinant of egocentric perceptions in cooperative groups. *Human Relations, 30*(11), 1039–1055.

Schmidt, U., McGuire, R., Humphrey, S., Williams, G., & Grawer, B. (2005). Team cohesion. In J. Taylor, & G. S. Wilson (Eds.), *Applying sport psychology: Four perspectives* (pp. 171–183). Champaign IL: Human Kinetics.

Schneider, B. (1987). The people make the place. *Personnel Psychology, 40,* 437–453.

Scholtes, P. R., Joiner, B. L., & Streibel, B. J. (2003). *The team handbook* (3rd ed.). Madison, WI: Oriel, Inc.

Schrage, M. (1990). *Shared minds: The new technologies of collaboration.* NY: Random House.

Schulz-Hardt, S., Mojzisch, A., & Vogelgesang, F. (2008). Dissent as facilitator: Individual- and group-level effects on creativity and performance. In C. K. W. De Dreu, & M. J. Gelfand (Eds.), *The psychology of conflict and conflict management in organizations.* NY: Lawrence Erlbaum Associates.

Schweiger, D. M., Sandberg, W. R., & Ragan, J. W. (1986). Group Approaches For Improving Strategic Decision-Making: A Comparative Analysis of Dialectical Inquiry, Devil's Advocacy, and Consensus. *Academy of Management Journal, 29,* 51–71.

Schweiger, D. M., Sandberg, W. R., & Rechner, P. L. (1989). Experimental effects of dialectical inquiry, Devil's advocacy, and consensus approaches to strategic decision making. *Academy of Management Journal, 32,* 745–772.

Schwenk, C. R. (1990). Effects of Devil's Advocacy and Dialectical Inquiry on Decision Making: A Meta Analysis. *Organizational Behavior and Human Decision Processes, 47,* 161–176.

Schwenk, C. R., & Valacich, J. S. (1994). Effects of devil's advocacy and dialectical inquiry on individuals versus groups. *Organizational Behavior and Human Decision Processes, 59,* 210–222.

Scott, C. R. (1999). Communication technology and group communication. In L. R. Frey, D. S. Gouran, & M. S. Poole (Eds.), *The handbook of group communication theory & research* (pp. 432–472). Thousand Oaks, CA: Sage.

Scott, W. G., Mitchell, T. R., & Birnbaum, P. H. (1981). *Organizational theory: A structural and behavioral analysis.* Homewood, IL: Irwin.

Seers, A. (1989). Team-member exchange quality: A new construct for role-making research. *Organizational Behavior and Human Decision Processes, 43,* 118–135.

Seers, A., Keller, T., & Wilkerson, J. M. (2003). Can team members share leadership? Foundations in research and theory. In C. L. Pearce, & J. A. Conger (Eds.), *Shared leadership: Reframing the hows and whys of leadership.* Thousand Oaks, CA: Sage Publications, Inc.

Seibert, S. E., Silver, S. R., & Randolph, W. A. (2004). Taking empowerment to the next level: A multiple-level model of empowerment, performance, and satisfaction. *Academy of Management Journal, 47*(3), 332–349.

Senécal, J., Loughead, T. M., & Bloom, G. A. (2008). A season-long team-building intervention: Examining the effect of team goal setting on cohesion. *Journal of Sport & Exercise Psychology, 30,* 186–199.

Shannon, C. E., & Weaver, W. (1949). *The Mathematical Theory of Communication.* Chicago: University Illinois Press.

Shapcott, K. M., Carron, A. V., Burke, S. M., Bradshaw, M. H., & Estabrooks, P. A. (2006). Member diversity and cohesion and performance in walking groups. *Small Group Research, 37*(6), 701–720.

Shepperd, J. A. (1993). Productivity loss in performance groups: A motivation analysis. *Psychological Bulletin, 113,* 67–81.

Sherif, M. (1935). A study of some social factors in perception. *Archives of Psychology, 27*(187).

Sherif, M. (1954). Integrating field work and laboratory in small group research. *American Sociological Review, 19*(6), 759–771.

Sherif, M., & Sherif, C. W. (1953). *Groups in harmony and tension: An integration of studies on intergroup relations.* NY: Harper & Brothers, Publishers.

Shin, Y. (2005). Conflict resolution in virtual teams. *Organizational Dynamics, 34*(4), 331–345.

Shonk, J. H. (1982). *Working in teams: A practical manual for improving work groups.* NY: AMACOM: A division of the American Management Associations.

Silver, S. R. (2008). Transforming professional relationships. *T +D: Training and Development, 62*(12), 63–67.

Silver, S. R. (2010). *The Workplace Covenant* [DVD]. Rochester, NY: Keith Jackson Directing.

Simons, T. L., & Peterson, R. S. (2000). Task conflict and relationship conflict in top management teams: The pivotal role of intragroup trust. *Journal of Applied Psychology, 85*(1), 102–111.

Simonton, D. (2006). In Kaufman, J. C., & Sternberg, R. J. (Eds.), *The international handbook of creativity.* Cambridge: Cambridge University Press.

Sims, H. P., Jr., & Manz, C. C. (1994). The leadership of self-managing work teams. In M. M. Beyerlein, & D. A. Johnson (Eds.), *Advances in interdisciplinary studies of work teams: Theories of self-managing work teams.* Greenwich, CT: JAI Press Inc.

Sivasubramaniam, N., Murry, W. D., Avolio, B. J., & Jung, D. I. (2002). A longitudinal model of the effects of team leadership and group potency on group performance. *Group & Organization Management, 27,* 66–96.

Smith, S. M. (2003). The constraining effects of initial ideas. In P. B. Paulus, & B. A. Nijstad (Eds.), *Group creativity: Innovation through collaboration.* Oxford: Oxford University Press.

Smith, S. M., Gerkens, D. R., Shah, J. J., & Vargas-Hernandez, N. (2006). Empirical studies of creative cognition in idea generation. In L. Thompson, & H-S. Choi (Eds.), *Creativity and innovation in organizational teams.* Mahwah, NJ: Lawrence Erlbaum.

Smither, J. W., & Reilly, S. P. (2001). Coaching in organizations. In. M. London (Ed.), *How people evaluate others in organizations.* Mahwah, NJ: Lawrence Erlbaum Associates, Inc.

Solansky, S. T. (2008). Leadership style and team processes in self-managed teams. *Journal of Leadership & Organizational Studies, 14*(4), 332–341.

Sommer, R., & Sommer, B. (2002). *A practical guide to behavioral research: Tools and techniques.* New York: Oxford.

Spector, P. E. (2008). *Industrial and organizational psychology: Research and practice.* NY: John Wiley & Sons, Inc.

Srivastava, A., Bartol, K. M., & Locke, E. A. (2006). Empowering leadership in management teams: Effects on knowledge sharing, efficacy, and performance. *Academy of Management Journal, 49*(6), 1239–1251.

Stagl, K. C., Salas, E., & Burke, C. S. (2007). Best practices in team leadership: What team leaders do to facilitate team effectiveness. In J. A. Conger, & R. E. Riggio (Eds.), *The practice of leadership: Developing the next generation of leaders.* San Francisco: Jossey-Bass.

Stangor, C. (2004). *Social groups in action and interaction.* New York: Psychology Press.

Stanovich, K. E., & West, R. F. (1999). Discrepancies between normative and descriptive models of decision making and the understanding/acceptance principle. *Cognitive Psychology, 38,* 349–385.

Stanton, N. (1996). Team performance: Communication, co-ordination, co-operation and control. In Stanton, N. (Ed.), *Human factors in nuclear safety* (pp. 197–215). Philadelphia, PA, US: Taylor & Francis.

Staples, D. S., & Webster, J. (2008). Exploring the effects of trust, task interdependence and virtualness on knowledge sharing in teams. *Information Systems Journal, 18,* 617–640.

Stark, E. M., & Bierly, P. E., III. (2009). An analysis of predictors of team satisfaction in product development teams with differing levels of virtualness. *R&D Management, 39,* 461–472.

Stasser, G. (1992). Pooling of unshared information during group discussion. In S. Worchel, W. Wood, & J. Simpson (Eds.), *Group process and productivity* (pp. 48–57). Newbury Park, CA: Sage.

Stasser, G., & Birchmeier, Z. (2003). Group creativity and collective choice. In. P. B. Paulus, & B. A. Nijstad (Eds.), *Group creativity: Innovation through collaboration.* Oxford: Oxford University Press.

Stasser, G., & Birchmeier, Z. (2003). In L. L. Thompson, & H-S. Choi (Eds.), *Creativity and innovation in organizational teams.* Mahwah, NJ: Lawrence Erlbaum.

Stasser, G., Stewart, D. D., & Wittenbaum, G. M. (1995). Expert roles and information exchange during discussion: The importance of knowing who knows what. *Journal of Experimental Social Psychology, 31*(3), 244–265.

Steiner, I. (1972). *Social Psychology: A serious of monographs, treatises, and texts.* New York: Academic Press.

Stephenson, B. Y., Michaelsen, L. K., & Franklin, S. G. (1982). An empirical test of the nominal group technique in state solar energy planning. *Group & Organization Studies, 7,* 320–334.

Sternberg, R. J. (2006). In Kaufman, J. C., & Sternberg, R. J. (Eds.), *The international handbook of creativity.* Cambridge: Cambridge University Press.

Stevens, M. J., & Campion, M. A. (1994). The knowledge, skills and ability requirements for teamwork: Implications for human resources management. *Journal of Management, 20,* 502–528.

Stevens M. J., & Campion M. A. (1999). Staffing work teams: Development and validation of a selection test for teamwork settings. *Journal of Management, 25,* 207–228.

Stewart, G. L., & Manz, C.C. (1995). Leadership for self-managing work teams: A typology and integrative model. *Human Relations, 48,* 747–770.

Stewart, G. L., Manz, C. C., & Sims, H. P., Jr. (1999). *Team work and group dynamics.* New York: John Wiley & Sons, Inc.

Stogdill, R. M. (1972). Group productivity, drive, and cohesiveness. *Organizational Behavior and Human Performance, 8,* 26–43.

Straus, D. (2002). *How to make collaboration work: Powerful ways to build consensus, solve problems, and make decisions.* San Francisco: Berrett-Koehler Publishers.

Straus, S. G. (1999). Testing a typology of tasks: An empirical validation of McGrath's (1984) group task circumplex. *Small Group Research, 30*(2), 166–187.

Stuhlmacher, A. F., & Halpert, J. A. (1998). Perceived fairness of arbitration: The impact of decision strategies. *Journal of Social Behavior & Personality, 13*, 359–373.

Sullivan, P. J., & Feltz, D. L. (2001). The relationship between intrateam conflict and cohesion within hockey teams. *Small Group Research, 32*, 342–355.

Tajfel, H., & Turner, J. C. (1986). The social identity theory of inter-group behavior. In S. Worchel, & L. W. Austin (Eds.), *Psychology of intergroup relations.* Chicago: Nelson-Hall.

Talbot, R. J. (1993). Creativity in the organizational context: Implications for training. In S. G. Isaksen, M. C. Murdock, R. L. Firestein, & D. J. Treffinger (Eds.), *Nurturing and developing creativity: The emergence of a discipline.* Norwood, NJ: Ablex Publishing Corporation.

Tata, J. (2002). The influence of accounts on perceived social loafing in work teams. *International Journal of Conflict Management, 13*, 292–308.

Tata, J., & Prasad, S. (2004). Team self-management, organizational structure, and judgments of team effectiveness. *Journal of Managerial Issues, 16*(2), 248–265.

Tekleab, A. G., Quigley, N. R., & Tesluk, P. E. (2009). A longitudinal study of team conflict, conflict management, cohesion, and team effectiveness. *Group Organization Management, 34*, 170–205.

Tenbrunsel, A. E., & Northcraft, G. (2010). In the eye of the beholder: Payoff structures and decision frames in social dilemmas. In R. M. Kramer, A. E. Tenbrunsel, & M. H. Bazerman (Eds.), *Social decision making: Social dilemmas, social values, and ethical judgments.* NY: Psychology Press.

The Ohio State Leadership Studies. (1957; 1962). Retrieved June 12, 2010 from https://fisher.osu.edu/offices/fiscal/lbdq/.

Thomas, K. W., & Kilmann, R. H. (1974). *Thomas-Kilmann conflict mode instrument.* Mountain View, CA: CPP, Inc.

Thomas, K. W., & Kilmann, R. H. (1978). Comparison of four instruments measuring conflict behavior. *Psychological Reports, 42*(3, Pt 2), 1139–1145.

Thompson, J. L. (2009). Building collective communication competence in interdisciplinary research teams. *Journal of Applied Communication Research, 37*(3), 278–297.

Thompson, L., & Choi, H.S. (2006). *Creativity and innovation in organizational teams.* Mahwah, NJ: Lawrence Erlbaum Associates, Inc.

Thompson, L., & Fox, C.R. (2001). Negotiation within and between groups in organizations: Levels of analysis. In. M. E. Turner (Ed.), *Groups at work: Theory and research.* Mahwah, NJ: Lawrence Erlbaum Associates.

Thompson, L. (2003). Improving the creativity of organizational work groups. *Academy of Management Executive, 17*, 96–6109.

Thompson, L. F., & Coovert, M. D. (2006). Understanding and developing virtual computer-supported cooperative work teams. In C. Bowers, E. Salas, & F. Jentsch (Eds.), *Creating high-tech teams: Practical guidance on work performance and technology.* Washington, D.C.: American Psychological Association.

Thye, S. R., Yoon, J., & Lawler, E. J. (2002). The theory of relational cohesion: Review of a research program. In S. R. Thye, & E. J. Lawler (Eds.), *Group cohesion, trust, and solidarity.* NY: Elsevier Science.

Tindale, R. S., & Larson, J. R. (1992a). Assembly bonus effect or typical group performance? A comment on Michaelsen, Watson, and Black (1989). *Journal of Applied Psychology, 77*(1), 102–105.

Tindale, R. S., & Larson, J. R. (1992b). It's not how you frame the question, it's how you interpret the results. *Journal of Applied Psychology, 77*(1), 109–110.

Tjosvold, D. (1985). Implications of controversy research for management. *Journal of Management, 11*(3), 21–37.

Tjosvold, D. (1986). *Working together to get things done: Managing for organizational productivity*. Lexington, MA: Lexington Books, D.C. Heath & Company.

Tjosvold, D. (1988). Cooperative and competitive dynamics within and between organizational units. *Human Relations, 41*(6), 425.

Tjosvold, D. (1995). Cooperation theory, constructive controversy, and effectiveness: Learning from crisis. In R. A. Guzzo, & E. Salas (Eds.), *Team effectiveness and decision making in organizations*. San Francisco: Jossey-Bass Publishers.

Tobey, D. D., (2005). *Needs assessment basics*. Washington DC: The American Society for Training and Development Press.

Tolbert, P. S., Andrew, A. O., & Simons, T. (1995). The effects of group proportions on group dynamics. In S. E. Jackson, & M. N. Ruderman (Eds.), *Diversity in work teams: Research paradigms for a changing workplace*. Washington, DC: American Psychological Association.

Topchik, G. S. (2007). Going from Conflict to Collaboration. *In The first-time manager's guide to team building* (pp. 105–115). NY: AMACOM.

Topchik, G. S. (2007). *The first-time manager's guide to team building*. NY: AMACOM.

Torrance, E. P. (1972). Can we teach children to think creatively? *Journal of Creative Behavior, 6*(2), 114–143.

Treffinger, D. J. (1993). Stimulating creativity: Issues and future directions. In S.G. Isaksen, M.C. Murdock, R. L. Firestein, & D. J. Treffinger (Eds.), *Nurturing and developing creativity: The emergence of a discipline*. Norwood, NJ: Ablex Publishing Corporation.

Triana, M. C., Kirkman, B. L., & Garcia, M. F. (April, 2009). Does the order of face-to-face and computer-mediated communication matter in diverse project teams? An investigation of communication order effects on minority inclusion, participation, and performance. Presented at the 24th Society for Industrial Organizational Psychology Annual Conference, New Orleans, LA.

Triplett, N. (1898). The dynamogenic factors in pacemaking and competition. *American Journal of Psychology, 9*, 507–533.

Tubbs, S. L. (1994). The historical roots of self-managing work teams in the twentieth century: An annotated bibliography. In M. M. Beyerlein, & D. A. Johnson (Eds.), *Advances in interdisciplinary studies of work teams: Theories of self-managing work teams*. Greenwich, CT: JAI Press Inc.

Tucker, J. C., Bullian, J., & Torrence, M. C. (2003). Collaborate or die! Collection development in today's academic library. In C.H. Mabry (Ed.), *Cooperative reference: Social interaction in the workplace*. Binghamton, NY: Haworth Information Press.

Tuckman, B. W. (1965). Developmental sequence in small groups. *Psychological Bulletin, 63*(6), 384–399.

Tuckman, B. W., & Jensen, M. A. (1977). Stages of small-group development revisited. *Group and Organization Studies, 2*(4), 419–427.

Tyler, T. R. (1998). The psychology of authority relations: A relational perspective on influence and power in groups. In R. R. Kramer, & M. A. Neale (Eds.), *Power and influence in organizations*. Thousand Oaks, CA: Sage Publications.

Tyler, T. R., & Blader, S. L. (2003). The group engagement model: Procedural justice, social identity, and cooperative behavior. *Personality and Social Psychology Review, 7*(4), 349–361.

US Department of Labor. (1999). *Futurework: Trends and Challenges for Work in the 21st Century* (Ch. 1). Retrieved June 14, 2009 from http://www.dol.gov/oasam/programs/history/herman/reports/futurework/report/pdf/ch1.pdf.

Van de Ven A. H., & Delbecq A. L. (1974). The effectiveness of nominal, delphi, and interacting group decision making processes. *Academy of Management Journal, 17*, 605–621.

Van de Vliert, E., & Janssen, O. (2001). Description, explanation, and prescription of intragroup conflict behaviors. In. M.E. Turner (Ed.), *Groups at work: Theory and research*. Mahwah, NJ: Lawrence Erlbaum Associates.

Van Dijk, E., Wit, A. P., Wilke, H. A. M., & de Kwaadsteniet, E. W. (2010). On the importance of equality in social dilemmas. In R. M. Kramer, A. E. Tenbrunsel, & M. H. Bazerman (Eds.), *Social decision making: Social dilemmas, social values, and ethical judgments*. NY: Psychology Press.

Van Dyne, L., Kossek, E., & Lobel, S. (2007). Less need to be there: Cross-level effects of work practices that support work-life flexibility and enhance group processes and group-level OCB. *Human Relations, 60*(8), 1123–1154.

Van Velsor, E. (1998). Designing 360-degree feedback to enhance involvement, self-determination, and commitment. In M. London, & W. W. Tornow (Eds.), *Maximizing the value of 360-degree feedback: A process for successful individual and organizational development*. SanFrancisco, CA: Jossey-Bass.

Van Vianen, A. E. M., & De Dreu, C. K. W. (2001). Personality in teams: Its relationship to social cohesion, task cohesion, and team performance. *European Journal of Work and Organizational Psychology, 10*(2), 97–120.

Vecchio, R. P. (1987). Situational leadership theory: An examination of a prescriptive theory. *Journal of Applied Psychology, 72*, 444–451.

Vodosek, M. (2007). Intragroup conflict as a mediator between cultural diversity and work group outcomes. *International Journal of Conflict Management, 18*(4), 345–375.

Voight, M., & Callaghan, J. (2001). A team building intervention program: Application and evaluation with two university soccer teams. *Journal of Sport Behavior, 24*, 420–431.

Von Glinow, M. A., Shapiro, D. L., & Brett, J. M. (2004). Can we talk, and should we? Managing emotional conflict in multicultural teams. *The Academy of Management Review, 29*(4), 578–592.

Vroom, V. H., & Yetton, P. W. (1973). *Leadership and decision-making*. Pittsburgh: University of Pittsburgh Press.

Vroom, V. H., & Jago, A. G. (2007). The role of the situation in leadership. *American Psychologist, 62*, 17–24.

Wageman, R. (1997). Critical success factors for creating superb self-managing teams. *Organizational Dynamics, 26*, 49–61.

Wageman, R. (2003). Virtual processes: Implications for coaching the virtual team. In R. S. Peterson, & E. A. Mannix (Eds.), *Leading and managing people in the dynamic organization*. Mahwah, NJ: Lawrence Erlbaum Associates.

Wageman, R., Hackman, J. R., & Lehman, E. V. (2005). The team diagnostic survey: Development of an instrument. *Journal of Applied Behavioral Science, 41*, 373–398.

Wageman, R., & Mannix, E. A. (1998). The uses and misuses of power in task-performing teams. In R. R. Kramer, & M. A. Neale (Eds.), *Power and influence in organizations*. Thousand Oaks, CA: Sage Publications.

Wagner, R. J., & Roland, C. C. (1992). How effective is outdoor training? *Training & Development, 46*(7), 61–64.

Wahrman, R. (2010). Status, deviance, and sanctions: A critical review. *Small Group Research*, *41*(1), 91–105.

Walther, J. B. (1992). Interpersonal effects in computer-mediated interaction: A relational perspective. *Communication Research, 19*, 52–90.

Warkentin, M. E., Sayeed, L., & Hightower, R. (1997). Virtual teams versus face-to-face teams: An exploratory study of a web-based conference system. *Decision Science, 28*, 975–996.

Watson, W. E., Kumar, K., & Michaelsen, L. K. (1993). Cultural diversity's impact on interaction process and performance: comparing homogeneous and diverse task groups. *Academy of Management Journal, 36*(3), 590–602.

Webber, S. S., & Donahue, L. M. (2001). Impact of highly and less job-related diversity on work group cohesion and performance: A meta-analysis. *Journal of Management, 27*, 141–162.

Wegge, J., & Haslam, S. A. (2005). Improving work motivation and performance in brainstorming groups: The effects of three group goal setting strategies. *European Journal of Work and Organizational Psychology, 14*, 400–430.

Wegner, D. M. (1987). Transactive memory: A contemporary analysis of the group mind. In B. Mullen, & G. R. Goethals (Eds.), *Theories of group behavior*. NY: Springer-Verlag.

Wellins, R. S., Byham, W. C., & Wilson, J. M. (1991). *Empowered teams: Creating self-directed work groups that improve quality, productivity, and participation*. San Francisco: Jossey-Bass.

West. M. A. (2004). *Effective teamwork: Practical lessons from organizational research*. Cambridge, MA: Wiley-Blackwell.

West, M. A., Sacramento, C. A., & Fay, D. (2006). Creativity and innovation implementation in work groups: The paradoxical role of demands. In Thompson, L. & Choi, H-S. (Eds.), *Creativity* and innovation in organizational *teams*. Mahwah, NJ: Lawrence Erlbaum.

Wheelan, S. A. (2005). *Creating effective teams: A guide for members and leaders* (2nd ed). Thousand Oaks, CA: Sage Publications.

Wheelan, S. A. (2009). Group size, group development, and group productivity. *Small Group Research, 40*(2), 247–262.

Whipple, R. (2009). Reinforcing candor: It builds trust and transparency. *Leadership Excellence, 26*(6), 17.

Whitman, L. E., Malzahn, D. E., Chaparro, B. S., Russell, M., Langrall, R., & Mohler, B. A. (2005). A comparison of group processes, performance, and satisfaction in face-to-face versus computer-mediated engineering student design teams. *Journal of Engineering Education, 94*(3), 327–334.

Whitney, J. C., & Smith, R. A. (1983). Effects of groups cohesiveness on attitude polarization and the acquisition of… *JMR, Journal of Marketing Research, 20*, 167–176.

Whitney, K. (1994). Improving group task performance: The role of group goals and group efficacy. *Human Performance, 7*(1), 55–78.

Widmeyer, W. N., Brawlery, L. R., & Carron, A. V. (1990). The effect of group size in sports. *Journal of Sport and Exercise Psychology, 12*, 177–190.

Wildermuth C., & Gray, S. (2005). *Diversity training*. Alexandria, VA: ASTD Press.

Willer, D., Borch, C., & Willer, R. (2002). Building a model for solidarity and cohesion using three theories. In S. R. Thye, & E. J. Lawler (Eds.), *Group cohesion, trust, and solidarity*. NY: Elsevier Science.

Williams, K., Harkins, S., & Latanè, B. (1981). Identifiability as a deterrent to social loafing: Two cheering experiments. *Journal of Personality and Social Psychology, 40*, 303–311.

Wilson, J. M., Straus, S. G., & McEvily, B. (2006). All in due time: The development of trust in computer mediated and face-to-face teams. *Organizational Behavior and Human Decision Processes, 99*, 16–33.

Winston, B. E., & Patterson, K. (2006). An integrative definition of leadership. *International Journal of Leadership Studies, 1*, 6–66.

Winquist, J. R., & Franz, T. M. (2008). Does the Stepladder Technique improve group decision making? A series of failed replications. *Group Dynamics: Theory, Research, and Practice, 12*, 255–267.

Winum, P. C., & Seamons, T. R. (2000). Developing a team-based organization: A case study in progress. *Consulting Psychology Journal: Practice and Research, 52*, 82–89.

Woodcock, M., & Francis, D. (1979). *Unblocking your organization*. La Jolla, CA: University Associates.

Woodcock, M., & Francis, D. (2005). *Resources for measuring and improving team performance*. Farnham, Surrey, UK: Gower Publishing Co.

Woodward, N. H. (2006). Doing town hall meetings better: town hall meetings enable senior leadership to keep employees informed, engaged, and in sync with business goals. *HR Magazine, 51*(12), 68–72.

Worchel, S., Wood, W., & Simpson J. A. (1992). *Group process and productivity*. Newbury Park, CA: Sage.

Yukl, G. A. (1970). Leader LPC scores: Attitude dimensions and behavioral correlates. *Journal of Social Psychology, 80*, 207–212.

Yukl, G. A. (2010). *Leadership in Organizations* (7th ed.). Upper Saddle River, NJ: Prentice Hall.

Zaccaro, S. J. (2007). Trait-based perspectives of leadership. *American Psychologist, 62*, 6–16.

Zaccaro, S. J., Heinen, B., & Shuffler, M. (2009). Team leadership and team effectiveness. In E. Salas, G. F. Goodwin, & C. S. Burke (Eds.), *Team effectiveness in complex organizations: Cross-disciplinary perspectives and approaches*. NY: Routledge/Taylor & Francis Group.

Zaccaro, S. J., & Klimoski, R. (2002). The interface of leadership and team processes. *Group & Organization Management, 27*, 4–13.

Zaccaro, S. J., Rittman, A. L., & Marks, M. A. (2001). Team leadership. *The Leadership Quarterly, 12*, 451–483.

Zander, A. (1983). *Making groups effective*. San Francisco: Jossey-Bass Publishers.

Zander, A. (1985). *The purposes of groups and organizations*. San Francisco: Jossey-Bass Publishers.

Zárraga, C., & Bonache, J. (2005). The impact of team atmosphere on knowledge outcomes in self-managed teams. *Organization Studies 26*(5), 661–681.

Zenger, J. H., Musselwhite, E., Hurson, K., & Perrin, C. (1991). Leadership in a team environment. *Training & Development, 45*(10), 46–52.

Zoghbi-Manrique-de-Lara, P. (2009). Inequity, conflict, and compliance dilemma as causes of cyberloafing. *International Journal of Conflict Management, 20*, 188–201.

Zucker, L. G., Darby, M. R., Brewer, M. B., & Peng, Y. (1996). Collaboration structure and information dilemmas in biotechnology: Organizational boundaries as trust production. In R. M. Kramer, & T. R. Tyler (Eds.), *Trust in organizations: Frontiers of theory and research*. Thousand Oaks, CA: Sage Publications.

Index